Laissez Faire Bks

AUSTRIAN ECONOMICS

NEW PERSPECTIVES ON AUSTRIAN ECONOMICS

In recent years there has been a spectacular revival of interest in the economics of the Austrian School. This volume collects together a range of contributions which illustrate both the richness of the Austrian heritage and the continuing validity of the Austrian tradition.

The volume begins with a keynote chapter by Israel Kirzner on subjectivism within Austrian economics. Subsequent contributions include:

- chapters on such major figures as Menger, Hayek and Schumpeter
- the socialist calculation debate
- Austrian perspectives on key theoretical issues including uncertainty, business cycle theory and evolutionary economics
- the implications of Austrian economics for current issues in competition policy, socialist economics and international economic policy.

Together they demonstrate that the Austrian tradition has made a unique and fundamental contribution to economic analysis for over a hundred years.

Gerrit Meijer is Senior Lecturer in Public Economics at the University of Limburg, at Maastricht, the Netherlands, having previously held a post at the University of Amsterdam. His research interests include the history of economic thought, comparative economic systems, the organization of the market economy, public finance and liberalism. He has published on these subjects in Dutch, English and German.

NEW PERSPECTIVES ON AUSTRIAN ECONOMICS

Edited by Gerrit Meijer

ROUTLEDGE

London and New York

First published 1995
by Routledge
11 New Fetter Lane, London EC4P 4EE

Simultaneously published in the USA and Canada
by Routledge
29 West 35th Street, New York, NY 10001

Typeset in Garamond by
J&L Composition Ltd, Filey, North Yorkshire
Printed and bound in Great Britain by
TJ Press (Padstow) Ltd, Padstow, Cornwall

British Library Cataloguing in Publication Data
A catalogue record for this book is available from the British Library

Library of Congress Cataloguing in Publication Data
A catalogue record for this book has been requested

ISBN 0–415–12283–X

CONTENTS

Part III Theoretical aspects of modern Austrian economics

Part IV Political applications of Austrian economics

CONTRIBUTORS

Jürgen G. Backhaus, Department of Economics, University of Limburg.
Eran Binenbaum, Department of Economics, University of California.
A. Godart-van der Kroon, Foundation Ludwig von Mises, Gent.
W.J.M. Heijman, Wageningen Agricultural University.
Yukihiro Ikeda, Keio University, Tokyo.
Willem Keizer, Department of Economics and Econometrics, Free University Amsterdam.
Israel M. Kirzner, New York University.
Auke R. Leen, Wageningen Agricultural University.
J.A.H. Maks, Department of Economics, University of Limburg.
Gerrit Meijer, Department of Economics, University of Limburg.
Aad van Mourik, Department of Economics, University of Limburg.
Jesús Huerta de Soto, Complutense University of Madrid.
Wladyslaw Sztyber, University of Warsaw, Poland.
Hans Visser, Department of Economics and Econometrics, Free University Amsterdam.
Ulrich Witt, University of Freiburg.
Emiel Wubben, Erasmus University, Rotterdam.
Rudy van Zijp, Department of Economics and Econometrics, Free University Amsterdam.
Roel P. Zuidema, Department of Economics and Econometrics, Free University Amsterdam.

PREFACE

This book includes articles on the history and relevance of the Austrian School. It concerns the keynote lecture of Professor Kirzner and, with one exception, papers originally written for the First European Conference on Austrian Economics held at Maastricht on April 9–10, 1992. The theme of the conference was 'The History and Relevance of the Austrian School of Economics'. The conference was organized by the Dutch research group Austrian School (also known as Austria Club).

The Dutch research group Austrian School was established in 1987 as a forum for exchanging ideas and in order to co-ordinate research activities. A joint research programme concerning the history and relevance of the Austrian School of economic thought was decided upon. The subject was not narrowly defined and the relationships between the Austrian school and other modern schools of economic thought were included in the programme.

The members of the group are teachers and researchers from several Dutch universities. Most of them are theoretical economists, but a few methodologists and philosophers are also included.

The authors were given the opportunity to revise their papers in the light of written or oral comments. Some of these comments are also included in this volume where it was thought expedient.

I wish to express my thanks to all the people who contributed to the conference. As an editor I am in debt to those who assisted me. They are mentioned at the appropriate places. Especially my thanks go to my wife Ria Meijer-Kuipers for her help in all phases of the project. I also thank Andries Nentjes, president of the Austria Club, for his contribution and support in the preparations of the organization. It was a pity that he was not able to take part in the conference due to illness.

The opening address by Hans Visser, vice-president of the Austria Club, gives more information, for example on other publications of the group. I only have to add that the papers delivered by members of the group, at the meeting of the International Society of Intercommunication of New Ideas (ISINI) in Paris 1990, have been published meanwhile in *The International Journal of New Ideas*, II, (1), 1993.

Gerrit Meijer, University of Limburg, Maastricht

INTRODUCTION

Gerrit Meijer

In this introduction a short overview is given of the contents of this volume, without giving way to the temptation to evaluate and discuss the contributions.

Kirzner gave a keynote lecture on 'The Subjectivism of Austrian Economics'. As he observes, this topic is both appropriate and important. He argues that the subjectivism that developed out of the pioneering insights of Carl Menger, who founded the Austrian School, has come to mean entirely different things to different doctrinal traditions within modern economics – each of which derives substantially or wholly from the Mengerian tradition. He argues that the variety that informs modern Austrian economics preserves and deepens most faithfully Menger's own fundamental insights. The deepening took place in three phases through the work of Mises, Hayek and Kirzner. The key elements in this modern extension of Mengerian subjectivism are the role of entrepreneurship in market processes (Mises), and the gradual expansion of knowledge generated in the course of the competitive market process (Hayek). Kirzner integrated these elements in his theory of entrepreneurship and equilibrium.

The other articles are arranged in three categories. Some of them have a historical content. Others are more relevant in the sense of being either theoretically orientated or applications to problems of economic policy (especially competition policy, socialist economics and international economic order).

The first series of articles, in Part II, is opened by Yukihiro Ikeda, who discusses the relationship between Roscher and Menger on the basis of the Menger papers deposited at Duke University. His main conclusion is that the traditional interpretation concerning the relationship between Menger and the German historical school is one-sided. They share common ground in substance. In his comment on Ikeda's article, Jürgen G. Backhaus remarks that Ikeda is right in insisting that the relationship between the Austrians and the Historical School needs to be looked at again.

This is followed by an exposition, by A. Godart-van der Kroon, of the impact on and contribution to economics of the Dutch economist Nicolaas

Gerard Pierson, who had affinity to the marginalist schools, especially the Austrian School. Pierson laid a new foundation for economics in the Netherlands. He contributed especially to the introduction and extension of the marginal utility theory and the ideas of the Austrian School, e.g. on economic calculation in the socialist society.

W.J.M. Heijman writes on 'Austrian Sustainability'. Extending the duration of durable goods is one aspect of the struggle for a sustainable economy. He applies and extends Böhm-Bawerk's theory of capital and interest to the duration of durable goods.

Auke R. Leen elaborates on the relatively unknown and neglected third-generation Austrian economist Schönfeld-Illy. The problem of how to abbreviate economic calculations was one of the core difficulties for the Austrian inventors of marginalism. Because of the mathematical mould of their theories, the problem was overlooked by the English and French co-inventors. In his article the author tries to formulate and formalize the abbreviating role of marginal utility as a short-cut in consumer calculations. He models the abbreviating role of marginal utility as a habit-forming process. Within a household production framework, an intertemporal model of consumer choice is used. Three groups of consumers are selected: first, immigrants; second, trendsetting consumers; and third, the well-established consumers of traditional theory. For the first group the abbreviating role of marginal utility is modelled as a beneficial rational addiction, for the second it is modelled as either of no concern or as a harmful rational addiction, and for the third it acts as an addiction *sine qua non*. He also looks at the producer's problem: who are the most susceptible to the advertising of new goods? The model explains why emigrants save more and buy relatively more new goods, though at a decreasing rate, than the well-established people do. Trendsetters, on the other hand, save less in buying new goods than the other groups.

Part III elaborates especially on the contributions of Mises, Hayek and Kirzner to Austrian economics.

The first article in this part is written by Ulrich Witt on 'Schumpeter vs. Hayek: Two Approaches to Evolutionary Economics'. He compares Schumpeter's and Hayek's approaches to evolutionary economics: the phenomena of process and change. Hayek, in contrast to Schumpeter, bases his theory on subjectivism. In evolutionary theory the emergence of novelty needs explication. The Schumpeterian tradition ignores this problem as a consequence of its attitude towards subjectivism. In Austrian economics both problems are treated. Therefore he argues that an appropriately interpreted evolutionary approach may be a fruitful basis for future research into the issues treated traditionally by Austrian economics. Concerning the problem of process and change the views of the Schumpeterian tradition can be useful for Austrian economists, because entrepreneurial alertness and arbitrage, according to Witt, cannot explain reality fully. This article is commented on by Willem Keizer. From his comments the most important may be that Austrian economics must turn itself into a more fruitful theory by interacting with other currents of thought, for example 'neo-institutional' economics. Useful new insights could also result from cross-fertilization with evolutionary economics.

The following two articles are closely related to the problems treated by Kirzner in his keynote lecture. These contain the rather lengthy but thorough analyses of Emiel Wubben and Eran Binenbaum on 'Austrian Economics and Uncertainty: On a Non-deterministic but Non-haphazard Future' and 'Kirzner's Core Concepts'.

Wubben applies Austrian economics to the problem of uncertainty. The oldest generation did not discuss uncertainty. This was done explicitly by Mises, Hayek, Kirzner and Lachmann. Wubben looks for answers to the following questions: (1) how is uncertainty introduced into Austrian economics and (2) what are the consequent implications for decision-making? Hayek more or less ignored the origination of new market information. Kirzner elaborated on this in his synthesis of the ideas of Menger, Mises and Hayek. Wubben concludes that Austrian economics takes a middle-ground position on the point of uncertainty between the extreme view-points of a deterministic and a haphazard or kaleidic future.

Binenbaum attempts to interpret Kirzner's core concepts in the field of economic methodology and positive economics. There is, according to him, a tension between praxeology and the concept of entrepreneurship. Binenbaum argues that there are some inconsistencies in Kirzner's main ideas. He concludes that the unequivocal abandonment of praxeology and the development of a solid epistemological and methodological alternative would contribute to the further development of Kirzner's valuable ideas on entrepreneurship and market processes.

The article by Rudy van Zijp and Hans Visser, 'On the Non-neutrality of Mathematical Formalization: Austrian vs. New Classical Business Cycle Theories', falls into the same category. The authors do not share the Austrian aversion to mathematical models. The available mathematical techniques should not, however, set or limit the research agenda. They observe that Austrians and new classicals differ considerably on the role of mathematical formalization in economics. The former downplay or even reject its usefulness, whereas the latter claim that formalization constitutes the main source of progress in economics. Their conclusion is that the new classical heuristic prescription of mathematical formalization is non-neutral, in the sense that its use of mathematical techniques, and particularly of the technique of optimalization under constraints, restricts the domain of economics. It eliminates Cantillon and other distribution effects from its domain. In contrast Hayek's business cycle theory, in their interpretation, stresses the complexity of social reality, and allows for inclusion of Cantillon and distribution effects at the cost of mathematical rigour.

Part VI begins with an article on competition policy written by J.A.H. Maks on 'Economic Theory and Competition Policy in the Netherlands'. Neo-Austrians hold that imperfect competition generally produces welfare results through improvements in the coordination of supply and demand. Chicago adherents declare perfect competition as the norm, saying that it leads to Pareto optimality and that real world competition emulates perfect competition under normal conditions. Ordo-Liberals also take perfect competition as the norm, but say that the government should establish an economic order such that perfect competitive results are closely approximated.

The Harvard school explicitly departed from perfect competition as the norm and strove towards a rating of the various forms of imperfect competition in markets by the workable competition concept, but got stuck in cruder studies of the concentration doctrine. The new industrial economics has also come to the insight that some forms of imperfect competition may be socially beneficial. It tries to identify the effects of the various types of barriers to entry. Welfare measurement is performed with consumers and producers. So all in all, the trend is towards allowing a certain amount of room for the concept of imperfect competition.

Maks observes that welfare economics proves to be a useful if not necessary instrument. Entrepreneurial action in the neo-Austrian approach leads to a Pareto improvement towards a second-best Ramsey allocation. The Chicago school position can be improved by the replacement of perfect competition Pareto optimal allocation by socially optimal Ramsey competition. Ordo-Liberals may prefer to ground competition policy on informational scarcity third-best insights. New industrial economists can improve their welfare analysis using the same insights. It is to be noted that this conclusion can be stated, despite the fact that third-best welfare economics, based on imperfect information and compatible with imperfect competition, is just beginning to explore its potential.

It is pretty clear that neo-Austrians and Chicagoans would give high marks to the permissive practice of Dutch competition policy and that Ordo-Liberals would be severely disappointed. Traditional industrial economists would emphasize the increase in the concentration in Dutch industries in the period 1950–1970 and expect higher profits. If they found these profits higher than necessary in some industries, they would have argued for a more active policy. New industrial economists would probably like to start an extensive research programme to investigate the question. They would not hesitate, however, to identify a likely shortcoming of the Dutch policy, in the law's lack of identified goals for the competition policy. A possible, systematic negligence of the consumer interest in defining the general interest may be a factor that the new industrial economist, who is concerned with producer and consumer surplus and optimal social welfare, would want to give explicit emphasis.

This is followed by two articles on socialist economics. Wladyslaw Sztyber writes on 'Early Views on the Socialist Economy'. He gives an exposition of the almost forgotten origins of the discussion on the functioning of the socialist economy. This discussion is still relevant for the problems of transition in the former communist countries.

De Soto's subject is 'Entrepreneurship and the Economic Analysis of Socialism'. According to him the theory of entrepreneurship, as developed by Kirzner in the footsteps of Mises and Hayek, is an essential element of the economic analysis of socialism. He proposes a new definition of socialism, not based on the criterion of state ownership, but on the concept of entrepreneurship. From the point of view of entrepreneurial theory he concludes the impossibility of socialist economic calculation. In addition he criticizes the traditional concepts of socialism.

The last article in Part IV is on international economic problems and is written by Roel P. Zuidema. In his article, entitled 'The Austrian Perspective for the European Economy Today', he asks the question: what message does neo-Austrian economic thinking have for (re-)shaping the economic institutions to the benefit of all European peoples concerned? In his comment on Zuidema's article, Aad van Mourik stresses the relation between these ideas and present problems. He applies them to the problems of the European Community today. All the contributions also clearly show in this way the actuality of the conference theme.

OPENING ADDRESS TO THE AUSTRIA CONFERENCE

Hans Visser

Most of us have been brought up on the idea that the great contribution of the Austrians was subjective value theory and that Schumpeter had had some interesting things to say. We also studied Hayek's business cycle theory, but only as one among many, from Haberler's *Prosperity and Depression* and that was it, more or less. It had been an interesting school which had left a legacy of fruitful contributions to economic theory, but its days were over. One of the leading economists in the Netherlands three decades ago depicted Mises and Hayek as a pair of old grumblers whose ideas were invariably proven wrong by the facts.

Those days are long past. Austrian economics has made a brilliant comeback. Hayek's ideas on currency competition sparked off a plethora of studies on the monetary constitution which spilled over into politics, leading Mr John Major in his guise as Chancellor of the Exchequer to advocate currency competition as an alternative to the road to monetary union as proposed in the Delors report. I doubt whether he was serious, because it could only be seen as a plea to his fellow Britons to shift from sterling to the Deutschmark and the Dutch guilder. The revival of Austrian economics is now riding the wave of the return of democracy in Eastern Europe and I can imagine Routledge shipping Hayek's *The Road to Serfdom* to Eastern Europe by the wagonload. As every age rewrites history from its own point of view and with its own problems in mind, we felt there were plenty of reasons to give renewed attention to the Austrian school, both to get a better understanding of the roots of Austrian economics and to gain an insight into the possible contributions of the Austrian approach to the study of present-day problems. The Austrian emphasis on entrepreneurial activities is of course especially relevant in this respect. Highlighting the role of the entrepreneur no longer meets with the hostility characteristic of large parts of the intellectual scene back in the 1970s.

Previous feats of the Austria Club were, among others, the publication of a special double issue of the *Journal of Economic Studies*, which has also been published separately as a book and to which Professors Hutchison and

Yeager contributed; the publication of a special issue of the Dutch economics magazine *Maandschrift Economie*; and the organization of a session at the ISINI conference in Paris in 1990. ISINI stands for International Society for the Intercommunication of New Ideas, and if papers on the Austrian approach are not deemed out of place in a conference on new ideas, this can only be seen as a testimony to the freshness of the Austrian approach after so many years.

Having said this, it is probably fair to say that most of the members of the Austria Club have not nailed themselves firmly to the Austrian mast. Rather, we have remained mainstream or eclectic economists who, however, have grown sympathetic to much of Austrian economics, in the way Leland Yeager has. Speaking for myself, I have always had a sneaking suspicion that general equilibrium models, elegant though they are, somehow fail to capture the full richness of life, and Austrian economics proved to provide welcome support. For one thing, general equilibrium models leave no place for the entrepreneur, and economics without the entrepreneur is like *Hamlet* without the prince, or the fifth Brandenburg concerto without the harpsichord. For another thing, I do not share the Austrian aversion to mathematical models, but if there is one thing that my study of Austrian economics has brought home to me, it is that you should not let available mathematical techniques set or limit the research agenda.

After having dipped a few toes in the water in the way I have just sketched, we at last felt free to organize our own conference and invite a leading Austrian economist to give the opening lecture; to go for the real thing, so to speak.

We were greatly honoured that Professor Kirzner from New York University accepted our invitation to be the keynote speaker at this conference. W. Duncan Reekie (1984: 188) wrote in his *Markets, Entrepreneurs and Liberty* that 'it is to Kirzner that most Austrians [. . .] look as the man who "Salvaged the Ideas" of Menger, Mises and Hayek' and after the demise of Hayek two weeks ago, Professor Kirzner must surely be seen as *the* leading Austrian economist.

In Professor Kirzner's work, for instance his book *The Economic Point of View* (1976) or his 1989 book *Discovery, Capitalism, and Distributive Justice*, we find the important Austrian themes such as economics as a science of action, competition as a discovery procedure and the role of entrepreneurial activity. In *Discovery, Capitalism, and Distributive Justice* entrepreneurial discovery occupies centre stage. The central themes are, to cite his own words: 'To discover an opportunity is to create it' (p. 40) and 'Resources and products have always had to be discovered. They have never "existed" up until the moment of their entrepreneurial discovery' (p. 174). Via a probably new element in the discussion, the finders-keepers ethic, this leads to a spirited defence of capitalism, at the least a welcome change from the 'appropriation of surplus value' so popular in the 1970s. This is unvarnished

Austrianism, and very stimulating too, even if one does not fully share Professor Kirzner's enthusiasm for capitalism and the price mechanism.

I myself would rather subscribe to the view of James Meade's intelligent radical, who can only give two cheers for the price mechanism, against the at least three cheers of the average Austrian. The intelligent radical recognizes that the world is a wicked place in which compromise is inevitable. He freely admits that the price mechanism is the worst possible form of economic system except the others, and his stirring political rallying cry is: 'Two Hearty Cheers for the Price Mechanism' (Meade 1975: 123).

All the same, it is gratifying to see that an insightful and incisive analysis of society is still possible without invoking Messrs Box and Jenkins or the combined might of an army of Hamiltonians, Jacobians and Hessians, both bordered and unbordered. Three cheers for Professor Kirzner.

REFERENCES

Kirzner, I.M. (1976) *The Economic Point of View*, 2nd edn, Kansas City: Sheed and Ward.

Kirzner, I.M. (1989) *Discovery, Capitalism, and Distributive Justice*, Oxford: Basil Blackwell.

Meade, J.E. (1975) *The Intelligent Radical's Guide to Economic Policy*, London: George Allen & Unwin.

Reekie, W. Duncan (1984) *Markets, Entrepreneurs and Liberty: An Austrian View of Capitalism*, Brighton: Harvester Wheatsheaf.

Part I

THE SUBJECTIVISM OF AUSTRIAN ECONOMICS

1

THE SUBJECTIVISM OF AUSTRIAN ECONOMICS

Israel M. Kirzner

I have chosen subjectivism as my topic for this paper and surely few will question the appropriateness and importance of this topic for an Austrian conference. Austrian economics has recently lost one of its great modern masters, Friedrich A. Hayek. It is therefore perhaps particularly fitting to open this paper with Hayek's often quoted tribute to the role of subjectivism in the growth of economic understanding. It is, he wrote, 'probably no exaggeration to say that every important advance in economic theory during the last hundred years was a further step in the constant application of subjectivism' (Hayek 1955: 31). Our thesis will be that the subjectivism that developed out of those pioneering insights of Carl Menger who founded the Austrian school, has come to mean entirely different things to different doctrinal traditions within modern economics – each of which derives substantially or wholly from the Mengerian tradition. In calling for the endorsement of that one variety of subjectivism which informs modern Austrian economics, we shall argue that it is this variety that most faithfully preserves and deepens Menger's own fundamental insights.

THE SUBJECTIVISM OF THE AUSTRIAN SCHOOL

Subjectivism has never, of course, meant any challenge to the possibility of 'objective truth' in economics. It has never claimed that 'everything is merely a matter of subjective interpretation' by the would-be economist. What the subjectivism of the 1870s challenged was the basic – if unstated – classical tenet that ultimately the only determinant of social–economic phenomena is the objective physical environment. All economic science has endeavoured to account for real-world phenomena. The classical economist believed that these phenomena are to be seen as having been inexorably determined by the underlying physical realities. The availability of scarce natural resources, in conjunction with population and its demographics, basically determine the course of human history. What emerges over history is inescapable, it cannot be substantially altered by human will. Economic history emerges as automatically determined by the objective conditions governing and surrounding production. It was against this premise that Menger did revolutionary battle in his 1871 *Grundsätze* – written, we are told, in what he himself described as 'a state of morbid excitement' (Hayek 1981: 16).

The central thrust of Menger's book, we argue, was not so much his articulation of a subjective (marginal utility) theory of value, as his vision of the entire economic process of production as expressing the imprint, upon external reality, of the human factor. It was this vision that led him to formulate his theory of goods of various 'orders', in which it is the preference of the final consumers that determines the place of each potential resource in the structure of production, and that ultimately assigns market values to all of them. It was this vision that led him (some twenty years earlier than his fellow pioneers in the marginalist revolution, in other schools) to glimpse, at least, the outlines of the theory of marginal productivity *within the very formulation of the marginal utility theory of value.* What ultimately determines the economic phenomena that we observe in the real world is, in this Mengerian vision, not the physical conditions governing production, but the needs of human beings. It is the latter that determine production methods, and the assignment of market values to goods, and incomes to owners of agents of production. Menger's vision is thus subjective in the fundamental sense that what emerges in real-world economies is the expression of human preferences as exercised against a background of given, passive resource constraints and endowments.

This subjectivist view of Menger differs not only, as already seen, from the classical view. It also differs, at least philosophically, from the Marshallian version of the neoclassical view. In this latter view (which has, largely due to the influence of Knight and his disciples, become the contemporary mainstream view in the United States) economic phenomena are seen as emerging from the interplay of the subjective and objective elements of supply (expressing objective cost conditions) and demand (reflecting consumer preferences). For Menger, as we have seen, the relevant insight is that – while, to be sure, the objective situation has much to do with the specific market outcomes that emerge in the course of the economic process – it is solely the actions of choosing consumers that in fact initiate and drive the process through which these outcomes emerge.

THE INCOMPLETENESS OF MENGER'S SUBJECTIVISM

As we shall see, and as is well known, Menger's subjectivism was incomplete in several respects. But we shall claim that the above kernel of Menger's subjectivist insight remains valid and central for economic understanding. It is this kernel that, during the long and checkered history of twentieth-century (and especially Austrian) economics, sometimes came to be obscured (especially in the early decade of the century). It is the revival of this kernel of subjectivism in the mid- and late twentieth century work of Mises, Hayek and their followers, that constitutes, in this economist's view, the most exciting feature of the resurgence of Austrian economics. And it is, paradoxically, this kernel that has unfortunately become threatened by certain recent developments within Austrian economics itself.

With the benefit of hindsight it is in fact possible to discern within Menger's work precisely those elements in his economic vision that we now see to have been, subjectivistically speaking, profoundly flawed, and relate them to those valid, enduring aspects of his subjectivism that have been, as it were, rediscovered and reaffirmed in modern Austrian economics. And, if we describe these latter, valid elements in Menger's subjectivism as being threatened, paradoxically, by certain developments within Austrian economics itself, the solution to the paradox is perhaps not far to seek. It has been an overenthusiastic tendency on the part of certain Austrian economists in recent years, to escape the legacy of incompleteness in Menger's subjectivism, that seems to have inadvertently led them almost to reject those paramount, valid expressions of Menger's subjectivist vision.

We have seen this vision to consist in the insight that the essential causal determinant shaping economic phenomena is not the physical environment within which economic activity proceeds, but the preference structure of the consumers whose needs inspire that activity. The prime flaw in Menger's vision – as seen from the subjectivist perspective – is his odd belief that this shaping influence exercised by human wants occurs inexorably and automatically, as it were without the intermediation of the human will (Menger 1981: IX). It seems plausible to link this unfortunate view to Menger's apparent (and equally unfortunate) assumption, in his price theory, that values (which he showed to be determined by marginal utilities) occur in the context of complete knowledge. Ignorance, Menger argued, is to be seen as a pathology which should not obscure the underlying economic laws relating to healthy, normal (i.e., omnisciently informed) economic activity (Menger 1981: 200; 1985: 56; Kirzner 1979: ch. 4 and 1992: ch. 4).

An example of the baneful influence of Menger's view of the 'automatic' translation of consumer needs into the appropriate market values and patterns of resource allocation, occurs in a passage in Schumpeter in which he criticized the Misesian thesis concerning the possibility of rational economic calculation under socialism. And the extent to which post-Mengerian Austrian subjectivism was able to escape these unfortunate influences is expressed in Hayek's sharp reaction to Schumpeter.

Mises has shown how, in the absence of markets for productive resources, socialist planners would simply be unable to plan rationally, because they lack indexes of the relative social importance of the relevant resources. Schumpeter rejected this on what we can see to have been solid Mengerian grounds. The appropriate pattern of resource allocation is implied, for any form of economic society, in the pattern of consumer desires. This follows, for the theorist, Schumpeter (1950: 175) argued, 'from the elementary proposition that consumers in evaluating ("demanding") consumer goods *ipso facto* also evaluate the means of production which enter into the production of those goods'. Clearly Schumpeter (correctly) understood Mengerian theory as implying an automatic, *logical* relationship linking consumer preferences to the correct valuation of productive resources.

And it was this that provoked Hayek to refer to this view of Schumpeter's as 'startling'. Only for a single mind to which not only the valuation of consumer goods are known but also the conditions governing the supply of the various factors of production, would it be valid to claim such a logical relationship. Schumpeter has simply slid into the (Mengerian) error of disregarding 'the unavoidable imperfection of man's knowledge and the consequent need for a process by which knowledge is constantly communicated and acquired' (Hayek 1949: 91).

MENGER'S SUBJECTIVIST HERITAGE: THE DIVERGENT PATHS

We have seen the central subjectivist thrust of Menger's vision. And we have seen the incompleteness of that vision (in its assumption of the normalcy of perfect knowledge.) It appears plausible to see this dominant, but flawed, subjectivism of Menger, as the reason for the divergent paths followed by subsequent generations of economists touched by Menger's influence. We may distinguish three such paths.

(a) *Mainstream economics.* Menger's influence has left a powerful imprint upon twentieth-century mainstream microeconomics. This influence was introduced, it can be shown, primarily through Lord Robbins' important 1932 book, *The Nature and Significance of Economic Science.* Robbins' work reflected (as made clear in his Preface to the book) the character of Austrian economics to which he had been exposed during the later 1920s. This economics expressed Menger's subjectivism – with all its incompleteness. Austrian economics in the 1920s paid virtually no attention to the problems of ignorance and uncertainty. While Robbins succeeded in shaping modern microeconomics in a subjectivist direction, by making the economizing decision the decisively important analytical unit, he did so while in effect retaining the Mengerian assumption of complete relevant information. In the Robbinsian approach adopted by mainstream microeconomics, as absorbed into the Walrasian context, each market participant is assumed to confront a given and fully known ends–means framework (created symmetrically by the decisions being simultaneously made by the remaining, similarly situated, market participants).

Clearly, what we identified as the disturbing flaw in Menger's subjectivism has, in this modern mainstream version of it, become its most central identifying feature.

As an almost natural result of this central feature (the assumption of perfect knowledge), mainstream microeconomics proceeded to extend the Robbinsian framework (in which the individual decision-maker is seen as facing a given, known ends–means complex) to the economy as a whole. The entire economy was seen as somehow facing an economizing problem, as if it was required to allocate given social resources in a pattern calculated to achieve maximum satisfaction of ranked social objectives. Although Robbins himself had assumed perfect relevant knowledge strictly at the level of each individual, the extension of his framework to encompass societal economizing decisions, in effect assumed the possibility of complete, centralized information concerning the entire economy and all its available options, desires and possibilities. With this extension the mainstream view had expanded the flaw in Menger's system to the point where the subjectivist element in Menger's heritage was virtually smothered. It was Hayek's 1945 paper, 'The Use of Knowledge in Society', that decisively rejected this assumption, for any realistic understanding of the operation of the market system.

(b) *Radical subjectivism.* The second path taken by post-Mengerian subjectivists is that which, in the second half of the twentieth century, has been represented most prominently by the work of Shackle and of Lachmann. Although Shackle was a student of Hayek in the 1930s, there is little to suggest that his subjectivism owes much to Menger's specific influence. Lachmann, on the other hand, explicitly drew his subjectivism from Austrian (and especially Mengerian) economics. The Shackle–Lachmann subjectivist path represents the outright rejection of those elements in the mainstream view that we have identified with the flaws in Menger's own subjectivism. But they go much further. Not only do Shackle and Lachmann reject the assumption of perfect knowledge, they tend to emphasize the virtual *impossibility* of relevant accurate knowledge. Decisions refer to courses of action that will have consequences in the future; the future is unknowable; hence even *individual* decisions (let alone imaginary societal decisions) must never be seen by economists as being made in the allocative mode central to mainstream microeconomics. The uncertainty of the future must confound and frustrate the (admitted) urge to rationality which humans display. No longer can we see decisions as dictated, in effect, by the given arrays of ends and means relevant to the respective decisions. Decisions are, in this view, made in a manner expressive of the decision-maker's own assessments of what the options are (and what consequences they are expected to generate). These assessments reflect the expectations held at the moment of the decision; they are held, in this view, to be *undetermined* by objective phenomena. This 'subjectivism of expectations', to use Lachmann's phrase, undermines traditional microeconomics because it injects an unprecedented degree of subjectivist-generated indeterminacy into the economic picture. One can no longer rely, as traditional microeconomics relied, upon equilibrating market forces (driven by rationally maximizing individual decisions) to generate systematic market outcomes. Market outcomes express the decisions made; the decisions made express the expectations that happen to be held at the moment of decision; that is all. This radical subjectivism has thus not only cast away the assumption of perfect knowledge which Menger's incomplete subjectivism had no qualms in making. It has at the same time entirely abandoned those central conclusions of Menger's economics in which, we argued, his subjectivism found expression. In the radical view we can no longer recognize any systematic processes in which consumer preferences come to leave any powerful imprint upon the production decisions governing the uses to which higher-order goods are to be allocated.

The preceding, mainstream 'path' had led to the smothering of Mengerian subjectivism as a result of the drastic deepening of the 'perfect knowledge' assumption. The radical path has, we have now seen, led to the denial of those central results of economic analysis in which Menger's own subjectivist view of the economic process was reflected. It is against this background that we turn to note the third path taken by economists touched by Menger's subjectivist influence.

(c) *The modern Austrian revival.* This path is that created by the work of Mises and of Hayek. It has brought about, during the past quarter of century, a significant revival of interest in Austrian, and especially Mengerian, economics. We shall argue that this path preserves what is sound and valid in Menger's subjectivism, steering clear of both the incompleteness in Menger's view (which led to the death of subjectivism in mainstream microeconomics) and the nihilism of the radical subjectivists (which has led to the abandonment of the central subjectivist conclusions of Mengerian economics).

The key elements in this modern extension of Mengerian subjectivism (on this see further Kirzner 1992: ch. 7) are the role of entrepreneurship in market processes, and the gradual expansion of knowledge generated in the course of the competitive market process. The first of these two key elements we owe to Mises; the second has formed the kernel of Hayekian economics since 1945. Briefly put, the Mises–Hayek theory of the market process sees it as a systematic process of knowledge expansion, the equilibrating character of which is the expression of entrepreneurial discovery. This vision of the market process not only preserves the key element of subjectivism in Menger's theory (i.e. recognition of the primary and dominant role exercised by consumer preferences). It does so without accepting the troubling Mengerian assumption of perfect knowledge. In fact, as we shall see, this modern Austrian view is able to reach Menger's central subjectivist conclusion *only* by introducing the new element of subjectivism needed in order to provide scope for entrepreneurial discovery. Not only are the flaws in Menger's subjectivism no longer necessary for his subjectivist conclusions, it turns out in fact that a new dimension for subjectivism is the necessary link in establishing anew the old Mengerian conclusions. All this deserves more careful attention.

THE MODERN AUSTRIAN SUBJECTIVISM

In this modern Austrian view subjectivist insights reveal two cardinally significant features of economic life. It is these features that make possible the claim (in Mengerian fashion) that markets do systematically tend to express the preferences of consumers. The first of these two features is in fact the direct denial of that feature in Menger earlier described as a flaw in his subjectivism. Whereas Menger's theory of price depended on the assumption of perfect knowledge, the Mises–Hayek understanding of markets emphasizes that, at any moment, markets are pervaded by widespread mutual ignorance on the part of market participants. Markets do *not* at each instant accurately reflect the patterns of consumer preferences of that moment. This recognition of ignorance is the foundation of all subsequent wisdom in regard to the systematic quality of market processes. And it is here that the second of the above two features in the modern Austrian subjectivist view enters our theoretical picture.

This second subjectivist feature recognizes that mutual error on the part of market participants *creates opportunities for pure entrepreneurial profits.* The emergence of these opportunities offers attractive incentives for entrepreneurial discovery. Subjectivism enters here by way of our appreciation for the way in which such entrepreneurial discoveries are made. The modern Austrian approach emphasizes that it is not sufficient, in order for these opportunities to be grasped (and thus eliminated), that they exist. Unnoticed opportunities are in fact the key feature of the economic world which is entailed by our understanding of market ignorance. For hitherto unnoticed opportunities to be noticed and grasped, they must be *discovered;* and such discovery requires a special characteristic on the part of potential discoverers, viz. the propensity to be alert. Entrepreneurial alertness is the new subjectivist element implicit, at least, in the work of Mises and Hayek, which is now seen to drive the Mengerian market process through which consumer preferences come to dictate productive decisions. This idea of entrepreneurial alertness was expanded in Kirzner (1973, 1979, 1985, 1989).

So long as unexploited opportunities for pure profit still remain, economic analysis demonstrates that consumer preferences have, in some sense, been defied. A pure profit opportunity expresses the situation where a unit of resource service is currently being assigned to a lower value use than is in fact available elsewhere in the market. This latter unfulfilled value is one through which 'more urgent' consumer desires (as measured by money offered) are failing to be served as a result of the current allocation of resources services. The incentive for discovery provided by the available profit opportunity is the element that excites entrepreneurial alertness and thus drives the tendency towards a resource allocation pattern which, in the context of available resources, conforms to consumer preferences (as expressed by their money-backed demand). Modern Austrian subjectivist insights have served to illuminate the validity of Menger's vision of consumer sovereignty in the formulation of allocative decisions.

SCYLLA AND CHARYBDIS AVOIDED

It is instructive to notice how this modern Austrian version of subjectivism avoids the pitfalls inherent in each of the other two varieties of subjectivism we have seen to have derived from the Mengerian heritage. The Robbinsian subjectivism emphasized the allocative choice of market participants. But it did so, it seemed, by tacitly assuming (as in Walrasian theory) that all such allocative choices somehow correctly anticipated one another. There was nothing in the Robbinsian framework that could explain how any pattern of choices that failed so correctly to anticipate each other could systematically generate a more 'correct' array of decisions. In other words, the perfect knowledge implicit in the Robbinsian framework (and thus in modern microeconomics) requires us to imagine that market outcomes are automatically dictated (to be sure, via the network of mutually compatible maximizing decisions) by the underlying data (i.e. production possibilities and consumer utility functions) without any human intervention that might be conceived of as arranging that appropriate choices in fact be made. It was this aspect of the Robbinsian system, we saw, that seemed to convert the flaw in Menger's subjectivism into one of its own central features. The modern Austrian subjectivism has avoided this trap both by explicitly rejecting the assumption of perfect knowledge and by introducing a new (subjectivism-friendly) analytical scheme for understanding the equilibrating propensity which markets display.

The Shackle–Lachmann more radical variety of subjectivism, we saw, pointed to the complete denial of systematically equilibrating market tendencies. Whereas Menger's subjectivism was, in Lachmann's terminology, the 'expression of human "disposition" ', modern radical subjectivism argues for subjectivism as 'a manifestation of spontaneous action' (Lachmann 1986: 55). In the earlier view choice is the '*result* of the impact of constraints on human dispositions. In the new view choice is not a result of anything, but a *creative act*' (Lachmann 1986: 55). The markets are not to be seen as the systematic result of any set of objective circumstances whatever. Each decision is, in Shackle's phrase, 'a new beginning' (Lachmann 1986: 55), in principle wholly disengaged from all previous history. In this radical view, although it is conceded that people's choices are to be seen as rational responses to their perceived circumstances, it is insisted that these perceived circumstances are always, at least in part, the creation of their own mind (and thus by no means necessarily correspond to any *actual* circumstances). From such a position it is a short distance to the conviction that market outcomes are wholly unlikely ever systematically to manifest any equilibrating tendencies.

The modern Austrian version of subjectivism escapes these nihilistic conclusions by the injection of the entrepreneurial element. This element, although fully consistent with the subjectivist's insights into the autonomy of the human mind, enables us to rescue economic science from the abyss threatened by that radicalism which can discern no systematic continuity whatever in the course of human history.

Although subjectivism indeed affirms the autonomy of the human mind, our awareness of the entrepreneurial element in human action enables us to postulate a systematic linkage which shapes discoveries and actions into patterns that do tend correctly to reflect and anticipate those external phenomena relevant to successful action. In this fashion the modern Austrian version of subjectivism is able to explain and understand equilibrating market tendencies. In fact, as we have seen, it is not merely that this version of subjectivism permits such equilibrating tendencies, it is in fact the pivotal explanatory element which enables us to understand how, in a world without centralized direction, spontaneous social coordination can possibly emerge. This issue separating the modern Austrian version of subjectivism from the radical one deserves further exploration. This is especially the case in the light of some explicit criticisms raised by the radical school, against what we have termed the modern Austrian view.

RADICAL CRITIQUES AND MODERN AUSTRIAN DEFENCES

From the radical perspective the modern Austrian version of subjectivism is so moderate and diluted as to approach incoherence. Instead of being able to enjoy the best of both worlds (equilibrium theory and subjectivism), modern Austrian economics appears, from the radical perspective, to be shot through with crippling inner inconsistencies.

From the radical perspective, the options facing the social scientist are clear cut. Either one recognizes the autonomy of the human mind – involving the subjectivism, not only of human tastes and preferences, but also of human expectations and human interpretation of current events – or one does not. If human beings are not to be reduced to automatons whose choices are fully determined by existing circumstances (including tastes), then we must recognize the inherent indeterminacy of individual behaviour (and hence of market outcomes). It is all very well, the radical view would argue, to talk of successful entrepreneurial discovery. But the freedom of the human mind requires us, surely, to recognize the ubiquity of human and entrepreneurial error. Such recognition surely snaps, the argument runs, any linkages between initial circumstances and market outcomes, that might render equilibration a plausible possibility. Moreover the inherent unknowability of the future injects, in the radical view, yet an additional element of implausibility into the idea of market outcomes somehow coming into benign coordination with the 'underlying realities' (see, for more detail on these radical criticisms of modern Austrian subjectivism, Kirzner 1992: ch. 1).

After all, the argument runs, the relevant underlying realities presumably mean the future events upon which one wishes one's present decisions to impinge. But such future events are themselves strictly created by current decisions, so that there is no independent existence at all to any realities to which human activities are to be adjusted. The future that one wishes to anticipate (in the course of one's decision-planning) is created by those self-same decisions. To believe, as modern economics (together with mainstream economics) believes, that markets display systematic tendencies in which market outcomes tend correctly to fit in with an independently conceived future, is to surrender (as mainstream economics has surely already surrendered) all claims to consistent subjectivist recognition of the autonomy and freedom of the individual mind.

The modern Austrian version of subjectivism defends itself against these criticisms not by arguing the merits of moderation in subjectivism (as against a more consistent version of it), but by maintaining that a correctly conceived, utterly consistent version of subjectivism does indeed yield the conclusions of modern Austrian economics. Everyday human experience surely teaches us that human beings do successfully formulate decisions (and even multiperiod plans) in dealing with the vagaries of natural events and the uncertainties inherent in dynamic social intercourse. Neither the admitted unknowability of the future nor the admitted human propensity to err, nor any combination of the two, is able totally to frustrate human efforts to act rationally for the uncertain future. Humankind is not simply a helpless piece of flotsam buffeted by the hydrodynamics of social changes. Markets do display remarkable tendencies towards coordination. Our task as economists is not to explain how mistakes in decision-making may occur; such mistakes offer no mystery challenging our powers of explanation. Our task is to explain the observed tendencies to coordination. Modern Austrian economics, building on the subjectivist tradition from Menger to Mises and Hayek, finds this explanation not, as the radical subjectivists imagine, by compromising our commitment to subjectivist insights, but rather by deepening these insights. In the modern Austrian version of subjectivism, the idea of human entrepreneurial alertness is the analytical device that enables us to see how human creativity is in fact geared towards a tendency pointing to the discovery of opportunities that are in fact 'waiting' to be discovered.

It is true that the future is created by current decisions. But it is equally true that that future is, from the perspective of the acting individual, something to be anticipated as if it were a datum of nature. Since each of the current decisions (which together generate the future course of events) is motivated and guided by entrepreneurial alertness, we can confidently assert that such alertness *is* able successfully to tend to link current decisions to the 'underlying realities'.

SUBJECTIVISM AND THE AUSTRIAN TRADITION

We saw earlier in this paper how Menger's subjectivist perspective enabled him to see how economic phenomena are the expression of consumer valuations operating to govern the prices and uses made of all consumer goods and productive resources. Throughout the history of the Austrian School it is this subjectivism, pioneered by Menger, that has served as the most prominent feature of the school.

This paper has traced the varied fortunes of the Mengerian subjectivist legacy during the twentieth century. In particular we have argued that the key Mengerian insights find their preservation in that version of subjectivism that has informed and illuminated the modern revival of interest in Austrian economics. It is because alternative versions of the Mengerian subjectivist legacy seemed to have led either to an unacceptable modern neoclassical formalism on the one hand, or to an equally unacceptable radically subjectivist nihilism, on the other, that this modern revival of Austrian economics appears so promising.

REFERENCES

Hayek, F.A. (1949) *Individualism and Economic Order*, London: Routledge and Kegan Paul.

Hayek, F.A. (1955) *The Counter-Revolution of Science: Studies on the Abuse of Reason*, Glencoe, Illinois: Free Press.

Hayek, F.A. (1981) 'Introduction', in Menger (1981). Originally published as the introduction to *Collected Works of Carl Menger*, London: London School of Economics, 1934.

Kirzner, I.M. (1973) *Competition and Entrepreneurship*, Chicago: University of Chicago Press.

Kirzner, I.M. (1979) *Perception, Opportunity and Profit*, Chicago: University of Chicago Press.

Kirzner, I.M. (1985) *Discovery and the Capitalist Process*, Chicago: University of Chicago Press.

Kirzner, I.M. (1989) *Discovery, Capitalism and Distributive Justice*, Oxford: Basil Blackwell.
Kirzner, I.M. (1992) *The Meaning of Market Process: Essays in the Development of Modern Austrian Economics*, London and New York: Routledge.
Lachmann, L.M. (1986) *The Market as an Economic Process*, Oxford: Basil Blackwell.
Menger, C. (1981) *Principles of Economics*, New York and London: New York University Press.
Menger, C. (1985) *Investigations into the Method of the Social Sciences with Special Reference to Economics*, translated by F.J. Nock, New York: New York University Press; originally published in German in 1883.
Schumpeter, J.A. (1950) *Capitalism, Socialism and Democracy*, 3rd edn, New York: Harper and Row.

Part II

HISTORICAL ASPECTS OF AUSTRIAN ECONOMICS

2

CARL MENGER IN THE 1860s:

Menger on Roscher's *Grundlagen*

Yukihiro Ikeda

INTRODUCTION

The purpose of this paper is to examine the relationship between Carl Menger and Wilhelm Roscher using unpublished papers written by Menger in the 1860s. These papers, the Menger Papers, now housed in the Special Collections Department of the Perkins Library, Duke University, cast new light on the interpretation of Menger's *Grundsätze der Volkswirtschaftslehre* (see Barnett 1990).

This paper concerns itself with three topics. The first one is the making of the *Grundsätze* (first edition). There had been scanty information as to how Menger wrote his *Grundsätze*, for almost all his unpublished material had been inaccessible to scholars. However, Emil Kauder, one of the leading figures in this field, transcribed Menger's comments (1963) on Rau's *Grundsätze*. Thus he made the first step towards the study of the making of the *Grundsätze*. Kiichiro Yagi (1981), following Kauder, transcribed Menger's comments on Ricardo's *Principles*.

As mentioned, further information is now available thanks to the donation of Menger's unpublished papers to Duke University by Eve Menger, his granddaughter. Perhaps Yagi (1993) was the first to trace the making of the *Grundsätze* using this new material.[1] Yagi's arguments can be summarized as follows:

(a) He found a close affinity between German economics and Menger; thus reconfirming the conclusions made by Erich Streissler (1990a; 1990b).
(b) He emphasized the importance of the inverted triangles; as he pointed out, theoretically these inverted triangles are marginal utility functions.
(c) He discovered several outlines, which Menger wrote in the preparation of his *Grundsätze*.

The second problem is a revision of the *Grundsätze*. Menger began to revise his *Grundsätze* after its publication in 1871, but he was never able to complete the task. The second edition, which was compiled from various manuscripts of Menger, was edited by Karl Menger, his son. It is interesting to note that there are some differences between the two editions of the *Grundsätze*. According to Yagi (1988), these differences can be attributed to concessions that Menger made to the German Historical School.

Third, we will comment on the problematic relationship between Menger and the German Historical School. It has been believed that only disagreements had existed between the two. Recent studies indicate, however, that the traditional view of this issue is one-sided. For instance Max Alter (1990) succeeded in drawing a beautiful picture of Menger's historicism.[2] Another remarkable example is Streissler (1990a; 1990b). He revealed a closer link between Menger and not only German economics, but also Roscher, than had previously been known.

This paper, along with Streissler's work, shares a similar viewpoint that Menger's *Grundsätze* can be understood within the context of German economics. Boos (1986: 16–17) also emphasizes the relationship between German economics and Menger. But, here, I confine myself to Menger's relation with Roscher, which allows me to scrutinize their relationships from a broader perspective.

In the next section I will introduce the contents of the Menger Papers. The third section discusses Menger's outline in 1867 and compares it with Roscher's *Grundlagen*. The fourth highlights Menger's comments on Roscher's definition of goods, while the fifth concerns itself with Menger's excerpts from Roscher, made from the methodological point of view. In the last section some concluding remarks will be given.

THE MENGER PAPERS

In a diary, Menger claimed to have commenced studying economics in earnest in September, 1867.[3] This can be confirmed by his notebooks written in this period.

First of all, let me explain these notebooks with numbers on the front pages. Menger began to write *Heft 1* on September 7, 1867, and the last date appearing in this notebook is September 17. The next day he started writing *Heft 2*. Below are the beginning dates of various notebooks. An asterisk means that these notebooks cannot be dated.

Heft 2 September 18.
Heft 3 September 24.
Heft 4 September 30.
Heft 5 October 10.
Heft 6 October 21.
Heft 7 October.
Heft 8 November 1.
Heft 9 November 21.

Heft 10 December 10.
Heft 11 *
Heft 12 *
Heft 13 *
Heft 14 *
Heft 15 *
Excerpte 16 *
Heft 16 December 25.
Literatur A nach 15 *
Literatur B *

Also noteworthy are notebooks with the titles *Geflügelte Worte*[4] and *Theoretisches Repertorium* respectively. While the former is a medium-sized notebook, including excerpts from Roscher's *Grundlagen* and comments on it, the latter is a bigger one containing excerpts from Rau's *Grundsätze* and Roscher's *Grundlagen* with comments. As can be verified by his remark in the *Theoretisches Repertorium*, Menger used the sixth edition of the *Grundlagen*. This copy is now preserved in the Menger Library at Hitotsubashi University, Tokyo. On page 46 of the *Geflügelte Worte* there is a comment on Roscher's theory of goods; however, there is no date, but on page 52 there is the date August 9, 1867. From this, we can assume that Menger had begun reading the *Grundlagen* as early as August. On page 86 is the date July, 1868, demonstrating that he had been working on this notebook for at least two years. As will be mentioned in the next section, there is an outline of the *Grundsätze* on page 2 of the *Theoretisches Repertorium*, with the date September 6, 1867. But a detailed outline on page 4 is dated June 9, 1867, which may be misleading, for it is difficult to believe that an outline itself is preceded by a detailed outline.

The diary contains his curriculum vitae and much information about his daily life. There are several worthwhile points to be elaborated on in future investigations.

It is fascinating to note that he had written a novel entitled *Ewige Jude in Wien*. Yagi (1992: 96) suggests a possibility that Menger wrote his novel for a newborn paper, *Wiener Tagblatt*. In addition, he wrote several comedies in March, 1867. Although he took a doctorate from Cracow University in March, 1867, it seems that he did not have a clear picture of what he would do in the future. Then suddenly we encounter a statement like this: '1867 Sept. Werfe mich auf Nationaloek. Studiere Rau etc.'[5]

Although he had begun writing the *Geflügelte Worte* in August, the above comment is not too far from the truth since he commenced writing his *Theoretisches Repertorium* in September. The above statement is followed by descriptions of the years 1868, 1869 and 1870, in which he wrote his *Grundsätze* while working at *Debatte, Tagespresse* and *Volkszeitung*.

It is widely known that Karl Menger was preparing a biography of his father. The publication of this biography was also announced by *Philosophia*

Verlag. A draft below is supposed to be a part of this very book. The draft has twelve typewritten pages with some handwritten insertions by Karl Menger himself. Let us take a look at the first part of the draft:

> X. BEGINN DER AKADEMISCHEN LAUFBAHN
> (1. Habilitation. 2. Persönlicher Kummer. 3. Auswärtige Angebote. Erste Schüler. Ausserordentliche Professur. 4. Erste Vorlesungen und Beginn des Seminars. 5. "Fasse Plan zur Methodologie." 6. Bericht an den Kaiser. Weitere Entwicklungen. 7. Die juridische Fakultät. 8. "Ursachen meiner Kränklichkeit." 9. Sorge für junge Wissenschaftler. 10. Wieser und Böhm-Bawerk.)[6]
>
> (K. Menger, Diary: 1)

X is supposed to mean that this is a tenth chapter of the draft. On the top of this quote is inserted 'final', probably by Karl Menger himself, showing that he was already on his last stage of his work. Although the other chapters of the draft are missing, the remaining draft will bring some new information to light, such as the role of Lorenz von Stein on the *Habilitierung* of Menger. It should prove to be a good starting point for a complete biography of Menger in the future.

MENGER'S OUTLINES

As Yagi pointed out, we have at least three outlines for the *Grundsätze*; an outline at the outset of the *Theoretisches Repertorium*, an outline at the outset of the *Literatur A nach 15*, and an outline of four pages with the date November 20, 1870. Considered here is the first of these, dated September 6, 1867.[7] On page 2 of the *Theoretisches Repertorium* he wrote:

> Vorrede Einleitung
> 1. Wesen der Güter ohne Rücksicht auf Verkehr
> 2. Entstehung der Güter
> 3. Austausch der Güter
> 4. Entstehung von Tauschwerten
> 5. Verteilung der Güter
> 6. Verteilung der Tauschwerte
> 7. Consumtion der Güter
> 8. Consumtion der Tauschwerte.[8]

Menger begins with the essence of goods; then comes to the production of goods, the exchange of goods, the distribution of goods and the consumption of goods respectively. This structure reminds us of the classic works of Say and Mill. Although Menger drops population theory, the basic similarity between the above outline and the table of contents of Roscher's *Grundlagen* cannot be denied, for the latter has the following structure:

Einleitung
Erstes Buch Production der Güter
Zweites Buch Güterumlauf
Drittes Buch Vertheilung der Güter
Viertes Buch Consumtion der Güter
Fünftes Buch Bevölkerung[9]

(Roscher 1866)

Menger continued to summarize his outline, this time in more detail. A detailed outline below has the date June 9, which he perhaps confused with September 6, as already noted:

Vorrede-Einleitung
I. Wesen der Güter
1. Stellung des Menschen in der Natur,
2. Abzweigung des Rechts, 3. Wert,
4. Gut, 5. Harmonie der Zwecke,
6. Wirthschaft, 7. Vermögen, 8. Reichtum
(relativ), 9. Schätzung (absolute) (nach
Verh. der Mittel zu d. Zweck)
II. Entstehung der Güter
1. Naturproducte 2. Producte der Arbeit
3. Mittel zur Production 4. Arbeitsgliederung
5. Productivität (vom Güterstandpunkte)
6. Einfluss pers. Güter auf Production
III. Austausch der Güter
1. Tausch, 2. Preis, 3. Angebote, Nachfrage,
4. Geld, 5. Objectiver Wert
IV. Entstehung von Werten
1. Capital, 2. Intelligenz, 3. Productivität
des Capitals, 4. Productivität der Arbeit,
5. Persönliche Güter
V. Verteilung der Producte
1. Grundbesitzer, 2. Arbeiter,
3. Entreprenneur, 4. Kapitalist
VI. Verteilung der Werte
1. Grundrente, 2. Arbeitslohn,
3. Capitalzins, 4. Unternehmergewinn
VII. Consumtion der Güter
1. Consumtion, 2. Luxus
VIII. Consumtion der Werte [10]

(Menger, *Theoretisches Repertorium:* 6)

Also here we can identify the origins of the outline. Chapter 1, entitled the essence of goods, includes the common topics with the introduction of chapter 1 of Roscher's *Grundlagen*, such as goods, value, property, wealth and the economy. We observe a close relationship between Menger and Roscher in exchange and distribution theories as well. The similarity in consumption theory is striking. Menger's consumption theory is separated into two sections: consumption and luxury. This indicates a correspondence between the two, for Roscher's consumption theory is also divided into consumption in general and luxury.

The question of whether or not there is continuity between the above outline and his *Grundsätze* is of crucial importance. If there is a discrepancy between the two, it is quite possible that the outline was aborted in the process of preparing the *Grundsätze*. A critical comment in the second edition of the *Grundsätze* seems to suggest that this was the case:[11]

> Die in den bisherigen wirtschaftstheoretischen Untersuchungen der Systematik der Nationalökonomie zugrunde gelegte Klassifikation der Wirtschaftserscheinungen in solche der Produktion, der Verteilung und der Konsumtion der Güter beruht demnach zum Teile auf einer bloß äußerlichen, zum Teile auf einer geradezu irrtümlichen Auffassung des Wesens der menschlichen Wirtschaft im subjektiven und im objektiven Sinne.[12]
>
> (Menger 1923: 64)

Although the above criticism was made directly against Say's trichotomy, the same can be applied to post-Ricardian classical economics in general represented by Mill. Does it mean that Menger threw away his initial outline of 1867?

Other important material to be considered is the outline presumably written after the publication of the *Grundsätze* in 1871:

> II. Teil: Kapitalzins, Arbeitslohn,
> Grundrente, Einkommen, Kredit, Papiergeld.
> III. Praktischer Teil: Theorie der Produktion
> und des Handels. Die technischen
> Erfordernisse der Produktion. Die
> ökonomischen Bedingungen einer Produktion.
> Die Ersparnisse an der Produktion. Handel:
> Theorie der Technik des Handels, der
> Spekulation, Arbitrage, Detailhandel.
> IV. Teil: Kritik der gegenwärtigen
> Volkswirtschaft und Vorschläge zur sozialen
> Reform.[13]
>
> (Menger 1923: VI)

While there are some ambiguities as to the relation between the last two parts of the outline quoted above and the outline of 1867, it is fairly apparent that part 2 of the outline above includes a distribution theory, which corresponds to the chapters 5 and 6 of the preceding outline. Furthermore, it is likely that the first edition of the *Grundsätze*, which was intended to form the first part of the above outline, corresponds to the first four chapters of the outline in *Theoretisches Repertorium,* thereby revealing the origins of the masterpiece. The first three chapters of the *Grundsätze* deal with the essence of goods and the production of goods, while the last four chapters deal with the exchange of goods. Distribution theory in the proper sense of the word was left over to be elaborated on in the future. Thus, it may safely be said that Menger also in 1871 maintained his initial outline, which was written under strong influences of Roscher's *Grundlagen.*

MENGER AND ROSCHER ON THE DEFINITION OF GOODS

A definition of goods in Roscher's *Grundlagen* interested Menger, as can be shown by his comments both in *Geflügelte Worte* and *Theoretisches Repertorium.* Before scrutinizing his comments, a word may be in order on Roscher's definition itself. Roscher (1866: 1), said: 'Güter nennen wir alles dasjenige, was zur Befriedigung eines wahren menschlichen Bedürfnisses anerkannt brauchbar ist'.[14]

This sounds like a standard definition made from subjective value theories. Nevertheless, Menger, finding the above definition not subjective enough, made a penetrating criticism. He wrote in the *Geflügelte Worte*:

> Roscher sagt: Gut sei alles dasjenige was zur Befriedig. Eines wahren menschlich. Bedu. anerkannt brauchbar ist. Ist Tabakrauchen ein wahres menschliches Bedürfnis, ist Casanova ein solches? Wo ist da die Gränze? Sehr relativ und stets sehr streitig. Wie es auch sehr streitig ist was ein menschliches Bedürfnis überhaupt ist.[15]
>
> (Menger, *Geflügelte Worte*: 46)

Menger continued his criticism against Roscher:

> Ich behaupte es kann ein Ding ein Gut sein wenn auch nur ein Mensch dessen Brauchbarkeit anerkannt . . . Das anerkannt hat bei Roscher offenbar den Sinn anerkannt von allen Menschen oder doch von vielen Menschen was aber unrichtig wäre.[16]
>
> (*Ibid.*: 46,47)

Seen from subjective value theory, a diversity of preferences must be admitted, whereas Roscher's definition above does not allow such a diversity, which could not be accepted by Menger. This indicates that he had reached a subjective way of thinking already by August, 1867. Nonetheless, the above criticism did not appear in the *Grundsätze*. On the contrary, he seems to have accepted Roscher's arguments when he wrote:

> Ein eigenthümliches Verhältniss ist überall dort zu beobachten, wo Dinge, die in keinerlei ursächlichem Zusammenhange mit der Befriedigung menschlicher Bedürfnisse gesetzt werden können, von den Menschen nichts destoweniger als Güter behandelt werden. Dieser Erfolg tritt ein, wenn Dingen irrthümlicherweise Eigenschaften, und somit Wirkungen zugeschrieben werden, die ihnen in Wahrheit nicht zukommen, oder aber menschliche Bedürfnisse irrthümlicherweise vorausgesetzt werden, die in Wahrheit nicht vorhanden sind. In beiden Fällen liegen demnach unserer Beurtheilung Dinge vor, die zwar nicht in der Wirklichkeit, wohl aber in der Meinung der Menschen in jenem eben dargelegten Verhältnisse stehen, wodurch die Güterqualität der Dinge begründet wird. Zu den Dingen der ersteren Art gehören die meisten Schönheitsmittel, die Amulette, die Mehrzahl der Medicamente, welche den Kranken bei tief stehender Cultur, bei rohen Völkern auch noch in der Gegenwart gereicht werden, Wünschelruthen, Liebestränke u. dgl. m., denn alle diese Dinge sind untauglich, diejenigen menschlichen Bedürfnisse, welchen durch dieselben genügt werden soll, in der Wirklichkeit zu befriedigen. Zu den Dingen der zweiten Art gehören Medicamente für Krankheiten, die in Wahrheit gar nicht bestehen, die Geräthschaften, Bildsäulen, Gebäude etc. wie sie von heidnischen Völkern für ihren Götzendienst verwandt werden, Folterwerkzeuge u. dgl. m.[17]
>
> (Menger 1968: 4)

Menger classified the situations under two cases. In the first case, things become goods due to the insufficient understanding of the causal relationship between goods and wants. In this case wants themselves are considered to be justified. In the second case, however, wants are said to be untrue, apparently from the viewpoint of Menger himself. Obviously he accepted the argument which he had considered to be unfounded in 1867. In a footnote in Chapter 1 of the *Grundsätze*, Menger (1968: 2) mentioned Roscher's definition of goods, this time without any critical comments. It can be said that Roscher's discussion contributed to the normative bias of the *Grundsätze*.[18]

SOME METHODOLOGICAL ISSUES

In this section we shall deal with two issues, which are favourite ones of the German Historical School: the possibility of economic laws and the role of self-interest in economic science. As already noted, it is widely accepted that there is a gulf between Menger and the German Historical School concerning these issues. Here I shall endeavour to show the one-sidedness of the traditional view, using Menger's manuscripts of the 1860s. In the first place let us see what Menger said in the *Theoretisches Repertorium*:

> Anm. 4) Der Zusammenhang des Ganzen ist meist viel wichtiger als die analysirten Einzelheiten. Der unerklarbare Hintergrund muss zugestanden werden, ob man ihn nun Lebenskraft, Volksgeist, Gedanken Gottes etc. nennt ist gleichgiltig.[19]
>
> (Menger, *Theoretisches Repertorium*: 3)

This is, in fact, a summary of a footnote on page 24 of Roscher's *Grundlagen*. Roscher intended to overcome mystical statements often made by radical historicists, while admitting the limits of economic science. In other words, he tried to keep distance from fanatic historicism or relativism, although he is known as a founder of the German Historical School. At least partially, this well-balanced standpoint of Roscher was shared by Menger in his criticism against Schmoller, in which he insisted on distinguishing himself from mystical historicism represented by Savigny.[20]

Next we will look at self-interest. See the following summary, which is again a digest from Roscher's *Grundlagen*:

> Roscher ibid Die Volkswirthschaft ist mehr, als ein Nebeneinander vieler Privatwirthschaften. Streit der Ansichten: Die Einen sagen Volksw. ist nur Organisation des Eigennutzes. Die Menschen handeln am gemeinnützigsten wenn sie ihr eigenes Interesse fördern. Läugnen die Idee der Nationalität. etc. Die Anderen führen an dass der Mensch Opfer für die Zukunft der Nation bringt. etc.[21]
>
> (Menger, *Theoretisches Repertorium*: 52)

The beginning of the above summary was taken from Roscher's *Grundlagen*, although Menger's citation slightly differs from the original. It is noteworthy that the basic ideas of the German Historical School were already presented in the above quote: such as the private economy being incompatible with the national economy, and the problem of nationality. Menger attempted to summarize two discrepant assertions in his own words later in the quote. According to the first, there is a harmony between self-interest and social welfare; whereas in the second, such a harmony is discredited. However, Menger avoided giving a definite answer as to which one is right.

Another important statement is found in the section *Ethische Momente* in the *Theoretisches Repertorium*. The title of the section itself reveals his strong concern with the framework of the German Historical School:

> Dass keine Privatwirthschaft ganz unabhängig von Gemeinsinn sein kann, ist schon daraus zu entnehmen, dass sie im Gemeinwesen ihre Wurzel hat und das Gemeinwesen selbst den Eigennutz sehr fördert. Wir haben nicht nur einen Verstand auch Gefühl. Je mehr wir in unserer allgemeinen Befriedigung von dem Urteile der Menschen abhängig werden, um so mehr haben die Ideen der Gesellschaft Macht über uns. Die Ideen, welche die Grundlage des Zusammenlebens des Menschen mit all den ungeheuren Vorteilen dieses letztern bilden,

> erscheinen als öffentliches Gewissen, mit dem der einzelne oft in Widerstreit ist im Ganzen jedoch nur selten.[22]
>
> (*Ibid.*: 48)

Menger's standpoint was rather ambivalent. On the one hand he knew well the importance of social welfare, thereby indicating concession to the German Historical School. But on the other hand, the discrepancy between self-interest and social welfare was considered to be generally rare, as the last sentence in the quote showed. Here Menger did not seem to be satisfied with the criticism of the German Historical School made against the English Classical School.

CONCLUDING REMARKS

This paper has shown that the traditional interpretation concerning the relationship between Menger and the German Historical School is one-sided. Menger had read Roscher's *Grundlagen* before the publication of the *Grundsätze*. Although he criticized Roscher, sometimes rather severely, Menger turns out to be his follower in some sense: on pages 28–31, I have shown that a prototype of Menger's outline can be found in Roscher's *Grundlagen*. On pages 31–32, it was demonstrated that Menger in his *Grundsätze* accepted Roscher's definition of goods notwithstanding his criticism in 1867. On pages 32–34, his view on the ethically oriented economics was examined; Menger shared a framework similar to the Historical School in 1867.

All these findings indicate that a re-examination is now necessary with regard to the relationship between Menger and the Historical School. Also for this aim, the new material at Duke University will continue to be a valuable source from which many inferences can be drawn.

NOTES

Comments from Harald Winkel, Jürgen Backhaus, Gerrit Meijer and Ulrich Fellmeth and anonymous referees have been helpful in revising the paper. My thanks also go to Hiroyasu Iida, Denzo Kamiya, Toru Maruyama and Kiichiro Yagi for their comments on the first version of the paper. Ken Gordon and Hussein Kotby helped to make my English readable. Needless to say the usual caveat applies. I am also indebted to the Special Collections Department of the Perkins Library, Duke University, for their assistance and permission to quote from the Menger Papers. Citing these materials, I tried to keep the original spelling. Today we have to write *Produkt* instead of *Product* or *gleichgültig* instead of *gleichgiltig* in German according to the rules of *Rechtschreibung*. But here I cited just like Menger wrote his notebooks. The same applies to the abbreviations, which the readers can often meet in these kind of notebooks. The citations are translated in English in the notes. Last but not least, I would like to thank the Nomura Tohshi Shintaku for grants for my research in the United States.

1 Yagi (1992), using this new material at Duke University, gives a full discussion about the activities of Carl Menger as a journalist and his relationship with Rudolf.

2 This does not mean that Alter's thesis is generally accepted. See for instance White (1990). The following characterization of Alter's assertions by White is quite right, when the latter says: 'I hypothesize that Alter's ultimate aim is to rehabilitate the doctrines of the Historical School. Alter's judgment of Menger thus boils down to: well, he was better than Walras, but not quite as good as Schmoller' (White 1990: 356–357).

3 This section draws heavily on Yagi (1993).

4 *Geflügelte Worte* means in German a book compiled from various familiar quotes in various nations. A typical example is a book edited by Georg Büchmann (1867). Presumably what Menger had in mind was Büchmann's book, for the first edition of the latter was published already in 1864, when Menger was 23 or 24 years old. This information is brought to me by courtesy of Backhaus.

5 C. Menger, *Tagebuch*: 14. English translation is as follows: 'September 1867. Threw myself into economics. Studied Rau etc.'

6 English translation is as follows:

X. BEGINNING OF THE ACADEMIC CAREER.

1. Appointment to university lecturer. 2. Personal worries. 3. Offers from foreign countries. The first students. Extraordinary professorship. 4. The first lectures and the beginning of the seminar. 5. 'Drawing sketch of methodology.' 6. Report to the Emperor. Further developments. 7. The faculty of law. 8. 'Reasons for my sicklyness.' 9. Worries about young scholars. 10. Wieser and Böhm-Bawerk.

7 For the details of these outlines see Yagi (1993). Yagi already mentioned a close link between the outline in the *Theoretisches Repertorium* and German economics in general. Here efforts are made to find a root of this outline in Roscher's *Grundlagen*.

8 Translation is as follows:

Introduction
1 Essence of goods
2 Formation of goods
3 Exchange of goods
4 Formation of exchange values
5 Distribution of goods
6 Distribution of exchange values
7 Consumption of goods
8 Consumption of exchange values

9 Roscher (1866), table of contents. Translation is as follows:

First book: Production of goods
Second book: Circulation of goods
Third book: Distribution of goods
Fourth book: Consumption of goods
Fifth book: Population

10 Translation is as follows:

Preface-Introduction.

I. Essence of goods. 1. Position of human being in nature. 2. Branch of law. 3. Value. 4. Good. 5. Harmony of purposes. 6. Economy. 7. Property. 8. Wealth (relative). 9. Estimation (absolute) (According to the relation of the means to the purpose).

II. Formation of goods. 1. Natural products. 2. Products of labour. 3.

Means of production. 4. Organization of labour. 5. Productivity (from the viewpoint of goods). 6. Influence of personal goods on production.
III. Exchange of goods. 1. Exchange. 2. Price. 3. Supply demand. 4. Money. 5. Objective value.
IV. Formation of values. 1. Capital. 2. Intelligence. 3. Productivity of capital. 4. Productivity of labour. 5. Personal goods.
V. Distribution of products. 1. Landlord. 2. Labourer. 3. Entrepreneur. 4. Capitalist.
VI. Distribution of values. 1. Rents. 2. Wages. 3. Interest on capital. 4. Entrepreneurial profit.
VII. Consumption of goods. 1. Consumption. 2. Luxury.
VIII. Consumption of values.

11 The following interpretation of the second edition of the *Grundsätze* is based on a comment from Ken Mizuta.

12 Translation is as follows: 'Until now the base of economic–theoretical investigations of the system of economics, namely the classification of economic phenomena into production, distribution and consumption of goods is partially based on the supervisional, partially wrong understanding of the essence of the humane economy in the subjective and objective meaning.'

13 Translation is as follows: 'Second part: Interest on capital, wages, rents, income, credit, paper money. Third part: Practical part: Theory of production and commerce. The technical conditions of production. The economic conditions of productions. Savings on productions. Trade. Theory of trade techniques, speculation, arbitrage and retail trade. Fourth part: Criticism of the present economy and suggestions for social reform.'

14 Translation is as follows: 'Goods are anything which can be used for the satisfaction of any true human needs, and whose utility for this purpose is recognized' (Roscher 1982: 53). The quotes from Lalor's translation, including this one, are changed slightly due to the differences between the thirteenth and the sixth edition. Furthermore some terminologies are translated differently, based on my own interpretation.

15 Translation is as follows: 'Roscher says: Goods are all things, which are recognized as useful for the satisfaction of true needs of human beings. Is smoking a true need of human beings? Is Casanova such a thing? Where is the border? Very relative and very controversial at all times. Just as the very definition of a human need is controversial.'

16 Translation is as follows: 'I maintain that a thing can be good, even if only one person recognizes the usefulness of that thing . . . Recognition in Roscher has the meaning that it is recognized by everybody or by many people, which would not be correct.'

17 Translation is as follows: 'A special situation can be observed whenever things that are incapable of being placed in any kind of causal connection with the satisfaction of human needs are nevertheless treated by people as goods. This occurs (1) when attributes, and therefore capacities, are erroneously ascribed to things that do not really possess them, or (2) when non-existent human needs are mistakenly assumed to exist. In both cases we have to deal with things that do not, in reality, stand in the relationship already described as determining the goods-character of things, but do so only in the opinions of people. Among things of the first class are most cosmetics, all charms, the majority of medicines administered to the sick by peoples of early civilizations and by primitives even today, divining rods, love potions, etc. For all these things are incapable of actually satisfying the needs they are supposed to serve. Among

things of the second class are medicines for diseases that do not actually exist, the implements, statues, buildings, etc., used by pagan people for the worship of idols, instruments of torture, and the like' (Menger 1950: 53).

18 As for the normative bias of Menger's economics, see Nakayama.

19 Translation is as follows: 'In many cases the connection of the whole is much more important than the analyzed parts. The inexplicable background must be admitted. Whether we call it vital force, spirit of the nation, or thought of God, makes no difference.'

The original footnote of Roscher is as follows: 'Ob man den unerklärbaren Hintergrund, vor dem unsere Analyse jeweilig stehen bleiben musz, Lebenskraft, Gattungstypus, Volksgeist oder Gedanken Gottes nennt, ist für jetzt wissenschaftlich gleichgültig. Um so nothwendiger im Allgemeinen die Selbsterkenntnisz und Ehrlichkeit, welche dasz Vorhandensein jenes Hintergrundes zugesteht und nicht durch Leugnung desselben den Zusammenhang des Ganzen leugnet, der meistens viel wichtiger ist, als die analysirten Einzelheiten. Ebenso entschieden vreilich musz ich gegen Verketzerungsgelüste protestiren, welche die heilige Pflicht der Wissenschaft nicht begreifen, durch immer weiter gehende Forschung jenen unerklärbaren Hintergrund immer weiter zurückzuschieben' (Roscher 1866: 24, fn. 4).

English translation of this footnote is as follows: 'Whether we call the inexplicable backgrounds, which our analysis cannot reach, vital force, generic form, spirit of the nation, or God's thought, is for the present a matter of scientific indifference. All the more necessary are the self knowledge and honesty, in general, which admit the existence of this background, and which do not, by denying it, deny the connection of the whole, which is for the most part much more important than the analyzed parts. But of course at the same time I must enter my energetic protest against the imputation of heresy made by those who do not comprehend the sacred duty of science, by never ceasing investigation, to push farther back the bounds of this inexplicable background' (Roscher 1982: 82, fn. 3).

20 Menger wrote: 'Schmoller macht mir den Vorwurf, dass ich "über W. Roscher's und B. Hildebrand's historische Arbeiten klage", er sucht bei seinen Lesern den Eindruck hervorzurufen, dass ich Knies mit einigen wenigen Worten "abgethan" habe, er bezeichnet mich als einen Anhänger des Manchesterthums, imputirt mir Sympathien für den Mysticismus des Savignyschen Volksgeistes u. dgl. m.' (Menger 1970: 90).

English translation is as follows: 'Schmoller blames me for my complaints about the historical works of W. Roscher and B. Hildebrand. He tries to evoke in the readers the impression that I did with Knies in a few words. He calls me a supporter of the Manchester School. He imputes sympathies for the mysticism of national spirit *à la Savigny* to me, etc.'

21 Translation is as follows: 'Roscher ibid. The national economy is more than the juxtaposition of many private economies. Differences of opinions: the one says that the national economy is only an organization of self-interest. People act socially optimal, when they promote their own interest. They deny the idea of nationality, etc. The other argues that people bring sacrifices for the future of the nation, etc.'

Roscher wrote: 'Die Volkswirthschaft ist mehr als ein bloszes Nebeneinander vieler Privatwirthschaften; gerade so, wie ein Volk mehr ist, als ein bloszer Haufe von Individuen, und das Leben des menschlichen Körpers mehr, als ein bloszes Gewühl chemischer Wirkungen.' This can be translated as follows: 'The national economy is more than the simple juxtaposition of many private economies, just like a nation is more than the simple aggregation of individuals, and the life of the human body is more than a simple turmoil of chemical influences' (Roscher 1982: 21). It seems that the latter part of Menger's summary is based on pages 21–22 of Roscher's *Grundlagen*.

22 Translation is as follows: 'That no private economy can be entirely independent of the public spirit, can be already deduced from the fact that the former has its roots in the community and that the community stimulates private interest. We have not only intelligence, but also feelings. The more we are dependent on the judgements of other people for our general satisfaction, the more the ideas of society have influence on us. The ideas, which form the basis of human society with all its huge advantages of the latter, appear as public conscience, with which the individual comes often into conflict – but on the whole only rarely.'

REFERENCES

Alter, M. (1990) *Carl Menger and the Origins of Austrian Economics*, San Francisco and Oxford: Boulder.

Barnett, M. (1990) 'The Papers of Carl Menger in the Special Collections Department, William Perkins Library, Duke University', in Caldwell, B.J. (ed.) *Carl Menger and his Legacy in Economics* (Annual Supplement to *History of Political Economy* 22), Durham and London: Duke University Press.

Boos, M. (1986) *Die Wissenschaftstheorie Carl Mengers*, Wien, Köln, Graz: Boehlau.

Büchmann, G. (1867) *Geflügelte Worte*, vierte umgearbeitete und vermehrte Auflage, Berlin. Neubearbeitet von Paul Dorpert, Zürich: Classen 1946.

Menger, C. (1923) *Grundsätze der Volkswirtschaftslehre*, 2. Auflage mit einem Geleitwort von Richard Schüller aus dem Nachlass hrsg. von Karl Menger, Wien und Leipzig: Hoelder-Pichler-Tempsky/Freytag.

Menger, C. (1950) *Principles of Economics*, translated and edited by James Dingwall and Bert F. Hoselitz, Glencoe, Illinois: Free Press.

Menger, C. (1963) *Carl Mengers erster Entwurf zu seinem Hauptwerk "Grundsätze" geschrieben als Anmerkungen zu den "Grundsätzen der Volkswirthschaftslehre", von K.H. Rau*, Bibliothek der Hitotsubashi Universität, Tokyo.

Menger, C. (1968) *Gesammelte Werke*, hrsg. von F.A. Hayek, Tübingen: Mohr/Siebeck, 2. Auflage, Bd. 1, *Grundsätze der Volkswirthschaftslehre*.

Menger, C. (1970) 'Die Irrtümer des Historismus in der deutschen Nationalökonomie', in *Gesammelte Werke*, hrsg. von F.A. Hayek, Tübingen: Mohr, 2. Auflage, Bd. 3.

Menger, C. *Geflügelte Worte*, Box 2, Menger Papers, The Special Collections Department, William Perkins Library, Duke University.

Menger, C. *Theoretisches Repertorium*, Box 4, Menger Papers, The Special Collections Department, William Perkins Library, Duke University.

Menger, C. *Tagebuch*, Box 21, Menger Papers, The Special Collections Department, William Perkins Library, Duke University.

Menger, K. *Diary Transcriptions and Notes on Carl Menger's Life by Karl Menger*, Box 21, The Special Collections Department, William Perkins Library, Duke University.

Nakayama, C. *Continuity and Discontinuity in the Marginal Revolution: The Case of Carl Menger* (in Japanese), unpublished.

Roscher, W. (1866) *Die Grundlagen der Nationalökonomie*, 6. Auflage, Stuttgart: Cotta.

Roscher, W. (1982) *Principles of Political Economy*, translated by John J. Lalor, Vol. I, Chicago.

Streissler, E. (1990a) 'The Influence of German Economics on the Work of

Menger and Marshall', in Caldwell, B.J. (ed.) *Carl Menger and his Legacy in Economics* (Annual Supplement to *History of Political Economy* 22), Durham and London: Duke University Press.

Streissler, E. (1990b) 'Carl Menger, der deutsche Nationalökonom', in B. Schefold (ed.) *Studien zur Entwicklung der ökonomischen Theorie X* (Schriften des Vereins für Socialpolitik, Band 115/X), Berlin: Duncker und Humblot.

White, L.H. (1990) 'Restoring an "Altered" Menger', in Caldwell, B.J. (ed.) *Carl Menger and his Legacy in Economics* (Annual Supplement *History of Political Economy* 22), Durham and London: Duke University Press.

Yagi, K. (1981) 'Menger on Ricardo: C. Menger's Notes on Ricardo's "Principles of Political Economy" ', *Okayama Economic Review* 13 (1).

Yagi, K. (1988) *Studies on the Austrian School* (in Japanese), Nagoya University Press.

Yagi, K. (1992) 'Carl Menger as Editor: Significance of Journalistic Experience for his Economics and for his Later Life', *Revue européenne des sciences sociales,* XXX (92).

Yagi, K. (1993) 'Carl Menger's *Grundsätze* in the Making', *History of Political Economy* 25 (4), Winter.

3

COMMENT ON YUKIHIRO IKEDA'S 'CARL MENGER IN THE 1860s'

Jürgen G. Backhaus

Yukihiro Ikeda, working with the Menger Papers now deposited at Duke University, and building on the work of Kiichiro Yagi, offers us a rare glimpse into the development of Menger's world of ideas. Looking at how these ideas were formed is important in understanding not only from whom Menger borrowed and where he felt that he was himself making important contributions. The formative period can also give us clues about further developments in the history of economic ideas that owed impulses to Menger's work and the way it was presented, yet by themselves and in their end results could not be determined by him. In particular, the turns taken in the *Methodenstreit* and the way this academic *Kräftemessen* has set the tone and influenced the substance of economic discourse appear in a very different light indeed when we note one of Yukihiro Ikeda's main results which shows the substantial common ground shared by Menger on the one hand and the Historical School on the other. This result is in line with other recent work on this subject, e.g. work published by Max Alter, and the author is right in insisting that the relationship between the Austrians and the Historical School needs to be looked at again.

This paper is particularly interesting in showing us how Menger went about his work. He started to study economics only fairly late, when he was 26 or 27 years of age, after having written novels and comedies and having received his law doctorate from the University of Cracow (apparently without a dissertation). Interestingly, during the same month of March, 1867, when he received his doctorate and when he had just turned 27 (on February 23), he wrote two of these comedies. Then, half a year later in September, he started to study economics seriously. And he did so with the most basic introductory book, the one by Rau (and not, for example, Adam Smith's *Wealth of Nations*). It did not take long and he had plans to write an introduction himself. After all, Menger was primarily working as a journalist for three Vienna newspapers. He patterned the outline primarily after the most successful introductory textbook, the one by Roscher. And he went about his work in a very systematic and idiosyncratic way: as was customary for law students, he tried to compile a teaching document (in this case for his own study) in which the material was summarized in the most compressed form possible. As is still customary in law studies, he called this a *Repertorium,* but the twist is the attribute: it is a *theoretisches Repertorium.* We learn that Menger familiarized himself with economics in the way one would do so with law. A second notebook has the title *Geflügelte Worte,* which is the German term for a book in which, typically in alphabetical order and by different languages, famous quotes from the works of classical and contemporary literary authors are compiled. (See for example one of the most famous ones: Georg Büchmann, *Geflügelte Worte und Zitatenschatz,* verbesserte neue Ausgabe mit über 3.500 Zitaten aus Deutschland, Russland, Frankreich, Dänemark, England, Spanien, Italien. Zürich: Classen, no year). This second notebook primarily contains definitions copied from other authors.

The difference to the working approach of his later contender in Berlin, Gustav Schmoller, could hardly have been greater. The latter, having defended a prize-winning dissertation in economics, set out to compile, from scratch, a large data set of industrial statistics, i.e. the industry census for his native kingdom of Württemberg, and published his first widely acclaimed scholarly article on basic principles of income taxation.

Ikeda shows clearly that Menger did not gather his material uncritically. He disagreed with Roscher's definition of an economic good which requires some objective, generally agreed-upon utilitarian characteristics. Roscher actually makes no distinction between the German terms *Bedürfnis,* designating some publicly or socially sanctioned need, and *Gut,* which is just an object of individual demand. Menger, despite criticisms, adopts Roscher's definition. However, I am not sure that we can, from the critical notes, conclude that 'this indicates that he had reached the subjective way of thinking already by August, 1867' (Ikeda, page 31). His qualms are less about objectivism than of a moral nature as they deal with smoking tobacco and reading Casanova. The main disagreement between Menger and the Historical School is said to have consisted of Menger's not sharing the German criticisms of some aspects of the English classical system. It is worth our while to look at the reason given for this reservation. The ideas that form the bases for human co-operation with their enormous advantages towards individual human beings appear as a public conscience with which the individual may be in disagreement - but on the whole fairly infrequently. This is an empirical statement which is certainly hard to test.

4

NICOLAAS GERARD PIERSON: HIS IMPACT ON AND HIS CONTRIBUTION TO ECONOMIC SCIENCE

*A. Godart-van der Kroon**

INTRODUCTION

Nicolaas Gerard Pierson (1839–1909) created the foundation for a fully developed theoretical economic science in the Netherlands. Before Pierson there had been important economists like Mees, van Rees and others (Hasenberg Butter 1969: 99–104). Pierson, however, aimed to construct a new economic theory (van Maarseveen 1981: 44). Dutch economics was dominated in those days by French economists like Bastiat and Say. Mees and Pierson introduced English economics and adapted it to the Netherlands.

Successive sections will treat: Pierson's life; his contribution to economic science; his contribution to the introduction of the marginal utility theory and the ideas of the Austrian School; and his contribution to economic theory in the international context. In the final section some conclusions will be drawn.

PIERSON'S LIFE

Pierson was born as the youngest son of Jan Lodewijk Gregory Pierson and Ada Oyens on February 7, 1839. He came from an extremely gifted family. His brother Allard, who was even more famous than Nicolaas, was a prominent theologian, philosopher and professor in the history of art in Amsterdam. Two sons of Allard, J.L. and H.D. Pierson, became bankers of the famous bank Pierson, Heldring en Pierson. Hendrik, another brother, studied theology in Utrecht. He became director of the Heldring Institutions. In this function he fought against prostitution, successfully in the end.

* I would like to thank Gerrit Meijer, and also Professor Charles H. Powers, University of Santa Clara, California and Visiting Professor at the University of Limburg, for helpful comments and other kinds of support. I also gratefully acknowledge the remarks by Hans Visser.

Pierson's parents formed part of the Reveil, a protestant movement opposed to conservatism and optimism (Allard Pierson 1904: 46–48). People of the Reveil were convinced that the human beings and society were deadly ill and the orthodox religion had not altered this (A. Pierson 1904: 48–49). The movement was originated in Geneva (Switzerland) about 1810.

Pierson's father was a merchant and that fact turned out to be important for Pierson's liberal economic opinions. At first Pierson intended to go into business, and was sent to England and the United States to study the cotton trade. Later he travelled to Germany (Verrijn Stuart 1911: 28). At the age of 20 he wrote a promising article, concerning trade and banking in Louisiana (USA), 'De handel en het bankwezen van den staat Louisiana (U.S.A.)' (1859), which was published in *Review for Economics and Statistics* of Mr W.A.E. Sloet tot Oldhuis. In this article Pierson explained the importance of a well-functioning banking system for the national economy. In fact this was a great problem in the United States: the banks produced too many banknotes, with the consequence that too much money was circulating (van Blom 1910: 4).

Pierson's attempt at starting a cotton shop and making a living out of it was not very effective. He had more success in studying for the examination in economics at the first Business School in Holland (in Amsterdam). On June 20, 1864 he passed his first and last examination with success (Verrijn Stuart 1911: 29). He continued to be attached to the Business School and to study economics. After that, success came very quickly. In 1868 the directorate of the Business School was offered to him, but he declined. He wrote to van Houten: 'One has to devote his life to this job. Do you want the job? That is the question. I, for one, do not have the ambition' (van Maarseveen 1990: 364). This job was also offered to van Houten, a close friend of Pierson and a politician, who turned it down also (van Maarseveen 1990: 369).

Pierson was also involved in the establishment of the Bank of Surinam (1864) and of the Kasvereniging. The intention of this last bank was to pay interest just like the joint stock banks in England (Verrijn Stuart 1911: 28–31). In 1868 he became one of the directors of De Nederlandsche Bank. Later he would become president of this bank. G.J. Goschen and W.C. Mees, both of whom he met during this period, were to have a very great influence on Pierson; Mees especially, concerning the question of bi-metallism.

Pierson occupied himself for much of the time with reorganization of the Dutch tax system. This system was obsolete and the tax burden was much heavier for poor parts of the population than it was for the richer parts. In order to discuss this matter a small circle of liberals was brought together, including Mees, Pierson, Buys, Geertsema, van Houten and Verkerk Pistorius. They did not propose an income tax. Instead, they pinned their faith to a combination of inhabited-house duty and death duties (Verrijn Stuart 1911: 32–36).

Besides these activities, Pierson was also a professor in economics and statistics at the University of Amsterdam from 1877 to 1885. In 1875 the University of Leyden conferred an honorary degree in law to Pierson. In 1881 the position of Minister of Finance was offered to Pierson, but he declined. In the same period the currency question was an important policy concern. In 1881 a Currency Conference was convened in Paris to discuss the comparative merits of the gold standard and bi-metallism. Pierson changed his mind about the subject twice.

In 1885 Pierson became president of De Nederlandsche Bank, later the Central Bank of the Netherlands. Also in 1885 the first tome of his *Leerboek der staathuishoudkunde* appeared, followed by the edition of the second tome in 1890.

From 1891 to 1894 Pierson took his seat in the Cabinet of van Tienhoven-Tak van Poortvliet (Verrijn Stuart 1911: 39). Although scientific work meant more to Pierson than his political career, he was the right person to bring about a change in social–economic policy (Verrijn Stuart 1911: 40). From 1897 to 1891 he was again Minister of Finance in the Cabinet of Pierson-Goeman Borgesius. New legislation appeared in the areas of education, child labour, (personal) military service, a new regulation of the health service, housing, and industrial injuries (Verrijn Stuart 1911: 42–43). This was a 'government of social justice' (van Maarseveen 1981: 221). However, Pierson himself admitted that 'the government had a too left-wing policy'.

In 1904 Pierson was at the very peak of his career: the University of Cambridge granted him the *doctor honoris causa* (Verrijn Stuart 1911: 44–45). In 1905 he put himself up for a Member of Parliament in order to end *the Kuyper-trend*. Kuyper was the leader of the Antirevolutionary Party, who aimed to re-establish religious education at schools. Kuyper had even established a pure Protestant (reformed) University at Amsterdam. It was not so much the aim of Abraham Kuyper that appalled Pierson, but his manner, which Pierson regarded as too demagogical and intolerant.

When Pierson was aging and in poor health, a special fund was created in his name in 1909. He died later that year on December 24 (van Maarseveen 1981: 222).

Pierson's personality was well balanced. Verrijn Stuart speaks of a 'totally honest, incorruptible personality, who would never surrender to improper policy. That is why he was a personality, that "reconciles and not divides" ' (Verrijn Stuart 1911: 42).

PIERSON'S CONTRIBUTIONS TO ECONOMIC SCIENCE

The philosophical background of Pierson

Pierson was a self-educated man who was a serious student of economic theories throughout his adult life. He was especially interested in English economists, not only because of his many visits to England and the United States, but also because these thinkers addressed practical economic questions (Verrijn Stuart 1911: 55).

A philosopher like Schopenhauer, highly praised by his friend van Houten, did not appeal to Pierson (van Maarseveen 1990: 163–164, letter of September 18, 1863 to van Houten). To Schopenhauer the individual person is nothing and, curiously enough for a liberal, Pierson agreed with Schopenhauer on that point. According to Pierson, the nineteenth century turned out to be too individualistic, in the field of religion, art, economics, etc. Pierson writes this to his friend van Houten in the same letter: 'We can see to what consequence this individualism takes us: in the United States (1863). The collapse of the United States is due solely to its individualism, which was so much praised in this country. It was not the question of slavery or democracy' (van Maarseveen 1990: 167).

Another subject covered by Schopenhauer was the denial of free will and determinism. Pierson approved this. 'Nothing speaks the free will', he wrote in the same letter of September 18, 1863. He does not agree, however, with the rejection of every form of religion by Schopenhauer. 'Schopenhauer speaks about God as a blind person about colours. Really, Schopenhauer is lacking any religious feeling. His whole existence lacks something because of that' (the same letter of September 18, 1863, van Maarseveen 1990: 170–171). Schopenhauer (1818) was definitely not Pierson's favourite philosopher.

Pierson felt more attracted to Marshall or Ricardo and – curiously enough for an adherent of the deductive method – the German Historical School. Marshall in particular fascinated Pierson. According to Verrijn Stuart the reason for this is the fact that Marshall was practically orientated (Verrijn Stuart 1911: 55). In his review of Marshall's book *Principles*, Pierson begins with a beautiful description. 'There are landscapes or books or people, which you see or read and enjoy immensely. They impress enormously. But once you must describe them, you cannot find the right words.' The same is the case with Marshall. No subject about which he has written can be described without consulting Marshall (Pierson 1891: 517). To recapitulate the content of the article, Marshall is not a fervent adherent of the laissez-faire policy. He feels sorry for the workers, and to ameliorate their misery is one of the reasons that Marshall studied economics (Pierson 1891: 522 and 538–539). Pierson also criticized Marshall's work, especially his treatment of production, but appreciated the fact that Marshall studied the German economists, at a time when the German and English schools were developing without noticing each other. On the whole Marshall sympathized with the German economists. He praised List, an economist who applied the method of historical comparison, and praised German economists for their contribution to the study of socialism and the economic role of the state (Pierson 1891: 525–526).

Adam Smith and Ricardo also influenced Pierson. In fact, Pierson never abandoned Ricardo's theory of rent (Verrijn Stuart 1911: 57). But he criticized Ricardo: 'Marshall is not a golddigger like Ricardo, who throws up everything that glitters a little, leaving it to us to make a choice and to say: this is ore, that is rubbish' (Pierson 1891: 517). And: 'Ricardo was at the same time the most genius and the most careless thinker we have ever known in the whole economic literature' (Pierson 1884: 342).

It was his feeling for applied economics that made Pierson study the English economists as well as the ideas of the Historical School (Verrijn Stuart 1911: 58). But members of the Historical School practised the method of induction and Pierson adhered only to the method of deduction. As Pierson summarized it: 'To generalize too quickly (like Adam Smith) is surely wrong. But if it is not allowed to generalize at all, how can we make the first step towards a real study of science? Because the aim of every science is first of all: to discover the unity in variety. The Historical School does not accept such a unity' (Pierson 1864a: 95–96).

Another figure who had a great influence on Pierson was the Dutch economist W.C. Mees. Mees was Pierson's teacher. Pierson wrote: 'He was a teacher for all the young ones' (Pierson 1890a: 501) and he praised Mees's brightness and original way of thinking (Pierson 1884: 326), and Mees's compelling arguments swayed Pierson in the bi-metallism controversy. Before he met Mees, Pierson had not even thought of accepting bi-metallism (Pierson 1866: 18 and 36). Mees was the only person at the Currency Conference (1881) in Paris to vote against the gold standard.

The same thing happened concerning the tax system. Pierson changed his ideas on this subject under the influence of Mees. Pierson initially shared the ideas of J.S. Mill regarding taxes on capital and interest. But Mees convinced Pierson that Mill's reasoning was a sophism. If capital produces interest, then it means that a new income has been shaped. The same capital will not be charged by the taxes. Pierson accepted this explanation by Mees (van Maarseveen 1981: 157).

The social problem (pauperism, wages)

Pierson was moved by the poverty of the working class. Most progressive liberals thought alike on this point. Pierson wrote about Marshall: 'He was prompted by emotions to his economic studies' and Verrijn Stuart adopted this phrase to describe Pierson. The basic ideas in his economic study were to raise production, to stimulate the formation of capital and to stop the destruction of capital, in order to relieve social distress. This was the *Leitmotiv* in his work (Verrijn Stuart 1911: 68). This stands in contrast to the socialist ideas of the day, for according to Pierson the equal division of income would not be sufficient to remove social distress. Workers would benefit much more from increasing production than from simple redistribution. He was not an advocate of strikes, unlike his friend van Houten, who wanted to abolish the prohibition of coalition, in order to make it easier for workers to strike (van Maarseveen 1981: 163).

The labour problem

Pierson's attitude towards this problem has been moulded by a 'warm sympathy with the underdog' (Verrijn Stuart 1911: 5–8). It was also a consequence of his education. The people who were adherent to the Reveil – so important for Pierson's way of life and thought (de Graaff 1929: 19–20) – were of the opinion that 'society was deadly ill' and for that reason 'the wealthy Christian had to make every effort to ease the fate of the underdog' (van Maarseveen 1981: 111 and A. Pierson 1904: 48). But after 1870 Pierson became more conservative. He corresponded with van Houten, and discussed this social problem with him. According to Pierson the cause was to be found in the extreme individualism of his time. He described in his letter (of March 18, 1863) how, over the ages, collectivism and individualism succeeded each other and that by the nineteenth century individualism prevailed in all aspects of life, including economics, poetry, painting and music. He wrote: 'Our century is now very individualistic. The consumer is king again, but the consumer is also producer, and according as he gets his rights on one hand, he is set apart on the other hand. He stops being the aim, he starts being the means. Almost all the improvements are for the benefit of the capitalists. The working class ride in the rear' (van Maarseveen 1990: 238, letter of January 9, 1866).

Pierson developed the notion of an organic society, with classes in equilibrium. Poverty results from a disturbance in this equilibrium (van Maarseveen 1981: 114). If wealth is the normal state of society as an organism, then poverty is a symptom of illness in society (Pierson 1864a: 90). According to van Maarseveen, Pierson reached this conclusion under the influence of the German Historical School (van Maarseveen 1981: 114). Pierson maintained that classes have to be dependent upon each other, for as soon as one class is less dependent than another, the social balance has been broken (Pierson 1864a: 90).

The problem of public finance (Taxation)

Public finance dominated much of the social scientific literature of the nineteenth century. Cohen Stuart, J.S. Mill, Wagner, Neumann and Schäffle all wrote about it. In the Netherlands the whole system of taxation (1821) was hopelessly out of date (Hasenberg Butter 1969: 91), for taxes were not levied according to tax-paying capacity.

From 1848 to 1893 – a very long period – a new and more just system of taxation was being created. In 1870 a committee including J.T. Buys, J.H. Geertsema, J.G. Gleichman, S. van Houten and W.A.P. Verkerk Pistorius was convened to advance ideas about the tax system. W.C. Mees was the chairman (Verrijn Stuart 1911: 34). Pierson seems to have taken charge of most activities (van Maarseveen 1981: 155). He wrote several articles about land tax, tax-paying capacity and the financial consequences of the tax reforms, etc. Van Houten, Geertsema and Buys wrote several memoranda. There was never a final statement (Verrijn Stuart 1911: 34–35). Pierson was opposed to income tax in that period (1870–1871). According to van Maarseveen, some Dutch economists were sceptical about the issue of income tax and rejected the idea out of hand (van Maarseveen 1981: 155). Pierson published a controversial article in 1871, *De inkomstenbelasting*, in which he stated that 'the income tax would not be advisable, not as such and not as a part of a tax system' (Pierson 1871: 49–56, spec. 55). He thought a combination of inhabited-house duty and death taxes would be sufficient. His argument against income tax was that pure income was very difficult to define. This point of view aroused the reaction of van Houten and Goeman Borgesius, who were in favour of income tax (van Maarseveen 1981: 158–159). This caused a discussion between Pierson and van Houten. Van Houten protested against Pierson's opinion about the taxes during a meeting at Felix Meritis in Amsterdam in January, 1871. Van Houten advocated income tax; according to him this tax was justifiable, but Pierson rejected at that moment the very idea of income tax, because of scientific analysis (van Maarseveen 1981: 159). However, Pierson did change the tax system after more reflection on theory and practice. Backed by van Houten, Pierson introduced the wealth tax in 1892 and the tax on business revenues in 1893, the so-called divided or two-tracked income tax (van Maarseveen 1981: 219–220 and van de Poel 1966: 141).

Value

Value was another of the many subjects discussed by Pierson. However, his interest in this subject was secondary and his treatment of it was not systematic. For example, he did not mention van Houten's thesis about value (1859), although Van Houten's thesis was considered a precursor of the Jevons' theory of value (van Maarseveen 1981: 71; Bordewijk 1931: 625). Nor did he mention Von Wieser's book, dedicated to the problem of value: *Der natürliche Wert* (1890). According to Verrijn Stuart this subject was too abstract to be of primary concern for Pierson, although later on he did accept the theory of marginal utility (Verrijn Stuart 1911: 56).

According to Hayek and Howey, Wieser was the first to use the term 'marginal utility'. 'He wrote the introduction specifically as a translation of Jevons' "terminal utility" or "final degree of utility".' Howey refers to an earlier book of von Wieser, *Uber den Ursprung und die Hauptgesetze des wirtschaftlichen Wertes* (Howey 1960: 144–146). Hayek refers to *Der natürliche Wert* (Hayek 1926: 512–530, especially 517–518).

Pierson tried to give a definition of value for the first time in his article about Ricardo's system: *De grondslagen van Ricardo's stelsel* (1864b: 126–211). Roughly translated, this means 'The Principles of Ricardo's Theory'. Although Ricardo made many mistakes, Pierson also appreciated the importance of his contribution. First these principles have to be clearly explained; then they can be properly criticized (Pierson 1864b: 128–129).

In the appendix of his article Pierson makes a distinction between exchange-value and use-value. In this he adopts the theory of Adam Smith (Pierson 1864b: 205). Adherents of the German Historical School, like Friedländer and Roscher, wanted to avoid this distinction in favour of only one notion of value: the value that goods have when they satisfy needs. Pierson did not agree with this notion and he maintained Smith's definition, which according to Pierson was informed by common sense (Pierson 1864b: 210).

One cannot find any tendency towards the marginal utility theory in Pierson's early work despite the influence of his friend van Houten (1859). Later – in his *Leerboek*, his greatest achievement – he introduced the theories of Menger and Jevons (Pierson 1885: 65).

Van Houten attacked Ricardo's theory of value, just as Menger, Walras and Jevons had. Ricardo, for instance, was of the opinion that value was defined by the costs of production, while Menger, Walras and Jevons were of the opinion that this was not decisive. They held 'that large costs incurred in producing goods will not necessarily result in their having high prices' (Landreth 1976: 203). Van Houten presumed that value was based on utility and adherents of the marginal utility school maintained that the value of a good is determined by marginal utility. They perceived 'another fundamental flaw in pre-classical and classical economic theory: its failure to recognize that the significant element in price determination is not total or average utility, but marginal utility'. They were able to elucidate the old diamond – water paradox: diamonds have high prices but little utility, while water has a low price but high utility. While classical theorists could not elucidate this paradox 'because they thought in terms of the total utility which diamonds and water give to consumers and did not understand the importance of their marginal utility' (Landreth 1976: 203). In fact we can say that van Houten has been more progressive than Pierson in this matter. In 1864 the latter still quoted Adam Smith and much later he adopted the theory of Jevons and Menger.

According to van Maarseveen, Pierson did not even accept the subjective theory of value. For that reason Pierson did not mention van Houten and Asser in his article. However, Pierson applied the theory of value to the distribution of income because services as well as goods have their value (Pierson 1885: 85), arguing that the division of goods not only depends on exchange value, but also on rent, lease, interest, profit and wages (Pierson 1885: 87). The very important article that Pierson wrote on 'The Problem of Value in the Socialist Society' (1902) will be discussed later.

Of course Pierson, as a director of De Nederlandsche Bank, was very interested in banking. He wrote various articles about this subject, in 1863, 1866, 1867 and 1883 (about the change in the value of gold since the discovery of gold in California and Australia). He also wrote on the history of economic thought. Later he applied himself to other aspects of economics.

Methodology

Already at the start of his career as an economic scientist, Pierson had decided on the matter of methodology (Pierson 1861): the method of deduction. In a later article he describes this as follows: to deduce knowledge from other knowledge (Pierson 1885: 39). One has to proceed as follows:

(a) To explain the elements of knowledge already obtained;
(b) To co-ordinate well-known truth in such a way that it produces a new truth (Pierson 1861).

Pierson noticed that the science of economics flourished when the deductive method had been applied, and was stationary when the inductive method had been applied (Pierson 1885: 39). Development of the new theory of value seemed to exemplify this. Pierson thought that operations of economic causes can only be understood by isolating them one after the other. Facts without a 'firm backbone of reasoning' were without meaning, according to Marshall, and Pierson shares this opinion (Pierson 1891: 527). In contrast, the method of induction implies that a cause will not be found by reasoning but by observation (perception). But Pierson questioned the reliability of the inductive method because a given event may have causes other than the one we happen to notice (Pierson 1885: 42). Pierson follows Mill by distinguishing four methods of induction: the method of agreement, the method of differences, the method of residues, the method of concomitant variations. The latter method does not deserve any consideration according to Pierson. The method of residues can be considered if the first two methods are useful. The first two methods can be applied to the natural sciences, but not to economics (Pierson 1861: 5–6). One of the reasons that the method of natural sciences has been applied to other branches of science, such as economic science, was the great success of the natural sciences. But the social sciences and the natural sciences differ because their data differ. We all know too well the *Methodenstreit* in the 1880s between Schmoller and Menger, so I will not continue to explain the difference between induction and deduction. However, Pierson's point of view still has to be described.

Pierson never neglected the science of statistics, which is an inductive method. On the contrary, he contributed to the advancement of statistics as a professor in Amsterdam and later by proposing in 1892 a central organization of statistics. Much later he saw the establishment of the Centraal Bureau voor de Statistiek (Central Office of Statistics, 1899) (Verrijn Stuart 1911: 60–65). But, as Pierson emphasized, statistics never explain something, but need explanation themselves. In this context he persisted in the belief that the inductive method is generally inappropriate for the social sciences. The development of statistics can be a blessing but also a disaster (Pierson 1879: 280). Pierson quoted Böhm-Bawerk who formulated this position as follows: 'The classical economists have studied theory without history; the economists of the Historical School studied history without studying theory. But in the future we can use a third possibility: history *and* theory' (Pierson 1890: 503–504, with reference to Böhm-Bawerk). In German the text is as follows: 'Die klassische Nationalökonomie hat Theorie ohne Geschichte getrieben, die historische Nationalökonomie ist im besten Züge Geschichte ohne Theorie zu treiben. Aber die Zukunft muss und wird einen dritten Wohlspruch gehören: Geschichte und Theorie.'

Most German economists rejected the economic laws of the English Classical School. Pierson regarded this as a scientific sin (Pierson 1890: 527), and he decried the lack of tolerance that British and German economists showed for one another. The above-mentioned remark of Böhm-Bawerk corresponds with Pierson's comment at the publication of Marshall's *Principles*: 'The English and the German (scientist) would agree more if the former widened their field of study and the latter worked more methodically' (Pierson 1891: 527).

This subject deserves some extensive treatment, for Pierson, who advocated the deductive method and rejected the inductive method, was an ardent supporter of the Historical School. According to Verrijn Stuart, it was his practical attitude towards his subjects combined with his sympathy for the poor, that turned Pierson into one of the first supporters of the Historical School outside Germany, despite his rejection of the inductive approach (Verrijn Stuart 1911: 58–59). Later in the same context Verrijn Stuart contradicted himself when he called Pierson 'the fighter of the Historical School' (Verrijn Stuart 1911: 60).

Pierson seems to have been carried away by the idea that he could describe economic phenomena, which fascinated him. In his early years

Pierson wrote a number of penetrating articles about the economic history of Italy in the seventeenth and eighteenth century (1866), the situation in villages in Russia (1867) and about ancient Athens (1870). Pierson reconciled his interest in history with his rejection of the inductive method by noting that

> The historical method is to me no system at all, no expedient, but a psychological phenomenon. I want to demonstrate what we owe to this Historical School: revival of the dogma of history, enrichment of knowledge, more mildness in judging those who think otherwise, a better historical view – but above all a higher idea of the task and vocation of science . . . Every dogma is narrow-minded, middle-class. Only the historical method can free us from this dogma.
>
> (Letter dated October 6, 1867 in van Maarseveen 1990: 293–294)

It is curious that Pierson wrote this in 1867, since he had adopted the method of deduction by 1861. The contradiction is clear enough, and perhaps it is due to his youth. But Pierson can also be credited with having tried to reconcile the English Classical School and the German Historical School (van Maarseveen 1981: 208). Pierson would be a warm adherent of econometrics today for, like Schumpeter, he wanted to combine history, statistics and deduction (Heertje 1987: 62).

PIERSON'S CONTRIBUTION TO THE INTRODUCTION OF MARGINAL UTILITY THEORY AND THE IDEAS OF THE 'AUSTRIAN SCHOOL'

Pierson's contribution to the introduction of marginal utility theory has been described by several writers. Yet Pierson did not accept this theory at the start of his academic career (van Maarseveen 1981: 70). Pierson rejected the theory of value based on subjective valuations, and did not mention the thesis of Asser and van Houten in his *Aantekening* (van Maarseveen 1981: 71 and Hasenberg Butter 1969: 143). But Pierson drew d'Aulnis de Bourouill's attention to the theory of Jevons, and de Bourouill wrote extensively about van Houten in his letters to Jevons: 'Ensuite nous avons le traité de m. S. van Houten sur la valeur [1859] Un petit chef d'oeuvre, d'originalité, de profondeur et de critique' (letter of October 11, 1874, Collison Black 1977: 73–74). Translated, he said: 'Then we have the thesis of m. S. van Houten about value. A small masterpiece, original, deep and serious.' D'Aulnis even connected the van Houten's theory with that of Jevons: 'Chez nous, nous avons un prédécesseur de votre théorie dans un Monsieur S. van Houten. Il est un des hommes les plus éminents de notre petit pays. Il a une influence énorme' (Collison Black 1977: 75). And later, 'La dissertation est, à mes yeux, le meilleur traité sur la valeur, qui ait paru avant votre livre, quoi que s'y trouvent encore beaucoup de passages obscurs et confus' (Collison

Black 1977: 89). Roughly translated this means that d'Aulnis considers van Houten's thesis the best book about value that has been published before Jevons' theory, and he thinks van Houten a forerunner of Jevons' Theory.

Did Pierson and d'Aulnis never discuss van Houten's thesis on value? This seems very strange since Pierson and van Houten were very good friends, and Pierson and d'Aulnis discussed this matter. It was Pierson who pointed out the importance of Jevons (1871). This fact was confirmed by van Maarseveen, who notes in his dissertation that Pierson was the first economist in the Netherlands to estimate the importance of the theory of marginal utility (van Maarseveen 1981: 196). In this context he refers to d'Aulnis de Bourouill's story of his meeting with Pierson. This meeting has been described extensively by d'Aulnis himself and repeated by van Maarseveen and Heertje. In short the story runs as follows:

> In autumn 1873 my professor, Prof. Buys, introduced me to Pierson. The early work of Pierson had inspired me to write a dissertation about theoretical economics. Soon I got into trouble. I asked Prof. Buys' advice and he told me to go to Pierson. Go to Amsterdam, he said, if it is possible to get an answer to your questions, then Pierson can give it to you. And so I went to Amsterdam, with a letter of recommendation from Prof. Buys. Pierson greeted me as a guest – very friendly – and answered my question. I had to study the new theory of value, written by William Stanley Jevons, professor in Economics at Manchester, and published under the title *The Theory of Political Economy* [1871]. I returned to Leyden, and studied this difficult book. I expanded his theory a little and completed my thesis . . . There had to be a new foundation on which the study of economics could be built. For the new theory of value inspired the rebirth of theoretical economics. For the last forty years, theoretical economics, like the theory of the Austrian school concerning capital and interest on capital, has been based on the method of Jevons. This method has been traced by Pierson in an English book full of mathematics, in which he employed differential calculus, inaccessible for the average economist. But Pierson was extraordinary.
>
> (d'Aulnis de Bourouill 1911: 26–27)

Apparently Howey was unaware of this meeting between Pierson and d'Aulnis, because he wrote: 'We have no idea of the circumstances that led d'Aulnis de Bourouill to turn to marginal utility as a dissertation topic at the university of Leyden' (Howey 1960: 203). Pierson's merit is not only that he directed d'Aulnis towards Jevons. Howey mentions Bordewijk's note that 'Pierson was one of the first economists to accept the theory of value of the Austrian school', and Greven said that 'through Pierson's work the latest improvements in economic theory initiated by Jevons,

Menger and others, and their application to problems of distribution, have penetrated wide circles of readers' (Howey 1960: 204; with reference to Bordewijk 1937: 134). Despite this statement, Howey is of the opinion that Pierson was interested in too many different topics and consequently spent too little time studying the theory of value. And it is true that Pierson did not accept Jevons' theory without criticism. In the first edition of *Grond-beginselen* (1875, 1876) he merely mentioned Jevons in a footnote, saying that the theory needed to be improved (Pierson 1876: 54).

In his *Leerboek*, Pierson rejected Jevons' suggestion that we replace the concept of value with exchange rate (Pierson 1885: 58). Pierson was more an adept of Marshall's theories. And Marshall criticized the theory of Jevons! As Marshall put it: 'He [Jevons] seemed perversely to twist his own doctrines so as to make them appear more inconsistent with Mill's and Ricardo's than they really were' (Howey 1960: 63–64; with reference to Marshall 1925: 99–100). Jevons was too casual in his rejection of the teachings of the great economists of the past, particularly the great English economists. Pierson was more inclined to accept Marshall's point of view and he continued to cling to the ideas of the English Classical School and of Ricardo concerning the theory of land rent, so much so that he could not wholeheartedly accept marginal utility theory. Hennipman (1964: 303–305) describes this ambivalence. On the one hand Pierson was the first to introduce the term 'marginal utility', and on the other hand he could not give up the ideas of the Classical School. Heertje (1987: 81) puts it clearly: 'Because he did not abandon the material notion of prosperity and the ideas of the Classical School, he could not accept openmindedly the subjective way of thinking' (Heertje 1987: 81). And Bordewijk, who mentioned Pierson as the first to accept Jevons' theory, notes that 'He advocates the modern theory of value, but it has not penetrated into his flesh and blood' (Bordewijk in Verrijn Stuart 1931: 13). Let us not forget, however, that Pierson had an enormous influence as an economist from the last two decades of the nineteenth century until his death, because his *Leerboek* (1885–1890), which described Jevons' theory (though not very deeply), reached a large audience and influenced them to accept marginal utility theory (Heertje 1987: 81).

One more observation is in order. It is commonly accepted that d'Aulnis drew the attention of Walras to the theory of Jevons (Howey 1960: 203). However, published correspondence (Collison Black 1977) between Walras and Jevons suggests Pierson's antecedent role in drawing d'Aulnis' attention to Jevons.

NICOLAAS GERARD PIERSON

PIERSON'S CONTRIBUTION TO ECONOMIC THEORY IN THE INTERNATIONAL CONTEXT

His work

Pierson was one of the first Dutch economists to have an international reputation. Several of his articles and books have been translated. In 1902 his *Leerboek der Staathuishoudkunde* was translated in English. In 1904 he was given an honorary degree by the University of Cambridge. In 1905 the same book was translated into Italian by Prof. Erasmo Malagali in Genoa. Later Pierson was appointed as a member of the Royal Academy in Rome (d'Aulnis de Bourouill 1911: 39–40). Also several of his articles have been translated: 'De Muntquestie' (about currency) (1881), was translated into German, in *Holtzendorff's Deutsche Zeit- und Streitfragen, Jahrgang XI, Heft 162;* 'La situation monétaire des Pays Bas' (written with Dr Vrolik, 1883) was translated into French; and translated into English were 'Further Considerations on Index Numbers' (*Economic Journal*, 1896), 'On Foreign Exchanges' (1901), 'The Railway Strikes' (*Economic Journal*, 1903) and 'Income Tax in Holland' (*Economic Journal*, 1907).

One article was very important and has been published in the book *Collectivist Economic Planning* edited by F.A. Hayek (Pierson 1902). It is called 'The Problem of Value in the Socialist Society'. Van Maarseveen considered this article to be pioneering work (van Maarseveen 1981: 222). It is more profound than the section in his *Leerboek* about socialism. But both articles demonstrate a rare foresight that few people had in those days (or later!). Pierson does not get confused: the phenomenon of value can no more be suppressed than the force of gravity. What is rare and useful, has value. Value, Pierson maintained, is not the effect, but the cause of exchange (Pierson 1902: 75–76).

Pierson compares the existing society (capitalism) with communism. The latter dissolves the connection between work performed and income received. That you must work, it says, is one thing; that you receive food, clothing and the means of subsistence is another. The principle presupposes an obligation on the part of everyone to work. The society of today is compatible with a free choice of vocation. Whoever does not wish to relinquish this freedom must oppose communism (Pierson 1902: 47–48). This does not mean, however, that communism is without advantages:

> We must grant it one thing: for the grave problem of unemployment it offers more than a solution; for in a communist society the problem cannot arise. Unemployment – I use the word in its technical sense – can only arise in a society in which income depends on service of one sort or another; and that precisely is what is absent from communism. (Pierson 1902: 51).

In his article concerning socialism Pierson described the pros and cons of socialism and communism (Pierson 1890a: 100–103). The disadvantages are little progress, no competition, no formation of capital and difficulties in international trade. The advantages are that industry can be more efficient, that a larger part of output will be used for the benefit of the community, that there will be no depressions in industry and that health care for the poor and for ill workers will be better (Pierson 1885: 100–101).

But despite these arguments he thought that international trade between socialist states could only be maintained according to the principles that govern international trade today. These principles are as follows:

(a) Unconditional recognition of the freedom of everyone to exchange or not to exchange at their own discretion.
(b) Exchange on a basis of equivalent services.

If these principles are not maintained, international trade will develop into a sort of international plunder (Pierson 1890a: 67).

Pierson tried to show that problems would persist even after a transition to socialism. In this case it would be the task of the governments concerned to maintain trade on the basis of an agreed code or by negotiation. But who would furnish the capital necessary for such trade (Pierson 1902: 56)? Pierson maintained that disparities in income and the business cycle would continue even if capitalist economies were transformed to socialism. There would be an everlasting depression because of lack of capital and total lack of competition (Pierson 1902: 108). 'We proceed; sixty, one hundred years have passed, what do we see? What has been changed and what has not? What has been left of the old system is exactly what most people disliked: the inequality' (Pierson 1902: 98). History has proved him to be right. And it was quite fitting that Pierson's article was published in *Collectivist Economic Planning* in 1935. Pierson's thesis was that international trade has to be conducted according to capitalist principles, and communist societies cannot function properly because no price calculation is possible when trade is absent.

Pierson (1878) also discussed academic socialism (see also Overbeek 1987: 1–4,8 and 12). In the nineteenth century the Historical School with Schmoller as its leader was predominant in Germany. This school even had its impact in the United States, according to Overbeek. The adherents of this school preferred historical studies in the examination of economic processes more than analytical theory. They neglected the deductive method (Overbeek 1987: 4).

According to Overbeek, Pierson's criticism of state socialism can be summarized as follows. First of all, state socialists assume that their teachings are the only authentic ones. Their opponents, the adherents of the Classical School, live, according to them, 'in the dark' (Pierson 1878: 221). They also believe that as soon as society has been changed by state intervention, the living and working conditions of the workers will be improved as well. According to Pierson this idea will only raise unrealistic expectations (Pierson 1878: 229).

The *Kathedersocialisten* (socialists of the chair) rejected the idea of unalterable laws. Human beings are not subject to economic laws, they have a free will. In connection with this argument the academic socialists assume that economic events cannot be predicted because opinions, ideas and institutions change during the centuries and differ from country to country. But in reality many fundamental ideas do not change, as Pierson pointed out. Socialists do not accept the concept of individualistic human behaviour, namely that people can be motivated by self-interest (Pierson 1878: 230–240). The most important charge against academic socialists is that they advocate state interventionism. However, if they repudiate the existence of economic rules and generalizations, how can they favour state intervention? The implications cannot be foreseen either. There exists in this connection, according to Pierson, *a contradictio in terminus* (Pierson 1878: 242 and Overbeek 1987: 8 and 12).

Pierson's contact with international economists

Pierson kept in close touch with several economists abroad. He corresponded with Marshall, Böhm-Bawerk and Jevons. He had no correspondence with Menger, but the latter did write about Pierson. Menger remarks that 'eine nicht mehr ganz kleine Gemeinde von älteren und jungeren (deutschen) Volkswirten *De economische geschriften* von Pierson mit Eifer liest und beachtet' (a no longer small group of older and younger [German] economists reads Pierson's *De economische geschriften* with zeal and attention) and 'dass wir ohne eine Lücke in unserem Wissen zu empfinden seine Arbeit nicht wohl übergehen konnten' (that we cannot neglect his work without feeling a lack in our knowledge) (Verrijn Stuart 1911: 73–74 with reference to *Rechtsgeleerd Magazyn* 1890: 269 etc.). In short, Pierson was the link between German and British economic traditions. It was no longer possible to study economics without consulting Pierson's work.

Böhm-Bawerk was also a German economist who corresponded with Pierson. The latter had reviewed Böhm's *Kapital und Kapitalzins* (1884, vol. I) and *Positive Theorie des Kapitals* (1889, vol. II) in *The Economist* of 1889 (published later in Pierson 1889). In his article he praised Böhm-Bawerk's work. And indeed the way that Böhm explained interest as the difference of value between goods we have now and those we may have in the future, is very explicit. In one of their first letters of correspondence (October 9, 1886) Böhm-Bawerk thanked Pierson for sending his *Grondbeginselen.* He praised Pierson's clear style of writing: 'You have given an example of how to describe economics. An example from which our slow-witted economists could learn a lot.' Böhm-Bawerk also announced the second part of his article about value, which would take at least a year. This article marked him as a member of the marginal utility school (Howey 1960: 156). In his letter of January 21, 1889 Böhm-Bawerk explained his theory about capital and interest. He agreed with Pierson's remark that his theory could be described as a *motivierbare Produktivitätstheorie* (an argued productivity theory).

He indicated the correspondence and the differences between his theory and the accepted theory. The most important difference is also the core of his theory: the idea of the difference in value of future goods and present goods. According to Böhm-Bawerk, future goods have less value. Böhm-Bawerk is of the opinion that, thanks to this theory, he is neither 'ein einseitiger Produktivitätstheoretiker wie Thünen', nor 'ein eklektiker wie Jevons' (a one-sided theorist like Thünen nor an eclecticist like Jevons). This was not a very flattering remark, considering the fact that Von Thünen (1783–1850), an adherent of the Classical School and Ricardo's theories, lived too early to evolve the marginal utility theory. Yet Marshall also referred to Thünen. In the first edition of the *Principles* he said that at first he borrowed the term 'marginal' from Von Thünen, and later adopted Jevons' term 'final' but gradually became convinced that 'marginal' is the better (Howey 1960: 84, with reference to Marshall's *Principles* 1890). Howey does not accept this statement by Marshall: 'He cannot correctly attribute his use of "marginal" to Thünen's *Grenze*' (Howey 1960: 85, etc.).

Böhm-Bawerk also wrote about Wieser to Pierson. Wieser, whose thinking was very close to the ideas of Böhm-Bawerk, did not accept the difference in value between future and present goods. This difference in value was described in his book *Kapital und Kapitalzins* and discussed by Pierson in his review. In his letter of January 26, 1889 Böhm-Bawerk continued to expand this theory of value. He also applied the notion of value to labour. According to him, labour is a future good, so it will be less appreciated than an existing product. He also explained the roundabout or capitalistic method of production. That creates an agio in favour of present goods. In his letter of March 24, 1889 Böhm-Bawerk thanks Pierson extensively for the review he wrote of his book *Kapital und Kapitalzins.* They also met each other, as described in his letter of January 21, 1889: 'Jener heisse Junitag . . . steht uns in bester und werther Erinnerung' (that hot day in June . . . gave us the best and most valuable memory).

In 1909 and 1910 Böhm-Bawerk wrote two letters to Pierson's wife. 'Ich bin auf das Tiefste bewegt und erschüttert von der Botschaft, die mir das Hinscheiden Ihres unvergesslichen Herrn Gemahls meldet. Es ist dies ein unendlich schweres Verlust für Sie, für sein Vaterland und für die Wissenschaft' (letter of January 6, 1910 N.G. Pierson Archives). Translated, this says: 'I was deeply moved to hear that your unforgettable husband has passed away. It is a great loss for you, for your country and for science.'

Pierson had a short correspondence with Jevons, from April 13, 1878 until September 9, 1878, from which Pierson wished to obtain some information about the monetary history of England (van Maarseveen 1981: 198; Collison Black 1977: 251). Pierson's question is as follows: 'I wish to know how and when the idea of correcting the exchanges by raising the rate of interest first presented itself' (Collison Black 1977: 251). Pierson was interested in the English example because in 1833 the Bank Act had been brought into force. In that act an exception was made to the English usury laws for the Bank of England: in those laws it was prohibited to raise more than 5 per cent interest (van Maarseveen 1990: 65 n. 7). In a letter of July, 1878 Jevons mentions having discovered Gossen's book *Entwicklung der Gesetze des menschlichen Verkehrs und der daraus fliessende Reglen für menschliches Handeln* (Braunschweig 1854). This book was a forerunner to the marginal utility theory. Jevons could excuse himself because of his want of knowledge of German (letter September 1, 1878), but it is astonishing that Pierson had never heard of Gossen before (letter of September 9, 1878; van Maarseveen 1990: 658–659).

Marshall was another economist who corresponded with Pierson. In his letter of April 8, 1891 he thanked Pierson for his review of Marshall's book *Principles*: 'You are too kind and good anyway.' But, later in the same letter, he rejected Pierson's characterization that the book had no central theme, a remark that hurt Marshall. Nevertheless, Marshall wrote of Pierson: 'You are one of those to whom it has been given to make the whole world better than it would have been if you had not been born into it . . . The world will class you with A. Smith, the thinker, the patriot and the cosmopolitan, and with Turgot the statesman-economist' (Marshall in his letter to Pierson December 21, 1909, Verrijn Stuart 1911: 75 and van Maarseveen 1981: 222).

CONCLUSIONS

From the foregoing sections it becomes clear that Pierson laid a new foundation for economics in the Netherlands. Thanks to Pierson the ideas of English, German, Italian and Austrian economists were integrated with the ideas of French economists like Bastiat and Say. Pierson contributed especially to the introduction of marginal utility theory and the ideas of the Austrian School.

Pierson was a versatile man: he was professor in economics at the University of Amsterdam, President of the Central Bank, Minister of Finance and Prime Minister.

Although more or less self-educated, Pierson was a liberal thinker. He was a sincere Christian who wanted to change society and make it more liveable. He was indeed a great man.

REFERENCES

Abbreviation: *VEG Verspreide Economische Geschriften*

d'Aulnis de Bourouill, J. (1911) 'Levensbericht van N.G. Pierson', in *Jaarboek der Koninklijke Akademie van Wetenschappen*, Amsterdam, 15–51.

Blom, D. van (1910) *Mr. N.G. Pierson: In de reeks Mannen en vrouwen van beteekenis in onze dagen,* Haarlem: Tjeenk Willink.

Bordewijk, H.W.C. (1931) 'Stoffelijke en a-stoffelijke economie' in *Economische opstellen aangeboden aan Prof. Dr. C.A. Verrijn Stuart*, Haarlem: Bohn.

Bordewijk, H.W.C. (1937) 'Nicolaas Gerard Pierson (1839–1909)', *Encyclopaedia of the Social Sciences*, Vol. XII.

Collison Black, R.D. (1977) *Papers and Correspondence of William Stanley Jevons, 1873–1878*, Vol. 4, London: Macmillan.

Graaff, A. de (1929) *Allard, Hendrik en Nicolaas Pierson, Portretten*, Zeist: Ploegsma.

Gossen, H.H. (1854) *Entwicklung der Gesetze des menschlichen Verkehrs un der daraus fliessende, Reglen für menschliches Handeln* Braunschweig: Vieweg.

Hasenberg Butter, I. (1969) *Academic Economics in Holland 1800–1870*, The Hague: Martinus Nijhoff.

Hayek, F.A. (1926) 'Friedrich, Freiherr von Wieser', *Jahrbücher für Nationalökonomie und Statistik* 125: 513–530.

Heertje, A. (1987) in A.J. Vermaat, J.J. Klant, J.R. Zuidema (eds) *Van liberalisten tot instrumentalisten: Anderhalve eeuw economisch denken in Nederland,* Leiden: Stenfert Kroese.

Hennipman, P. (1964) 'Pierson, Nicolaas Gerard' in *Handwörterbuch der Sozialwissenschaften*, Bd. 8: 303–305.

Houten, S. van (1859) *Verhandeling over de waarde*, Groningen: Wolters.

Howey, R.S. (1960) *The Rise of the Marginal Utility School 1870–1889*, The University of Kansas: Lawrence, Kansas.

Jevons, W.S. (1871) (4th edn: 1911) *The Theory of Political Economy*, London: Macmillan.

Landreth, H. (1976) *History of Economic Theory*, Boston: Houghton-Mifflin.

Maarseveen, J.G.S.J. van (1981) *Nicolaas Gerard Pierson, handelsman, econoom en bankier, Eerste periode 1839–1877*, Rotterdam.

Maarseveen, J.G.S.J. van (1990) *Briefwisseling van Nicolaas Gerard Pierson 1839–1909*, Deel I: 1851–1884, Amsterdam: NIBE/DNB.

Overbeek, J. (1987) 'Nicolaas Pierson and Socialism' in *Austrian Economics Newsletter*, Summer 1987: 1–4, 8 and 12.

Pierson, A. (1904,2) *Oudere tijdgenooten*, 2nd edn, Amsterdam: van Kampen.

Pierson, N.G. (1861) 'De logica der staathuishoudkunde', *VEG I*: 1–13.

Pierson, N.G. (1864a) 'Het begrip van volksrijkdom', (*Gids* 1864) *VEG I*: 14–103.

Pierson, N.G. (1864b) 'De grondslagen van Ricardo's stelsel', (*Gids* 1964), *VEG I*: 126–211.

Pierson, N.G. (1866) 'Bijdrage tot de geschiedenis der economische studieën in Italië gedurende de 17e en de 18e eeuw' (*Economist* 1866), *VEG II*: 1–131.

Pierson, N.G. (1867) 'De dorpsinstellingen in Rusland' (*Tijdschrift voor Nederlands-Indië* 1867), *VEG III*: 58–99.

Pierson, N.G. (1870) 'Een economische blik op oud Athene' (*Gids* 1870), *VEG III*: 3–57.

Pierson, N.G. (1871) 'De inkomstenbelasting' (*Gids* 1871), *VEG V*: 20–56.

Pierson, N.G. (1875) *Grondbeginselen der Staathuishoudkunde*, Deel I, Haarlem: Bohn.

Pierson, N.G. (1876) *Grondbeginselen der Staathuishoudkunde*, Deel II, Haarlem: Bohn.

Pierson, N.G. (1878) 'Het Katheder-Socialisme' (*Gids* 1878), *VEG I*: 211–247.

Pierson, N.G. (1879) 'Werkkring en methode der staathuishoudkunde' (*Gids* 1879), *VEG I*: 248–286.
Pierson, N.G. (1881) 'De muntquestie' (*Gids* 1881), *VEG IV*: 224–260.
Pierson, N.G. (1884) 'Levensbericht van W.C. Mees', *Jaarboek der Koninklijke Akademie van Wetenschappen*, Amsterdam, *VEG II*: 326–358.
Pierson, N.G. (1885) (2nd edn: 1896) *Leerboek der Staathuishoudkunde*, Deel I, Haarlem: Bohn.
Pierson, N.G. (1889) 'Boekaankondigingen. E. von Böhm-Bawerk: *Kapital und Kapitalzins*', *VEG I*: 412–446.
Pierson, N.G. (1890a) (2nd edn: 1902) *Leerboek der Staathuishoudkunde*, Deel II, Haarlem: Bohn.
Pierson, N.G. (1890b) 'Economisch overzicht IV' (*Economist* 1890), *VEG II*: 487–516.
Pierson, N.G. (1891) 'Boekaankondigingen. Marshall's *Principles*' (*Economist* 1891), *VEG II*: 516–544.
Pierson, N.G. (1902) 'The Problem of Value in the Socialist Society' in *Collectivist Ecnomic Planning*, ed. F.A. von Hayek, London: Routledge, 1935.
Poel, J. van der (1966) *Sijmen betaal! Belastingen toen en nu*, Alphen aan den Rijn: Samson.
Schopenhauer, A. (1818) (2nd edn: 1916) *Die Welt als Wille und Vorstellung*, Leipzig: Brockhaus, Reclam.
Verrijn Stuart, C.A. (1911) 'N.G. Pierson', in *Levensberichten der afgestorvene medeleden van de Maatschappij der Nederlandsche letterkunde*, Leiden: Brill, 26–81.
Verrijn Stuart, C.A. (1931) *Economische opstellen aangeboden aan Prof. Dr. C.A. Verrijn Stuart*, Haarlem: Bohn.

Collected works of N.G. Pierson

Verspreide Economische Geschriften van N.G. Pierson, verzameld door C.A. Verrijn Stuart, Haarlem: Bohn 1910/11.
Deel I: *De methode en theorie der staathuishoudkunde.*
Deel II: *De geschiedenis der staathuishoudkunde.*
Deel III: *De economische geschiedenis.*
Deel IV: *Handel, crediet en muntwezen.*
Deel V: *De financiën van rijk en gemeenten.*
Deel VI: *Sociale vraagstukken.*

Archives

Gemeentelijke Universiteit Amsterdam, University Library.
Manuscript collection N.G. Pierson Archives (letters to and from Pierson).

5

AUSTRIAN SUSTAINABILITY

*W.J.M. Heijman**

Extending the lifetime of durable goods is an important aspect of the struggle for a sustainable economy. Indeed, extending the lifetime of goods will probably cause a decrease in the use of depletable resources. Therefore, it is important to analyse the forces that influence lifetime. For a general description of the relation between sustainability, depletion speed of resources and interest rates, see Heijman (1991). In their work, Böhm-Bawerk and other Austrians provided an explanation for capital and interest. These insights can be extended to account for changes in the lifetimes of durable goods. It has to be stressed that the classical Austrian theory of interest will be used here and not the slightly different modern Austrian version as has been put forward by, amongst others, Faber and Bernholz (see Zuidema 1993).

BÖHM'S THEORY

In his explanation for the paying of interest, Böhm-Bawerk states that there are three reasons why current means of satisfaction are more highly valued than future means. The so-called third reason is that a more roundabout way of production is, as a rule, more productive. He illustrated this with an example taken from Roscher and modified. Suppose that there is a nation of fishermen with no capital, living on a diet of fish which are caught during ebb tide. Suppose that one fisherman can catch 3 fish a day. If he had a boat, he could catch 30 fish a day. Building a boat will take a month. He is not able to build a boat entirely on his own because he has to keep on catching fish to feed himself. Now suppose that another fisherman lends him 90 fish against the promise that after two months he will give 180 fish back. The fisherman agrees and builds his boat with which, in the second month, he is able to catch 900 fish. After giving back 180 fish he still has a

* The author gratefully acknowledges the comments by Prof. Dr. R.P. Zuidema and Prof. Charles H. Powers, University of Santa Clara, California and Visiting Professor at the University of Limburg.

'profit' of 720 fish, which proves that the value of the fish borrowed must be higher than 90 and even higher than the 180 future fish he used to pay for them (Böhm1889: 350; Heijman 1991).

Böhm then noted the following as an important parallel phenomenon. It refers to the fact that the effort of creating a more long-lasting commodity containing more utility than a commodity with a shorter lifespan takes a more roundabout method of production which yields a greater productivity. He illustrated this relation between duration and 'roundaboutness' with the following 'classic' example (Böhm 1889: 352–354). Suppose that a house which has an expected lifetime of sixty years contains the same amount of utility as two houses each with a duration of thirty years. Building a house with a duration of thirty years costs thirty years of labour, while building a house with a duration of sixty years costs forty-five years of labour. Building two houses, one after the other, each with a duration of thirty years, would take sixty years of labour. Böhm realized that this phenomenon fits entirely into the third reason for paying interest.

Böhm maintained that a more roundabout method of production results in a lower rate of interest than a less roundabout method because of decreasing marginal productivity of capital (Zuidema 1970, 1989). But his analysis contains a fundamental error, for a lower rate of interest actually results in longer lifetimes for durable goods (consumer durables as well as capital goods). This has tangible consequences. For example, the relatively long lifetime of pre-war durable goods can be attributed in part to the low real interest rates in those days.

DURATION OF CONSUMER GOODS

The useful lifespan of durable commodities is influenced by the rate of interest (Heijman 1989). But the relationship is not as it was described by Böhm. Suppose that the two possibilities of building houses mentioned above are valued equally. In that case fifteen present years of labour are valued as high as thirty years of future labour. Then the rate of interest i can be computed as follows: $30/(1+i)^{30} = 15$, so $i = 0.023$. If the rate of interest is higher than 2.3 per cent, a consumer would decide on two houses each with a duration of thirty years. If the rate of interest is lower than 2.3 per cent, then the buyer would decide on one house with a duration of sixty years. From this example we may conclude that a high rate of interest is combined with a low duration of durable commodities, while a low rate of interest is combined with a long duration of durable commodities. In other words, high rates of interest imply relatively short production periods, while a low rate of interest implies long periods of production.

Now, let us generalize this example of buying a house. Suppose that the consumer can choose between a house which lasts for $2n$ years and two houses (the second being bought after the first has been worn out) which each last n years. Which option will the consumer choose if the prices (p_1 for the first option and p_2 for each of the two houses in the second option) are known and if the consumer would like to minimize his or her costs? The solution to this problem depends entirely on the rate of interest i. This can be proved as follows. First I calculate the break-even point, which means:

$$p_1 = p_2 + \frac{p_2}{(1+i)^n}$$

$$(1+i)^n = \frac{p_2}{p_1 - p_2}$$

with $p_1 > p_2$. This can be written in a continuous form as

$$e^{in} = \frac{p_2}{p_1 - p_2}$$

$$in = \ln \frac{p_2}{p_1 - p_2}$$

$$i = \frac{\ln\left[\frac{p_2}{p_1 - p_2}\right]}{n}$$

Now, if

$$i > \frac{\ln\left[\frac{p_2}{p_1 - p_2}\right]}{n}$$

then the consumer chooses option number two (two houses). The consumer chooses option one (one house) if

$$i < \frac{\ln\left[\frac{p_2}{p_1 - p_2}\right]}{n}$$

Of course, this proof can be extended to a choice of more than two houses.[1]

The conclusion of this section is that, as far as durable consumer goods are concerned, the duration is determined by the interest rate *ceteris paribus*.

DURATION OF CAPITAL GOODS: THE CASE OF A FIXED BUDGET

What determines the average lifespan n of a capital good (Krabbe and Heijman 1986)? The situation of choice for the firm is characterized by the following three equations:

$$q = s\left\{\frac{1}{(1+i)} + \frac{1}{(1+i)^2} + \ldots + \frac{1}{(1+i)^n}\right\} \tag{5.1}$$

$$b = p_s\, s + p_t n,$$

$$Max\ q$$

In equation (5.1), q represents the discounted cash flow of a capital good. Annual cash flow is represented by s. It is assumed here that the cash flow per unit output equals 1, so that, in this case, s equals production per period. Further it is assumed that this capacity is constant.

The second equation is the budget function. Total budget for one capital good can be spent on either a good with a high production per period s and a relatively short duration n or a capital good with a low production per period and a long lifetime. It is assumed that the budget, as well as the shadow prices for duration p_t per period (for example per year) and capacity (production per year) p_s, are fixed parameters. So, with given prices of duration (for example in years) and capacity (production per year), a machine will be expensive if it has a long duration combined with a high capacity. Finally, the last equation represents the optimum condition: maximize the total of the discounted cash flows under the constraint of the given budget. Through a Lagrange procedure we arrive at the optimum condition:

$$\frac{\partial q/\partial s}{p_s} = \frac{\partial q/\partial n}{p_t} \tag{5.2}$$

From this equation it can be deduced that the capacity of a capital good and the duration of this capital good are two quality attributes of the capital good. In order to gain maximum production with a given budget, the ratio between marginal productivity and price must be equal for each quality attribute (Steenkamp 1989: 24).

A continuous form for equation (1) is

$$q = s\int_0^n e^{-it}\,dt$$

$$q = \frac{s}{i} - \frac{se^{in}}{i}$$

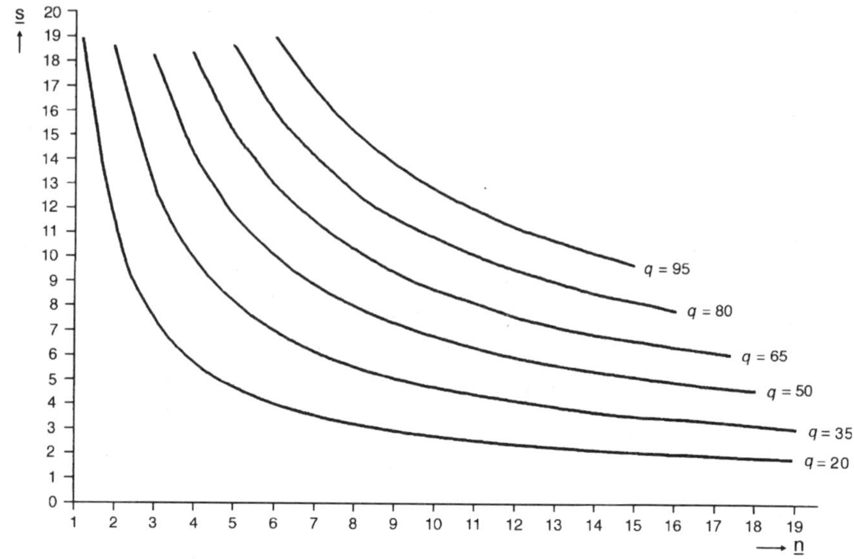

Figure 5.1 Iso-production curves combining s and $n(i=0.06)$. (*Source*: Heijman 1991.)

This equation can be seen as a 'production function'. In Figure 5.1, a field of six possible iso-production curves is shown, the rate of interest being equal to 0.06. It is also clear from this figure that the iso-production curves are convex, which means that the optimization procedure delivers a maximum. Partial differentation of q with respect to s and n gives:

$$\frac{\partial q}{\partial s} = \frac{1 - e^{-in}}{i}$$

$$\frac{\partial q}{\partial n} = se^{-in}$$

Substitution of these equations into the optimum condition (5.2) yields the equation of the producer's expansion path:

$$s = \frac{p_t(e^{in} - 1)}{ip_s}$$

Differentiation of s with respect to n yields the tangent of the angle of inclination of the expansion path:

$$\frac{ds}{dn} = \frac{p_t}{p_s} e^{in}$$

It appears that the expansion path is steeper in proportion to the rate of interest, which means that, with a given budget, a high rate of interest provides a short duration of the capital good, while a low rate of interest causes a long duration of capital goods. However, one might wonder whether a long duration of capital goods is always favourable to the conservation of natural resources. When the duration of capital goods is relatively long, then the introduction of nature-sparing technological innovations will take, relatively, a great deal of time. Indeed, a lot of (nature-sparing) innovations are bound to new capital goods. In other words, many technological innovations are embodied.

FLEXIBLE BUDGET: A PARADOX

If the budget is not fixed, the firm will decide according to the following rules:

$$\frac{\partial q}{\partial s} = \frac{1 - e^{in}}{i} = p_s$$

$$\frac{\partial q}{\partial n} = se^{-in} = p_t$$

This means:

$$s = \frac{p_t}{1 - ip_s}, \frac{ds}{di} > 0$$

$$n = \frac{-\ln(1 - ip_s)}{i}, \frac{dn}{di} > 0$$

This is surprising because, when the budget is not fixed, it is not only the capacity of the machine that increases when interest goes up, which is to be expected, but also the duration.[2] The explanation is that a high interest rate stimulates the scale of production, in other words a high interest rate stimulates the capacity of the machine s. When a machine has a high capacity it pays to buy one with a longer duration. However, the conclusion of the preceding section, i.e. that with a constant scale or capacity (s is constant), duration will be longer with a low interest rate than with a high rate of interest, still stands.

NOTES

1. If there are J options, every option containing the same amount of *housing time* with a different duration of houses for every option, then the 'general' equation of costs K for option $j(l \ldots J)$ to be minimized is:

$$K_j = p_j + \frac{p_j}{(1+i)^{n_j}} + \frac{p_j}{(1+i)^{2n_j}} + \ldots + \frac{p_j}{(1+i)^{hn_j}} + \ldots + \frac{p_j}{(1+i)^{Hn_j}}$$

with $(H + 1)n_j$ constant for all houses j (h and H are non-negative integers).
The continuous form for this equation is:

$$K_J = \frac{p_j}{in_j} - \frac{p_j e^{-Hin_j}}{in_j}$$

2.

$$\frac{dn}{di} = \frac{\frac{ip_s}{1-ip_s} + \ln(1 - ip_s)}{i^2} > 0$$

REFERENCES

Böhm-Bawerk, E. von (1889) (1921) *Kapital und Kapitalzins II, 1: Positive Theorie des Kapitales*, 4th edn, Jena: Fischer.
Heijman, W.J.M. (1989) 'Böhm-Bawerk on Time Preference', in J.J. Krabbe, A. Nentjes and H. Visser (eds), *Austrian Economics: Roots and Ramifications Reconsidered*, Rochester: MCB University Press.
Heijman, W.J.M. (1991) *Depletable Resources and the Economy*, Wageningen: PUDOC.
Krabbe, J.J. and Heijman, W.J.M. (1986) *Economische theorie van het milieu*, Assen: van Gorcum.
Steenkamp, J-B.E.M (1989) *Product Quality*, Assen: van Gorcum.
Zuidema, R.P. (1970) *Produktie, kapitaal en produktiviteit: Een analyse van produktie in de tijd*, Haarlem/Leiden: Bohn/Stenfert Kroese.
Zuidema, R.P. (1989) 'On the Austrian Contribution to Capital Theory', in J.J. Krabbe, A. Nentjes and H. Visser (eds), *Austrian Economics: Roots and Ramifications Reconsidered*, Rochester: MCB University Press.
Zuidema, R.P. (1993) 'The neo-Austrian View on Interest', *International Journal of New Ideas* 2 (1).

6

THE SHORT-CUT APPROACH TO CONSUMER CALCULATIONS: A NEO-MARGINALIST SOLUTION

*Auke R. Leen**

INTRODUCTION

In economic textbooks, the presentation of the standard model of consumer choice is often followed by a disclaimer: 'People aren't that smart' (Parkin 1990: 167) or 'We consumers are not expected to be wizards' (Samuelson and Nordhaus 1989: 451). But, suppose the present-day economist's model is not only a formal model that helps thinking but reflects the reality of the maximization process of the consumer too. Then, what wriggles most? It is neither the beginning nor the end. We all intuitively accept the start: a budget constraint and a set of preferences (including Gossen's first law of decreasing marginal utility). Didn't economists in the early phases of the history of economics think that Gossen's first law signified a real-world psychophysical phenomenon: the so-called Weber–Fechner law? We also accept the result: the optimal allocation of goods (Gossen's second law of equi-marginality). No, what wriggles most as highly unrealistic is the maximization process that lies in between both Gossen's laws. Whatever it is the consumer does, it certainly is not solving a Lagrangean function: the constrained maximization of a utility function. Indeed, consumers can't be that smart.

From a theoretical point of view, to compute the marginal utilities a consumer has a lot to do. First, one has to line up all the alternatively possible combinations of goods one can get. Second, one has to assess the needs that successive units of the various goods can satisfy. Third, one has to find out at what point in the row satisfaction breaks off. See for instance the Mengerian Table 6.1. It shows the marginal utility that a consumer derives from various amounts of food and cloth. Each physical unit of food or cloth costs $1. Suppose a consumer's budget is $4; how much of each good should one buy? Table 6.1 shows that, if rational, one would allocate $3 to food and $1 to cloth.

The problem of how to abbreviate economic calculation was one of the

* The author gratefully acknowledges the comments by Prof. Dr. R.P. Zuidema.

Food		Cloth	
Quantity	*Marginal utility*	*Quantity*	*Marginal utility*
4	4	0	0
3	5	1	5
2	8	2	4
1	10	3	3
0	0	4	2

core problems for the neo-marginalists. The neo-marginalists were a generation of economists of the Austrian school of economics. They worked from the early 1920s until the end of the 1940s. The first generation was the founder Carl Menger; the second generation, his two heralds Eugen von Böhm-Bawerk and Friedrich von Wieser; the neo-marginalists, Hans Mayer, Paul Rosenstein-Rodan and Leo Schönfeld-Illy are the third generation. For them, marginal utility was not only the solution to a problem but also gave rise to this new problem. Marginalism, the solution to the well-known value paradox, posed the problem of finding an overall goods allocation with its astonishing amount of individual comparisons. Economic theory had to be in congruence with reality.

The abbreviation problem was overlooked by the English and French co-inventors of marginalism. For them, because of the mathematical mould of their theories, the problem was a mathematical one: solving a Lagrangean function. In the classical objective value theory, too, the problem had no place in the core of economics and could be neglected by the theoretical economists. Value was given with outside labour costs. With subjective use value, however, this changed. At least for the Austrians, value had to be calculated by each person. The problem was further aggravated with the transition from a cardinal to an ordinal utility concept; it changed from a quantitative to a qualitative one, which was even more difficult to handle. The problem becomes even more complex if we use a household production function. For then the consumer has to state not only the needs to be fulfilled by the goods themselves but also by their intermediate products.

In this paper, first I give the logical development of the idea of taking short cuts (abbreviations) in consumer calculations; it is related to the role of marginal utility in equilibrium and disequilibrium. Second, a first formalization is given of taking short cuts in an intertemporal model of consumer choice. Saving and consumption patterns are explained for different groups of consumers.

SHORT CUTS IN EQUILIBRIUM

According to Böhm-Bawerk (1886: 74–77), experience shows that calculations do not give us much trouble. Why? First, we do have a lot of practice.

We are great virtuosi in our value calculations. Calculations, after all, do not have to be more exact than is worthwhile. Second, we have all sorts of reliefs, e.g. our memory, things we have learned from other people and our everyday routines. All the reliefs can be used as long as our situation does not drastically change. This is practically the case for most of the people most of the time.

Rosenstein-Rodan asked: how do we find the initial equilibrium situation that holds on in the first place and is of relevance if nothing changes? His answer was that we cannot create this situation *uno actu*, it is the result of a historical process of trial and error. If, however, we are in equilibrium, the attained marginal utilities fulfil their function as a short cut without which there simply could be no rational economic conduct. The marginal utilities are the *sine qua non* for any real-world economic calculations.

> The utilities of the new uses [changes in allocation] which are contemplated are compared with past marginal utilities in these uses; if they are larger, the new uses are expedient, if smaller, the new uses are not expedient. The marginal utility in different need classes (kinds of uses) thus fulfils a watch-dog function with respect to consumption.
>
> (Rosenstein-Rodan 1927: 85)

The complementarity of utilities seems to pose a problem. Even with a relatively small change in the data, it suggests that the whole economic plan has to be revised; one is forced to go through all calculations again and again each time a situation changes. This, according to Rosenstein-Rodan, is not so. A consumer, usually, does not substitute a house for a car but a hamburger for a cheeseburger. The layers of goods allocation are the marginal ones; complementarity is the lowest and the utilities are the smallest. Small changes in the data have no great repercussions. Mayer, the successor of Wieser, added the time element to the watch-dog function of marginal utility. Generally, a consumer plans the purchase of goods not for one but for more than one time period (Mayer 1922: 15). All consumers have to ration their supply of goods so that it lasts until new goods become available. The Mengerian table has to be multiplied for each time period. Consequently, if the consumer's horizon is one time period, the marginal utility of a stock of goods appears only once: it is unique. If, however, the consumer's horizon is more than one time period, the same marginal utility appears more than once. This is due to the periodical repetition of the same needs (Mayer 1922: 17–18).

In short, for the neo-marginalists the essential function of marginal utility was to abbreviate economic calculations. To apply the abbreviated procedure we need (a) an initial equilibrium situation, and (b) relative constancy of needs and ends.

Short cuts in disequilibrium

Almost unnoticed by the other neo-marginalists, Schönfeld-Illy changed the use of the consumer's abbreviation procedure. He was dissatisfied with a theory that described small changes in equilibrium only, and not how the equilibrium came about. His favourite examples of budget allocation were students who receive their first income after graduation, people who marry and start a family, and immigrants in a foreign and strange country (Schönfeld-Illy 1948: 125–126 and 321). For him, marginal utility as an instrument of abbreviation is not only used in equilibrium but in disequilibrium too. Abbreviation is no longer linked with small changes but with abrupt, great changes in means and ends.

Schönfeld-Illy developed his use of marginal utility from what he thought was an inconsistency in Wieser's thought. Wieser, the brother-in-law of Böhm-Bawerk, took the definition of marginal utility from the last stage of calculation. 'The measure of marginal utility is got from the least useful of the most important uses . . . conditional on the highest use of the supply and the most careful inquiry of the needs' (Schönfeld-Illy 1924: 75; cf. McCulloch 1977: 254). On the other hand, he drew the description of the function of marginal utility from the situation that actually starts calculation. 'All uses that stand below are forbidden . . . all uses that stand above or are equal are permitted' (*op. cit.*: 75). Schönfeld-Illy wondered whether the last stage of calculation contains all the things that have been used during the start. Isn't a definition based on the last stage too narrow? What is the correct definition of marginal utility consistent with its function?

A consumer rarely deals with a single good. A consumer calculates mostly with stocks of goods that contain many different intensities of utility. For a consumer the marginal utility of a stock is the utility of the economically smallest part of the stock. It lies at the margin of use of the stock and is of relevance to the whole stock with regards to the plans one has for using it. For the price a consumer is willing to pay for a good at the margin of a stock, based on its marginal utility, has an economic relevance for all other units. 'A fortiore: for the utility of these other units is higher than the utility of the marginal unit and therefore the same, marginal price paid for the other units certainly must be justified' (Schönfeld-Illy 1948: 60). The cumulative validity of the subjective demand price makes it possible to shorten the calculation process: we do not have to state and compare the other utilities anymore. Buying bread, a parent does not think, nor needs to think, that the family might die without it. The possibility of abbreviation is a direct result of Gossen's first law of decreasing marginal utility. Marginal utility becomes an instrument in a process of trial and error; it is used to discover the optimal consumption pattern (Schönfeld-Illy 1948: 67 and 126).

In short, marginal utility fulfils two special roles. It acts no longer only as a watch-dog that precludes all utility under it and sustains all utility above it. Its function, too, is its economic relevance: the relevance of the economic use at a margin for a whole. More correctly, its function can grow from economic relevance only, to being watch-dog too.

A FIRST MODEL OF CONSUMER ABBREVIATION

To show the difference between the abbreviating role of marginal utility in equilibrium and disequilibrium, I select three groups of consumers. First, consumers who are in disequilibrium by choice, and second, those who are in disequilibrium by necessity. Examples of the first group are trendsetting consumers; examples of the second, immigrants on arrival in a foreign country and people who marry and start a family. All these consumers are discovering what their optimal allocation looks like. The third group are the familiar consumers from the traditional theory of consumer choice. They are the well-established consumers, who are in equilibrium by definition.

I model the abbreviating role of marginal utility as a habit-forming process. A good not only provides immediate satisfaction but also affects the marginal utility derived from subsequent consumption. The familiar results of habit formation (cf. Stigler and Becker 1977; Becker and Murphy 1988; Chaloupka 1991) are used and reinterpreted as follows. In a simple intertemporal model of consumer choice a household maximizes the utility function

$$U = U\,(Z_t, Z_{t+1}, \ldots, Z_{t+n}) \tag{6.1}$$

where Z_t stands for the composite commodity from which utility is directly obtained in period t. The commodities are produced in a household production function

$$Z_t = Z\,(X_t, T_t, S_t) \tag{6.2}$$

with a composite market good X_t, the consumer's time allocated to calculation T_t, and the consumer's human capital specific to calculation skill S_t. All other inputs of time and (human) capital are ignored. I assume that

$$\frac{\partial Z_t}{\partial X_t} > 0, \ \frac{\partial Z_t}{\partial T_t} > 0, \ \frac{\partial Z_t}{\partial S_t} > 0$$

and also that

$$\frac{\partial^2 Z_t}{\partial T_t \partial S_t} > 0$$

S_t is produced through learning by doing: consumers learn to calculate by calculating. It accumulates the effects of earlier commodity allocation. A simple investment function is chosen:

$$S_t = S\,(Z_{t-1},\ Z_{t-2},\ \ldots,\ E_t) \tag{6.3}$$

E_t registers education and other human capital relevant for calculation, i.e. abbreviation skills. I assume that

$$\frac{\partial S_t}{\partial E_t} > 0, \text{ and } \frac{\partial^2 S_t}{\partial Z_{t-v}\partial E_t} > 0,\ v = 1,\ 2,\ \ldots$$

The ratios of the marginal utilities and the shadow prices, the marginal costs of adding a unit of the composite commodity, set the optimal allocation of consumption over time

$$\frac{MU_{Z_t}}{MU_{Z_{t+n}}} = \frac{\frac{\partial U}{\partial Z_t}}{\frac{\partial U}{\partial Z_{t+n}}} = \frac{\pi_{Z_\tau}}{\pi_{Z_{\tau+n}}} \tag{6.4}$$

The term π_{Z_t}, the shadow price, is the full price of commodity Z_t. It can be deduced from the first-order condition of the maximization of the utility function (6.1) subject to the combined time and budget constraint

$$\sum \frac{pX_t + wT_t}{(1+r)^t} - \sum \frac{wT_t^* + b_t}{(1+r)^t} = 0$$

where w is the wage rate, r the interest rate, b the non-wage income and T^* the total available time (absence of time preference is presupposed). The shadow price consists of two parts: the full money price of the composite commodity,

$$\frac{p\partial X_t}{\partial Z_t} + \frac{w\partial T_t}{\partial Z_t}$$

and the change in the discounted money value of future time inputs from the effect of the production of Z_t on subsequent S,

$$-\ w \sum_{i=1}^{n-t} \left(\frac{\partial Z_{t+i}}{\partial S_{Z_t+_i}} \Big/ \frac{\partial Z_{t+i}}{\partial T_{Z_t+_i}} \right) \cdot \frac{dS_{Z_t+_i}}{dZ_t} \cdot \frac{1}{(1+r)^i}$$

where n is the length of life (cf. Stigler and Becker 1977: 79, n. 5); to be simplified to

$$\pi_{Z_t} = \frac{p\partial X_t}{\partial Z_t} + \frac{w\partial T_t}{\partial Z_t} - A_t \tag{6.5}$$

If S is a beneficial habit, $\frac{dS_{Z_t+i}}{dZ_t} > 0$ and A_t becomes positive, consumption of Z decreases the price of consumption at a later point in time. If S is a harmful habit, however, $\frac{dS_{Z_t+i}}{dZ_t} < 0$ and A_t becomes negative, consumption of Z increases the price of consumption at a later point in time. In other words, the marginal utility of time allocated to calculating $\frac{\partial^2 Z}{\partial T_t \partial S_t}$ increases by the consumption of Z if S is a beneficial habit; it decreases if S is a harmful habit.

DIFFERENT SAVING AND CONSUMPTION PATTERNS

How does the model explain the consumption and saving patterns of the selected consumers? For well-established consumers, the ones we know from traditional economic theory, the last term of equation (6.5), A_t, is zero. The price is the familiar marginal cost formula. These consumers are in equilibrium by definition: they move from one equilibrium to another and make marginal comparisons only. Marginal utility functions as a watchdog. To develop an abbreviation skill is neither intended nor necessary: they have it already. The relative price of consumption now and in the future does not change.

For those who are in disequilibrium by choice, our trendsetting consumers, calculation can be short-sighted (myopic) or far-sighted. When short-sighted, just as with the well-established consumers, A_t is zero. Only this time, one is short-sighted because one does not want to be far-sighted. When far-sighted, A_t is negative. Trendsetters do not see the allocation process as a positive investment. On the contrary, after the discovery of a new consumption pattern, human capital specific to abbreviation loses its value. For the trendsetter, abbreviation is a harmful habit. Abbreviation breeds a habit one does not want to have; it takes time and energy to get rid of it.

For the short-sighted trendsetter, the future price rises. For the trendsetters who see their abbreviation skill as a harmful habit the value of saving in future inputs is negative. The full shadow price rises; it is cheaper to consume now than in the future. The rise is greater for the far-sighted than for the short-sighted consumer, since for the latter the future harmful effects are not discounted at all. With an inelastic demand curve for the commodity, however, for the short-sighted as well as for the far-sighted trendsetter, the consumption of goods and time spent on calculating does not fall in the future. An inelastic demand curve seems a realistic assumption. Trendsetting can only be shown by conspicuous consumption. The abbreviating role of marginal utility as a short cut in calculations results in consumption as a harmful rational addiction: an increase in present consumption raises future consumption.

For far-sighted consumers who are in disequilibrium by necessity, e.g. our immigrants, A_t is positive. The abbreviating role of marginal utility as a short cut in calculations results in consumption as a beneficial addiction. In other words, the marginal utility of time allocated to figuring out the present composite commodity increases by the growth in calculating capital. The relative price of consumption now declines versus the price in the future. If the demand curve is sufficiently elastic, consumption will rise and savings decline. A long-run elastic demand curve is likely; these consumers are not yet spending much.

Now, let me look at the producer's problem: who are the most susceptible to the advertising of new goods? Advertising of new goods lowers the search costs, but it also makes human capital obsolete. The investment function can show the influence of advertising on human capital through a depreciation rate, δ, of human capital specific to abbreviation, S_t:

$$S_t = S\,(Z_{t-1}, Z_{t-2}, \ldots, E_t, \delta) \tag{6.6}$$

For the well-established consumers who have the biggest investment in human capital, δ is strongly negative. The ultimate abbreviation skill, i.e. marginal utility as a watch-dog, is their defining characteristic; without it they cannot exist. For consumers who are in disequilibrium by necessity, although δ is still negative, the odds at stake are much lower. By trial and error, immigrants and young couples are still discovering their optimal consumption pattern. For trendsetters, who are in disequilibrium by choice, the fact that human capital specific to abbreviation becomes obsolete is either of no concern, if they are short-sighted, or, in the case of abbreviation as a negative addictive good, a positive fact. δ is zero for the short-sighted and positive for the far-sighted trendsetter.

Because for all groups the relative prices change, saving and consumption patterns will change too. Well-established consumers buy the least new goods, short-sighted trendsetters buy more, and far-sighted trendsetters with a positive depreciation rate buy the most new goods. As time goes by, immigrants and just-married couples buy fewer new goods.

CONCLUSION

First, all this reminds one of the present-day work of Herbert A. Simon. He, too, bases his theory on certain limitations of the human mind described as 'bounded rationality'.

> The capacity of the human mind for formulating and solving complex problems is very small compared with the size of the problems whose solution is required for objectively rational behaviour in the real world - or even for a reasonable approximation to such objective rationality.
> (Simon 1957: 198)

The difference, however, between Simon and Schönfeld-Illy is that the simplifying devices of Simon result in a lack of optimality, but those of Schönfeld-Illy do not. Simon's consumers calculate solutions that are good enough. Schönfeld-Illy's consumers calculate solutions that are optimal.

Second, I can get the same results by introducing the present-day notions in addiction literature of tolerance and reinforcement (Chaloupka 1991: 723). Tolerance means that the utility from a given amount of consumption is lower when past consumption is greater, $\frac{\partial Z}{\partial S} < 0$. Reinforcement means that increases in past use raise marginal utility of current consumption, $\frac{\partial Z}{\partial T \partial S} > 0$. A habit is addictive by definition. It is called a beneficial addiction if $\frac{\partial Z}{\partial S} > 0$ and a harmful one if $\frac{\partial Z}{\partial S} < 0$. For an addiction it is a necessary and sufficient condition that reinforcement exceeds tolerance. This means that, given time preference, σ, and the depreciation rate, δ,

$$(\sigma + 2\partial) \frac{\partial^2 Z}{\partial T \partial S} > - \frac{\partial^2 Z}{\partial S \partial S} \tag{6.7}$$

(Becker and Murphy 1988: 680).

For the abbreviation problem the notions of tolerance and reinforcement are not easily intuitive to interpret. The notions of a positive and negative habit in terms of marginal utility, and the elasticity of demand, however, are straightforward to understand. So I stick to the terminology of Stigler and Becker's original article.

Third, the way I handled abbreviation may strike some readers as rather old-fashioned at its best or completely wrong at its worst. Isn't one of the blessings of modern economic theory that it is not expected to be a description of reality? Shouldn't one look for the implications of utility-maximizing theory for observable behaviour (Stigler 1965: 153)? I believe, however, that the paper proved there is still something to be gained from looking at the neo-marginalist phase of the development of utility theory. It gave us just what we wanted: testable predictions.

In other words, I did not take marginal utility as a shorthand but as a short cut. It was no shorthand for, but a short cut in, actual consumer calculations.

REFERENCES

Becker, G.S. and Murphy, K.M. (1988) 'A Theory of Rational Addiction', *Journal of Political Economy* 96: 675–700.

Böhm-Bawerk, E. von (1886) 'Grundzüge der Theorie des wirtschaftlichen Güterwerts', *Jahrbücher für Nationalökonomie und Statistik*, Bd. XIII, NF: 1–82.

Chaloupka, F. (1991) 'Rational Addictive Behavior and Cigarette Smoking', *Journal of Political Economy* 99: 722–42.

McCulloch, J.H. (1977) 'The Austrian Theory of the Marginal Use and of Ordinal Marginal Utility', *Zeitschrift für Nationalökonomie* 37:249–280.

Mayer, H. (1922) 'Untersuchung zu dem Grundgesetz der wirtschaftlichen Wertrechnung', *Zeitschrift für Volkswirtschaft und Sozialpolitik*, NF II: 1–23.
Parkin, M. (1990) *Economics*, Wokingham: Addison-Wesley.
Rosenstein-Rodan, P. (1927) 'Marginal Utility', *Handwörterbuch der Staatswissenschaften*. Reprinted in Alan T. Peacock, Ralph Turvey, Wolfgang F. Stolper, and Hans Liesner, (eds) (1960) *International Economic Papers*, no. 10, London and New York: Macmillan: 70–106.
Samuelson, P. A. and Nordhaus, W.D. (1989) *Economics*, New York: McGraw-Hill.
Schönfeld-Illy, L. (1924) *Grenznutzen und Wirtschaftsrechnung*, Wien. Reprinted with an introduction by Kurt R. Leube, München and Wien: Philosophia Verlag, 1982.
Schönfeld-Illy, L. (1948) *Das Gesetz des Grenznutzes, Untersuchung über die Wirtschaftsrechnung des Konsumenten*, Wien: Springer Verlag.
Simon, H.A. (1957) *Models of Man*, New York: John Wiley & Sons.
Stigler, G.J. (1965) *Essays in the History of Economics*, Chicago: University of Chicago Press.
Stigler, G.J. and Becker, G.S. (1977) 'De Gustibus Non Est Disputandum', *American Economic Review* 67: 76–90.

Part III

THEORETICAL ASPECTS OF MODERN AUSTRIAN ECONOMICS

7

SCHUMPETER VS. HAYEK: TWO APPROACHES TO EVOLUTIONARY ECONOMICS

*Ulrich Witt**

INTRODUCTION

Although two of the original protagonists of evolutionary thinking in economics – Schumpeter and Hayek – were born in Austria and educated in Vienna, Austrian economics and the evolutionary approach are usually considered to be two distinct and independent developments. This distinction has something to it and the present paper will give some hints as to why. However, the two schools also have much in common. It seems worthwhile, therefore, to examine whether matching the two lines of thought could yield a promising research strategy. An exploration of this question is complicated, unfortunately, by the fact that within the Austrian School there is considerable disagreement about various issues (see, e.g., Shand 1981). The same is true with respect to the evolutionary approach which still suffers from a significant lack of coherence (see Witt 1991). Before the possible gains from matching ideas from the two camps can be assessed, a thorough review of similarities and differences between, and shortcomings and strengths of, several positions in both schools seems necessary.

The paper proceeds as follows. The next section (pp. 82–83) briefly summarizes core notions of the two schools and seeks to discover the relationships that exist between them. Core notions of the Austrians, it will be argued, are the subjectivist creed and the predominant interest in the phenomena of process and change in the economy. The evolutionary approach shares the latter, while the problem of subjectivism has, up to now, been grossly ignored. As explained on pp. 84–86, this attitude, which can be traced back to Schumpeter (1912), is unfortunate. It prevents the evolutionary approach from fully understanding the implications of a

* I wish to thank Hans Albert, Howard Baetjer, Stephan Boehm, Peter Boettke, Juli Irving-Lessmann, Israel Kirzner, Don Lavoie, Mario Rizzo and William Tulloh for helpful comments on earlier drafts. The paper has also been published under the title 'Turning Austrian Economics into an Evolutionary Theory' in B.J. Caldwell and S. Boehm (eds), *Austrian Economics: Tensions and New Directions*, Dordrecht: Kluwer Academic Publishers 1992.

crucial feature of evolution, namely the emergence of novelty. In order to come to grips with novelty, subjectivism must, on the other hand, not be associated with Mises' (1949) apriorism. The next section (pp. 86–88) shows that apriorism conflicts with basic research interests of the evolutionary approach. The subsequent section (pp. 88–90) therefore advocates a fallibilist methodology which may also help to resolve the epistemological intricacies involved in dealing with novelty. Such a methodology has been worked out by Hayek (1967a). Yet, surprisingly, at the core of his later work – his theory of cultural evolution (Hayek 1979, epilogue; 1988) briefly reviewed on pp. 90–92 – the individual and its subjectivity does not seem to play a role any more. The theory relies on quasi-biological group selection criteria. As explained on pp. 92–94, population features – as the one implied in Hayek's criterion – are indeed crucial elements of evolutionary theories. They are not, in principle, incompatible with an individualistic methodology but necessitate some qualifications. Having reached this point, evolutionary theorizing is suggested in the conclusions on pp. 94–95 as a promising way of developing Austrian economics further.

HOW CORE NOTIONS OF THE TWO SCHOOLS RELATE

Economic decision-makers pursue their aims on the basis of their current views of ends–means relationships. This empirically almost trivial hypothesis can easily be confirmed by introspection. Simple as the hypothesis is, it provides a foundation for subjectivism, a core notion of Austrian economics, once it is recognized that – unlike in the neoclassical fiction of uniform, perfect information – the views that the agents hold, and the information they have, may differ. Their understanding of ends–means relationships may, as a result of ignorance and subjective interpretation, be incomplete, biased and even illusory, in an idiosyncratic way. Accordingly, not only tastes and preferences represent a subjective domain, as generally accepted in economics, but also the current state of perceptions, knowledge and expectations.[1] All this is not directly observable and may (sometimes) be rather volatile. As economic activities depend on the hidden, inner state of mind, the explanation and prediction of the former requires hypotheses about the latter.

There is a second core notion, which seems generally accepted in Austrian economics: the idea that individual economic activities may be in – and must potentially be explained as emerging from – permanent flux.[2] It is closely related to, or may even be seen as, an implication of the first core notion, because it is for the imperfections and insufficiencies of the subjective state of knowledge that there is room for discovering and realizing improvements. The agents learn and work out superior possibilities for acting and, accordingly, readjust their plans. As a consequence, the economy changes continually and thus has to be portrayed in terms of a theory of process rather than static theory.

Process and change also represent core notions in the evolutionary approach to economics where evolution has to be understood as more than just dynamics. Evolution is a process in which a system under consideration transforms itself over time. Thus, focus is on endogenously caused change as opposed to change induced by external forces. To use Schumpeter's formulation, the task is to explain 'the possibility of development intrinsically generated from within itself'.[3]

Given this task, it is natural to ask what counts as the reason for and as the ultimate source of endogenously created change. As a simple consideration shows, the ultimate source of endogenous change is the emergence of novelty. Unless novelty is continually created, change would sooner or later come to an end. The adaptive efforts of the agents would converge simultaneously to an equilibrium state in which everything has been learned and all possible advantageous readjustments have been exploited.[4]

Once novelty has been created somewhere in the economy, the question arises whether and how this novelty diffuses through the economy. As it diffuses, novelty potentially induces adaptive efforts at a growing number of points in the economy and, perhaps, has a self-amplifying effect. The evolutionary approach can therefore be characterized as an attempt to explain the continuing change in, and the transformation of, the economy as a process governed by regularities in the emergence and dissemination of novelty (Witt 1993). What seems important here is that a continually ongoing creation of novelty by economic agents does not only explain why change may, for endogenous reasons, never come to an end, it also provides a powerful argument for a subjectivist position in economics (see Witt 1989a). This connection has already been suggested by Shackle (1959, 1972: ch. 37; 1983) in his work on the imaginative element in decision-making and on kaleidic economics.

In the realm of economics, new information emerges from the creative activity of the individual human mind. This information obtains a specific meaning, as new private knowledge, by the particular interpretative framework which has grown out of the individual's experience. Initially, novelty is therefore necessarily subjective. It may be disseminated in communication processes and may then be shared, as a common view, by other agents. Nonetheless, the information sets of the agents in the economy never completely converge as long as creative activities go on: first, because interpersonal communication is time-consuming, disseminates new information selectively (often even discriminatingly) and is certainly not unambiguous; second, because new information may be interpreted in different ways and may thus mean different things to different people.

SCHUMPETERIAN EVOLUTION: THE DENIAL OF SUBJECTIVISM

In the previous section the emergence of novelty has been identified as a crucial feature of evolutionary theories. To the extent to which novelty, as in the domain of economic theory, originates from the human mind, it has been argued that it is inherently subjective. This seems to suggest a subjectivist perspective in evolutionary economics. However, such a perspective is absent and the subjectivism problem is grossly ignored, notably in the Schumpeterian line of evolutionary economics. This seems remarkable in view of the fact that Schumpeter had Böhm-Bawerk and Wieser among his teachers. It is no secret, of course, that Schumpeter wanted to achieve a standing of his own and thus tended to distance himself from standard Austrian positions from the very beginning (cf. Lachmann 1982: 34; Boehm 1987). Thus the approach he adopted in his first major work, his habilitation thesis (Schumpeter 1908), was consciously heterodox. The splendid, albeit rather eclectic, discussion of contemporary theoretical problems synthesizes themes, thoughts and tools from various schools in economics – chiefly, however, ideas from the neoclassical school as represented by Pareto.

In writing his thesis, in particular in the passages where he deals with the restoration of equilibrium after exogenous changes (*ibid.*, part IV), Schumpeter must have noticed that a crucial feature of the historical economic record was missing in the predominant economic theories of his time. There was no explanation for the driving forces of economic change. He sat down to develop the missing – evolutionary – theory in Schumpeter 1910 and 1912 publications. As is well known, this theory portrays economic evolution as a perennial gale of creative restructuring and expansion which is driven by disruptive, innovative activities of pioneering entrepreneurs. The original theory is inspired especially by the attempt to make sense of the cyclical pattern of 'prosperity and depression' (Schumpeter 1910).[5] Nonetheless, Schumpeter takes pains in attempting to explain the development in terms of a self-transformation process, the driving element of which is an innovating 'entrepreneur-hero'. In no instance, however, does Schumpeter confront the reader with a consideration of the subjectivism problem or with any subjectivist reservation.[6]

The 'trick' by which Schumpeter evades such considerations is simple. He contrasts the notion of innovation, 'the carrying out of new combinations', which he discusses at length, with the notion of invention. On the basis of this distinction the emergence of novelty can be referred to the domain of inventions. But inventions, Schumpeter postulates, are trivially and abundantly available and known to all sorts of people. Their coming into being is declared irrelevant for economic analysis. All that matters in his theory is the pioneering initiative, the 'doing it', the carrying out of what is already available but which no one has yet ventured to realize. Consequently, Schumpeter elaborates upon the psychology of his 'entrepreneur-hero'. He talks about what nowadays is labelled achievement motivation and about the skills needed to attract and command resources into the first ventures. Once these have been performed, an entire wave of imitative enterprises is supposed to follow suit – a metaphor clearly indicating that Schumpeter's theory is all about the dissemination of novelty in the market and the economy as a whole.

The flaw in the construction that was intended to treat the dissemination aspects without going into the problems involved in the emergence of novelty, is easy to identify. The dichotomy of invention and innovation builds on the fiction that the meaning and the relevant implications of new information, once invented or discovered, are instantaneously, exhaustively and unambiguously revealed to everybody. What actually happens, however, is quite different. First, lack of experience with a newly invented item has to be compensated by imagining what might be attainable with the invention. One and the same invention can mean different things to different people depending on their subjective, speculative assessments of the implications of the invention. What else but their visionary capacity makes entrepreneurs discern a venture where others see nothing? It is evident that this implies an idiosyncratic, subjective element in perceptions or expectations. Second, because of lack of experience, the process of innovating is experimental by nature. This means that it is a sequential, and usually highly subjective, revelation process into which further discoveries can intervene so that inventive and innovative activities actually interact recursively. Even if Schumpeter's exclusive focus on entrepreneurial innovations were acceptable, novelty – together with its subjectivist implications – would still be encountered in the diffusion process and would thus need to be taken into account.

It is important to note these flaws, because the construction with which Schumpeter tried to circumvent both the problem of emergence of novelty and the related problem of subjective action knowledge has later proved to be the vantage point for neoclassical adaptations of his theory of innovation. Just two decades after the first publication of his evolutionary theory Schumpeter himself started reinterpreting it, (e.g. in Schumpeter 1935), probably as a result of the intellectual influences he experienced after moving to Harvard (see Stolper 1979). Today there is a vast neoclassical literature on industrial innovation and R&D. Although it usually relates itself to Schumpeter it has, by completely ignoring the question of how novelty emerges, abandoned even the last traces of his evolutionary elements.[7]

Even if he does not create the new information himself, the 'entrepreneur-hero' in Schumpeter's original outline at least had to decide which new information to take up in the attempt to make his way forward. Furthermore, there was room for individuality with respect to willpower and achievement motivation. By contrast, 'innovative' activities in the neoclassical literature become competitive races in which everybody chases in the same way after the same success along the same well-known tracks. Correspondingly, 'innovation' turns into a particular kind of investment problem under probabilistic perfect information. The problem is portrayed as one of investing in the development of a new product or process where, entirely at odds with the subjective and insecure nature of the tentative knowledge actually involved in pursuing novel ventures, all properties of the new items and even the revenues to be earned are supposed to be common knowledge. What motivates these assumptions is, of course, the attempt to meet the prerequisites for applying neoclassical constrained maximization calculus and equilibrium analysis.

In opposition to such an attempt, increasing efforts have been undertaken to reconstruct, on the basis of loose analogies to natural selection in biology, a theory of Schumpeterian evolution without subscribing to the optimization hypothesis and expectational equilibrium (Winter 1964, Nelson and Winter 1982, Day 1987, Dosi *et al.*(1988). These contributions provide important new insights into how novelty disseminates (see Witt 1991). However, the source from which, over and again, new diffusion processes spring – the emergence of novelty – is, here too, left unexplored. As a consequence the problems resulting from the subjectivity of new knowledge are ignored here as they have been in Schumpeter (1912).

WHAT KIND OF SUBJECTIVISM?

The subjectivism problem, it has been argued above, is at the core of Austrian economics. The evolutionary approach, too, must come to terms with it, if the emergence of novelty is not neglected altogether as in the Schumpeterian tradition. However, the consequences to be drawn from the fact that individual action hinges upon subjective knowledge which, if at all, is only indirectly and partially accessible to the outside observer, may differ. The more recent discussion, in particular in the Austro-American school, has been strongly influenced by Mises' aprioristic methodology, a position difficult to reconcile with the evolutionary approach.[8]

As is well known, Mises (1949: ch. 2) tries to solve the problem by defining economics as a praxeological science. 'Praxeology' is a label for the logic of hypothetical associations of ends and means by which, according to the maxim of 'rationality', the most appropriate means is to be derived for the chosen ends. As a mere logical operation, praxeology produces only analytical judgements which, as Mises rightly points out, cannot be subjected to empirical evaluation. Nonetheless, he claims 'Praxeology conveys exact and precise knowledge of real things [namely of action as it appears in life and history]' (*ibid.*: 39). Mises wants to achieve this knowledge not by adding empirical hypotheses but by deriving from pure ratiocination what he calls the 'essence' of an action.[9] How this can work is not clear. In order for the asserted empirical judgement to be feasible to (extended) praxeology, two things would actually have to be added: first, an empirical hypothesis about which ends and means an individual perceives; second, the – empirical – conjecture that individuals decide in a logically consistent way. If economics were a (faultless) logic of hypothetical ends–means relationships, as defined by Mises, the second query would be inappropriate. Indeed, Mises (1949: ch. 1) explicitly refers the explanation of behaviour deviating from full logical consistency to the domain of psychology.

With this definition of economics as a prerequisite, Mises' solution to the subjectivism problem is almost self-defeating. The fact that decision anomalies have turned out in recent research to be pervasive (see Meyer 1986) would render economic behaviour largely an object of psychology. Even worse, the dynamics of purposive behaviour, learning and creativity, can hardly be put in terms of a logic of hypothetical ends–means relationships, a point already made by Lachmann (1951). These aspects, too, would have to be referred to psychology. The narrow definition of the realm of economics, which corresponds to Mises' aprioristic approach, thus conflicts with basic research interests of the evolutionary approach. Methodological apriorism cannot be expected to provide insights as to how novelty emerges and disseminates in the economy.[10]

A different attitude towards the subjectivism problem has been suggested by Hayek (1952a) in his fallibilistic approach. This attitude is much closer to the empirical orientation prevailing in most of the contributions to evolutionary economics, notably in Schumpeter's work and the Schumpeterian tradition, except that the latter ignores the subjectivism problem. Since one can argue about what other individuals perceive, understand and conclude, it must be possible to pose empirical conjectures about the subjective state of mind of some individual(s). These conjectures are, in principle, falsifiable, even though they can, at best, be tested indirectly by implications which should be independently observable if the conjectures are correct. Introspection as well as the (fallibilistic) methodology of *Verstehen*, that is an attempt to find intelligible elements in observed action, may play a role in deriving such hypotheses (Hayek 1967b).

In line with this general orientation Hayek (1952b) develops an empirical theory on how the human mind organizes incoming information. Note that putting questions like these requires discarding both aprioristic methodology *and* Mises' restrictive definition of economics. It does not necessarily mean, however, uncritically mimicking the methodology of the empirical sciences, especially physics. In fact, Hayek (1967a) takes pains to draw attention to, and to elaborate on, the particular conditions that a fallibilist position meets in the life sciences and social sciences. While physics faces relatively simple phenomena, economics, for instance, is confronted, not least because of the subjective character of the data, with complex phenomena. Complexity does not allow all information necessary to completely specify and control the antecedence conditions of the theories to be obtained. Because of the rough and usually incomplete approximation of the preconditions, the explanations or predictions derived this way can only cover certain general features and may be compatible with a great number of circumstances. Such 'explanations of the principle' and 'pattern predictions' (Hayek 1967a) reduce the possibilities of falsifying the underlying theory. However, as long as the theory still rules out something, it is testable and thus fallible. Hayek's theory of cultural evolution, to be discussed below, provides an example of such a theory.

HOW TO DEAL WITH NOVELTY

According to the considerations so far, the Schumpeterian variant of evolutionary economics is, because of its lack of recognition of the role of novelty, as irreconcilable with the subjectivist tenet as Misesian praxeology is, because of its narrow, aprioristic methodology, with the evolutionary approach. A different theory is thus needed as a basis of evolutionary economics, ideally one that discerns both the emergence of novelty and its dissemination as relevant objects of inquiry. The theory should recognize the subjectivism problem, yet be based on a fallibilistic methodology. In fact, as will be explained now, such a methodological orientation is also needed in order to come to grips with the amorphous nature of novelty which poses an intricate problem for evolutionary theories. Although the emergence and dissemination of novelty jointly constitute the evolutionary process, there is a fundamental epistemological difference between the two, and the problems involved here sometimes motivate scientific treatments to neglect the emergence aspects.

The problems can best be approached by noting, first, that novelty may mean different things in the context of emergence on the one hand and in the dissemination context on the other. By definition, the very concept of novelty rules out positive foreknowledge of its informational content. Yet, two cases can be distinguished in terms of who is unable to anticipate the meaning of novelty. Non-anticipatability may be confined to the individual agent who is confronted with something which (s)he does not yet know, but which other agents may very well be familiar with. This may be called the case of 'subjective novelty'. It is the typical, almost trivial prevailing case where novelty diffuses in markets or the economy as a whole. New businesspeople or consumers continue to 'discover' for themselves what others may already be used to.

The characteristic of this case is that the scientific observers can reasonably be assumed to have the same status as those individuals already acquainted with the new item. They can use the existing knowledge to develop and test, according to scientific standards, empirical conjectures about the reactions of those individuals exposed to the new item for the first time (cf. Witt 1989a). Since the subjective meaning of the new item may differ for each single adopter (or non-adopter) and, hence, the individual reaction hinges upon the subjective state of mind, the scientific observer is confronted here with the subjectivism problem as explained in the previous section. Thus, within the context of disseminating novelty, evolutionary theory faces no particular new epistemological or methodological problems as long as the diffusion process can indeed be explained as a sequence of independent individual adoption or non-adoption decisions (the discussion of the slightly more complicated case where the independency assumption is not valid being deferred to on pp. 92–94).

The situation changes, however, once the context of emergence is entered. This may happen even within an ongoing diffusion process, if the diffusing item 'mutates' significantly in consecutive adoptions. In that case, non-anticipatability is no longer confined only to the individual adopter/non-adopter. The informational content of what newly emerges is unknown in general and thus also to the scientific observer. To distinguish this situation one may thus speak of 'objective novelty' here. As a consequence, the methodological strategy developed for explaining what happens in the dissemination context no longer works: hypotheses and predictions contingent on specific knowledge about the informational content of novelty are no longer feasible. It is here that the notions of 'explanation of the principle' and 'pattern prediction' as developed by Hayek in his fallibilistic methodology become relevant once more.[11] They suggest the following strategy.

One may easily speculate about the information that novelty might reveal. The number of conceivable variants is only constrained by the limitations of imagination, but not all of them will appear equally plausible, given the existing scientific knowledge. Thus, it seems straightforward to develop hypotheses that predict that certain variants of information will *not* occur. These 'there-will-be-no-such-thing-like . . .' hypotheses clearly have empirical content in the sense that they can be tested and, in principle, be falsified. This means that even though 'objective novelty' cannot be positively anticipated, evolutionary theory is capable, in principle, of developing hypotheses that impose limitations on what can be expected to emerge and, presumably, on how novelty emerges.

Such hypotheses may be used for explanatory and for predictive purposes. In view of the unlimited number of conceivable realizations not excluded by the hypotheses, the predictive power and the explanatory value of such hypotheses will, of course, be rather weak. It will be confined to elucidating the principles governing the emergence of novelty. Detailed prevision – anything that goes beyond mere pattern predictions – cannot be expected. Since in the case of novelty which is created by the human mind, the underlying processes seem to be extremely complex, these principles may be even less telling than the principles governing the production of genetic novelty.[12] But, as long as the underlying hypotheses still exclude something, they can help to gain insights that would otherwise not be feasible.

HAYEKIAN EVOLUTION: A DENIAL OF INDIVIDUALISM?

While Schumpeterian evolution deals with novelty diffusing, in the form of innovations, through the given institutional framework of the economy, Hayek goes beyond this to focus on the evolution of the institutional framework itself.[13] The competitive societal evolution on which his theory centres is an instance of 'complex phenomena'. Accordingly, what Hayek aims at is not to reconstruct or foretell any specific course of events, but an 'explanation of the principle' or a 'prediction of the pattern' of the evolution of rules of conduct in society and the economy. On a closer look it turns out that the explanations he seeks to give are less concerned with the emergence of new rules than with the various aspects of their competitive dissemination.

Three levels of evolution are distinguished in Hayek (1971, 1979: epilogue): genetic evolution, evolution of rational thought, and cultural evolution, as it operates 'between instinct and reason' (Hayek 1988: ch. 1), i.e. between the former two levels. Hayek's major interests lie in cultural evolution. Culture, he submits, 'is neither natural nor artificial, neither genetically transmitted nor rationally designed. It is a tradition of learned rules of conduct which have never been "invented" and whose functions the acting individuals usually do not understand' (Hayek 1979: 155). Which rules come into play, and how – the context of the emergence of novelty here in the form of new rules – is to Hayek a question of historical accident to which he does not pay much attention. The question his theory is concerned with is which of the rules survive. To Hayek, the answer is determined by the outcome of a largely unplanned and not consciously controlled process of selective transmission and replication – a theory which clearly belongs to what has been called here the dissemination context.

In a nutshell, selective cultural transmission is conceived of as working as follows. Those groups that succeed in developing and passing on rules better suited to governing their social interactions are supposed to grow and feed a larger number of people. Their relative superiority may enable such groups to conquer and/or absorb less well-equipped competing groups and thus, unintentionally, propagate the superior sets of rules. A growing population requires specialization and division of labour which, in turn, presuppose that the spontaneous order that governs impersonal interactions is increasingly extended. The rules become ever more differentiated, abstract and difficult to understand. Over thousands of years during which human civilization grew, an 'extended order' has thus spontaneously evolved. It is assumed to embody super-individual intelligence incorporated in the impersonal rules that have been accumulated during the endless cultural transmission and selection process. The most important achievements according to Hayek (1988: ch. 3) are trade and the emergence of a system of markets.

Thus, Hayek's theory underlies the 'twin ideas of spontaneous order and evolution'. The backbone of the former is a system of impersonal rules of conduct (cf. Vanberg 1989 for a concise scheme). The backbone of the latter is differential selection of groups with different rules. Taken together this implies that natural selection not only 'chooses' between competing species, but also between competing human sub-populations as the unit to which acquired cultural norms and rules – more or less suited to co-ordinate social interactions efficiently – are fixed. The group selection hypothesis sounds familiar from sociobiology. Indeed, Hayek (1979: epilogue), refers to, among others, Huxley (1943), Waddington (1960), Dobzhansky (1962) and Campbell (1965) who are inspired by Darwinian concepts of evolution. Hayek (1967c) rightly points out that the very idea of evolution is older than Darwin's theory.[14] Still, his group selection hypothesis comes very close to the theory of natural selection with only two exceptions. First, the traits on which variation and selective replication operate are not genetic but cultural. Second, acquired properties can therefore be transmitted directly in a Lamarckian fashion, thus speeding up evolution significantly compared to variation and selection operating only on genetic codes.[15]

The second element in Hayek's theory, the idea of a spontaneous order in social and economic interactions, is to him, in the last resort, the outcome of the cultural transmission and selection processes that generate, and still continue to form, the impersonal rules of conduct. Originally, however, the idea goes back to the Scottish moral philosophers David Hume, Adam Smith, Adam Ferguson and their forerunner Bernard Mandeville who conceived first of the division of labour and a system of multilateral, anonymous markets as a spontaneous order. Spontaneous here refers to something not deliberately planned or only conceived of. Spontaneous order is understood as an unintended side effect of individual actions which, despite their possibly purely self-seeking motives, work out to the mutual advantage of all. A notion of the process through which spontaneous order comes into being is not provided in the Scottish moral philosophy.

The idea of spontaneously emerging institutions has, in a similar vein, but apparently independently, been advocated by Carl Menger (1883/1963) in considerations of his 'causal-genetic' method of analysis. Menger submits that regularities in social interactions may be constituted by the individual choices of all participants without anybody having intended or even understood this effect. All individual actions taken together spontaneously establish mutually co-ordinated behaviour. Through habit formation, this comes to be taken for granted. Manifest institutional regularities emerge in this way. Already at the rather primitive societal level of self-sufficiency and a household economy one can, for example, observe regularities such as language and common law – examples Hayek often refers to. Menger's conjecture does not encompass, of course, a clear notion of the actual process by which the institutions mentioned emerge.

By synthesizing the spontaneous order conjecture and the theory of the selective cultural transmission (or rule dissemination) process, Hayek achieves an explanation of the principle of cultural evolution which leads to spontaneous order. None of the single components of the synthesis, taken by themselves, is able to provide such an explanation. This is an important achievement although various facets of the theory still need careful reconstruction, extensions and improvements.[16] One question arises, however, which seems particularly important for assessing the relevance of evolutionary theorizing in the further development of Austrian economic thought. Is the gist of the quasi-sociobiological, population-oriented selection argument, which figures so prominently in Hayek's explanation of the principle, compatible with methodological individualism as defended, in pursuit of the Austrian tradition, by Hayek (1948) himself? What role is played by the individual in cultural evolution? What relevance can the individual's subjective beliefs have at all, if it is an impersonal selection process that determines the regularities in social interactions?

EVOLUTIONARY THOUGHT AND METHODOLOGICAL INDIVIDUALISM

Methodological individualism is usually taken to mean the attempt to explain social phenomena by reducing them to individual actions from which they are supposed to emerge, where these individual actions are then explained independently (Hayek 1948). By contrast, the criterion that governs the Hayekian rule selection or dissemination process is 'group success' – something that does not seem reconcilable with an individualistic perspective. The contrast has repeatedly been felt as a tension impairing Hayek's theory of cultural evolution (Gray 1984: 52; Vanberg 1986). Indeed, a shift in the level of argumentation can hardly be denied.

Suppose an individual comes up with a variation of a hitherto prevailing rule of conduct. An attempt to explain the innovator's motives and expectations would be fully in line with methodological individualism, as would be all efforts to explain the motives and expectations of other individuals who are, or are not, going to imitate the innovator. Yet, for the logic of Hayek's cultural selection process such considerations appear irrelevant. Whatever the underlying beliefs and motives may be, a variation of rules is successful and survives if, and only if, it helps to improve, or is at least not detrimental to, the economic performance of the group. In fact, it does not even matter whether individual action concerning the rules is purposeful or purely random, i.e. intelligible or not, for the result of cultural evolution. The competing groups' relative success explains where the entire process ends up and which of the individual innovative rule variations, for whatever reasons they have been undertaken, eventually become socially successful and which are doomed to fail. Even though Hayek relies on the criterion of group success without even trying to relate it to the level of the individual, this does not necessarily mean, of course, that his theory is incompatible with an individualistic approach. In the domain of the social sciences, novelty emerges from and is disseminated through individual action. Hence, an attempt to explain the evolutionary process by reduction to individual innovative and imitative activities is quite natural, notwithstanding the fact that the very notion of dissemination implies a population as a reference base. One reservation must, however, be made. This reservation reflects a significant feature of evolutionary theories: whenever the individual innovative and imitative activities are not perfectly independent, the evolutionary process cannot entirely be reduced to the level of the individual. Some population-bound criterion or variable remains.

The independency assumption is commonly violated, for instance, in dissemination processes, where it may not be irrelevant for the behaviour of some particular individual at which position in the diffusion sequence they are exposed to the new item. Sometimes this kind of dependency is hidden in a self-sorting hypothesis according to which individuals with systematically changing attributes successively act in, and thereby carry on, the diffusion process.[17] More often, however, the dependency effect comes along in evolutionary theories in the form of a frequency-dependency hypothesis which presupposes otherwise identical individuals. The individual choice among a fixed number of reactions is viewed as hinging upon the relative frequency with which the reactions have been chosen previously during the diffusion process by other individuals in the population. Relative frequency is, of course, a population-related variable.[18]

The latter case seems to apply to an individualistic foundation that could be constructed for substituting the group success criterion in Hayek's theory of cultural evolution. A new rule of conduct is retained, it is claimed, if it enhances the success of a subgroup obeying it. The rule tends to propagate in the population, whether for the sub-group's growth or for an imitation of the new rule by other sub-groups. If this is interpreted as the outcome of a sequential adoption process in which each member of the population decides on whether or not to follow the new rule, the explanatory task can be reduced to explaining the individual adoption behaviour.

The implications of this individualistic model are consistent with Hayek's conjecture if the 'group success' is composed of a positive net advantage which each individual can internalize by adopting, rather than not adopting, the new rule. As has been shown elsewhere (Witt 1989b), the frequency-dependency effect plays a role here, in so far as the extent to which the new rule disseminates in a given population depends on how the size of the individual advantage varies with the relative frequency of adopters. However, as Vanberg (1986) has rightly pointed out, a problem arises in such an individualistic reconstruction, where the adoption of a new rule involves social dilemmas such as, e.g. a prisoners' dilemma. Adopters may then find themselves collecting the 'sucker's pay-off', if collective adoption would be advantageous, i.e. enhances the group's success, but is vulnerable to individual defection.

In such a case, the individualistic model does not support Hayek's argumentation on the basis of the group success criterion as easily as before. Looked at more closely, it turns out that the frequency-dependency effect is now decisive for whether a positive net advantage from adopting can be internalized by an individual. If a sufficiently large number of members of the population have adopted the collectively advantageous new rule, the individual mean gain from following the rule may outweigh the mean loss caused by the remaining free riders.[19] This means that an individualistic theory of the evolutionary process now necessarily has to account for population aspects in the form of population-bound variables or criteria.

However, notwithstanding this reservation, which may have to be made quite often in evolutionary theorizing, an individualistic perspective is still possible. There is no doubt that, in evolutionary economics, the individual decision-maker may be, and should be, chosen as the basic explanatory unit, for this is the level where novelty emerges and is disseminated. The frequency-dependency effect does require a consideration beyond the single economic agent. But what provides the key for understanding the ongoing activities is, in the last resort, still the situation as the individual perceives it.

CONCLUSIONS: WHAT CAN BE GAINED?

In economics, evolutionary theorizing is often identified with the Schumpeterian tradition. This paper has argued that such a view is not appropriate. Evolutionary theorizing requires that the emergence of novelty is recognized as a crucial feature. Due to the subjective nature of novelty in the domain of the social sciences, this necessitates, in turn, finding a solution to the subjectivism problem. The Schumpeterian tradition ignores both issues. An evolutionary theory in which the two problems are taken up is congenial in many respects to Austrian economics with its core notions of process and change and its subjectivist creed. An appropriately interpreted evolutionary approach may therefore be suggested as a fruitful basis for future research into those issues with which Austrian economics is traditionally concerned.

If this suggestion is accepted, sacrifices and adjustments will have to be made. In particular, apriorism will have to be abandoned because evolutionary theorizing presupposes a solution to the subjectivism problem on the basis of a fallibilistic and empirically oriented methodology. This is not only a prerequisite for inquiring more deeply into individual innovative behaviour and the particular dynamics it induces in the economy, but also for encountering the epistemological problems involved in the non-anticipatability of novelty. Furthermore, as explained in more detail above, the interpretation of methodological individualism will have to be adapted in order to accommodate population-bound features.

In return, evolutionary theorizing may help in enhancing the understanding of how spontaneous order in economy and society emerges and changes. This encompasses not only the institutional regularities, the rule-governed basis of spontaneous order, on which Hayek's theory of cultural evolution focuses, but no less the very process of co-ordination of the mass of individual economic ventures and activities taking place within the institutional framework and on the basis of established rules. Concerning this process Austrian economics may also profit from results and insights obtained in the Schumpeterian tradition. What happens here cannot fully be captured by the mere postulates of entrepreneurial alertness and arbitrage in the markets. The reasons for, and the dynamics of, innovative activities and their diffusion through the economy can provide new insights into how an economy works and why the pace and direction of its evolution varies so greatly in history and place.

NOTES

1 See Mises (1949: 18–21), Hayek (1952a: ch. 3), Kirzner (1979: chs. 8 and 9), Boehm (1982) and the thoughtful discussion in O'Driscoll and Rizzo (1985: chs. 2 and 3). There is now also a British subjectivist tradition (cf. Shackle 1972, Loasby 1976, Wiseman 1983) with origins and views related to Austrian economics, see Lachmann (1976) and Wiseman (1985); the connection has recently also been taken up by Loasby (1991: ch. 2).

2 See Kirzner (1973, 1979: chs. 1 and 2), Lachmann (1986), Boettke, Horwitz and Prychitko (1986); see also Shackle (1943).

3 Schumpeter (1912: 75), my translation according to the second German edition; the appendix to the first chapter in this edition has not been included

in the English edition of 1934); cf. also Nelson and Winter (1982: ch. 2), Day (1987), Allen (1988), Faber and Proops (1990: part III), Witt (1991).

4 Cf. Fehl (1986). If it happens that, because of mutually interfering adjustments of the agents, the adaptive efforts become cyclic, motion would persist but would be confined to a closed set of states. In a broader sense, such equilibrium motions show no change.

5 At a time when ordinary business and routine dominate, i.e. in a phase of 'circular flow' of the economy, entrepreneurs are assumed to come up with major technical or organizational innovations or with creating new markets. The multiplier effects of these path-breaking activities at once attract and support imitative ventures by growing numbers of less creative and less skilled entrepreneurs. The economy takes off into a boom phase until, after a while, the wave of innovations and imitations has led to overcapacity. Increasing competitive pressure squeezes prices and profits, the expansion ceases. Credit repayments induce a deflationary tendency and negative multiplier effects. Depression drives inefficient productive capacity out of business until, eventually, the economy is back in 'circular flow', albeit at a higher level of output and welfare.

6 Schumpeter thus adopted a popular notion as far as the entrepreneur is concerned. See Streissler (1972, 1983) who attributes it to Wieser. Schumpeter refrained from taking up the presumably even more prominent discussion on subjectivism, or even pointedly ignored it as Lachmann (1986: 144) argues.

7 See Kamien and Schwartz (1982), Scherer (1984), Baldwin and Scott (1987) and Reinganum (1989).

8 There are, of course, considerable differences of opinion in this question: see O'Driscoll and Rizzo (1985: ch. 2), Boettke, Horwitz and Prychitko (1986) and the recent reflections in Mäki (1990). Although the methodological intricacies of the subjectivism problem seem to have already been recognized by Carl Menger, the founder of the Austrian school did not develop a clear position in this respect, cf. Meyer (1990).

9 He argues that 'action' is the result of human reasoning, namely the logical implication of a hypothetical ends–means calculus; hence the essential features of action should be reconstructible by analytical reasoning. For a recent reconstruction of essentialism – not apriorism – in terms of realism see Mäki (1990).

10 Symptomatically, the Austro-American school has not been able to make much out of its early insight that a significant role could be played by novelty. Discovery or creation of novelty is related here to an entrepreneurial human element (Mises 1949: 252–256, High 1986, Kirzner 1989: ch. 2). But the theoretical underpinnings of this relationship have still not been developed beyond the rather vague concept of alertness from which the discovery of novelty is somehow believed to spring. For example, Kirzner (1979: 8–9) states: '. . . indeed, we do not clearly understand how entrepreneurs get their flashes of superior foresight. We cannot explain how some men discover what is around the corner before others do . . . As an empirical matter, however, opportunities do tend to be perceived and exploited.'

11 In fact, Hayek (1967a) himself explicitly relates them to the emergence of novelty in Darwinian evolutionary theory. In that theory the non-anticipatability condition concretely means that positive predictions as to what phenotypic traits will occur as a result of genetic mutations in a certain species cannot be made.

12 For the latter cf. Eigen (1988); a discussion of the former can be found in Witt (1992: ch. 1).

13 Hayek came to appreciate the role of evolutionary phenomena only in his later work on what he labelled 'social philosophy', cf. Hayek (1973: 5). In his earlier studies of economic theory in the narrower sense, which engaged most of his attention until the end of the 1940s, no attempt is made to introduce evolutionary theorizing. Symptomatically, there is, to my knowledge, no reference in Hayek's oeuvre in which Schumpeter (1912) is recognized as a seminal contribution to evolutionary economics – and not simply as yet another business cycle theory.

14 It can already be found in a line of thought in the arts, social sciences and law beginning in Germany in the eighteenth century, and linked to names such as Herder, Savigny and Wilhelm von Humboldt. See also Bowler (1989: 104–108).

15 Similar ideas have recently been advocated more rigorously as an extension of sociobiology in the so-called 'co-evolutionary view' (Cavalli-Sforza and Feldman 1981, Lumsden and Wilson 1981, Boyd and Richerson 1985).

16 For an excellent appraisal see Vanberg (1986). A discussion of the critical points is beyond the space available here. In generalizing the underlying idea, Lavoie, Baetjer and Tulloh (1990) have recently attempted an application to the domain of artificial intelligence. An equivalent to cultural evolution has a certain tradition in this field, see Schwefel (1992).

17 An explanation of what is going on here cannot avoid specifying a distribution of attributes over a population and the relative position that has been reached in that distribution. A case in point is Schumpeterian evolution. Even though much emphasis is placed here on the role of the innovative entrepreneurial individual, the actual process can only be understood if the population-bound variable 'relative entrepreneurial skill' is recognized which ranges from the 'promoter' to the 'plain business person', cf. Schumpeter (1912: 74–94). It is argued there that innovative activities are gradually turning into imitative, and eventually ordinary, business practices the further the process works its way through each new 'swarm of entrepreneurs'.

18 Note that the frequency-dependency hypothesis describes only a general feature so that it may be taken as a typical example of an 'algebraic theory' (Hayek 1967a) from which only pattern predictions result.

19 Several different hypotheses have been suggested in order to explain the spontaneous solution of the dilemma along these lines (Boorman and Levitt 1973, Axelrod and Hamilton 1981, Witt 1986, Güth and Yaari 1992). They all share the crucial reliance on the frequency-dependency effect.

REFERENCES

Allen, P. (1988) 'Evolution, Innovation, and Economics', in G. Dosi, C. Freeman, R. Nelson, G. Silverberg, L. Soete (eds) *Technical Change and Economic Theory*, London: Pinter, 95–119.

Axelrod, R. and Hamilton, D. (1981) 'The Evolution of Cooperation', *Science* 212: 1390–1396.

Baldwin, W.L. and Scott, J.T. (1987) *Market Structure and Technological Change*, New York: Harwood.

Boehm, S. (1982) 'The Ambiguous Notion of Subjectivism: Comment on Lachmann', in I.M. Kirzner (ed.) *Method, Process, and Austrian Economics*, Lexington: Heath, 41–52.

Boehm, S. (1987) 'Einleitung', in S. Boehm (ed.), *Joseph A. Schumpeter – Beiträge zur Sozialökonomie*, Wien: Böhlau, 13–37.

Boettke, P., Horwitz, S. and Prychitko, D.L. (1986) 'Beyond Equilibrium Economics: Reflections on the Uniqueness of the Austrian Tradition', *Market Process* 4: 6–25.

Boorman, S.A. and Levitt, P.R. (1973) 'A Frequency-dependent Natural Selection Model for the Evolution of Social Cooperation Networks', *Proceedings of the National Academy of Sciences, U.S.A.* 70: 187–189.

Bowler, P.J. (1989) *Evolution – the History of an Idea*, revised edn, Berkeley: University of California Press.

Boyd, R. and Richerson, P.J. (1985) *Culture and the Evolutionary Process*, Chicago: University of Chicago Press.

Campbell, D.T. (1965) 'Variation and Selective Retention in Socio-Cultural Evolution', in H.R. Barringer, G.I. Blanksten and R.W. Mack (eds) *Social Change in Developing Areas: A Reinterpretation of Evolutionary Theory*, Cambridge, Massachusetts: Schenkman.

Cavalli-Sforza, L. and Feldman, M. (1981) *Cultural Transmission and Evolution*, Princeton: Princeton University Press.

Day, R.H. (1987) 'The General Theory of Disequilibrium Economics and of Economic Evolution', in D. Batten, J. Casti and B. Johannson (eds) *Economic Evolution and Structural Adjustment*, Berlin: Springer, 46–63.

Dobzhansky, T.G. (1962) *Mankind Evolving: The Evolution of the Human Species*, New Haven: Yale University Press.

Dosi, G., Freeman, C., Nelson, R., Silverberg, G. and Soete, L. (eds) (1988) *Technical Change and Economic Theory*, London: Pinter.

Eigen, M. (1988) 'Macromolecular Evolution: Dynamical Ordering in Sequence Space', in D. Pines (ed.) *Emerging Syntheses in Science*, Redwood City: Addison-Wesley, 21–42.

Faber, M. and Proops, J.L.R. (1990) *Evolution, Time, Production, and the Environment*, Berlin: Springer.

Fehl, U. (1986) 'Spontaneous Order and the Subjectivity of Expectations: A Contribution to the Lachmann-O'Driscoll Problem', in I.M. Kirzner (ed.) *Subjectivism, Intelligibility, and Economic Understanding*, New York: New York University Press, 72–86.

Gray, J. (1984) *Hayek on Liberty*, New York: Basil Blackwell.

Güth, W. and Yaari, M. (1992) 'An Evolutionary Approach to Explaining Reciprocal Behavior in a Simple Strategic Game', in U. Witt (ed.) *Explaining Process and Change – Approaches to Evolutionary Economics*, Ann Arbor: Michigan University Press, 23–34.

Hayek, F.A. (1948) 'Individualism: True and False', in *Individualism and Economic Order*, London: Routledge, 1–32.

Hayek, F.A. (1952a) 'The Subjective Character of the Data of the Social Sciences', in *The Counter-Revolution of Science*, Glencoe: Free Press, 41–60.

Hayek, F.A. (1952b) *The Sensory Order*, London: Routledge & Kegan Paul.

Hayek, F.A. (1967a) 'The Theory of Complex Phenomena', in *Studies in Philosophy, Politics, and Economics*, London: Routledge & Kegan Paul, 22–42.

Hayek, F.A. (1967b) 'Rules, Perception and Intelligibility', in *Studies in Philosophy, Politics, and Economics*, London: Routledge & Kegan Paul, 43–65.

Hayek, F.A. (1967c) 'Dr Bernhard Mandeville', *Proceedings of the British Academy*, Vol. 12, London: Oxford University Press.

Hayek, F.A. (1971) 'Nature vs. Nurture Once Again', *Encounter* 36: 81–83.

Hayek, F.A. (1973) *Law, Legislation and Liberty. Vol.1, Rules and Order*, London: Routledge & Kegan Paul.

Hayek, F.A. (1979) *Law, Legislation and Liberty. Vol.3, The Political Order of a Free People*, London: Routledge & Kegan Paul.

Hayek, F.A. (1988) *The Fatal Conceit*, London: Routledge.

High. J. (1986) 'Equilibration and Disequilibration in the Market Process', in I.M. Kirzner (ed.) *Subjectivism, Intelligibility, and Economic Understanding*, New York: New York University Press, 111–121.

Huxley, J.S. (1943) *Evolutionary Ethics*, Oxford: Oxford University Press.

Kamien, M.I. and Schwartz, N.L. (1982) *Market Structure and Innovation*, Cambridge: Cambridge University Press.

Kirzner, I.M. (1973) *Competition and Entrepreneurship*, Chicago: University of Chicago Press.

Kirzner, I.M. (1979) *Perception, Opportunity, and Profit*, Chicago: University of Chicago Press.

Kirzner, I.M. (1989) *Discovery, Capitalism, and Distributive Justice*, New York: Basil Blackwell.

Lachmann, L.M. (1951) 'The Science of Human Action', *Economica* 18: 412–427.

Lachmann, L.M. (1976) 'From Mises to Shackle: An Essay on Austrian Economics and the Kaleidic Society', *Journal of Economic Literature* 14: 54–62.

Lachmann, L.M. (1982) 'Ludwig von Mises and the Extension of Subjectivism', in I.M. Kirzner (ed.) *Method, Process, and Austrian Economics*, Lexington: Heath, 31–40.

Lachmann, L.M. (1986) *The Market as an Economic Process*, London: Basil Blackwell.

Lavoie, D., Baetjer, H. and Tulloh, W. (1990) 'High-Tech Hayekians: Some Possible Research Topics in the Economics of Computation', *Market Process* 8: 120–146.

Loasby, B. (1976) *Choice, Complexity, and Ignorance*, Cambridge: Cambridge University Press.

Loasby, B. (1991) *Equilibrium and Evolution – An Exploration of Connecting Principles in Economics*, Manchester: Manchester University Press.

Lumsden, C.J. and Wilson, E.O. (1981) *Genes, Mind, and Culture: The Co-evolutionary Process*, Cambridge: Harvard University Press.

Mäki, U. (1990) 'Scientific Realism and Austrian Explanation', *Review of Political Economy* 2: 310–344.

Menger, C. (1883) *Untersuchungen über die Methode der Socialwissenschaften*, Leipzig: Duncker & Humblot. English translation: (1963) *Problems of Economics and Sociology*, Urbana: University of Illinois Press.

Meyer, W. (1986) 'Beyond Choice', in I.M. Kirzner (ed.) *Subjectivism, Intelligibility, and Economic Understanding*, New York: New York University Press, 221–235.

Meyer, W. (1990) 'A Note on Menger's Philosophy of Science', *Methodus* 2: 46–47.

Mises, L. von (1949) *Human Action – A Treatise on Economics*, New Haven: Yale University Press.

Nelson, R.R. and Winter, S.G. (1982) *An Evolutionary Theory of Economic Change*, Cambridge, Massachusetts: Harvard University Press.

O'Driscoll, G.P. and Rizzo, M.J. (1985) *The Economics of Time and Ignorance*, Oxford: Basil Blackwell.

Reinganum, J.F. (1989) 'The Timing of Innovation: Research, Development, and Diffusion', in R. Schmalensee and R.D. Willig (eds), *Handbook of Industrial Organization*, Vol. I, Amsterdam: North-Holland, 849–908.

Scherer, F.M. (1984) *Innovation and Growth: Schumpeterian Perspectives*, Cambridge, Massachusetts: MIT Press.

Schumpeter, J.A. (1908) *Das Wesen und der Hauptinhalt der theoretischen Nationalökonomie*, Leipzig: Duncker und Humblot.

Schumpeter, J.A. (1910) 'Über das Wesen der Wirtschaftskrisen', *Zeitschrift für Volkswirtschaft, Sozialpolitik und Verwaltung* 19: 271–325.

Schumpeter, J.A. (1912) *Theorie der wirtschaftlichen Entwicklung*, Berlin: Duncker & Humblot. English translation: (1934) *Theory of Economic Development*, Cambridge, Massachusetts: Harvard University Press.

Schumpeter, J.A. (1935) 'The Analysis of Economic Change', *Review of Economics and Statistics* 17: 2–10.

Schwefel, H.P. (1992) 'Imitating Evolution: Collective Two-Level Learning Processes', in U. Witt (ed.) *Explaining Process and Change – Approaches to Evolutionary Economics*, Ann Arbor: Michigan University Press, 49–63.

Shackle, G.L.S. (1943) 'The Expectational Dynamics of the Individual', *Economica* 10: 99–129.

Shackle, G.L.S. (1959) 'Time and Thought', *British Journal for the Philosophy of Science* 9: 285–298.

Shackle, G.L.S. (1972) *Epistemics and Economics*, Cambridge: Cambridge University Press.

Shackle, G.L.S. (1983) 'The Bounds of Unknowledge', in J. Wiseman (ed.) *Beyond Positive Economics?*, London: Macmillan, 28–37.

Shand, A.H. (1981) *Subjectivist Economics – The New Austrian School*, Oxford: Short Run Press.

Stolper, W.F. (1979) 'Joseph Alois Schumpeter – A Personal Memoir', *Challenge* 21: 64–69.

Streissler, E. (1972) 'To What Extent was the Austrian School Marginalist?', *History of Political Economy* 4: 426–441.

Streissler, E. (1983) 'Schumpeter and Hayek: On Some Similarities in their Thought', in F. Machlup, G. Fels and H. Müller-Groeling (eds) *Reflections on a Troubled World Economy*, London: Macmillan, 356–364.

Vanberg, V. (1986) 'Spontaneous Market Order and Social Rules', *Economics and Philosophy* 2: 75–100.

Vanberg, V. (1989) 'Hayek as a Constitutional Political Economist', *Wirtschaftspolitische Blätter* 36: 170–182.

Waddington, C.H. (1960) *The Ethical Animal*, London: Allen & Unwin.

Winter, S.G. (1964) 'Economic "Natural Selection" and the Theory of the Firm', *Yale Economic Essays* 4: 225–272.

Wiseman, J. (ed.) (1983) *Beyond Positive Economics?*, London: Macmillan.

Wiseman, J. (1985) 'Lionel Robbins, the Austrian School, and the LSE tradition', *Research in the History of Economic Thought and Methodology* 3: 147–159.

Witt, U. (1986) 'Evolution and Stability of Cooperation Without Enforceable Contracts', *Kyklos* 39: 245–266.

Witt, U. (1989a) 'Subjectivism in Economics – a Suggested Reorientation', in K.G. Grunert and F. Ölander (eds) *Understanding Economic Behavior*, Boston: Kluwer, 409–431.

Witt, U. (1989b) 'The Evolution of Economic Institutions as a Propagation Process', *Public Choice* 62: 155–172.

Witt, U. (1991) 'Reflections on the Present State of Evolutionary Economic Theory', in G.M. Hodgson and E. Screpanti (eds) *Rethinking Economics: Markets, Technology and Economic Evolution*, Aldershot: Edward Elgar, 83–102.

Witt, U. (1992) *Individualistic Foundations of Evolutionary Economics*, Cambridge: Cambridge University Press.

Witt, U. (1993) 'Emergence and Dissemination of Innovations – Some Problems and Principles of Evolutionary Economics', in R.H. Day and P. Chen (eds) *Evolutionary Dynamics and Nonlinear Economics – A Transdisciplinary Dialogue*, Oxford: Oxford University Press.

8

COMMENT ON ULRICH WITT'S 'SCHUMPETER vs. HAYEK'

Willem Keizer

Witt's paper actually deals with two separate issues: the first half explores the possibilities of a cross-fertilization between Austrian Economics (AE) and Evolutionary Economics (EE), as far as it concerns the crucial issue of EE according to Witt: to explain the emergence of 'novelty' (specific new items), which causes endogenous change in economies. This part of the paper searches for a theoretical basis for this major element of EE in the subjectivist core of AE. The second half of the paper concerns a wholly different subject: the social processes of the selective transmission and continuation of novelty, *i.e.* the matter of its dissemination, as propounded in Hayek's social philosophy (as in his *Law, Legislation and Liberty*, 1973–1979). This is a different subject, and one not really amenable to subjectivist-individualist treatment. This part of the paper is essentially a critique of Hayek's apparent 'objectivist-collectivist' stance in explaining the success of particular social rules or institutions, from the viewpoint of the Austrian (and originally Hayek's own!) subjectivist-individualist paradigm.

My comments will mainly deal with the first section of Witt's paper, concerning the theoretical issues of EE and AE. It is noticeable that Witt, when speaking of EE, uses the qualifications 'school' and 'approach' interchangeably, as if they are synonymous. However, if that is not the case and the two terms denote different concepts (as they should and surely do), then the question arises: what is evolutionary economics – is it a 'school' or an 'approach'? Another way of putting this is: what is the present scientific status of EE? The term 'school' suggests a far greater conceptual coherence and crystallization of its main body of theory than the term 'approach' does. The latter suggests an as yet unco-ordinated *manner* of approaching the issues concerned. We speak of the 'property rights approach', implying that there is as yet no such thing as a more or less integrated body of property rights theory, but that it is more a particular way of looking at specific problems. The denotation of EE as an 'approach' also suggests that as yet it consists of diverse attempts to construct a new theory, but that it is not a developed and coherent body of theory yet (as Witt points out himself). This point is supported by the fact that Witt is seeking a theoretical basis for what he calls 'the crucial element' of EE: the 'emergence of novelty'. If a new body of thought still has to *find* its theoretical basis, it is still in a very underdeveloped stage indeed.

This impression is strengthened by Witt's description of the core elements of EE as compared with AE. The core of AE is defined as the two elements of 'subjectivism' and 'process of change' or 'permanent flux', both of which are clearly explained. The core of EE is *also* defined as the concepts of 'process' and 'change', so that the whole core of EE comprises only one of the two elements of AE. It is therefore not only smaller than that of AE, but it also introduces no new elements. 'Process' and 'change' as used above are very similar anyway, adding to the impression that the core of EE is rather empty and unoriginal. One wonders whether there is much point in trying to create a new body of theory on the basis of such a small and unoriginal core. Would it not be better to graft the institutional and evolutionary elements in which EE theorists are interested in regard to the existing body of AE? After all, according to Witt, EE originates in the evolutionary theory of the 'Austrian' Joseph Schumpeter, who may have ignored the subjectivist core of the Austrian tradition himself, but whose entrepreneurial theory certainly fits in it. EE is defined as the study of the regularities in the emergence and dissemination of novelty, in order to explain the continuing endogenous change and transformation of the economy.

The purpose of the paper is to 'match' EE with AE to see if any cross-fertilization can be achieved. What can both schools gain from this exchange? Witt states that EE has neglected subjectivism, which has prevented it from understanding the *emergence* of novelty. The paper is about what EE can gain from AE, which seems to be a great deal: a theoretical basis for its core. According to Witt, EE stands to gain insight into the emergence of novelty from the subjectivism of AE. This is lacking in (at least Schumpeterian) EE and must be provided. What Witt is searching for is a theoretical basis for EE. The cross-fertilization spoken of seems to be rather one-sided. Witt's paper tries to introduce subjectivism into EE; and it is EE that has a 'problem' with subjectivism, not AE. It is not clear what this subjectivist 'problem' is for AE, which Mises did not manage to solve, according to Witt. He explains that it means that 'The subjective meaning of a new item may differ for each single (novelty) adopter . . . and hence the individual reaction hinges upon the subjective state of mind.' If this is what the subjectivist problem is all about, I do not believe that it poses much of a problem for AE. No 'Austrian' should have any trouble in admitting that the interpretations and reactions of the economic subjects depend upon their subjective states of mind.

One can therefore ask: what can AE gain from EE? Apparently AE can gain 'powerful support' for its subjectivism. With reference to Shackle it is said that 'a continually ongoing creation of novelty provides a powerful argument for a subjectivist position in economics'. This is then demonstrated by arguing that 'novelty' is subjective. According to Witt, the existence and importance of 'novelty' form a strong argument in favour of subjectivism. But the tenor of the paper is more about the importance of subjectivism to EE than of EE to AE.

Yet the present author believes that AE also stands to gain from an interchange of ideas with EE. If it wishes to avoid sterility (Johnson's much-quoted charge of 'therapeutic nihilism') and endless exegesis on the writings of Mises and (to a lesser extent) Hayek, as seems to be the case with many of the 'libertarians' in the United States, then AE must turn itself into a more fruitful theory by interacting with other currents of thought. I believe that the fertilization of AE with elements of modern 'neo-institutional' economics should lead to useful new insights. In this sense I think that grafting the elements of EE onto the existing body of AE theory could be more fruitful than trying to devise a new body of EE theory.

Apart from these basic doubts, there is much in Witt's paper with which I agree, especially his critique on pp. 88–90 of the denial of the subjectivist origins of 'novelty' in Schumpeterian economics, which is about the dissemination of novelty, and not its origination. In the hands of its neoclassical adapters, Schumpeter's theory was transformed into a mechanistic problem of investment in R&D, in the process losing all its evolutionary aspects (not to mention its potential subjectivist aspects, which Schumpeter himself ignored). EE tries to redress this matter, by focusing on the origination or emergence of novelty and by (re)introducing its subjectivist and evolutionary aspects. Hence Witt's concern with a proper subjectivist basis for a theory about the emergence of novelty as the cause of ongoing endogenous change. He rejects Mises' apriorism on account of the narrowness of its purported 'pure logic of choice' approach, which cannot encompass creativity, the emergence of novelty and learning. Here one wonders if Mises is really guilty of viewing economics as a 'pure logic of choice', as L. Robbins and the neoclassical economists who took the term over from him undoubtedly were. According to Mises' pupil Kirzner, Austrians expressly reject the mechanistic 'logic of pure choice' view of human behaviour and base their theory instead on the 'alert actor' view of the economic subjects (Kirzner 1973).

Witt next looks to Hayek for a subjectivist explanation of the emergence of novelty, but is also disappointed in his treatment of this topic. It turns out that Hayek is also primarily interested in the intersocietal and intergenerational transmission of his 'successful social rules and institutions'. That is, his evolutionary theory also deals with the *dissemination* of novelty, like Schumpeter's. The rest of the paper is an analysis of the compatibility of Hayek's 'objectivist' and 'sociobiological' theory of the selection and transmission of 'successful' rules with the individualist-subjectivist paradigm of the Austrian School. Witt concludes that under certain assumptions concerning the definition of 'group interests', the individualist perspective can be maintained in Hayek's evolutionary theory, which could therefore serve as a theoretical basis for the development of EE.

REFERENCES

Hayek, F.A. (1973–1979) *Law, Legislation and Liberty*, 3 vols, London: Routledge and Kegan Paul.

Kirzner, I.M. (1973) *Competition and Entrepreneurship*, Chicago: University of Chicago Press.

9

AUSTRIAN ECONOMICS AND UNCERTAINTY: ON A NON-DETERMINISTIC BUT NON-HAPHAZARD FUTURE

*Emiel Wubben**

> That man acts and that the future is uncertain are by no means two independent matters. They are only two different modes of establishing one thing.
>
> (Mises 1949: 105)

INTRODUCTION

In this paper, I will apply Austrian economics to the problem of uncertainty. Economists of the Austrian School of economics acknowledge the prevalence of uncertainty in economic practices. With regard to future conditions, uncertainty prevails in both long-term and short-term activities (Mises 1962: 51). 'This uncertainty of the future is one of the main marks of human condition. It taints all manifestations of life and action' (Mises 1962: 65).

We may, albeit sketchily, distinguish between three generations of writers in the Austrian tradition. The three generations are represented by, first, C. Menger, F. von Wieser and E. von Böhm-Bawerk as the older of the three generations; second, Ludwig von Mises and Friedrich von Hayek as the second generation; and third, I.M. Kirzner, M.N. Rothbard and L.M. Lachmann as the third generation. The oldest generation did not discuss economic uncertainty at all, so I will begin with the work of Mises. Mises is often called the intellectual father of the *Neo*-Austrian School. In order to prevent irrelevant quibblings about terms and to give variety to this paper, I will use the terms 'Austrians' and 'Austrian economics'. In order to facilitate

* I would like to thank T. Vandevelde, R. van Zijp, B. Elzas, H. van den Berg, A. Leen, W. Keizer, R. Dullaart, J. Salerno, G. Woltjer and participants of the conference for their comments on earlier drafts. The research for this paper was part of a larger project which resulted in a 1993 PhD thesis, entitled *Markets, Uncertainty, and Decision-making: A History of the Introduction of Uncertainty into Economics* (Amsterdam: Thesis Publishers, Amsterdam). This dissertation has been awarded the 1994 Joseph Dorfman Dissertation Award by the History of Economics Society.

an organized description of the relevant theoretical developments within this school, I feel obliged to concentrate on the writings of Mises, Hayek, Kirzner and Lachmann.

The focus of this paper will be to answer questions about (a) how uncertainty has been introduced into Austrian economics, and (b) what the consequent implications for decision-making are. I will begin with a discussion of Austrian epistemology, because the relationship between uncertainty and economic theory has been drawn at this fundamental level by Mises himself. The key problem resulting from this discussion will be the co-ordination of actions directed at an uncertain future. Hayek gained prominence in this respect by elaborating on the dispersion of information, and on the necessary means of facilitating the co-ordination of individual activities. We will see that the theoretical profundity of Austrian argumentation evolved and became refined during an interwar *capitalism–socialism debate*, also called the *(socialist–)calculation debate* (Lachmann 1977: 192; Kirzner 1988). I will use this debate to illustrate the confrontation of the quickly maturing Austrian and neoclassical paradigms. From the outset, the authors involved were unaware of the sharp differences between the two (Kirzner 1988: 2). Furthermore, this debate illustrates the exclusion of the dynamic conception of uncertainty from economics (Lavoie 1981: 42).

Despite the originality and fruitfulness of the approach taken by Hayek, he was unable to solve the problem of the open-ended context of the market process, leaving both the pioneering *finding* of new information and the individual interpretation of market information hanging in the air. It was Kirzner who tried to solve the first of these two problems. It is the entrepreneur who creates the future by making decisions embedded in an alertness for possible profitable opportunities. Lachmann took up the second problem by investigating the formation of expectations. The two viewpoints have been integrated by O'Driscoll and Rizzo. They did so by distinguishing between the unique and the recurrent features of developments, related to rule-following and entrepreneurial behaviour respectively.

HUMAN ACTION

Ludwig von Mises (1881–1973) linked uncertainty directly to his key epistemological concept of *human action*. Fundamental to Mises' approach is his thesis that to act is to choose. Action is directed at improving the future state of affairs. 'The uncertainty of the future is already implied in the very notion of action. That man acts and that the future is uncertain are . . . only two different modes of establishing one thing' (Mises 1949: 105).

Human action is purposeful, is a teleological concept and assumes each individual to use means–ends frameworks. In other words: (a) action is caused by the desire to better one's situation; (b) it is directed at realizing an *individually* imagined more satisfactory state of affairs, and (c) every individual must expect that purposeful behaviour can at least alleviate the uneasiness. These are the general conditions for human action according to Mises (Mises 1949: 13–14).

One must beware, however, of subsuming all human conduct under human action. In order to make human behaviour a human action there must be room for human interference. There is no human action when people cannot influence their situation. In other words, in the absence of freedom to do otherwise, human behaviour does not involve actions. A stimulus-response (S-R) approach towards human activities is out of the question. A conscious choice to do nothing in the presence of at least one alternative, must be called a human action.

Under these conditions, uncertainty is clearly a permanent attribute of all calculations and decisions. When using the category of action, the perceived future cannot at the same time be considered to be deterministic. Mises states, almost analogous to Frank Knight: 'If man knew the future, he would not have to choose and would not act. He would be like an automaton, reacting to stimuli without any will of his own' (Mises 1949: 105). But people cannot predict all choices of their fellows. 'The future for which he plans will be codetermined by the actions of people who are planning and acting like himself' (Mises 1962: 46). Thus, particular expectations about the future must remain uncertain and inherently involve guesswork.

As a consequence, uncertainty is regarded as subversive with respect to the possibility of avoiding harm. '[W]ell-being ultimately depends on the operation of forces beyond man's wisdom, knowledge, prevision, and provision' (Mises 1962: 66). Engineering merely restricts a little the field of possible events. Natural sciences only supply us with information about the specific results of particular actions. Only *ex post* do we know to what extent an action would have attained the desired end and if it was the best choice possible.

PRAXEOLOGY

Praxeology is 'the general theory of human action' (Mises 1949: 3). It is meant to explicate the *a priori* category of human action. 'The science of human action that strives for universally valid knowledge is the theoretical system whose hitherto best elaborated branch is economics . . . It is as it were, the logic of action and deed' (Mises 1933: 12–13). That people purposively intend to bring about changes differentiates the subject matter of praxeology from its analogue in the natural sciences (Mises 1949: 352).

Both human thinking and human action are generated by the same source, the human mind. 'There is nothing in the structure of action that the human mind cannot fully explain. In this sense praxeology supplies certain knowledge' (Mises 1962: 64). The categories of means and ends, time and causality are implied in the category of human action (Mises 1949: 2, 64, 99).

The axiom of human action is a synthetic *a priori* proposition (Mises 1962: 8). Mises rejects the position taken by logical positivists claiming that *a priori* knowledge is necessarily always analytical. Rejecting the logical positivistic approach, Mises argues that human action is a Kantian category, supplying one with universally valid knowledge, telling us something about reality as we may know it (Huussen 1989). *A priori*, to Mises, means independence of time and place, but it does not imply independence of potential experience. Mises refers to the experiences of introspection and self-examination. It is for this argumentation that the axiom of human action may be called a synthetic *a priori* proposition (Mises 1962: 71).

The following two implications may now be discussed: (a) praxeological predictions are totally unconditional and absolutely valid, but they do not tell us anything about individual future value judgements or about their influence on specific actions (Mises 1949: 65), and (b) praxeological theories are not open to empirical confirmation or refutation. To elaborate:

(a) Praxeological laws are asserted universally valid, referring to the *form* of economic behaviour. Ultimately, all general knowledge is deductively derived from the *a priori* category of action. *General knowledge* refers to knowledge applicable to time-independent constellations (Mises 1949: 64). Nevertheless, praxeology presumes uncertainty with respect to means and ends. The latter are part of the black box *producing* actions to better one's situation. The rationality involved is not a rigid deterministic one, aimed at explaining and predicting individual behaviour. The rationality within praxeology deals with the logical patterns of purposeful behaviour. An example is the analysis of entrepreneurial activities in Mises' own business cycle theory.

(b) Concerning the second implication, it will be clear that Mises disagreed with Popper on the scientific status of praxeology. Praxeological laws do not relate to ideal-typical economic concepts. Ideal-typical economic concepts supply us with contingent laws. Praxeology provides us with necessary instead of contingent laws. Therefore, these laws are not open for empirical testing (Selgin 1988: 24). Nevertheless, following Popper's scientific demarcation criterion, all *a priori*stic theories, such as logic, mathematics and praxeology, would be unscientific, for *in principle* they cannot be refuted by experience. But the fallibility of our apprehension of sense data (Mises 1962: 71) and the problem of induction induce Mises to conclude against historicism and empiricism: 'There is no reason to ascribe to the operation the mind performs in the act of becoming aware of an external object a higher epistemological dignity than to the operation the mind performs in describing its own ways of procedure. In fact, nothing is more certain for the human mind than what the category of human action brings into relief' (Mises 1962: 71).

The aid of technology and the sciences may at best somewhat restrict the field of pure chance. What is more important, though, is the finding out of how the different economic actions of the individual persons co-ordinate. Entrepreneurs in particular must peer into the dark and appraise the mutual effects and their intensity actually brought about by an action. They must deal with the relevance of each motive and each action. This is called *understanding.*

UNDERSTANDING

The uncertain future may be tackled with the aid of (a) the faculty of understanding, and (b) the experience of past events. Experience of past events serves as no more than a starting point for a planning procedure. After trying to guess what is apt to change in the relevant future, people will adjust their actions as well as they can to foreseeable future want satisfaction (Mises 1949: 210–214).

Understanding, *Verstehen*, is according to Mises the only appropriate method for dealing with the uncertainty of future conditions. Understanding is trying to grasp what is going on in the minds of other people (Mises 1949: 118; Mises 1962: 50). It supplies one with expected future exchange ratios. It refers not to the praxeological side of human action, but to the field of history: 'Understanding deals with judgments of value, with the choice of ends and of the means resorted to for the attainment of these ends, and with the valuation of the outcome of actions performed' (Mises 1962: 48).

In principle, both scientists and children alike use the method of understanding. 'The methods of scientific inquiry are categorically not different from the procedures applied by everyone in his mundane comportment' (Mises 1962: 48). Observed dissimilarities may be traced back to differences in refinement, as well as to the number of inconsistencies and contradictions.

Austrians seem unwilling to let quantities prevail over qualities. Quantitative problems must be approached with understanding, based on incomplete knowledge. This knowledge will always be defective, because we can never exclude the possibility that we have erred (Mises 1949: 112). Valuations are neither necessarily constant nor continuous. In contrast with it, qualitative predictions may be based on praxeological knowledge. Recall that praxeological knowledge is asserted to be certain.

In line with the distinction made by Frank Knight (1921) between risk and uncertainty as measurable and unmeasurable uncertainties, Mises states that there are two different instances of probability: (a) class probability and

(b) case probability. A statement is probable if our knowledge concerning its content is deficient: we do know something, but we do not know everything about the problem concerned.

(a) Class probability (or frequency probability) means: 'We know or assume to know, with regard to the problem concerned, everything about the behaviour of a whole class of events or phenomena; but about the actual singular events or phenomena we know nothing but that they are elements of this class' (Mises 1949: 107). Insurance may be characterized by its dealing with a whole class of events. It is based on pooling and distributing risks, in order to compensate for the losses which regularly occur. The word *regularly* denotes that '[t]he amount of these losses is known as far as the whole class of the various items is concerned' (Mises 1949: 109).

(b) Case probability means: '[W]e know, with regard to a particular event, some of the factors which determine its outcome; but there are other determining factors about which we know nothing' (Mises 1949: 110). Statements in this field deal with unique events which are not, as such, members of any class. Case probability is 'not open to any kind of numerical evaluation' (Mises 1949: 113).

Mises is rather strenuous in separating the two types: The former is fit for the field of the natural sciences. The latter is a feature of the sciences dealing with human actions. Every human action, every experience, every event is unique, for each one of them changes our perspective. Unique events are no more than classes by themselves. This is called *methodological singularism* (Mises 1949: 45). Measurement and quantification in the sphere of human action are, consequently and inevitably, impossible.

> The fundamental deficiency implied in every quantitative approach to economic problems consists in the neglect of the fact that there are no constant relations between economic dimensions. The negligence of this fact is the deficiency implied in every quantitative approach to economic problems.
>
> (Mises 1949: 118)

Mises' radical conclusion that the use of class probabilities in economics is to be rejected as impossible originates in his adherence to subjectivism. It is often concluded that the most prominent feature of Austrian economics is radical subjectivism (Lachmann 1978: 1). But beware of equating this variant of subjectivism with the neoclassical one as used in relation with, e.g. subjective probabilities and marginal utility theory. In neoclassical theory subjectivism refers to individual numerical comparisons and rankings. Radical subjectivism differs also from the interpretation of subjectivism as the isolation of the economic subject.

According to the subjectivist stance taken by Austrians, we know about the physical world from without only, but about the world of human action from within. The method of the social sciences is the method of understanding. However, no questions can be posed with regard to the veracity of these chosen ends and means. The reason is that the facts of the social sciences consist of individual preferences and understood adequate means. 'Value judgments are necessarily always subjective' (Mises 1949: 395). No ideal decision rule may be derived from praxeology. For what is best to decide when dealing with merely unique events? It is the greater or lesser ability to understand the future that determines one's relative success or failure in this regard.

The future may be dealt with by gambling, engineering and speculating. With regard to the non-controllable influences, humankind is always the gambler, handling incomplete relevant knowledge. When concentrating on engineering, economic humankind is trying to enlarge its knowledge and reduce uncertainty as much as possible. Technologically satisfactory solutions will, however, never eliminate the importance of the element of speculation altogether.

The prevalence of the negative connotation of speculation may be caused by the lack of noticing or acknowledging the existence of uncertainty. Every investment is really a form of speculation. This occurs because people try to adjust their actions to only imperfectly known actions of others. 'Action is always speculation . . . In any real and living economy every actor is always an entrepreneur and speculator' (Mises 1949: 253).

ECONOMIC CALCULATION

In order to act in an economy with considered judgement one cannot act without economic calculation. For economists writing in the Austrian tradition, economic calculation is calculation with the use of a common denominator. The only suitable common denominator is *money*. Note that Mises had in mind, first and foremost, investment and trading activities, and not the buying decisions of the consumer. Thus, monetary calculation is based not on individual subjective use value, but on exchange value, 'arising out of the interplay of the subjective valuations of all who take part in exchange' (Mises 1920: 97). The value of the money unit itself is subject to fluctuation, but money is still the best denominator for economic calculations, especially for practical purposes (Mises 1920: 97–99,107–109).

'Economic calculation is either an estimate of the expected outcome of future action or the establishment of the outcome of past action' (Mises 1949: 211). The purpose of the establishment of the outcome of past action is, according to Mises, only to show the extent of the surplus free for consumption. But economic calculation does not offer certainty about the future. Moreover, economic calculation is, first of all, aimed at making plans for the future, but does not, by itself, supply any extra information about that future. Because things are perpetually fluctuating, action will always remain speculative (Mises 1949: 215).

It will most probably enhance our understanding of Mises' idea of economic calculation if we look at the first stage in the socialism–capitalism debate. Mises brought forward the problem of economic calculation as early as 1920, in his fierce attack on socialist economic organization, which he believed to be the then truly approaching commonwealth (Mises 1920: 88; Mises 1922: 511–515). Besides, with regard to his fight against socialism Mises became more outspoken, lucid and consistent in his later works. In these writings one finds most clearly relationships with praxeology and economic understanding.

What was Mises' argumentation? Along the standard line of thought, Mises' critique is interpreted as the denial of the *logical credentials* of socialism. Under socialism, it is expected that the community will determine the allotment of all means of production in production processes. But even if the planners, who somehow represent the community, happen to know the actual needs of the population, it is still impossible to calculate the required production structure (Mises 1920: 107). The fundamental reason for this is the impossibility of finding a non-market alternative for homogenizing various degrees of capacity and dexterity of labour. The labour equalization process, necessary in a socialist economy, 'is a result of market transactions and not its antecedent' (Mises 1920: 115). In the absence of private property rights, there is no motivation to search for the most efficient production and transactions. This inhibits the emergence of genuine relative scarcity prices for nationalized means of production. For example, it is impossible to find the cheapest way to produce under socialism, with regard to goods created in a combination of production processes, e.g. the building of a new railroad. 'But then we have the spectacle of a socialist economic order floundering in the ocean of possible and conceivable economic combinations without the compass of economic calculation' (Mises 1920: 110). This groping in the dark will end in chaos.

It was soon shown that E. Barone had already solved the problems involved in proving the theoretical possibility of rational calculation under socialism by 1908. Drawing on work by Pareto, Barone demonstrated that a socialist economy could be modeled analogue to Walras' general equilibrium model of choice. Barone's simultaneous equation model includes such elements as a numeraire, a collective maximum and an equilibrium situation (Barone 1908: 245–290).

It was also claimed, e.g. by J.A. Schumpeter, that a socialist economy may eliminate the *internal uncertainties* inherent in a market economy with its dispersed decision-making, the 'uncertainties about the reaction of one's actual and potential competitors and about how general business situations are going to shape' (Schumpeter 1942: 186). The practical solution of economic problems would be easier under socialism than under capitalism, when the economic efficiency of an economic system is reduced to productive efficiency, and the central planning board is taken both as a clearing house for information and as a co-ordinator of decisions (Schumpeter 1942: 186–189).

We may conclude that a general agreement has evolved about the position that a calculation may in principle incorporate all the consequences from and for activities in other parts of the economy. Socialism was considered to be better than capitalism in certain cases; for example, in a situation of going from one theoretically specified economic equilibrium position to another one. What is more, in the case of reserve capacity, 'as a matter of blueprint logic it is undeniable that the socialist blueprint is drawn at a higher level of rationality' (Schumpeter 1942: 196; cf. Schumpeter 1954: 989). Thus, the neoclassical general equilibrium approach provided most economists, including many socialists, with a satisfactory answer to the problem put forward by Mises.

But according to adherents of a nowadays prominent, radically different interpretation of the socialism–capitalism debate, there has been a critical misunderstanding of Mises' argument. The misinterpretation may have been caused by implicit differences in the blurred picture of the market (Kirzner 1988; Lavoie 1981; Keizer 1989). The Austrian version of the market with its Mengerian background pointed towards the process view of the market. Economic problems, by definition, involve change. Therefore, the main task of economic calculation is 'not to deal with the problems of unchanging or only slightly changing market situations and prices' (Mises 1949: 213); the main task of economic calculation is to deal with changes. The misinterpretation of the concepts used by the Austrians was inevitable, because their opponents used another view of the market, based on the Walrasian equilibrium approach. According to Mises, '[t]he static state can dispense with economic calculation' (Mises 1920: 109). Economic calculation ceases to be a problem in the stationary and structurally unchanging economy. The neoclassically oriented socialist model of the economy holds such a static equilibrium view of markets.

However, even if one accepts the possibility of a static state, the transition to a socialist state will itself change all economic data. In the actual economy, filled with persons coping with an imperfectly known future, one cannot do away with economic calculation, because of the changing economic data.

According to these authors, in the course of the debate Mises and his followers only gradually became aware of the fundamental differences between their view and the neoclassical view: the controversy began with *dynamic* issues, and was diverted to *statics* by the market socialists. 'Where there is no uncertainty concerning the future, there is no need for any cash holding. Money in itself is an element of change; its existence is incompatible with the idea of a regular flow of events' (Mises 1949: 414). Barone's work established only the formal similarity between capitalism and socialism under static conditions. Therefore, it is considered to be inapplicable.

Furthermore, it is claimed that no proper answer has yet been given by the socialists in regard to the necessity of using money prices for rational calculation. The price system connected with markets is claimed not to offer the best but the *only possible* method of allocating resources. Other objective values such as labour hours offer no alternative.

In his later work, Mises is still highly dissatisfied with the way in which most economists deal with the fundamental problems involved in economic calculation. For Mises, the crucial problem is the disregard for the non-neutrality of the denominator: '[T]hey do not comprehend that money prices are the only vehicle of economic calculation' (Mises 1949: 202). The *money* he meant is money under an institutional system of dispersed private property and markets for means of production. His concentration on the role of prices in society and his neglect of discussing extensively the presupposed competition may be due to the diversity of groups he was attacking at the same time.

Relevant for our argument is the fact that Hayek, when replying to the market socialists, stressed the importance of these neglected elements of the presupposed competition and its relation to private property. But before I am able to introduce and discuss the ideas of Hayek, another element must first be introduced: the element of *co-ordination*. It is important to distinguish co-ordination from equilibrium.

EQUILIBRIUM vs. CO-ORDINATION

Mises made the deduction from the *a priori* category of human action that there is an equilibrium as soon as there is no longer any action, nor any uncertainty. However, in the economy consisting of individuals coping with an uncertain future it is almost always easy to imagine a more favourable situation. As a consequence, the relevant situations are those where individuals interact, while all striving for an individually preferred position. But how are these subjective calculations resulting in human actions integrated into one huge harmonious pattern that agrees with the economic possibilities? Mises was unable to fit this co-ordination of entrepreneurial activities in his praxeological framework. The introduction of co-ordination makes it necessary to leave praxeology behind, and to focus on the role of knowledge and the function of learning in economic behaviour. To understand more completely the difference between co-ordination and equilibration, I want to discuss his views on economic equilibrium.

When one defines equilibrium as the absence of endogeneous change, then the informational structure is implicit; it is one of perfect information.

Such an equilibrium is, for both Mises and Hayek, not more than a limiting case. According to Mises, it is useless to consider an equilibrium, because in such a situation there are no economic problems. Using its praxeological meaning, no one would *act* any more. Hayek, however, considers the study of equilibria useful for the sake of studying some elements of economics.

In the absence of a feeling of dissatisfaction, there is no Misesian action, and thus a situation of equilibrium. Equilibrium is no more than an intermediate tool of thought, a heuristic, in analysing some logical aspects in which the economy works. It is not claimed that an equilibrium actually exists at a specific moment, because it would be analogous to stating that all economic problems are solved.

One may say that Mises' conception of human action implies the existence of disequilibrium. In a situation of a disequilibrium there is a subjective feeling of not being in the most favourable situation possible. 'The statement that action is *equilibrating* merely refers to the logical proposition that action continuously accounts for changes in the imagined framework of means and ends, i.e. changes in the structure of imagined profit opportunities' (Selgin 1988: 38).

As we have discussed before, Mises claims that the price system is necessary for establishing an equilibrating tendency. Market prices are necessary for making possible understanding, calculation and subsequent human action. The price system, although imperfect, provides the framework for guiding competitors under disequilibrium conditions. Profits are the result of noticing shortcomings in markets, and they direct the activities of entrepreneurs.

Within the context of praxeology, profit opportunities exist only when persons understand them as such. Such an imagined opportunity will be eliminated by the logically subsequent action. In principle, the equilibrating tendency is devoid of a real-world content, because understanding is a subjective element (Selgin 1988: 34). The profits involved are not necessarily equal to the profits in, for example, fiscal accounting systems. As a consequence and to take as an example, it is perfectly possible to state praxeologically the presence of an equilibrium, while simultaneously but in reality huge monetary profits and/or losses are being made. Understanding merely depends on subjective feelings of satisfaction.

The methodology of praxeology runs into fundamental problems when co-ordination is about to be introduced. The primary reason for this is that co-ordination, itself dependent on the reliability of expectations, is not a praxeological concept. Mises did not discuss this concept. Moreover, co-ordination requires adequate foresight. But the aim to better one's situation does not bring about, either by definition or by deduction, perfect mutual, and thus social, co-ordination: 'While we cannot think of free action as non-equilibrating, we may conceive of actions that are non-coordinating' (Selgin 1988: 43). It is the consequence of breaking up the relationship between the past and the future, and of introducing uncertainty with regard to the future. No mechanism for learning from past experiences has been presented by Mises.

Without such a mechanism, praxeology, in principle, cannot refute the statement that the future is radically uncertain, or kaleidic. Kaleidics refers to the absence of steady linkages between different time periods. As in a kaleidoscope, a small change in the situation makes the prevalent conception of the economic relations and how they interact wholly obsolete. The position that the future is kaleidic, taken for instance by Shackle, leaves human action to be haphazard (Shackle 1955). Admitting the presence of an imaginable but completely unknowable future would render praxeology merely tautological. As a consequence, the step from praxeology to humans in their environment cannot be made without introducing historical aspects.

Mises has written extensively on themes like the economic process and the role of the entrepreneur in society. However, praxeology appears to be mainly useful in studying understanding, calculation and action at the level of the individual. Ultimately, Mises must let his *a prioristic* viewpoint behind, and introduce empirical hypotheses, in order to be equipped to link up his theoretical conclusions with market phenomena. He has been criticized for this shortcoming, e.g. by Kirzner (1988: 7). Mises has been unable to solve the problem of integrating subjective calculations into a coherent pattern. Other writers in the Austrian School of economics, questioning the empirical meaningfulness of the idea of praxeology, emphasize the necessity of introducing time and place elements into economic theorizing. Their aim is to be able to make statements about the development of the economy, and about the possibility of co-ordination of actions under uncertainty. Already in the 1930s, Friedrich A. von Hayek (1899–1992), Mises' pupil, directed the attention of economists to the empirical element of local dispersed knowledge, and of human interactions.

ECONOMICS AND KNOWLEDGE

An important idea reflected in Hayek's writings is the notion of purposefulness of human action, where humankind is guided by expectations of an uncertain future (Hodgson 1989: 18). Hayek concentrated his investigations more on the consequences of starting with scattered bits and pieces of subjective knowledge, than on the consequences of uncertainty itself. He brought together problems of incomplete information, disequilibrium and expectations, which were already heavily disputed in the interwar years (O'Driscoll 1977: 20). He proposed emphasizing the role of learning and thus making economics not only a science of human action but also of human interaction, i.e. of co-ordination.

An analysis of Hayek's epistemological stance will most probably enhance our understanding of his views on planning, co-ordination and information. They will prove to be closely related. I will therefore now discuss his epistemological stance.

Hayek is thought to have broken with praxeology as early as 1937. Some supporting material may be found in his famous series on economic coordination, written in the period 1936–1947, when he was deeply involved in the socialism–capitalism debate. For instance, Hayek seems to accept Popper's demarcation criterion (Hayek 1937: 33), to which Mises was fiercely opposed. T.W. Hutchison called it Hayek's U-turn (Hutchison 1981: 215).

However, Hutchison's opinion is an unsatisfactory one. For instance, how can we link this interpretation to Hayek's opinion that the phenomena connected by means of a model can exclusively possess attributes derived from that model? 'Experience can never teach us that any particular kind of structure has properties which do not follow from the definition (or the way we construct it)' (Hayek 1943: 74). Theory, which is the mental construct for interpretation, cannot be verified or falsified by facts any more than mathematics or logic. It may 'only be tested for its consistency' (Hayek 1943: 74).

Furthermore, knowledge of other minds is based on reasoning by analogy from one's own mind. We see another person's action and supplement it by projecting our own classification of objects. '[W]e can understand less and less as we turn to beings more and more different from ourselves' (Hayek 1943: 66). It is by means of the connotation of a concept, not the empirical factor of the denotation, by which we form classes (Hayek 1943: 60–65). We may no longer understand the actions of others when we cannot apply analogies or patterns from our own way of thinking. Hayek's case for pattern predictions cannot be reconciled with Popper's philosophy because pattern predictions are immune to falsification (Paqué 1990: 282, 291).

Evaluating this information, it is not surprising to find another interpretation that takes the opposite position. According to this point of view Hayek did not leave praxeology behind, but merely *adjusted* it; support may be found in several of his writings.

First of all, Hayek's training in philosophy was in the school of E. Mach and later with the logical positivists.

> *Yet* all this had the effect only of creating an awareness, which became more and more definite as time went by, that, certainly in economics, all the people who are universally regarded as talking sense are constantly infringing the accepted canons of scientific method evolved from the practice of the natural sciences.
>
> (Hayek 1943: 58; emphasis added)

He emphasizes that natural scientists stepping into the social sciences left behind the methodology of the natural sciences, and those who did not usually ended up in disaster.

Second, when one wants to explain social processes, one has to introduce hypotheses, in particular assertions about causal connections, that concern the actual acquisition of knowledge. In other words 'the question to what extent and how his knowledge corresponds to the external facts' (Hayek 1937: 47). But Hayek engages merely in conjectural history. It is essential to choose the most relevant ideal types among the infinite variety of possible situations. The function of testing is diminished to finding out whether a theory fits actuality or not. Corroboration does not make the theory empirically true (Huussen 1990: 119).

Third, the formal aspects of social processes are the elements from which to construct a theory for explaining social interaction (Huussen 1990: 125). They supply us with a causal explanation of social structures. According to Hayek, it is a part of psychology, not economics, to explain individual behaviour. Economics does not (have to) explain individual behaviour (Hayek 1943: 67).

Finally, the pure logic of choice – Mises called it praxeology – is acknowledged to cover all conceivable situations. It begins with facts common to all human thought that are universally applicable and therefore *a priori* true (Hayek 1937: 47–48).

Hayek's opinion on scientism is related to this epistemological stance (Hayek 1943: 58). The fight against scientism has always been one of his major themes, and he believed that social science knowledge is fundamentally different from that of natural sciences. In 'Economics and Knowledge', published in 1937, Hayek introduced the distinction between scientific or objective knowledge, *knowledge that*, and private or positional knowledge, *knowledge how*:

> To employ a useful metaphor: while at the world of nature we look from the outside, we look at the world of society from the inside . . . in the world of society at least some of the most familiar concepts are the stuff from which that world is made . . . a common structure of thought . . . is also the basis on which we all interpret such complicated social structures as those which we find in economic life or law, in language, and in customs.
>
> (Hayek 1943: 76)

The conclusion to be drawn is on the impossibility of talking about subjective probabilities that tend to objective probabilities. The dimensions are not on the same footing but cover different *levels* of knowledge.

Hayek calls the result of this kind of theorizing the *compositive method*, 'which *constitutes* the social *wholes* by constructing models from intelligible elements' (Hayek 1943: 73). Theories are not about facts, but 'assist us in connecting individual facts' only (Hayek 1943: 73). 'We cannot speak about the behaviour of wholes as wholes, because we never deal with the whole of reality but always with a selection made with the help of our models'

(Hayek 1943: 74). Theories constitute these wholes, but are not about the social wholes. The complex phenomena discussed in the social sciences 'are never found ready given as are the persistent structures in the organic . . . world' (Hayek 1943: 72).

The following three points may be raised against this compositive method:

(a) The hierarchical order is broken once one acknowledges the existence of social institutional influences on individual preferences and actions, even if social *wholes* are themselves explained in reference to individuals. This is even more relevant because of the process orientation that Austrians take. It would result in an infinite regress, leaving us with a chicken-and-egg problem.

Writers in the Austrian tradition can present problems of observational individualism and ontological individualism to support their position. An analysis of individuals' actions is considered to be the only way to a cognition of social wholes, because we cannot observe social wholes (e.g. Mises 1949: 42–43). I would counterargue that the strength of this mind construct may be undervalued. It is often more appropriate to talk about social wholes, e.g. factory, divisions, firms and holdings, than to talk about the individuals that comprise them, because directives, investments, etc., are a crucial output for other collective wholes, and for the individuals involved. The second argument, ontological individualism, states that social wholes are no more than useful mind constructs. It is individuals who decide and act, although they may act differently under different external conditions. I do not know how to discuss individuals outside a specific environment, when it is acknowledged that even their revealed preferences are situation-dependent.

(b) The fallacy of composition asserts that the whole is more than the sum of the parts, and is another point against the compositive method. Building blocks, the basic elements in this hierarchical structure, must be the human individuals. All activities in society must now be wholely explained by means of basic elements and their interactions (Hodgson 1986: 220). I tend to disagree. The compositive method originating from Menger and elaborated by Hayek involves the genetic explanation. Social phenomena are explained in terms of their origin and their functioning, allowing for the unintended consequences of rational economic actions. The Austrians use a different method than the one discussed in combination with the fallacy of composition.

(c) The parts do not function 'merely because of their inherent qualities, after taking in inputs (information, etc.) from outside' (Hodgson 1986: 221). There is an original and thus unpredictable element in choices. It may cause the composition of social wholes out of smaller elements to lack a strong foundation in reality.

Already in the 1930s, Hayek distances himself from the then new but soon common definition of the economic problem, which was defined by Robbins as the problem of allocating scarce means to ends. More specifically, Hayek objected to the use of the standard assumption of complete knowledge on the part of all transactors, because it assumed away the problem (Hayek 1937: 33; Hayek 1945: 89–91). For him the central question for social sciences is the following: 'How can the combination of fragments of knowledge existing in different minds bring about results which, if they were to be brought about deliberately, would require a knowledge on the part of the directing mind which no single person can possess?' (Hayek 1937: 54).

Thus, the central research goal of economics as defined by Hayek is the problem of the usage of dispersed knowledge (Hayek 1937: 50–51). 'Throughout all his work he maintained his conception of the *economic problem* as a co-ordination problem, for the analysis of which the method of *logical implication* is the appropriate tool' (O'Driscoll 1977: 28). Hayek's pupil Kirzner would later call it *Hayek's knowledge problem* (Kirzner 1984: 407–408). Hayek's conceptions of the economic problem and the price mechanism continued to evolve until he completed his contribution to the calculation debate and especially the tetrad on economic co-ordination.

In line with Hayek's deviating definition of the economic problem is his plea for a reformulation of the concept of equilibrium. He objects to the 'excessive preoccupation with the problems of the pure theory of stationary equilibrium' (Hayek 1940: 188). Equilibrium analysis is no more than a useful preliminary to the study of practical problems. It has no direct relevance (Hayek 1945: 91; Hayek 1946: 96). 'What is relevant is not whether a person as such is or is not in equilibrium but which of his actions stand in equilibrium relationships to each other' (Hayek 1937: 36).

With regard to individuals, actions stay in equilibrium with each other during the period in which their anticipations prove to be correct. Any change in the knowledge used by a person and resulting in an alteration of their plan may be called a disruption of the equilibrium relation. Subsequent actions are no longer mutually related (Hayek 1937: 36).

The main difference between an individual and a societal equilibrium may be traced back to a crucial difference in the concept of the data. Correctness of individual anticipation does not imply the usage of objective data, but the absence of a need to change relevant, subjective knowledge. Change is defined as 'any divergence of the actual from the expected development, irrespective of whether it means a *change* in the absolute sense' (Hayek 1937: 40).

An equilibrium for a society at a given point of time means that different plans, made by individuals for action in time, are mutually compatible. But there is no necessity to restrict the discussion to a stationary state or a situation of constant data only (Hayek 1937: 41, 49). 'Hayek's view of the competitive process depends on progressive learning that must take place in virtue of the presumed stability of the market in question' (Boland 1986: 37). An equilibrating tendency means that 'the knowledge and intentions of the different members of society are supposed to come more and more into agreement' (Hayek 1937: 45). People act on the basis of partial ignorance and engage in a learning process.

Hayek's view of the optimal social co-ordination of actions – the mutual compatibility of plans – is dependent on the presumed stability of the market system. A stable economic system will, one way or another, find its best outcome, by solving its own economic problems, such as deadlock situations.

As a consequence, correct foresight is not a precondition in order to arrive at an equilibrium. Moreover, correct foresight is the defining characteristic of the state of equilibrium. Such a static equilibrium will last as long as the external data correspond to the common expectations of all the members of the society, 'as long as the anticipations prove correct' (Hayek 1937: 42). When we want to discuss a process, foresight need only be correct as far as it is relevant for the decisions of the individuals. Hayek calls it relevant foresight.

The institutional framework matters in the spread of knowledge. In opposition to the models using the assumptions of perfect knowledge, decisions made by different persons are not assumed to be optimal by definition. It raises the question of how we may create the situation for persons having knowledge suited to a particular task, to perform that task (Hayek 1946: 95). Nobody is able to overview the totality of adaptive events.

> Nonetheless, the whole structure of activities tends to adapt, through these partial and fragmentary signals, to conditions foreseen by and known to no individual, even if this adaptation is never perfect. There can be no deliberately planned substitutes for such a self-ordering process of adaptation to the unknown.
>
> (Hayek 1988: 76)

This practical (im)possibility of planning an economy is widely considered to be the main point of discussion in the second phase of the calculation debate. The first round of the calculation debate, about the theoretical (im)possibility of a socialist economy, was considered to be won by the socialists. The second round would be concerned with the practical problems involved (e.g. Hayek 1935a; 1935b; 1940). Both the collection of the necessary quantity of data, and the subsequent solving of the large amount of detail necessary for a simultaneous equations model, would render a socialist economy impossible. Hayek and Robbins were the prime proponents of this viewpoint. The standard interpretation is that the debate was effectively closed with publications by Oscar Lange in 1936.

Lange (1936) reflects the neoclassical viewpoint, with the state as substitute for the Walrasian auctioneer and long-run average cost minimization, as the leading principle for productive activities. Lange showed the parallels 'in both the formal conditions for a determinate equilibrium and in the trial and error procedures for *finding* equilibrium, between the neoclassical perfect competition model and his market socialist scheme' (Lavoie 1985: 161). His market socialist approach has long been accepted as the definitive answer to the critics (Schumpeter 1942; 1954: 989, n. 12).

However, the idea of the state as a substitute for the Walrasian auctioneer contrasts sharply with the Austrian view of the dynamic market. Placing the date of the end of the debate around 1937, while the development of argumentation on the Austrian side ended only in the 1940s, marks the mutual misunderstanding. Other interpretations of the discussion may be, and have been, given, among which the next interpretation features prominently.

The problem of central planning is, according to most writers in the Austrian tradition, the problem of scattered information. 'Hayek's knowledge problem consists in the dispersed character of available information' (Kirzner 1984: 410). It is acknowledged that a socialist scheme is logically compatible with a stationary economy (Mises 1949: 257). Such an *evenly revolving economy*, as the Austrians termed it, is irrelevant for the calculation problem.

Hayek's knowledge problem is the collective analogue of the basic knowledge problem, functioning at the level of the individual. The basic knowledge problem consists of inadequacies in a person's knowledge of the relevant circumstances. The central planner is subject to the same problems as the individual decision-maker. The central planner must evaluate the adequacy of the available dispersed bits of information, but lacks the instruments to do so. Furthermore, the knowledge problem confronting central planners cannot be solved by something like the market mechanism that solves the basic knowledge problem of individual decision-makers (Kirzner 1984: 409–410, 414).

Mises, in the first round of the debate, and Hayek, in the second round of the debate, are in essence discussing the same problem. Their arguments reflect the Austrian understanding of markets as a competitive discovery process. 'For Austrians, prices emerge in an open-ended context in which entrepreneurs must grapple with true Knightian uncertainty' (Kirzner 1988: 14).

Hayek emphasizes that prices hold two important functions: (a) they communicate information about the relative scarcity of resources, and (b) they improve co-ordination of transactors' plans under definite assumptions.

These functions serve to solve the equilibrating and the co-ordination process respectively.

He argues that the market system is the best possible method of allocating resources, because it is a relatively cheap communication network and works as a system of signals (Hayek 1937: 45; Hayek 1945: 87). Without pretending to attain perfect adjustment, it is claimed that only by means of market prices may a multitude of individuals use dispersed, specific information. '[P]rices can act to co-ordinate the separate actions of different people in the same way as subjective values help the individual to co-ordinate the parts of his plan' (Hayek 1945: 85). Knowledge with regard to valuation is scattered, but is reflected in the free communication system. 'The information created by means of the price system relates to changing market conditions' (Hayek 1945: 87). This mechanism is not a product of human design, but the result of human action.

Although the market system is not perfect itself, it entails not only the economy-wide consequences of good but also of bad decisions as inherent in a planned economy. Furthermore, the market system leaves it open to the individual (not) to use inarticulated, non-price information. This individual economic freedom makes the market process flexible and adaptation to changes proceeds quicker than by any alternative decision-making procedure. The real proof with regard to the best decision-making procedures is, however, according to Hayek, to be found in reality itself.

Evaluating this position, one might say that Hayek discusses information at two levels: first at the level of the individual planner, and second at the level of the economic process itself. Persons are faced with no more than distributions or a series of prices. But Hayek explains neither how these persons recognize (dis)co-ordinating processes, nor how information about product characteristics and qualities is to be recognized individually. Given only sets of prices it is unclear how one induces the relative scarcity and takes those actions that enhance co-ordination. Hayek did not succeed in solving the problem of the open-ended context of the market process. That is the problem of co-ordination: the problem of uncertainty.

To conclude my discussion of the calculation debate, I consider *both* the Misesian calculation critique of socialism and the Hayekian relative inefficiency critique of it to be right, within their own contexts, and as yet to remain unanswered. The Misesian calculation argument, discussed for the first time in economics in the 1920s, is consistent with the praxeological epistemology. The Hayekian knowledge argument refers to the slowness and ineffectivity of a socialist economy to concentrate, calculate and spread local and partially inarticulate information. It does not refer to its creative origination.

Hayek does discuss, however, the influence of the structure of an economic system on its progression. But his panacea, the market system, is assumed always to mobilize the best possible maximum of information. If the market cannot co-ordinate, no other economic system can.

Hayek may be criticized for neglecting the problems of the perception of information, and the creation of information from scratch. He suggests neither how individuals discover entirely new information, nor how they perceive already existing information. Although economic co-ordination and information dispersion are among the prominent members of his cast, Hayek gave learning procedures and the finding out of new data unsatisfactory supporting roles.

As said, Hayek discards the influence of individual perceptions on the economic process. No explanation is given to account for the difference between data and knowledge. In fact, these are not even distinguished. On the one hand, he acknowledges his inability to answer the following question: 'What could lead the subjective knowledge of agents to come into conformance with objective reality?' (Caldwell 1988: 529–530). On the other hand, he argues that it is a part of psychology to explain individual behaviour. This does not seem convincing, though, because individual learning mechanisms and individual imagination fundamentally influence economic developments.

For example, how and at what speed is one to learn if a piece of information represents some structural change or incidental error? Furthermore, learning in a state of disequilibrium is different from learning in one of equilibrium. '[I]nformation, therefore, requires interpretation (the messages have to be *decoded*) in order to be transformed into knowledge, and all such knowledge is bound to be imperfect' (Lachmann 1956: 21–23). About this aspect, Hayek's ideas are in agreement with standard conventionalist choice theory. Both ways of reasoning take inductive learning for granted (Boland 1986: 37). We will discuss this problem and Lachmann's solution to it below.

Next, Hayek may be criticized for evading the problem of the origination of (local) information. Is it by imagination or by observation that people come up with *new* information? It cannot be by purely subjective guesses that people come to find local information, because we ask ourselves how, in such a situation, will agreement result between the guesses and reality.

Israel M. Kirzner tried to provide an alternative analysis. Our understanding of economic processes can, according to him, be founded on the pure logic of choice, praxeology. Therefore, we do not have to wait for empirical work before we may discuss the economics of the market process. He devoted numerous articles and books to the discussion of subjects like uncertainty, discovery and economic understanding. Next, we will discuss his solution to the problem of knowledge creation.

UNCERTAINTY vs. ERROR

Kirzner wants to prevent action explained solely (a) by the Scylla of deliberately sought out or learned knowledge, or (b) by the Charybdis of pure coincidences, luck (Kirzner 1979: 144; 1981: 55–57; 1989: ix). The first category is the subject of an extensive literature, i.e. *search literature.* In this literature, a partial ignorance of knowledge is defended as potentially optimal, persisting until exogenous changes occur.

The second category, ignorance of information that is learned coincidentally, cannot be explained in terms of conscious individual decision-making. The reason is that ignorance of information expresses the 'sheer failure to notice what is there to be seen' (Kirzner 1979: 145). A substantial part of knowledge, beliefs and expectations, results from such unplanned learning experiences (Kirzner 1979: 142). One does not look for it, but nevertheless does notice it.

Uncertainty is defined as 'the essential freedom with which the envisaged future may diverge from the realized future' (Kirzner 1982a: 151, 157; 1985: 58, 66). Uncertainty reflects our awareness that the correspondence between the envisaged and the realized future is far from complete (Kirzner 1985: 55). Scope for the creative, unpredictable expressions of humankind is to be found here.

One must first of all select the relevant means–end framework. The actual economic calculation takes place within such a framework. However, one will never be sure of the adequacy of a chosen framework, because the *ex ante* selection between alternative scenarios takes place in an open-ended uncertain world. Every person is aware of the fact that they know only *some components* of what will determine tomorrow. Different persons may, therefore, end up with different calculations from different frameworks. We all make errors in the exercise of judgement when choosing a means–end framework (Kirzner 1979: 124; 1982a: 147–148). Deliberations about risks and probabilities are possible with reference to a specific, chosen, means–end framework only. As a consequence, it is not sufficient to broaden the standard framework to incorporate the acquisition of information. Purposeful limitation of the input of information, resulting in an optimum degree of ignorance, is beside the point. Experience may lead to a revision of forecasts and actions.

Kirzner takes the stance that modern economic theory lacks a theory of error (Kirzner 1979: 121), while 'economic analysis *depends* on this kind of error for its most elementary and far-reaching theorems' (Kirzner 1979: 131). People do not purposefully fail to achieve the most preferred available outcome, but they fail to notice relevant facts. Mises acknowledged the fact that people make mistakes. But to him errors constitute irrationality, and are therefore no subject of scientific research. Errors hold primarily a derived function, e.g. as the prime disturbing factor in the explanation of the business cycle, which is the result of wrong impressions. Therefore, errors were of no prime interest to Mises (Kirzner 1979: 121).

Kirzner defined such error as 'a decision being made in unwitting ignorance of pertinent information' (Kirzner 1979: 207). Errors do not, however, constitute irrationality. Although erring does imply ignorance, it does not necessarily imply uncertainty. In general, however, 'past error . . . may be attributed to the pervasive uncertainty that characterizes our world (and to the inevitably kaleidic changes responsible for that uncertainty)' (Kirzner 1982a: 147). Moreover, it is one thing to escape ignorance, but to deal with uncertainty is another (Kirzner 1982a: 148). An equilibrium consists of the absence of error. But already a dispersion of prices is caused by sheer error (Kirzner 1979: 124–135).

Kirzner takes a pragmatic attitude towards the resulting epistemological problem of the indeterminate future. On the one hand, he agrees with Lachmann and Shackle on the troublesome predictability of human knowledge. We do not know how entrepreneurs attain a superior foresight of unexploited opportunities (Kirzner 1979: 8; 1984: 415). On the other hand, he states that the observed tendency of opportunities being perceived and exploited results in a belief in a market process that is determinate (Kirzner 1979: 116–117): '[W]e do, in talking of human action, assume at least a tendency for man to notice those [facts] that constitute possible opportunities for gainful action on his part' (Kirzner 1979: 29).

The use of the perfect-knowledge assumption for an auctioneer discards the study of economic changes, of price dispersions, of information dissemination of dovetailing tendencies, etc. (Kirzner 1979: 17–24).

> At any given time people will, on the one hand, be blissfully ignorant of opportunities staring them in the face; on the other hand, they will be delightedly proceeding to exploit newly noticed opportunities of which they had been unaware yesterday.
>
> (Kirzner 1979: 32)

Empirical research is useful only for finding the details of the tendency of opportunity discovery.

Metaphorically speaking, present uncertainty and past errors are merely two sides of one coin, called entrepreneurship. The tension between present uncertainty and past error can be attenuated by the quality of alertness. The entrepreneurial element, 'of ensuring alertness to and awareness of the data' (Kirzner 1979: 116), is called entrepreneurial alertness (Kirzner 1982a: 150–151).

ENTREPRENEURSHIP

Entrepreneurial activities grapple with the inescapable uncertainty, by manner of spontaneous, undeliberate discovery (Kirzner 1979: 137–153). While not noticing available information is a troublesome factor in decision-making, it is not inconsistent with purposefulness: '[T]here is nothing in purposeful action that by itself guarantees that every available opportunity must be instantaneously perceived' (Kirzner 1979: 130).

Kirzner underscores the difference between discovering opportunities and learning facts (Kirzner 1979: 29). 'And it is the distinction between being alert and possessing knowledge that helps us understand how the entrepreneurial market process systematically detects and helps eliminate error' (Kirzner 1979: 8). Alertness is itself no guarantee for finding the truth – note our continuous erring. Dealing with uncertainty appears to be primarily motivated by the profit gained from avoiding possible difference between the future reality and the individual vision of the future. Kirzner's entrepreneur is first of all alert (Loasby 1982: 119).

It is entrepreneurship, deduced from the concept of human action, that makes the difference between a theory of market equilibria and a theory of the market process (Kirzner 1979: 7, 26–29). Entrepreneurship is absent in Robbinsian allocative activity, but it is present in Misesian human action (Kirzner 1982a: 146–147). 'Market entrepreneurship reveals to the market what the market did not realize was available, or, indeed needed at all' (Kirzner 1979: 181).

Thus, the analysis of the specific relationship between uncertainty and entrepreneurship, for example important for Knight and Schumpeter, has been developed by Kirzner. Schumpeter considers development as disequilibrating, spontaneous, given to disjointed changes in which the entrepreneur generates disturbances in the circular flow situation. According to Kirzner, however, the entrepreneur ensures a tendency towards an equilibrium, responding to intertemporal profit possibilities, grasping the yet unexplored available opportunities (Kirzner 1979: 117–119). The alternative affiliation of entrepreneurship is with the discovery of earlier error.

An explanation for the contrast between these viewpoints is to be found in the divergence of their respective status quo understanding. As Kirzner puts it: 'Instead of seeing how the entrepreneur has disturbed the placid status quo, we must see how the status quo is nothing but a seething mass of unexploited maladjustments crying out for correction' (Kirzner 1979: 119). Or, 'at each moment, enormous scope exists for improvements that are in one way or another ready to hand and yet are simply not noticed' (Kirzner 1979: 135).

Kirzner has been criticized by other Austrians for his interpretation of the relationship between uncertainty and entrepreneurship. The critique concentrates on the reduction of entrepreneurs, who are the bearers of uncertainty, to their quality of alertness. Mises defines the entrepreneur as '[a]cting man exclusively seen from the aspect of the uncertainty inherent in every action' (Mises 1949: 254). Kirzner agrees with this definition. The dispute on viewing the Misesian entrepreneur as the bearer of uncertainty versus the discoverer of errors, corresponds to the tension between present uncertainty and earlier error (Kirzner 1982a: 148).

It must be acknowledged, however, that Kirzner often discusses the role of the entrepreneur coping with uncertainty in a static context, as if the entrepreneur is just waiting for profitable opportunities to show up. This image is confirmed by his choice of metaphors, such as opportunities 'lurking around the corner', or 'staring them in the face', and entrepreneurs who 'pierce the fog of uncertainty'. Kirzner is aware of the mechanical flavour of them. 'But surely these metaphors are useful and instructive' (Kirzner 1982a: 157).

In fact, Kirzner is perfectly aware of the fact that in the multiperiod case, thereby multiplying the dimensions along which mutual ignorance may develop, an entrepreneur is more than a calculator, who needs 'qualities of boldness, determination and creativity . . . to create the future in an uncertain world' (Kirzner 1982a: 155). The entrepreneur plays an active role in giving shape to the evolving economy.

Further support of Kirzner's understanding of the entrepreneur may be found in his revised description of entrepreneurship. Earlier, it had meant no more than alertness to opportunities. More recently, however, it became the (by the lure of market profits) motivated prospensity to formulate an accurate image of the future and to implement it thereafter, thereby enhancing consistency between different parts of the market (Kirzner 1982a: 152–153).

With regard to decision-making in the market economy two problems must be posed. First, we have the calculation problem of planning the best action. Second, there is the problem of how to ensure that the best option is carried out. The former problem has been treated extensively, and is covered by the category of deliberate learning. The two problems are relevant to both the level of individual decisions and that of the society.

By now it will be no surprise that Kirzner concentrates on the latter problem which has to do with entrepreneurial alertness. Alertness is not just an ingredient in the decision-making process, but consists of a decision embedded in entrepreneurial alertness. At the individual level it is the problem of how to ensure that one observes the necessary optimal action. At the social level, one should take trouble to ensure that existing opportunities will be found and exploited.

There are thus two levels for discussing entrepreneurship. 'What the entrepreneurial element in individual decision making is to the individual, the entrepreneurship is to the market economy' (Kirzner 1979: 117). The correspondence between entrepreneurship at the level of individual action and in the context of the market will be obvious when considering Table 9.1 (Kirzner 1982a: 148–153).

Will widespread alertness nullify all the profit opportunities, and thus stop all human actions (Loasby 1982: 117)? No, entrepreneurship cannot be reduced to any kind of arbitrage, because alertness does not remove all ignorance. The abundancy of unnoticed profitable opportunities will leave the ideal of an equilibrium for what it is, i.e. no more than a limiting case in which 'each decision correctly anticipates all other decisions' (Kirzner 1979:

Table 9.1 Two levels of discussing entrepreneurship

Individual entrepreneurship	*Entrepreneurship in the market*
I. Endeavour: Consists of the endeavour to increase correspondence between the individually envisaged future and the actual future.	Consists of the function of securing greater consistency between different parts of the market.
II. Scope: Scope provided by the uncertainty of the future.	Scope provided by imperfect knowledge resulting in price divergences.
III. Incentive: Avoidance of entrepreneurial error as not merely a matter of being more truthful, but also profitable; the potential profit is the incentive.	The incentive seen as the pure gain to be won by market entrepeneurial activity.

110). An economy with just alert people may ultimately result in a stable equilibrium.

Another element to be mentioned is what I would call the paradox of evident opportunities. In the presence of many alert individuals, all deciding on their own, it is unclear if all, some or none will take the opportunity to gain a profit. Kirzner's viewpoint with regard to entrepreneurship would require him to state that individually perceived opportunities should, in general, remain unnoticed for a while in order to make exploitation profitable (Loasby 1982: 117). Kirzner acknowledged this, when he wrote that it was necessary that profit opportunities 'on the surface do not appear to exist' (Kirzner 1979a: 149–150). Once they *become obvious* to many alert persons in the market the profit margin will be squeezed out. The presence of widespread ignorance is a sufficient and satisfied condition for making alertness profitable.

A major problem related to Kirzner's argument about entrepreneurial alertness is the possibility of economic losses. This is caused by neglecting problems of interpretation. Following the simple argumentation that when people look for and act only in the presence of profitable opportunities, one does not usually end up with losses.

Mises dealt with losses by introducing understanding. He deduced that profits and losses are corollaries, both being important in the functioning of the social order. Profits (losses) result from superior (inferior) foresight and judgement because opportunities are as yet only possible sources of income.

Kirzner leaves us without an explanation for the possibility of the existence of errors and ensuing losses. The missing link is judgement. It was submerged by Kirzner in entrepreneurial alertness. But alertness is not the same as and cannot function well without interpretation, judgement. Entrepreneurs are modelled as if they were merely on the lookout for and discover profitable opportunities (High 1982: 166–168). Kirzner emphasizes, as Mises and Hayek did, the institutional facets of providing opportunities to the persons who are most suited to notice them; thus those persons who are most alert to them. Individuals differ to quite a considerable degree in their ability to notice what has so far been overlooked (Kirzner 1979: 148–149). But Kirzner concludes that '[a]lertness thus appears to possess a primordial role in decision making' (Kirzner 1979: 131). As a consequence, entrepreneurship is a scarce resource of a special kind: costless, not a potential stock and not something to be deployed in decision-making (Kirzner 1985: 20–29).

Therefore, institutional circumstances must be arranged so as to make the discovery and exploitation of socially advantageous opportunities into personal advantages (Kirzner 1985: 19,29). Kirzner judges the market process to be the most effective organization. The market process disseminates hitherto unknown knowledge. The knowledge that results in different kinds of actions must embody learning that was not sought after. We know something about the pattern of spontaneous learning, namely that spontaneous learning will take place more rapidly when the opportunities will be advantageous to the person involved. In a market economy money 'represents a social arrangement with the ability to present existing overlooked opportunities in a form most easily recognized and noticed by spontaneous learners' (Kirzner 1979: 150). The author wants us to recognize the 'extent to which both individual action and social co-ordination through the market can occur significantly despite the uncertainty of the future' (Kirzner 1982a: 156).

Profits are the result of noticing market shortcomings, and directing the activities of entrepreneurs. Entrepreneurs recognize the possibility of attaining a better monetary situation. 'The Misesian theory of entrepreneurial profit may be described as an *arbitrage* theory of profit' (Kirzner 1979: 94). Those that understand their environment better (worse) will realize bigger profits (losses).

Let's take stock. We began this paper with a discussion of uncertainty in relation to individual human action, moved over to economy-wide dissemination of information and finished with entrepreneurial alertness and individual spontaneous learning. Mises concentrated on the equivalence between uncertainty and human action. One tackles uncertainty with the help of experience and the faculty of understanding, to deal with the unique events of purposeful actions. Entrepreneurial activities take place only after monetary calculations have shown what outcome can be expected of an action. However, the problem of the co-ordination of entrepreneurial activities, a problem of dealing with mutually inconsistent expectations, has not been solved by Mises. Presumably he could not solve the problem partially because it does not fit praxeology, and partially because he concentrated on the decision-making individual, thereby underrating the importance of the acquisition of knowledge.

Hayek focused on the assumption of dispersed information and the consequences for economics. Each one of us is guided by expectations of an uncertain future. Market prices are supposed to communicate scattered information, and improve the co-ordination of plans. An economic process evolves stationary under relevant foresight only as long as the expectations are correct for the decisions at hand. One of the major fields of research neglected by Hayek concerns the creation or origination of information. It has been taken up by Kirzner.

According to Kirzner, uncertainty reflects our awareness of possible deviations of the envisaged future from the realized future. Past error and present uncertainty are two sides of the same coin which is called entrepreneurship. The entrepreneur is alert for as yet unnoticed profitable opportunities, i.e. existing maladjustments, but is unable to find them by deliberate search only. The other major field of research neglected by Hayek is judgement, i.e. the linking of information to expectations. This field has also been neglected by Kirzner. But how may co-ordination prevail when both errors and their concomitant uncertainty are possible at the same time?

EXPECTATIONS

Possibly as a consequence of the uncomfortable settlement of the problem of co-ordination of actions taking place under uncertainty, an increasing number of scientists writing in the Austrian tradition concentrate on the problems related to the formation of expectations. Ludwig M. Lachmann (1906–1990) was the most prominent among them. From the 1930s onwards he wrote primarily about the problems of the subjectivity and diversity of expectations. His writings correspond to the opinion that expectations are taken seriously in economics since the 1930s, with Knight (1921) and Schumpeter (1912) as exceptions.

Lachmann's ideas about economic activities have been inspired by the views of Mises, Hayek, Weber and Shackle. He believes that economics may enhance our understanding of economic activity, but cannot provide us with useful predictions. The interpretation of economic activity as the result of human actions, implying changes and purposeful choices, must influence the perceived function of economics. Lachmann's position on the function of the social sciences, invariable over more than a four-decade time period, is that social scientists ought to strive for achieving intelligibility of human activities and not their determinateness (Lachmann 1943: 14; 1977: 71).

Lachmann's Law, the name Boulding gave to Lachmann's view on prediction, asserts the following: 'The impossibility of prediction in economics follows from the fact that economic change is linked to change in knowledge, and future knowledge cannot be gained before its time' (Lachmann 1977: 90). For Lachmann, to introduce time is to introduce a fundamental unknown into the analysis, for it introduces a categorical distinction between the present and the future (Garrison 1986: 91, 93). Although the future is not unimaginable, it remains unknowable (Lachmann 1976: 59).

In a trial to merge Mises and Shackle, Lachmann stresses the negligence by Mises, Hayek and Kirzner of introducing expectations in their theories. Mises hardly ever mentioned expectations (Lachmann 1976: 58). In our evolving economy, prices are assumed to transmit information about expressed expectations. Once transmitted, the information may be speculative or outdated. Already for this reason *decoding* of price information is necessary (Lachmann 1956: 20–22).

Expectations are 'acts of the entrepreneurial mind which constitute his *world*, diagnose *the situation* in which action has to be taken, and logically precede the making of plans' (Lachmann 1956: 15). They are neither economic results, such as prices, nor data such as consumers' tastes. Furthermore, expectations may function differently in different markets. Expectations incarnate interpreted or *filtered* experiences.

The transformation process that takes place in the human mind, using experiences as inputs, results in *indeterminate* expectations. The *filter* is the subjective nature of our beliefs in the major forces causing and governing change in the economic process (Lachmann 1977: 66–73). Because of continuous and unpredictable change, expectations will deviate among individuals. Divergent expectations are the individual images of new, but rather blurred, knowledge.

Lachmann's main proposition is that, because an undisputed single *ex ante* criterion of success does not exist, the market cannot diffuse *superior expectations*. There is only a day-to-day balancing of *arational* expectations by anticipating humankind, the *homo divinans* (Lachmann 1976: 58–61). Arational expectations and behaviour are necessitated by the condition of genuine uncertainty. 'Market participants must make decisions without knowing what the relevant true probabilities are and even without knowing what the full range of possible outcomes are' (Garrison 1986: 94).

One is able to comprehend all human action contingencies only by reducing them to a mental pattern of relative simplicity (Lachmann 1977: 71). What is commonly called the *normal level*, e.g. of prices and interest rates, is 'determined by what are believed to be permanently operative forces' (Lachmann 1977: 78).

In this respect, Lachmann had already been discussing the phenomenon of price inflexibility since the 1940s. The analytical framework consists of a normal price range and an enveloping wider price range. Price movements are split between meaningless (functionless) and meaningful (significant) ones. One may also interpret this mental pattern as a distinction between minor or *random* forces and major or *permanent* market forces.

Inelastic expectations will stabilize the price movements, within the inner price range. As long as price movements remain within the *inner range*, they will be discarded and attributed to random influences. When prices stay within the *outer range*, but are already outside the inner range, some market participants will take heed. When this situation continues for some time, expectations are bound to change sooner or later.

The actual price will be interpreted as the resultant of a new constellation of permanent forces. If actual prices break through the outer range, then a new diagnosis and new expectations with regard to the different forces will be necessary (Lachmann 1956: 23–34; 1977: 73–79).

The European Monetary System (EMS), as it functioned in the 1970s and 1980s, may serve as an illustration of an analogous construction. It had a normal exchange level, as well as an upper and a lower exchange level limit, calling for accommodating actions by the central banks, and a range in-between, outside which restructuring of the system would have been necessary. Although the construction is analogous to his own, it is unlikely that Lachmann would applaud this normative system. For him the establishment of normal price ranges was only felt to be necessary because plans are based on the individual's subjective judgement of information, and made in the perspective of earlier expectations.

Equilibrium will only be reached by chance. The equilibrating forces will be thwarted by typically unexpected changes. 'What emerges from our reflections is an image of the market as a particular kind of process, a continuous process, without beginning, or end, propelled by the interaction between the forces of equilibrium and the forces of changes' (Lachmann 1976: 61).

Some convergence of expectations is ensured by the evolution of adequate market institutions. Interpersonal and intertemporal inconsistencies will be mitigated by the evolved institutions (Lachmann 1956: 25). Expectations that are consistently mistaken will result in lower profits/higher losses, and will therefore be removed from the market.

As already discussed, the importance of the adequate nature of institutions, in order to promote the prevalence of expectations in agreement with the underlying economic reality, is stressed also by other Neo-Austrians ever since the socialist-calculation debate took place. For them, as for Lachmann, a market economy is the only useful mechanism, rewarding adequate expectations via the profits to be acquired with the ensuing actions.

TIME AND TYPES

O'Driscoll and Rizzo brought together different lines of argument in regard to the relations between the future, the present and the past, especially between explanation and prediction. In 1985, these two relatively young authors, writing in the Austrian tradition, published the book *Economics as a Co-ordination Problem* on the problem of economic co-ordination under uncertainty. They attempted to synthesize, and build upon, the writings and ideas that have been discussed in this paper.

O'Driscoll and Rizzo use the term *genuine uncertainty* to refer to 'the recognition that all attempts to characterize the future involve both unique, and recurrent (*typical*) features' (O'Driscoll and Rizzo 1985: 72). The main features of genuine uncertainty are (a) ignorance, or the inherent unlistability of all possible outcomes of a course of action, and (b) the complete endogeneity of uncertainty, or real time (O'Driscoll and Rizzo 1985: 71; 1986: 258–259). The neoclassical 'counterparts' of these features are (subjective) probability distributions and the static concept of time. Genuine uncertainty contrasts sharply with neoclassical uncertainty, and it is incompatible with standard notions of equilibrium (O'Driscoll and Rizzo 1985: 4), as well as being inherently ineradicable (O'Driscoll and Rizzo 1985: 66). I will first discuss the two features of genuine uncertainty to be followed by a discussion of the element of types, which used to be part of their theory.

The first feature of uncertainty is ignorance. Individual decision-making is partly autonomous, and partly dependent on what others choose to do. The Austrian interpretation of subjectivism refers to this meaning: 'A world in which there is autonomous or creative decision-making is one in which the future is not merely unknown, but *unknowable*' (O'Driscoll and Rizzo 1985: 2). Action under uncertainty, that which Mises called human action, and subjectivism are inseparable ideas. The economic future is unknowable, because the future is *underdetermined* by the present state of the economic world.

The idea of ignorance is not captured by the presumption of perfect (stochastic) knowledge and foresight. Its fundamental aspect is the, at least perceived, unlistability of all possible outcomes of a course of action. Since all outcomes are affected by other's activities, choices are never made with complete knowledge of their consequences. The possibility set itself is unbounded. Therefore, it is not to be defined as some form of incomplete knowledge (O'Driscoll and Rizzo 1985: 4).

Real time is the second feature of genuine uncertainty. It must be compared with what O'Driscoll and Rizzo call Newtonian, or static, time. Both are special cases in a more general continuum. Genuine uncertainty may be characterized by both time-independent and time-dependent features.

Most economists use the Newtonian time concept. The perspective of Newtonian time is dominant, when one talks, for example, about a stable decision-making environment. Newtonian time may be characterized by at least three aspects:

(a) Time is homogeneous, and therefore it is a static category. Newtonian time may pass without anything happening.

(b) Time is mathematically continuous. Each time instant is merely one bead in a string of beads and in principle independent of the others.

(c) Newtonian time adds nothing to its content, and is therefore causally inert.

The consequence is a deterministic theory, or to put it in another way, the neglecting of the problem of economic change, and of process (O'Driscoll and Rizzo 1985: 53–58).

Real, subjective, historical, dynamic or endogeneous time is not perceived as some homogenous quantity, or as isolated points, but as a flow of events (O'Driscoll and Rizzo 1986: 255). It is the concept of time which Bergson called 'la durée', or duration (O'Driscoll and Rizzo 1985: 59). The continuous flow of novel experiences constitutes time. Memory and expectation are the structural components of real time, connecting successive periods through their non-deterministic continuous influence on individual perceptions. Furthermore with the enrichment of memory which links previous periods with the present, one's perspective changes. Finally, the perception of time is creative and causally potent instead of causally inert (O'Driscoll and Rizzo 1985: 60–62). To sum up, O'Driscoll and Rizzo use the metaphor that Lachmann used: 'The growth of knowledge is the endogeneous force that endlessly propels the system' (O'Driscoll and Rizzo 1985: 62).

The effects of real time are twofold. Real time (a) is irreversible, and (b) produces unpredictable change. As a consequence *movements along curves* are no longer neutral in a given situation. Furthermore, there should be scope for surprise and for creative evolution (O'Driscoll and Rizzo 1985: 56–62).

The critical contrast involved with uncertainty is between purely time-dependent, or endogenous, uncertainty and Newtonian, or time-independent, forms of uncertainty. Neither the subjective versus objective probability, nor the Knightian measurable versus unmeasurable uncertainty are the most fundamental contrast (O'Driscoll and Rizzo 1985: 75).

Genuine uncertainty is ineradicable because actions dealing with genuine uncertainty may only transform uncertainty (O'Driscoll and Rizzo 1985: 66). This will be evident once we refer to the gathering of information by what Shackle called *crucial experiments*. Such experiments affect the whole future course of relevant events (Shackle 1955: 6, 63). A further reduction of uncertainty may also be inhibited by certain characteristics of the markets, especially independent decision-making. Because of the unending relevance for one's own predictions of information on what others predict, extra information will only result in an extra level of guesses and counter-guesses. Keynes' beauty contest may serve as an illustration (O'Driscoll and Rizzo 1985: 234, 272).

Different types of human activities take different places in the time continuum. Maximizing behaviour is close to the Newtonian extreme. Creative decision-making tends towards the real-time extreme.

The more explicit a problem solution is, the greater the Newtonization of time, and the more narrow is the mnemic link. The leaping over logical steps, itself sometimes only clarified with a reconstruction, is the creative element in a decision. 'Therefore, the actual content of the thought or decision-making process determines the appropriateness of the particular concept of time' (O'Driscoll and Rizzo 1985: 67). An enlargement of the creative component goes together with a widening of the mnemic link (O'Driscoll and Rizzo 1985: 67).

Creativity, planning and purposeful actions all create a paradox of uncertainty, because some degree of both indeterminateness and predictability is needed (O'Driscoll and Rizzo 1985: 11). The paradox of uncertainty may be stated more suitably as follows: 'While complete stability and predictability are incompatible with time, their absence is incompatible with action' (O'Driscoll and Rizzo 1985: 76). The fundamental problem with any attempt to dispose of a denial of regularity and uniformity is the necessity to refer to ideal-typical representations. Such representations already presuppose the existence of social causation and co-ordination (Selgin 1988: 46).

The solution to the paradox of uncertainty is to be found in the given critical contrast. It is here that the writings of Alfred Schutz on the scientific interpretations of human actions come into play.

The philosopher and sociologist Alfred Schutz (1899–1959) applied Husserl's phenomenology to the structure of human action (Lachmann 1977: 96). Action, that is the execution of a projected act (Schutz 1932: 61), is based on a common-sense scheme of reference consisting of unquestioned past experiences. This common-sense knowledge is based on a basic fact of life that 'we live in a world of more or less well circumscribed objects with more or less definite qualities' (Schutz 1953: 307). This common-sense knowledge is subjective, not necessarily coherent, and is altered by experiences, but is given at the moment of choice.

The author emphasizes the distinction between the typical and the unique features of phenomena. In contrast to Weber, Schutz uses a narrow definition of ideal types, thereby signifying that all conceivable action conforms to these constructs. This definition makes his construction universally applicable and suited as foundation of praxeological theories.

Choices are made by way of a process of deliberation, that is a process of making combinations of selected knowledge components. The world is typically made up of a system consisting of more or less empty, ideal types, to be filled by the unique features of the individual occurrence. It involves what Husserl called the idealization of *I-can-do-it-again* (Schutz 1953: 319, 329).

The basic uncertainty as to the outcome of rational action involving social interaction is reduced with further standardization of the prevailing action pattern. The uncertainty is expressed by our hopes and fears. One orients one's actions on socially approved standards of rules of conduct. These standards find shape in norms, manners and mores, and are supported by habits, traditions, organizational frameworks, rules, regulations, laws, etc. The frame of typical constructs is taken for granted by the in-group. The evaluation of projected interactions will always carry a character of plausibility, of subjective likelihood, but not of mathematical probability. The reason for it is the undetermined future. The subjective chance that actions will be more successful is greater when the relevant behaviour pattern is more standardized (Schutz 1953: 325–333).

However, a major problem involved in this way of reasoning must be noted: with regard to the question of choice, it denies a proper place for the perhaps crucially important novelty of circumstances. It is not made clear how novel ideas and experiences change the types used by the actors. In fact Schutz more or less omits the element of creativity, that of novelty.

Mises refers positively to the writings of Schutz (Mises 1933: 125–126, n.27), and promised to discuss his ideas in another paper. He did use the ideas of Schutz in another work:

> If an ideal type refers to people, it implies that in some respect these men are valuing and acting in a uniform or similar way. When it refers to institutions, it implies that these institutions are products of uniform or similar ways of valuing and acting or that they influence valuing and acting in a uniform or similar way . . . Ideal types are expedients to simplify the treatment of the puzzling multiplicity and variety of human affairs. In employing them one must always be aware of the deficiencies of any kind of simplification.
>
> (Mises 1957: 316, 320)

The promised extensive discussion of the work and ideas of Schutz has never appeared (Selgin 1988: 52, n.29).

Typification is the process of 'extracting what stability and regularity there is in the flow of reality. Stable features are called types' (O'Driscoll and Rizzo 1985: 76). Events may be broken down into their (a) stable and typical, and (b) unique, aspects. This way of theorizing under genuine uncertainty received the support of, for instance, Langlois, Ebeling and Selgin (Langlois 1986: 182; Ebeling 1986: 51–52; Selgin 1988: 46).

Typical features are those elements of reality that we discover to be repeatable. Finding types or patterns is dependent on the stability of physical laws, and on mutual reinforcing and stabilizing effects of human interaction. The typical aspect may be anticipated with certainty or probability because it cannot be open-ended. The totality of possible alternatives are known. It makes pattern prediction possible.

The unique aspect is the specific time-dependent element in a stable pattern. 'Unique features are the idiosyncratic, nonrepeatable aspects of reality, that are tied to history and to particular concrete circumstances in which they occur' (Langlois 1986: 182). The unique aspect remains open-ended because the details are filled in as events occur. It constitutes, for instance, the endogenous market process. The typical features change only with exogenous shocks, for example a change in the institutional framework. Such shocks will produce a change in the class of results (O'Driscoll and Rizzo 1985: 85–87).

The interpretative-predictive schedule must be changed: (a) when the actual outcomes make beliefs change, (b) if a predicted typical event is falsified, and/or (c) when a unique event is of major influence. O'Driscoll and Rizzo expect only slow changes in these frameworks because types are, by definition, relatively stable elements (O'Driscoll and Rizzo 1985: 76–79). They leave unanswered the lingering and urgent question about the empirical recognition of these three possible occurrences. In other words, O'Driscoll and Rizzo do not solve the induction problem.

ENTREPRENEURSHIP vs. RULES

Both entrepreneurship and the adherence to rules reflect the individual response to uncertainty (O'Driscoll and Rizzo 1986: 253). '[M]arket economies do *not* rely solely on prices but depend on entrepreneurial activity, rules of thumb, contracts and other institutions to convey information and co-ordinate behavior' (O'Driscoll and Rizzo 1986: 256).

Rule-following behaviour is defined as a 'situation of the general type X, [in which] a relatively specific action or a limited set of actions A is observed' (O'Driscoll and Rizzo 1986: 258). These routines are the present representation of slowly evolved patterns of behaviour. A conscious explicit calculation with regard to the individual costs and benefits may not be found in this case (O'Driscoll and Rizzo 1986: 258).

Rules of thumb are adopted when the computational demand for maximization is excessive, or when maximization is made impossible by the informational demands of time-dependent uncertainty. These rules make behaviour more predictable by bounding individual behaviour and by providing regularities. Rules of thumb form a crucial factor in, for example, bargaining situations and in cases of collusion.

Continuous utility maximization in a situation of genuine uncertainty may result in unpredictable results. An example is the famous Keynesian beauty contest, in which the right expectation depends on guessing and counter-guessing, in principle never-ending, the expectations of the other participants. 'Rules may produce more satisfactory long-run results insofar as they reduce the errors attributable to fine tuning without sufficient knowledge, or insofar as they prevent destabilizing behaviour' (O'Driscoll and Rizzo

1986: 258). The endogenous uncertainty is reduced by these rules in both situations, often resulting in relatively higher social returns (O'Driscoll and Rizzo 1986: 259–263). Thus we may conclude that uncertainty, not certainty, is the source of predictable or stable behaviour (O'Driscoll and Rizzo 1986: 254).

The concept of entrepreneurship, presented by O'Driscoll and Rizzo, is an amalgam of the Schumpeterian and the Kirznerian theory of the entrepreneur. Entrepreneurs may stabilize economic activities by *shouldering uncertainty* or by better foresight of the future. 'The market function of entrepreneurial activity is to fill gaps in the knowledge of market participants . . . [It] consists in *outguessing* market prices when the prices do not seem consistent' (O'Driscoll and Rizzo 1986: 257). O'Driscoll and Rizzo consider entrepreneurship to be, by and large, more a stabilizing than a disruptive element in the economy.

The authors conclude that with non-zero information costs we will often go through sudden, if not catastrophic, changes (O'Driscoll and Rizzo 1985: 134–151). Quality certificates, product information, etc., may be considered as supplying the information not provided by the prices (O'Driscoll and Rizzo 1985: 234). Deregulation, privatization, reorganization and other environmental changes render much accumulated knowledge obsolete. Such changes create great dangers to decision-makers because the need to adopt new behavioural rules necessitates a whole new learning process. This only partly manageable process involves the acquisition of new information and new learning functions.

This learning process differs from the one referred to by Frank Knight. In his opinion it meant acquiring information on relevant prices and quantities. Rules are relevant for, for example, the development of firms.

Although each is at the opposite end of the behavioural continuum, entrepreneurship and rules of thumb are not incompatible. Opposite to what is commonly thought, they are mutually reinforcing. 'Entrepreneurial alertness, for example, may be the source of the perception of an opportunity, but rule following may be the only feasible way in an uncertain world' (O'Driscoll and Rizzo 1986: 256).

A self-stabilizing circle may exist with regard to economic behaviour. With genuine uncertainty one may find individual rule-following behaviour. Institutions are the social crystallizations of these activities. The rules themselves bound individual behaviour, providing regularities while reflecting a high degree of uncertainty. Both the social institutions and the individual rule-following behaviour bound the economic system, thereby stabilizing economic activities. This may be a self-reinforcing circuit (O'Driscoll and Rizzo 1985: 6).

General equilibrium is no more than a conceptual tool in the mind of the economist. It does not exist in the real world (Rizzo 1979a: 82). There are many equilibria depending on the operative institutional processes

(O'Driscoll and Rizzo 1985: 76–79). Because equilibrium concepts indicate directions for actions, via predictions, and are of use as a frame of reference, it is judged necessary to keep some sort of equilibrium concept as a tool of analysis. Introducing pattern co-ordination may be an enrichment of this conception using the Hayekian compatibility of plans and the distinction between unique and typical features. 'Pattern coordination consists of coordination among the typical but not the unique aspects of individual behaviour' (O'Driscoll and Rizzo 1985: 114). There is a societal (stochastic) pattern co-ordination in cases when we have compatible plans insofar as the typical features of plans being (probabilistically) co-ordinated (O'Driscoll and Rizzo 1985: 86).

A point of criticism concerns the split between typical and unique aspects of events. It might be useful in order to escape the problem of accepting the deterministic or the kaleidic viewpoint. However, we want to question the spectrum from a totally static time up to full dynamic real time. It does not reappear in the method of typification where a distinction is made between typical and unique aspects. We propose to extend the method to different combinations of creative, and rule-following, i.e. standardized, behaviour.

The approach taken by O'Driscoll and Rizzo may present a satisfactory solution to the problem of uncertainty, although we must assume the stability of certain patterns of behaviour. This assumption has to be used with the utmost caution, to beware of overstretched conclusions.

CONCLUSIONS

We are now able to answer the questions posed in the introduction. First, how has uncertainty been introduced into Austrian economics? Second, what are the consequent implications for decision-making? Note that writers in the Austrian School do not regard uncertainty as a negative factor. Mises has said that the same thing can be denoted both by stating that the future is uncertainty and by that people act; uncertainty is a pervasive fact of the economic process. If there were no uncertainty there could not be any evolving economic process.

According to Mises, we handle uncertainty with the help of experiences and the faculty of understanding, using case probabilities to deal with the unique events of purposeful actions. Mises, however, could not have solved the problem of dealing with mutually inconsistent expectations, partially because it did not fit praxeology, partially because he concentrated on the thoughtful individual, thereby underrating the importance of dispersion of knowledge by information. Therefore, we concentrated our attention on problems related to the co-ordination of economic activities. It was Hayek who showed economists the importance of the consequences of the dispersed information assumption. Each one of us is guided in our actions by expectations of an uncertain future. Market prices are supposed to communicate scattered information and improve the co-ordination of plans.

Hayek more or less ignored the origination of new market information. How do the persons who keep the economic process evolving, i.e. the entrepreneurs, come to find totally unknown opportunities? Kirzner tried to fill this gap. According to him, past error and present uncertainty are two sides of the same coin, and this is called entrepreneurship. Uncertainty reflects our awareness of possible deviations in the envisaged future from the realized future. The entrepreneur is alert for as yet unnoticed profitable opportunities and existing maladjustments, but is unable to find them solely by deliberate learning.

But how may co-ordination prevail when errors and their concomitant uncertainty are possible at the same time? It is in this respect that one must discuss economic judgement, i.e. the decoding or transformation of (price)information into individual expectations. This is the second major element neglected by Hayek. According to Lachmann, *filtered* experiences result in indeterminate expectations. The market cannot diffuse superior expectations because there is no *ex ante* criterion of success. Events may be broken down into stable or typical aspects and unique aspects. As a consequence, price movements may be distinguished by individuals in minor or *random* forces and major or *permanent* market forces.

An important contribution of the Austrian school of economic thought is that individual decision-making about an uncertain future is related to economic development in a systematic way. Economies must be modelled so as to facilitate the one that is best suited to perform a particular task with an adequate information-finding mechanism. The importance of the adequate nature of institutions, that is to say, a market economy with profits and losses so as to promote the prevalence of expectations in agreement with the underlying economic reality, has been stressed by the Neo-Austrians ever since the calculation debate.

More recently, there is a strong inclination to stress the necessity of analysing both entrepreneurial activities and the adherence to rules as individual responses to uncertainty. These analyses are directed at synthesizing ideas from Kirzner with ideas from Lachmann. Rules make behaviour more predictable, by bounding individual behaviour and by providing regularities. The function of entrepreneurial activity is to fill gaps in the knowledge of market participants. Together, by enlarging our knowledge, it propels the economy into the uncertain future.

To conclude, Austrian economics may be regarded as representing a middle-ground position on the point of uncertainty, knowledge, decision-making and predictability. It is a middle-ground position between the extreme viewpoints of a deterministic and a haphazard or kaleidic future, respectively. A more radical position is taken, however, on the capacities of individuals evaluating what is the best action for them, on the possibility of the market to cope with external and interdependency effects and on the speed with which new activities may be undertaken in a market economy.

REFERENCES

Barone, E. (1908) 'Il Ministro della produzione nello stato collettivista', *Giornale degli Economisti*, reprinted in Hayek (1935) as 'The Ministry of Production in the Collectivist State, Appendix A', 245–290.

Boland, L.A. (1986) 'Methodology and the Individual Decision Maker', in Kirzner, I.M. (ed.)(1986), 30–38.

Caldwell, B.J. (1988) 'Hayek's Transformation', *History of Political Economy* 20,4: 513–541.

Ebeling, R.M. (1986) 'Towards a Hermeneutical Economics: Expectations, Prices, and the Role of Interpretation in a Theory of the Market Process', in Kirzner (1986), 39–55.

Garrison, R.W. (1986) 'From Lachmann to Lucas: On Institutions, Expectations, and Equilibrating Tendencies', in Kirzner (1986), 87–101.

Hayek, F.A. von (ed.)(1935) *Collectivist Economic Planning: Critical Studies on the Possibility of Socialism*, London: George Routledge & Sons Ltd.

Hayek, F.A. von (1935a) 'The Nature and History of the Problem', in Hayek (1935), 1–40.

Hayek, F.A. von (1935b) 'The Present State of the Debate', in Hayek (1935), 201–243.

Hayek, F.A. von (1937) 'Economics and Knowledge', *Economica* IV: 33–54, reprinted in Hayek (1948), 33–56.

Hayek, F.A. von (1940) 'Socialist Calculation III: The Competitive Solution', *Economica* VII (26), reprinted in Hayek (1948), 181–208.

Hayek, F.A. von (1943) 'The Facts of the Social Sciences', *Ethics* LIV (1): 1–13, reprinted in Hayek (1948), 57–76.

Hayek, F.A. von (1945) 'The Use of Knowledge in Society', *The American Economic Review* XXXV (4): 519–530, reprinted in Hayek (1948), 77–91.

Hayek, F.A. von (1946) 'The Meaning of Competition', in Hayek (1948), 92–106.

Hayek, F.A. von (1948) *Individualism and Economic Order*, Chicago: University of Chicago Press, Midway reprint (1980).

Hayek, F.A. von (1988) *The Fatal Conceit: The Errors of Socialism*, in Bartley, W.W. (ed.), *Collected Works of F.A. von Hayek*, Vol. 1, London: Routledge & Kegan Paul.

High, J. (1982) 'Alertness and Judgment: Comment on Kirzner', in Kirzner (1982), 161–168.

Hodgson, G.M. (1986) 'Behind Methodological Individualism', *Cambridge Journal of Economics* 10: 211–224.

Hodgson, G.M. (1989) 'Evolution and Institutional Change', Newcastle upon Tyne: Newcastle upon Tyne Polytechnic, unpublished manuscript.

Hutchison, T.W. (1981) *The Politics and Philosophy of Economics: Marxians, Keynesians, and Austrians*, Oxford: Basil Blackwell.

Huussen, G.M. (1989) 'Mises and the Praxeological Point of View', *Journal of Economic Studies* 15: 121–133.

Huussen, G.M. (1990) 'Maakte Hayek een methodologische ommezwaai?', *Maandschrift Economie* 54 (2): 115–127.

Keizer, W. (1989) 'Recent Reinterpretations of the Socialist Calculation Debate', *Journal of Economic Studies* 16 (2): 63–83.

Kirzner, I.M. (1979), *Perception, Opportunity, and Profit: Studies in the Theory of Entrepreneurship*, Chicago: University of Chicago Press.

Kirzner, I.M. (1979a) 'Comment: X-inefficiency, Error, and the Scope for Entrepreneurship', in Rizzo (1979), 140–152.

Kirzner, I.M. (1981) 'Mises on Entrepreneurship', *Wirtschaftspolitische Blätter* 28: 51–57.

Kirzner, I.M. (ed.)(1982) *Method, Process, and Austrian Economics*, Lexington: Lexington Books.

Kirzner, I.M. (1982a) 'Uncertainty, Discovery, and Human Action: A Study of the Entrepreneurial Profile in the Misesian System', in Kirzner (1982), 139–159.

Kirzner, I.M. (1984) 'Economic Planning and the Knowledge Problem', *Cato Journal* 4 (2): 407–418.

Kirzner, I.M. (1985) *Discovery and the Capitalist Process*, Chicago: University of Chicago Press.

Kirzner, I.M. (ed.)(1986) *Subjectivism, Intelligibility and Economic Understanding: Essays in Honor of L.M. Lachmann on his Eightieth Birthday*, London: Macmillan.

Kirzner, I.M. (1988) 'The Economic Calculation Debate: Lessons for Austrians' *Review of Austrian Economics* 2: 1–18.

Kirzner, I.M. (1989) *Discovery, Capitalism, and Distributive Justice*, Oxford: Basil Blackwell.

Knight, F.H. (1921)(1948) *Risk, Uncertainty, and Profit*, Boston: Houghton Mifflin.

Lachmann, L.M. (1943) 'The Role of Expectations in Economics as a Social Science', *Economica* X (37): 12–23.

Lachmann, L.M. (1956) *Capital and its Structure*, London: Bell and Sons Ltd.

Lachmann, L.M. (1976) 'From Mises to Shackle: An Essay on Austrian Economics and the Kaleidic Society', *Journal of Economic Literature* 14: 54–62.

Lachmann, L.M. (1977) *Capital, Expectations, and the Market Process: Essays on the Theory of the Market Economy*, Kansas City: Sheed Andrews and McNeel Inc.

Lachmann, L.M. (1978) 'On Austrian Stocktaking: Unsettled Questions and Tentative Answers', in Spadaro, L.M. (ed.)(1978) *New Directions in Austrian Economics*, Kansas City: Sheed & Ward, 1–18.

Lange, O. (1936) 'On the Economic Theory of Socialism', in Lippincott, B.E. (ed.)(1964) *On the Economic Theory of Socialism*, New York: McGraw-Hill.

Langlois, R.N. (1986) 'Coherence and Flexibility: Social Institutions in a World of Radical Uncertainty', in Kirzner (1986), 171–191.

Lavoie, D. (1981) 'Introduction' and 'A Critique of the Standard Account of the Socialist Calculation Debate', *The Journal of Libertarian Studies* 5 (1) Winter: 1–5, 41–87.

Lavoie, D. (1985) *Rivalry and Central Planning: The Socialist Calculation Debate Reconsidered*, Cambridge: Cambridge University Press.

Loasby, B.J. (1982) 'Economics of Dispersed and Incomplete Information', in Kirzner (1982), 111–130.

Mises, L. von (1920) 'Die Wirtschaftsrechnung im Sozialistischen Gemeinwesen', *Archiv für Sozialwissenschaften*, 47, reprinted in Hayek (1935) as 'Economic Calculation in the Socialist Commonwealth', 87–130.

Mises, L. von (1922) *Socialism: An Economic and Sociological Analysis*, London: Jonathan Cape, translated second edn 1951.

Mises, L. von (1933) *Epistemological Problems of Economics*, New York: New York University Press, second translation 1981.

Mises, L. von (1949) *Human Action: A Treatise on Economics*, London: William Hodge and Company Ltd, third edn 1966.

Mises, L. von (1957) *Theory and History*, New Haven: Yale University Press.

Mises, L. von (1962) *The Ultimate Foundation of Economic Science: An Essay on Method*, Kansas City: Sheed & Ward Inc., second edn 1978.
O'Driscoll, G.P. (1977) *Economics as a Co-ordination Problem*, Kansas City: Sheed Andrews & McMeel Inc.
O'Driscoll, G.P., and Rizzo, M.J. (1985) *The Economics of Time and Ignorance*, Oxford: Basil Blackwell.
O'Driscoll, G.P., and Rizzo, M.J. (1986) 'Subjectivism, Uncertainty, and Rules', in Kirzner (1986), 252–267.
Paqué, K.-H. (1990) 'Pattern Predictions in Economics: Hayek's Methodology of the Social Sciences Revisited', *History of Political Economy* 22 (2): 281–294.
Rizzo, M.J. (ed.)(1979) *Time, Uncertainty, and Disequilibrium*, Lexington: Lexington Books.
Rizzo, M.J. (1979a), 'Uncertainty, Subjectivity, and the Economic Analysis of Law', in Rizzo (1979), 71–90.
Schumpeter, J.A. (1912) *The Theory of Economic Development*, Oxford: Oxford University Press, subsequent edns 1934 and 1980.
Schumpeter, J.A. (1942) *Capitalism, Socialism, and Democracy*, London: Allen & Unwin, 7th edn 1987.
Schumpeter, J.A. (1954) *History of Economic Analysis*, London: Allen & Unwin.
Schutz, A. (1932) *The Phenomenology of the Social Sciences*, Northwestern University Press, translated edn 1967.
Schutz, A. (1953) 'Common-Sense and Scientific Interpretations of Human Action', *Philosophy and Phenomenological Research* XIV (1): 1–37, reprinted in Natanson, M. (ed.)(1963) *Philosophy of the Social Sciences*, New York: Random House, 302–348.
Selgin, G.A. (1988) 'Praxeology and Understanding: An Analysis of the Controversy in Austrian Economics', *The Review of Austrian Economics* 2: 19–58.
Shackle, G.L.S. (1955)(1968) *Uncertainty in Economics, and Other Reflections*, Cambridge: Cambridge University Press.

10

KIRZNER'S CORE CONCEPTS

*Eran Binenbaum**

INTRODUCTION

This paper contains an attempt to interpret I.M. Kirzner's core concepts in the fields of economic methodology and positive economics. Professor Kirzner is a leading figure in the 'Austrian revival' of the 1970s and 1980s.[1]

The following section sketches the *context* of Kirzner's conception of economics as he developed it in his book *The Economic Point of View* (1960). In that book, Kirzner follows his teacher Ludwig von Mises in regarding economics as a branch of 'praxeology'. The main principles of the praxeological conception of economics are elucidated on pp. 150–158.

However, there is a tension between praxeology and Kirzner's best-known contribution to economic theory – his concept of entrepreneurship. Thus, as pointed out on pp. 156–158, Kirzner no longer appears to be entirely comfortable with one basic praxeological tenet, the unpredictability and indeterminacy of human beings. Non-Austrian economists have often had difficulties in understanding the most important praxeological tenet, the purposefulness of human action, which is the subject matter of the subsequent section. After mentioning some ambiguities surrounding this concept, I present my highly critical interpretation of it. The next section, on pp. 164–171 deals with Kirzner's core concept of entrepreneurship and its implications for the theory of economic order. For Kirzner, the ability of the entrepreneur to discover spontaneously worthwhile opportunities is *the* argument in favour of the free market economy. As will be explained on pp. 169–171, in addition to the axiom of rationality, there are a few other pivotal premises that are necessary for Kirzner to arrive at his *laissez-faire* conclusions. However, the discussion is being confined to the *positive* underpinnings of Kirzner's theory of economic order. The ethical side of the story falls outside the scope of this essay, although Kirzner has written a good deal on it.

Thus, the following four sections contain an account of Kirzner's core

* I would like to thank Gerrit Meijer, Rob Teijl, Casper M. v.d. Tak and D.D. v. Geet for helpful comments and other kinds of support. Of course remaining errors are mine.

concepts in positive economics, all the way from the praxeological conception of economics to some of Kirzner's main theoretical conclusions. However, having provided a faithful account of Kirzner's main economic ideas, I cannot help but conclude that they involve a number of inconsistencies. The final section summarizes these inconsistencies.

THE CONTEXT OF KIRZNER'S CONCEPTION OF ECONOMICS

Kirzner's perspective on the history of economic thought

The history of conceptions of 'the economic' is the subject matter of Kirzner's first book, *The Economic Point of View* (1960). Kirzner follows L.M. Fraser in his distinction between Type A and Type B definitions of economics.

> Type A definitions consider economics as investigating a particular *department* of affairs, while Type B definitions see it as concerned with a particular *aspect* of affairs in general. The specific department singled out by type A definitions has usually been wealth or material welfare. The aspect referred to in Type B definitions is the constraint that social phenomena uniformly reveal in the necessity to reconcile numerous conflicting ends under the shadow of an unescapable scarcity of means.
> (Kirzner 1960: 17)

Although Kirzner certainly is aware of the fact that this classification of definitions is far from exhaustive, he contends that

> The most outstanding development in the history of the problem [of defining economics] is the switch from the search for a department of human affairs to which the adjective 'economic' applies, to the search for the appropriate *aspect* of affairs in which economic concepts are of relevance.[2]

While Lionel Robbins provided the first comprehensive account of the Type B conception of economics, in Kirzner's eyes it was Ludwig von Mises who consistently pursued this line of thought to the most adequate solution of the problem of defining economics, namely, the *praxeological conception of economics*[3]. Kirzner portrays Mises' work as being the culmination of the entire history of thought on the problem, or, as Laurence Moss, who belongs to the same creed, aptly summarized Kirzner's position (in his introduction to Kirzner 1960): 'It took two hundred years for economists to discover that the subject matter of their discipline was none other than the structure of human action itself.' However, according to Kirzner, contemporary economists have largely failed to appreciate the importance of Mises' praxeology: 'The path-breaking work of Mises has a significance that, in the writer's opinion, has not been sufficiently recognized because it has not yet been brought into historical perspective' (Kirzner 1960: 18). Thus, the main purpose Kirzner seems to have had in mind when he wrote his *Economic Point of View*[4] was to draw attention to Mises' praxeological conception of economics by bringing it into historical perspective.

Robbins' contribution, contrary to that of Mises, *did* gain widespread attention and acclaim. Kirzner recognizes its great importance in the history of economic ideas: 'If modern neoclassical microeconomics sees itself as based upon the analysis of *choice*, this is in no small measure due to the influence of Robbins's book. When a modern textbook devotes an entire chapter to credit Robbins with the breakthrough leading up to the contemporary view that "the core of pure economic science is the general theory of choice"[5], this is by no means an exaggeration. What is now commonplace was, in 1932, something of a revolutionary idea; since then this idea has decisively governed the direction of mainstream economic thought' (Kirzner 1986: 124). Thus, Kirzner identifies the core of modern mainstream economics with the Robbinsian conception. Kirzner's appraisal of this conception is ambivalent. If we attempt to understand Kirzner's (and thus Mises') conception of economics, an outline of those elements in Robbins' conception that Kirzner approves of, and those elements Kirzner proposes to amend, respectively, provides a useful starting point.

Kirzner and Robbins

As is well known, Robbins defined economics as 'the science which studies human behavior as a relationship between ends and scarce means which have alternative uses' (Robbins 1932: 16). This definition requires some clarification which can be found in the following statement:

> When the time and the means for achieving ends are limited *and* capable of alternative application, *and* the ends are capable of being distinguished in order of importance, then behavior necessarily takes the form of choice . . . It has an economic aspect.
>
> (*ibid.*: 14)

Thus, probably the best three-word summary of Robbins' conception is that economics is the science of choice.

Robbins did not consider the factors and processes underlying means and ends as falling within the scope of economics. Hence, the means–ends formula enabled Robbins to draw a dividing line between economics and other disciplines. For example, in Robbins' conception, the study of human motivation belongs to the realm of psychology. Robbins, following Mayer, also attempted to distinguish between economics and technology (as Kirzner (1960: 126–127) points out, previous definitions had failed to do so): 'The problem of technique arises when there is one end, the problem of economy when both the ends and the means are multiple' (Robbins 1932: 35).

Kirzner (1960) finds great merit in Robbins' definition for a number of reasons. First, Kirzner prefers 'Type B' to 'Type A' definitions. Both Kirzner and Robbins reject 'the idea that economics is concerned with specific *kinds* of ends' or 'certain *kinds* of behavior' such as the acquisition of wealth; economics 'attempts, on the other hand, to bring out the economic *aspect* of behavior of all kinds' (Kirzner 1960: 110). Second, as it focuses on an aspect of behaviour, Robbins' formulation is *analytical* instead of *classificatory* (*ibid.*: 118). It results from contemplation on the nature of choice. The Robbinsian conception provides a foundation on which the edifice of economic theory can be constructed, while the earlier conceptions merely attempt to demarcate the construction site. Although this metaphor is not Kirzner's, he would probably approve of it. Third, Robbins' approach accords a central role to *scarcity*. Before Robbins, there had been a long series of definitions of economics that referred to scarcity, but Kirzner considers Robbins' formulation clearer and more vigorous than any of these:

> There was thus a long tradition in economic literature in which the importance of the limitation of recources was recognized, and there were, moreover, many indications pointing to the possibility of using the administration of scarce means as *the* distinguishing criterion of the economic. In pressing the scarcity of means into service as the very core of everything economic, and by discovering in the effects of coping with such scarcity an economic aspect to activity in general, Robbins was crystallizing ideas that had already been in ferment for some time.
>
> (Kirzner 1960: 114)

Fourth, Kirzner approves of Robbins' demarcation of economics *vis-à-vis* the other social sciences. Finally, Kirzner wholeheartedly endorses Robbins' case for the strict ethical neutrality of economics. Here, too, Robbins had many precursors, but Robbins' approach in this respect was new in that he claimed 'to have demonstrated that . . . ethical neutrality on the part of the economist follows with rigorous necessity from the very definition of the economic problem' (*ibid.*: 137). The argument briefly runs as follows: 'If the economist is, as such, exempted or interdicted from choosing particular ends of action as his special concern, then the results of his researches will be achieved with ethical indifference towards the data with which he deals' (*ibid.*: 119).

Let us turn to Kirzner's critique of Robbins back in 1960. This critique is fully in line with his later work. Kirzner criticizes the Robbinsian conception of economics on a number of counts. He thereby makes reference to earlier critics such as Talcott Parsons, R.W. Souter and A.L. McFie.

First, Robbins' treatment of ends and means is too static:

> Robbins's structure of ends and means . . . ignores the fact that ends are never presented to the actor coincidentally with the means . . . Ends can be conceived as observable states of affairs only *after* their achievement. At the time of the contemplation of action, ends are to the actor only anticipations of future hoped-for states of affairs.
>
> (Kirzner 1960: 125)

Furthermore, Robbins portrays ends as being objective entities, ignoring their essentially subjective character. Hence, Robbins is being charged with 'behaviourism' and 'positivism'. This second criticism of course is closely related to the first. Third, the ends–means dichotomy is an oversimplification: 'Ends may be considered as means to further ends, and . . . means may be equally well considered as the ends of earlier actions' (*ibid.*: 125). This renders the Mayer–Robbins distinction between economics and technology (see above) invalid (*ibid.*: 127)

KIRZNER'S CONCEPTION OF ECONOMICS

As will become apparent in the course of my argument, subjectivism is to be considered more fundamental to Kirzner's position than praxeology. Therefore, this section starts with a few basic remarks on Kirzner's subjectivism.

Subjectivism, part one

The subjectivist position can be described as follows: *Insofar as human action (as opposed to non-human phenomena) is concerned, physical reality counts only through people's subjective perceptions of it and the valuations they make in accord with it.*[6] Kirzner seeks to adhere to this principle throughout his works,[7] and on several occasions[8] he quotes with approval Hayek's well-known dictum (written in 1952): 'It is probably no exaggeration to say that every important advance in economic theory during the last hundred years was a further step in the consistent application of subjectivism.'

Below, Kirzner's subjectivism will be discussed in two parts. In this subsection, the two subjectivist principles on which the praxeological method is based are introduced. On pp. 156–158, the subjectivist foundations of Kirznerian entrepreneurship are introduced.

In his 1976 essay *The Foundations of Modern Austrian Economics*, Kirzner identifies 'two distinct insights about the economic world' (p. 42) as 'basic tenets of Austrian economics' (p. 43): 'First, there is the insight that *human action is purposeful*, and second, there is the insight that *there is an indeterminacy and unpredictability inherent in human preferences, human expectations, and human knowledge*' (p. 42). According to Kirzner, the first of these two propositions is obviously true, in the sense that we arrive at it by introspection. The truth of the second insight is not equally obvious, because it 'cannot be arrived at by introspection . . . [Instead,] it depends on our observations of our fellow men, that we do as a matter of fact find them to be unpredictable in their actions and expectations about future states of the world' (*ibid.*: 43). The second proposition reflects the Misesian position embodied in Kirzner's earlier writings. Together with the first proposition it provides the key to understanding the subject matter of the next two paragraphs, namely, the fundamentals of the praxeological conception of economics.

Kirzner's 1976 essay contains an – albeit cautious and vague – proposal to amend the second proposition. It will be discussed only in the last paragraph of this section.

Praxeology

Several Austrian economists[9] regard *praxeology* as an inseparable part of the Austrian paradigm. For Mises and Kirzner, economics is a branch of praxeology, and any attempt to define it so as to distinguish it from other branches of praxeology cannot be but arbitrary (Kirzner 1960: 182). Misesian praxeology can be defined by its subject matter as well as its method: (a) *it is the science (or set of sciences) that comprises exclusively statements that are valid for* all *human actions*, and (b) *it employs exclusively the aprioristic method.* Let me clarify this definition.

Kirzner stresses the point that the praxeological conception of economics can only be properly understood if it is placed within the context of the 'complete epistemological system of the social sciences' (*ibid.*: 147) as developed by Mises (1933; 1949; 1957; 1962).

Mises sharply distinguishes between the natural sciences and the sciences of human action. He divides the latter into two main categories: praxeology and history. From the point of view of Misesian epistemology, each of these groups of disciplines – the natural sciences, history and praxeology – is entirely different from both other groups. The first 'basic tenet of Austrian methodology', the purposefulness of human action, can be regarded as the epistemological basis of the methodological distinction between the natural sciences and the sciences of human action. The 'second tenet', the inherent indeterminacy of human preferences and knowledge, can be regarded as the epistemological basis of the methodological distinction between praxeology and 'history'. Let us consider both distinctions in turn.

In the world of the natural sciences

> there is cause and effect. There is what appears to be an inexorable regularity in the concatenation and sequence of phenomena. There are constant relations between entities that enable the scientist to establish the process called measurement . . . [But in that world] there is nothing

> that would suggest aiming at ends sought; there is no ascertainable purpose.
>
> (Mises 1962: 8)

One cannot explain human behaviour solely by postulating chains of cause and effect that depend only on *externally observable* phenomena. In human behaviour a force is operative to which the physical scientist's measuring equipment is insensitive – *purpose*. It is the category of purpose that distinguishes human action from other phenomena. The importance of this category to Mises' and Kirzner's thought cannot be overemphasized. If people aim at purposes, other categories, such as goods, labour, exchange and money, follow.

The task of economics, and of the sciences of human action in general, in a nutshell is 'to make the world intelligible in terms of . . . human purposes' (Kirzner 1976: 44). Thus, Kirzner believes that economics is capable of performing this task. This belief is predicated on the first basic tenet of Kirzner's methodology, the *purposefulness of human action.*

Kirzner provides the following example. A researcher from Mars observes a particular location on Earth and discovers a certain regularity. Every day at 7.30 a.m. a moving box comes to a stop, swallows up a body and moves on. Observing this, the investigator postulates a definite law, the law of moving boxes and bodies. As he goes on with his research, however, he discovers that sometimes the box moves away without the body having entered it, while sometimes the body moves at an unusually rapid speed, arriving just in time to be swallowed up before the bus moves on. Now the Martian researcher may be able to explain the movements of the body and the box entirely without reference to the fact that someone is trying to catch the bus because he is trying to get to work on time. 'But,' runs Kirzner's (*ibid.*: 318) conclusion, 'if he does so, he has not told us everything there is to be learned about this situation. A theory of moving boxes and bodies that does not draw attention to the dimension of purpose gives a truncated view of the real world. *This* is what economics, in the Austrian view, is all about.' And, it may be added, this is what praxeology in Mises' and Kirzner's conception is all about. As said above, Kirzner tells us there is no clear-cut objective criterion to distinguish economics from other branches of praxeology. There is, on the other hand, a sharp distinction between praxeology and 'history' – at least in the work of Mises, and Kirzner appears to follow him in this – as far as the substance of Misesian 'history' – as opposed to the term itself[10] – is concerned.

According to Mises (1949: 30), *history* is

> the collection and systematic arrangement of all the data of experience concerning human action. It studies all human endeavors in their infinite multiplicity and variety and all individual actions with all their accidental, special, and particular implications. It scrutinizes the ideas

> guiding acting men and the outcome of actions performed. It embraces every aspect of human activities.

This includes *inter alia* 'ethnology and anthropology, as far as they are not a part of biology . . . psychology as far as it is neither physiology nor epistemology nor philosophy'; and (as Mises adds in a footnote) economic history, descriptive economics and economic statistics.

An essential feature of 'all historical sciences' is that 'their subject matter . . . is the past. They cannot teach us anything which would be valid for all human actions, that is, for the future too' (*ibid.*: 30). Kirzner, at least in his earlier writings, shares this view[11] which essentially rests on the 'second basic tenet of Austrian methodology' mentioned above – the inherent indeterminacy of human preferences and knowledge.

Kirzner's division of labour and apriorism

Kirzner (1960: 173–177) does not include *constancy of wants over time* in his definition of *purposefulness*. The former premise, however, is bound up with Kirzner's praxeology no less inextricably than the latter: '[both] the notion of "given ends" and the assumption of a constancy of wants . . . are inevitably involved in . . . a praxeological theorem' (Kirzner 1960: 173). The reason for this is that praxeology is radically aprioristic: 'A theorem of a praxeological science provides information that has been derived by sheer reasoning; it is the product of pure logic without the assistance of any empirical observation' (Kirzner 1960: 177). The reader may dismiss this extreme position as absurd and indefensible. But not so fast! We must first bear in mind that Kirzner here refers to economic *theory*.[12]

As explained above, Misesian praxeology does not include psychology, economic history and statistics. Correspondingly, Kirzner envisages a division of labour between economic theory on the one hand, and applied economics, that *does* refer to empirical evidence, the human sciences and moral philosophy (praxeology does not involve moral philosophy because of its strict ethical neutrality) on the other:

> The severely circumscribed applicability of the propositions enunciated by the economic theorist, far from being the necessary result of a crudely unrealistic methodology, is but the properly incomplete contribution of the specialist whose skills have been developed by a judicious and fruitful division of labor. Specific policy recommendations on economic affairs may require long and careful study of the actual attitudes of human beings, their wants, valuations, and expectations.
>
> (Kirzner 1960: 132–133)

In Kirzner's definition, the scope of economic theory is limited:

> Unquestionably the most 'interesting', and, for the business of living, the most important [level of discussion] is the consideration of the way in which men have acquired their particular interests; the development of particular programs that men believe worthy of undertaking; the forces that determine people's value judgments and the emergence of their sense of absolute moral appraisement. The level of interpretation on which praxeology has a contribution to make, is, however, a more modest one. It is willing to accept the interests and programs of man as data . . . The principles of human action make it possible to ascribe and refer back historical events to such interests and programs as 'final causes' that can be accepted without further explanation.
>
> (*ibid.*: 177)

Praxeology and reality

At this point it is useful to summarize the discussion thus far. Probably the most succinct statement of the core idea of praxeology is the following combination of two quotations: 'Praxeology rests . . . on the primordial fact that individuals engage in conscious actions toward chosen goals. The praxeological method spins out by verbal[13] deduction the logical implications of that primordial fact' (Rothbard 1976: 19). '[The scope of praxeology] is human action as such, irrespective of all environmental, accidental, and individual circumstances of the concrete acts . . . Its statements . . . are not derived from experience. They are, like those of logic and mathematics, a priori' (Mises 1949: 32). However, there is a fundamental difference between praxeology on the one hand, and logic and mathematics on the other:

> The theorems attained by correct praxeological reasoning are not only perfectly certain and incontestable, like correct mathematical theorems. They refer, moreover, with the full rigidity of their apodictic certainty and incontestability to the reality of action as it appears in life and history. Praxeology conveys exact and precise knowledge of real things.
>
> (Mises 1949: 39)

The main reason for this is that the axiom of purposefulness of human action is 'true': 'Since praxeology begins with a true axiom, A, all the propositions that can be deduced from this axiom must also be true' (Rothbard 1976: 19–20), provided, of course, that these propositions are deduced by correct reasoning. This implies that 'apart from the fact that these conclusions cannot be "tested" by historical or statistical means, there is no need to test them, since their truth has already been established' (*ibid.*: 21). Thus, the claim is made that praxeology conveys exact knowledge of *reality* without any reference to *experience*.

Naturally, the question arises: does the derivation of economic theorems not require any axioms other than that of action? We will consider the answers 'yes, it does' and 'no, it does not' in turn.

Yes, more axioms are required. Examples of such necessary axioms are causality; the axiom that action takes place through time, and the related axiom that knowledge of the future is uncertain; and the axiom of disutility of labour.

No, the axiom of action is sufficient. 'The concept of human action is sufficient, in the praxeological view, for the deduction of complex chains of reasoning concerning the choices men will make, the alternatives from which they will be forced to choose, and the like' (Kirzner 1960: 179). Consider the aforementioned examples. Causality is contained in the concept of action. That action takes place through time is not only self-evident but also is contained in the concept of action. That knowledge of the future is uncertain is not an additional axiom, but is also contained in the concept of action.[14] Even the disutility of labour can be derived from the action axiom.[15] Kirzner (*ibid.*: 179–180) refers to labour disutility as follows:

> In order to be of service in the understanding of reality, praxeology must direct its attention exclusively to the analysis of situations that correspond to the actualities of the external world. It would be possible, for example, to examine the consequences of a world in which labor was preferred over leisure. Economics could certainly deduce theorems concerning prices, incomes, and production in such a world. But this would be intellectual gymnastics of a fruitless kind . . .

The rejection of formalization

As a rule, Kirzner does not use any mathematics,[16] and this methodological 'constraint' is closely connected to his apriorism. Mainstream economists often conceive of models as a, or even *the*, means for testing their theories – and praxeological theories cannot and need not be tested.[17] Furthermore, the building of a model requires a relatively high degree of specification of a group of premises. In order to derive such premises, one would have to resort to some method other than apriorism; in other words, it would be necessary to refer, directly or indirectly,[18] to empirical facts in order to vindicate the premises. But, as pointed out above, the 'second basic tenet of Austrian methodology' tells us that regularities discovered in empirical facts concerning human beings can never safely be generalized. Hence, according to this approach, models will never convey reliable information, and testing their premises makes as little sense as testing their predictions.

Subjectivism, part two

As Kirzner (1986: 122–123) explains in a recent paper, there are (at least) two different levels of subjectivism. These have been described as 'static' and 'dynamic' subjectivism. Each will be discussed in turn.

'The "statically subjectivist" view . . . makes it appear as if preferences . . . are somehow separate from . . . the decision itself, and as if these preferences then "determine" the specific decision taken' (*ibid.*: 23). The subjectivist quality of this view can only be found in the insight that preferences are the expression of independent subjective likes and dislikes. If preferences are given, the decision is being treated as flowing inexorably out of the objective circumstances prevailing at the instant prior to the decision.

Dynamic subjectivism has been most radically embodied in the work of G.L.S. Shackle: 'Shackle has been concerned to emphasize the radical *creativity* and *indeterminacy* of the human decision. Each decision is a spontaneous new beginning' (*ibid.*: 122). Shackle and Kirzner reject 'static' subjectivism for its 'mechanical' model of decision-making:

> The very circumstance that the 'chosen' course of action is seen as already inexorably implied in the given configuration of preferences and constraints . . . makes the choice 'mechanical' or 'automatic' – and thus not a true choice at all . . . A machine can calculate a required optimal solution; we would not wish to say that the machine can *choose.*
>
> (*Ibid.*: 123)

Kirzner criticizes Robbins and modern mainstream microeconomics for their exclusive focus on 'static' subjectivism; he describes this static version of choice as 'Robbinsian maximizing' (Kirzner 1973): 'The world populated entirely by Robbinsian economizers is in fact the world of contemporary neoclassical microeconomics' (1986: 127). In a radically uncertain world, one cannot speak of preferences as given independently of (or prior to) a decision, because preferences depend on 'alternative imagined future scenarios' (*ibid.*: 126). Kirzner identifies some basic insights of Mises and Hayek, respectively, as advances in the development of dynamic subjectivism.

Kirzner praises Mises *inter alia* for the latter's introduction of the concept of *entrepreneurship* into subjectivism (Kirzner 1986: 131). Kirzner's elaboration of this concept today is his best-known contribution to economic thought. The pith of Mises' concept is that every actor in the economy is an entrepreneur, in the sense that the human agent 'is endowed not only with the propensity to pursue goals efficiently, once ends and means are clearly identified, but also with the drive and alertness to identify which ends to strive for and which means are available' (Kirzner 1973: 34).

> Subjectivism in the analysis of Misesian human action includes the insight that any ends–means framework relevant to a human action

> has *itself been actively chosen* in the course of that very action – and that choice expresses and reflects that agent's dreams, aspirations and imagination, his expectations and his knowledge, his hunches and his biases.
>
> (Kirzner 1986: 131)

As to Hayek, he enriched subjectivism by establishing the pivotal role of knowledge and learning in the market process. Kirzner has repeatedly and with great acclaim quoted the following 'classic' 1945 passage of Hayek's:

> The peculiar character of the problem of a rational economic order is determined . . . by the fact that the knowledge of the circumstances of which we must make use never exists in concentrated or integrated form but solely as the dispersed bits of incomplete and frequently contradictory knowledge which all the separate individuals possess.
>
> (For example, Kirzner 1990a: 163)

Already in 1937, Hayek had identified market equilibrium as being characterized by 'complete mutual knowledge on the part of market participants' (Kirzner 1986: 132). Together, these two statements imply that the market is always in disequilibrium. But in the course of the market process agents are constantly *learning* from the consequences of previous choices: 'Hayek . . . demonstrated . . . the nature of hypothesized equilibrating market processes as consisting of specific patterns of mutual *learning*' (*ibid.*: 132–133).

One important consequence of Hayek's emphasis on learning for Kirzner's thought has been Kirzner's reluctant and partial relaxation of the aforementioned 'second basic tenet of Austrian economics':

> If we are to be able to say anything about the process of equilibration . . . we shall have to rely upon the particular empirical proposition that men learn from market experience in a systematic manner. This is inconsistent with the second tenet underlying Austrian economics that there is an inherent indeterminacy in the way by which human knowledge changes.
>
> (Kirzner 1976: 48–49)

Kirzner's (1973, 1979, 1985) work on entrepreneurship can essentially be described as an attempt to merge Misesian entrepreneurship and Hayekian learning. Kirzner regards Mises' and Hayek's contributions to subjectivism as pointing the way to an understanding of market processes as systematic 'discovery procedures', i.e. spontaneous mutual learning procedures 'continually being set in motion by entrepreneurial human agents'.

Kirzner does not share Shackle's radical brand of dynamic subjectivism: 'Despite continual buffeting by unpredictable exogenous changes in the basic data, it is still possible, on this modern Austrian view, to perceive the powerful co-ordinative forces of entrepreneurial alertness' (Kirzner 1986: 135). Thus, Kirzner's subjectivism is neither static, nor radically dynamic. This middle-ground position is characteristic of Austrian economics in general (Garrison 1982, Kirzner 1985: ch. 1, Kirzner 1992: ch. 1).

THE 'PURPOSEFULNESS OF HUMAN ACTION'

As explained above, praxeologists regard the 'purposefulness of human action' as the foundation of their system. Other economists have had difficulties understanding this notion.[19] Let us explore its meaning.

The terms 'action' and 'purposefulness'

To begin with, it must be noted that Kirzner and other Austrian economists sometimes use 'rationality' as a synonym for the specifically Austrian term *purposefulness*. However, Kirzner himself emphasizes that there is a difference in meaning between *rationality*, as the term is commonly interpreted, and his own notion of *purposefulness*:

> For many non-Austrian economists [the rationality] hypothesis is invoked with apologies and is considered something of a necessary evil . . . For Austrian economists, on the other hand, the notion of purposefulness is not merely a useful tool to obtain results but an essential element of economic reality that cannot be omitted.
>
> (Kirzner 1976: 47)

According to Kirzner (1960: 149), praxeology defines *human action* as 'a path of conduct . . . that has been selected by reason'. This definition consists of three elements. First, *action* falls within the broader category of *conduct* or behaviour. Second, note the metaphor 'path' that points to the fact that action takes place in *time* – which is an insight fundamental to Kirzner's economics (and Austrian economics in general), and a recurrent theme in his critique of stereotype 'static' mainstream economics. Third, 'in the praxeological view, action is rational *by definition*' (*ibid.*: 167, italics added).

What, then, does Kirzner mean by *purposefulness*? First, purposefulness implies *consciousness* (*ibid.*: 166: 'Rationality involves the conscious effort'). Second, repeated and careful perusal of some relevant statements of Kirzner's leads me to interpret purposefulness as consistency between preferences and behavior.[20] This sounds like a mainstream conception of rationality, but as will be explained below, this is not the case.

In order to obtain a complete picture of Kirzner's concept of rationality, or purposefulness, it must also be pointed out what Kirzner does *not* mean by it. Consider a man 'who does not wish to indulge in gluttony, who has in fact budgeted all his money for other, more highly valued purposes, but who, yielding to the temptation of the moment, buys and drinks Rhenish wine'.[21] Is the man acting rationally? In Kirzner's view, he is. Kirzner's 'purposefulness' does not require *constancy* of preferences (or 'ends'): 'In the praxeological view, the man has simply substituted a new set of ends . . . for the previously chosen ends' (*ibid.*: 168–169). Furthermore, judgements concerning the *wisdom* of an end do not make any difference to the issue whether its pursuit is rational or not:

> The fact that in the eyes of an outside observer, or even in the eyes of the man himself at a cooler moment, it is the original set of ends that constitutes the man's 'best interests', is not sufficient to justify our labeling the man's pursuit of his newly selected goal as 'irrational'.
>
> (*ibid.*: 169)

Hence, both thoughtfulness and *paternalism* (I hope the reader will forgive my usage of terms not used by Kirzner) fall outside the scope of Kirzner's 'purposefulness'. I use the term 'paternalism' to denote the circumstance that another person ('an outside observer' in the above quotation) judges which ends constitute the subject's best interest, irrespective of the subject's own judgement. By thoughtfulness I mean 'a state of sufficient mental clarity ('a cooler moment' in the above quotation) to allow the subject to retrieve relevant knowledge he already possesses. The knowledge to be retrieved concerns both ends (the subject's own ideas about his 'best interests')[22] and means.

We can now understand the difference between 'purposefulness' and more common notions of rationality. According to the latter, the 'Rhine wine' behaviour would be irrational, either because the man's preferences change so abruptly, or because the man's choice is inconsistent with his own true preferences (as opposed to the preferences he is aware of).

An assertion, or only a definition?

Consider the following two statements: 'Action is rational by definition' (Kirzner 1960: 167); 'Praxeological ideas . . . hinge on a conception of rationality as a pervasive quality of all human action' (*ibid.*: 168). If we combine both statements, it is evident that the result is meaningless. Kirzner appears to assert that rationality is a pervasive quality of all rational behaviour! Here, a definition is being confused with a substantive assertion.

However, if we are to make sense of praxeology, we must choose: either the purposefulness of action is given by definition, or it must be interpreted as a meaningful assertion. Only if we follow the latter avenue can we conceive of the purposefulness of action as being the foundation of an entire system. Thus, there must be some assertion contained in the concept. This conclusion is strongly supported by Kirzner's contention that

> for many non-Austrian economists [the rationality hypothesis] is invoked with apologies and is considered something of a necessary evil . . . For Austrian economists, on the other hand, the notion of purposefulness is not merely a useful tool to obtain results but an essential element of economic reality that cannot be omitted.
>
> (Kirzner 1976: 47)

This leaves us with the question: what is being asserted? Let us have a look at two possible interpretations.

An obvious assertion?

Kirzner's following formulation seems to be pretty straightforward: 'The first of the basic tenets of Austrian theory [is] that there is a realm of reality constituted of human motives, interests, and purposes, and that, although purposes cannot be seen or touched, they are nonetheless "there"' (Kirzner 1976: 44). Now if this is all that is being asserted, it is easy to understand that Kirzner considers it sufficiently vindicated by his reference to introspection: 'The purposefulness of human action is something we arrive at by introspection. In this sense it is "obviously" true' (Kirzner 1976: 47).

If purposes exist, action exists. But is it possible to use this obvious fact as a premise for economic theory, or even as its foundation? No, because 'unpurposeful' behaviour is not excluded; it may interfere with purposeful behaviour. Hence, the mere existence of action in itself cannot be of any direct use to the construction of economic theory. Surely, there must be more to the purposefulness of action than the mere existence of purposes.

A substantive assertion?

As we saw, purposefulness encompasses consciousness and consistency between preferences and behaviour. Now consider the hypothesis that there is a hidden assertion in praxeology (as represented by Mises, Rothbard and Kirzner), namely, that if behaviour is accompanied by consciousness, there is consistency between those preferences that are present in consciousness on the one hand, and behaviour on the other. In short: *all conscious behaviour is purposeful.* Which arguments support this interpretation?

First, Kirzner follows Mises in claiming 'the insight that men are purposeful' (Kirzner 1979: 128). This implies that 'if one has become sufficiently alerted to the existence of an opportunity – that is, one has become sufficiently convinced regarding the facts of a situation – it becomes virtually impossible to imagine *not* taking advantage of the opportunity so discovered' (Kirzner 1980: 22). Similarly,

> No matter how compelling the physiological or physical factors that crave action may seem, it is within the power of reason to resist them.

> No matter how strong the psychological pressures on man may be, his actions have necessarily passed the scrutiny and gained at least the tacit assent of his reason.
>
> (Kirzner 1960: 151)

Second, the hypothesis is fully consistent with the praxeologists' conception of *un*purposeful behaviour. If 'Rhine wine' behaviour is purposeful, then what is unpurposeful behaviour? The answer is provided by Mises:

> Conscious or purposeful behavior is in sharp contrast to unconscious[23] behavior, i.e., the reflexes and the involuntary responses of the body's cells and nerves to stimuli. It is sometimes not easy to establish whether concrete behavior is to be considered voluntary or involuntary. But the distinction between consciousness and unconsciousness is nonetheless sharp and can be clearly determined.
>
> (Mises 1949: 11)

'The opposite of action is not *irrational behavior*, but a reactive response to stimuli on the part of the bodily organs and instincts which cannot be controlled by the volition of the person concerned' (*ibid.*: 20). The same sharp contrast between unconscious and conscious behaviour can be found in the following quotations:

> Praxeology rests on the fundamental axiom that human beings *act*, that is, on the primordial fact that individuals engage in conscious actions toward chosen goals. This concept of action contrasts to purely *reflexive*, or knee-jerk, behavior, which is not directed toward chosen goals.
>
> (Rothbard 1976: 19)

> [Action is] conduct that is accompanied by the consciousness of volition, of something more than a bundle of reflexes responding to specific stimuli.
>
> (Kirzner 1960: 151)

Thus, Mises, Rothbard and Kirzner all take it for granted that if behaviour is not purely reflexive, it is purposeful. There is a sharp distinction between these two categories of behaviour; there is no in-between.

Here we have the substantial assertion we were looking for. Once it has been established that unpurposeful behaviour is nothing more than bodily reflexes, the latter category can be dismissed as irrelevant to economic analysis.

Still, we may rightfully ask: why should consciously perceived preferences at all times be consistent with behaviour?

Preferences: a circularity

The clue to the riddle can be found in a circularity in Mises' and Kirzner's concept of preferences.

Suppose the 'Rhine wine' man, while indulging in his fleeting pleasure, is well aware of the fact that he is forsaking his previous budget plan. Could the man's preferences be inconsistent? Kirzner, as I interpret him, would say: 'No. The man's decision to buy the wine reveals his preferences at the time of the decision.' According to Kirzner, the reason that some would regard the man's decision as irrational is 'the artificial creation of a "plan" in the form of a prior selection of ends' (Kirzner 1960: 170). Thus, for Kirzner, the man's preferences have *changed* and the man is no less purposeful than he was before; any criterion to judge whether or not the man has behaved rationally is arbitrary.

I interpret Kirzner to agree on the (im)possibility of inconsistent preferences with his teacher Mises, who wrote on it:

> The attempt has been made to attain the notion of nonrational action by this reasoning: If *a* is preferred to *b* and *b* to *c*, logically *a* should be preferred to *c*. But if actually *c* is preferred to *a*, we are faced with a mode of acting to which we cannot ascribe consistency and rationality. This reasoning disregards the fact that two acts of an individual can never be synchronous. If in one action *a* is preferred to *b* and *b* to *c*, it is, however short the interval between the two actions may be, not permissible to construct a uniform scale of value in which *a* precedes *b* and *b* precedes *c* . . . All that the example proves is that value judgments are not immutable and that therefore a scale of value, which is abstracted from various, necessarily nonsynchronous actions of an individual may be self-contradictory.
>
> (Mises 1949: 103)

Thus, for Mises, a person's action is the one and only means of telling what the person's preferences at the time of the action (or rather, at the time of the decision leading to the action) are. Both Mises and Kirzner implicitly deny the possibility, or at least the possible relevance, of inner conflict. Preferences cannot be but consistent.

This argument involves a circularity. Actions are being explained by reference to preferences. How are we to know what a person's preferences are? By looking at the person's actions!

If this interpretation is correct, Mises and Kirzner have fooled themselves into believing that the (almost magic) concept of purposefulness has any meaning. They have got trapped in a complex system of definitions that depend on each other. This seems the only remaining plausible interpretation that is able to encompass the interpretations contained in the preceding four paragraphs. We must therefore conclude that *the axiom of the 'purposefulness of human action' is meaningless after all, and cannot serve as the ultimate foundation of economics.* Instead, Kirzner's economics depends on the standard assumption of consistent preferences which, however, is not unproblematic.

Praxeology and constancy of preferences

As we saw above, an important element of Kirzner's praxeological conception of economics as set forth in his *Economic Point of View* (1960) is that preferences, being the object of study of disciplines other than economics, are among the 'final causes' of economic analysis that 'can be accepted without further explanation'. This implies that if preferences *change*, such changes fall outside the scope of economics. Praxeology can only analyse the interaction of purposeful agents who have *constant* preferences (during the period that is analytically relevant):

> Analysis of human action can proceed only by the treatment of given purposes as data; the effects of a change in surrounding circumstances can be deduced only on the assumption that these purposes are adhered to with constancy, that no new 'program' has been substituted for the old . . . The crucial point is that the perception of any kind of explanatory framework has been made possible only by prescinding from any conceivable change in a given set of programs.
>
> (Ibid.: 174 and 176)

According to Kirzner, the assumption of constancy of preferences does not prevent economists from recognizing causal chains in empirical data; moreover, the assumption is a necessary condition for such scientific achievements:

> It is the outstanding achievement of economic theorists to have been able to recognize determinate causal chains within the tangles of statistics; they were able to succeed in this only by treating social phenomena as the systematic working out of the praxeological consequences of *given programs* that were adhered to.
>
> (*Ibid.*: 176)

As explained above, constant preferences are not included in the definition of purposefulness. Although in *The Economic Point of View*, constancy of preferences (like purposefulness) is portrayed as a distinguishing feature of economic theory, it is no article of faith (unlike purposefulness):

> A particular program may not necessarily be adhered to, but the emergence of human action at all presupposes the existence of *some* program that was adhered to, and it is in reference to *this* that praxeological reasoning provides the explanatory key.
>
> (Ibid.: 176)

ENTREPRENEURSHIP

If one concept can be singled out as the most important in, and the most characteristic of, Kirzner's economic thought, then it is *entrepreneurship*. Kirzner (1985: 11) claims 'that *only* by incorporating entrepreneurship into microeconomic theory can the core of that theory be salvaged'. Many descriptions of both entrepreneurship and the related notion of (entrepreneurial) alertness can be found in Kirzner's work. In order to understand these concepts we have to combine and interpret elements from various publications.

The terms *entrepreneur, entrepreneurial* and *entrepreneurship* all have a wider and a narrower meaning. In the wider meaning reference is being made to *all* human decision-making, while the narrower meaning refers to business decisions (decisions on production or trade of goods and services; they are neither political nor consumptive) with profits accruing to (or losses borne by) the decision-maker (see pp. 167–168). It is in this narrower sense that Kirzner mostly uses the terms *entrepreneur* and *entrepreneurship*.

As pointed out above, the broad conception of entrepreneurship goes back to Mises' work. It is an attempt to come to grips with the tension between purposefulness and ignorance. How can a person act, or be purposeful, with less than complete relevant knowledge? Kirzner's answer to this question is the subject matter of the next section.

Entrepreneurial alertness

The basic idea behind Kirznerian entrepreneurship is that there is a very important element in human decision-making that is not captured by the standard notion of Robbinsian economizing. The fundamental cause of the existence of this extra-Robbinsian element is widespread ignorance – incompleteness of knowledge relevant to decisions.

One may ask, in turn, why, for Kirzner, ignorance is so pervasive. He does not explicitly address this question; apparently he considers the matter obvious. Two principle causes of ignorance can be found in Kirzner's work. First, it is very difficult to observe the preferences and plans of other actors: 'Many [decisions] . . . erroneously anticipate and depend upon other decisions which are in fact not being made' (Kirzner 1973: 9). Second, the relevant information is subject to change. Kirzner follows Hayek in regarding the equilibrating market process as a *learning* process (see above). This process never ceases due to 'the incessant injection of unexpected changes and surprises' (Kirzner 1985: x). Equilibrium is never achieved due to the frequency and momentum of the changes.

One obvious but important argument vindicating a radical rejection of the assumption of full information is the enormous quantity and complexity of the relevant information. I have not yet come across explicit use of this argument in Kirzner's work, but it can be safely assumed that he considers it important. For example, resource characteristics, employee abilities, technical and organizational possibilities and consumer tastes all are very complex. The final products are highly differentiated; the product itself is an economic variable.[24]

Under conditions of ignorance, that is, if there are gaps in the decision-maker's ends–means framework, pure Robbinsian economizing, which exclusively consists in 'the task of calculation' (Kirzner 1980: 16), is impossible.

Thus, the extra-Robbinsian or 'entrepreneurial element in human action . . . is that element in individual decision making that cannot be pressed into the standard "maximizing" model of the decision', namely, '*the very identification of the ends-means configuration itself*, within which action is being conducted' (Kirzner 1979: 158). This formulation requires some clarificatory remarks. First, if the decision-maker already possesses part of the required knowledge, it is not the *entire* configuration but only the missing parts of it that must be identified. Second, 'identification' here is being used as a synonym of 'perception'. Third, as Kirzner (1980: 16–17) explains,[25] we can speak of an 'entrepreneurial element' (as opposed to the Robbinsian or computational element) in a decision if and only if the decision-maker lacks both the 'first-order' and the 'higher-order' knowledge needed to *compute* the decision. By first-order knowledge I mean the knowledge directly relevant to the decision. Second-order knowledge is knowledge about the nature or worth of, or about the means and cost of obtaining, the missing first-order knowledge. Somehow the decision-maker must perceive, that is, become aware of, the missing information in order to make a decision. This perception, or awareness, then, constitutes the *entrepreneurial* element in the decision. If the perception is quick and accurate, then the entrepreneur is said to be *alert*. The combination of quickness and accuracy of perception is particularly important because of the complexity and pace of change of the missing information. Thus, *entrepreneurial alertness* is one of Kirzner's core concepts; the equilibrating market process depends on it. Disequilibrium, the perennial state of the economy, is characterized by the existence of unnoticed worthwhile opportunities; hence, 'Entrepreneurial alertness consists . . . in the ability to notice without search opportunities that have been hitherto overlooked' (Kirzner 1979: 148).

As Kirzner (1979: 141) points out, 'The literature on the economics of information has, at least since Stigler's pioneer article 'The Economics of Information', stressed the role of *deliberate search* for information.' In Stigler's approach, the acquirement of information is being regarded as the result of maximizing decisions that take into account all the relevant costs and benefits. Kirzner challenges this approach and forcefully makes a case for the importance of undeliberate learning:

> The theory of search cannot, it is clear, avoid making the assumption that, before undertaking the search, one *already* knows enough . . . to be able to calculate rewards and costs . . . One may, of course, imagine a long sequence of searches for knowledge, each set in motion by the information gathered deliberately from the preceding search. But this cannot free us from the conclusion that at the *start* of the necessarily finite sequence of searches, at least, some knowledge was possessed that was not itself the result of deliberate search.
>
> (Ibid.: 142)

If we translate this argument into the terminology introduced above, Kirzner is saying that Stigler's approach is adequate for dealing with the problem of incomplete first-order knowledge *only insofar as complete higher-order knowledge can be assumed.* The problem about the latter assumption is that the number of orders of knowledge cannot be infinite.[26]

For Kirzner, deliberate search for information along the lines of Stigler's scheme is just another kind of Robbinsian maximizing; therefore, it is no part of *entrepreneurial alertness* and *entrepreneurship.*

A related aspect of entrepreneurial alertness is that one does not choose being alert (or not being alert, for that matter), and alertness cannot be transferred from one person to another. Alertness implies 'being good at perceiving opportunities';[27] it results in knowledge concerning opportunities and must be sharply distinguished from the knowledge itself. Contrary to knowledge and other resources, alertness can neither be bought nor deployed; hence, it is costless, unlike knowledge and other resources (Kirzner 1979: ch. 10; 1980: 21–26). The element of choice is implicit in the notion of deployment. One cannot meaningfully speak of an agent 'deploying' a resource, unless the agent has the option not to deploy the resource.

Knowledge and entrepreneurship

This section contains a brief discussion of three of Kirzner's insights that are closely related to his concept of entrepreneurship.

First, for our understanding of Kirzner's entrepreneur, the distinction between missing information that concerns present facts[28] on the one hand, and elements of information about uncertain future events[29] on the other, is essential. In his earlier (1973) work, Kirzner emphasized the former, and was subsequently criticized for neglecting the latter (Kirzner 1982: 141–142). In his (1982, chapter 12) paper 'Uncertainty, Discovery, and Human Action', he does shift his emphasis to uncertainty. This leads him to regard the entrepreneur as a person who 'secures greater correspondence between [his] future as he envisages it and his future as it will in fact unfold' (Kirzner 1982: 151). This he does not only by 'peering through the fog', but also by *creating* opportunities for the future. This implies a widening of the meaning of 'alertness': Kirzner now speaks of 'metaphorical alertness' which 'may consist in the vision to *create* something in the future' (Kirzner 1982: 155). Or, as Kirzner puts it elsewhere:

> *Alertness* is a concept sufficiently elastic to cover not only the existence of existing arbitrage opportunities, but also the perception of intertemporal speculative opportunities that can be definitively realized only after the lapse of time, and even also the perception of intertemporal opportunities that call for creative and imaginative innovation.
>
> (Kirzner 1984a: 85)

I agree with High (1982) and Wubben (1992: 22) that this shift in Kirzner's emphasis constitutes an improvement. However, this use of the term 'alertness' may be criticized on semantic grounds.

Second, a closely related and equally important point is that the initially missing information very often does *not* present itself to the entrepreneur in an *exact* form. Hence, *intuition* is a major element of entrepreneurial alertness.[30] Here we have another reason for Kirzner's aforementioned rejection of formalization; it is very hard, or even impossible, to translate intuitive knowledge into mathematical terms.

Third, the subjectivist distinction between objective and subjective reality should be directly applied to the problem of knowledge. Actors may hold erroneous beliefs. They may even be ignorant of their ignorance; if one takes a particular decision on the assumption that one possesses all the relevant knowledge, this assumption may in fact be wrong. Furthermore, *availability* of information is no guarantee for *perception*;[31] it is precisely for this reason that Kirzner has introduced his concept of *alertness*.

Profit accrual and the profit motive

One important element of Kirzner's definition of *entrepreneur*[32] is that they are the people to whom profits resulting from their decisions accrue. This becomes apparent when Kirzner attempts to separate the entrepreneurial function from both ownership and management (represented by A and B, respectively): 'If A gets the profits, he is acting as an entrepreneur, not as a mere owner. If B gets the profits, he is acting as an entrepreneur for himself, not as a mere hired factor' (Kirzner 1973: 62). However, Kirzner does not draw a clear-cut distinction between profit *accrual* and the profit *motive*, so that at times his entrepreneur emerges as a profit maximizer *by definition*; for example: 'A feature common to all kinds of entrepreneurial discovery is the incentive of pure profit, arising out of the respective price discrepancies[33] of which the entrepreneurial opportunities consist' (Kirzner 1984a: 86).

On a few occasions does Kirzner acknowledge the variety of human motivations. In one rather vague passage he remarks that profit maximization 'includes self-enrichment in non-pecuniary ways' (Kirzner 1973: 63). Talking of 'the promise of pure gain as an entrepreneurial incentive', Kirzner points out that 'gain' is to be 'broadly understood to include fame, power, prestige, even the opportunity to serve a cause or to help other individuals' (Kirzner 1980: 28). Similarly, in reply to criticism of the assumption of self-interest as a foundation of economic theory, Kirzner pronounces the view that

> In [market] processes, self-interest is indeed a central element, but this self-interest must . . . be understood with a certain subtlety. Properly understood self-interest does not exclude altruistic motivation; it depends on purposefulness, but not on any selfishness of purpose. The point to be stressed is that it is one's *own* purposes which inspire one's actions and excite one's alertness.
>
> (Kirzner 1990b: 208)

Nonetheless, in all of Kirzner's economic analyses – which invariably concern market processes – entrepreneurs are out to maximize their money profits. Moreover, Kirzner (1979: ch. 10) introduces the category of *pure entrepreneurial profit* as a direct extension of his concept of entrepreneurship. This is the net gain that arises as a consequence of the exercise of entrepreneurial alertness (as opposed to purely Robbinsian maximizing).

The 'uncharted frontier'

In a section entitled 'The Qualities of Entrepreneurship – the Uncharted Frontier', Kirzner (1980: 25–26, italics added) concludes that research on psychological aspects of entrepreneurship is desirable:

> It would certainly be desirable to be able to identify with precision those human qualities, personal and psychological, which are to be credited with successful entrepreneurial alertness, drive, and initiative. It would be most valuable to be able to study the short-run and long-run impact upon the development of these 'entrepreneurial' qualities of alternative social, economic, and institutional frameworks. It would be important to know, for example, if a comfortable sense of security discourages noticing new opportunities. If 'independence' or 'economic freedom' encourages entrepreneurial drive and initiative, this would be significant information. Likewise, does 'competition' encourage alertness to new opportunities? . . . Up to the present, little systematic work appears to have been done on these questions. Observations made are likely to be based on 'common sense' or on anecdotal foundations. *It is indeed necessary to go beyond this elementary stage.* Indeed, an important frontier of knowledge, largely unexplored, appears to consist of those

> aspects of psychology, such as temperament, thirst for adventure, ambition, and imagination, that are likely to throw light on the development of the qualities of entrepreneurship and on the ways alternative institutional arrangements may affect such development. It is to be expected and very much to be desired that research should proceed on this frontier during the years ahead . . . My tentative observations here will suggest that a number of important general statements can be made even before we enjoy the systematic knowledge I anticipate will emerge from research into the psychology of entrepreneurship.

As will be seen (pp. 170–171), the 'important general statements' that can be made without psychological research are necessary for Kirzner's conclusions on economic order. Essentially, they seem to be reducible to two basic propositions. First, *alertness in general is powerful enough to cope with the level of uncertainty and the turbulence of the real world.* Second, *whether or not something is being noticed by an agent depends to a significant degree on its profitability to the agent.* These two propositions and their implications are the respective subject matters of the following two sections.

Uncertainty: the 'middle ground'

This section is a continuation of the subsection 'Subjectivism, part two'. As we saw there, Kirzner seeks to occupy the middle ground between 'static subjectivism' and 'radical dynamic subjectivism'. These three paradigms have correspondingly different opinions on the question of equilibrium. On the one hand, Kirzner envisages the market as being in perennial disequilibrium, which is a view diametrically opposed to that of static subjectivism; on the other hand, Kirzner insists that there are strong equilibrating tendencies, which is denied by the radical subjectivists. For Kirzner, the existence of such tendencies is due to the powerful force of entrepreneurial alertness.

At the bottom of Kirzner's difference of opinion with the radical subjectivists is the problem of uncertainty. Kirzner's middle-ground position is one 'between the extreme viewpoints of a deterministic and a haphazard or kaleidic future, respectively' (Wubben 1992: 35). Kirzner (1992: ch. 1) uses a number of arguments to defend his position against radical charges. First,

> We endeavour to grasp [the] future somehow in our imaginations. Some of us are more successful at this endeavour than others are . . . We must, that is, recognize something like 'entrepreneurial ability', understood as the capacity independently to size up a situation and more correctly reach an imagined picture of the relevant (as yet indeterminate) future.
>
> (Ibid.: 26)

Second, there does exist some relation between present 'underlying realities' and 'future realities'. Hence, although entrepreneurial action is future-oriented, 'the equilibrating process set in motion by entrepreneurial profit-oriented activity is inspired by the underlying realities, after all' (*ibid.*: 27).[34] Third, Kirzner refers to historical experience with markets:

> As elementary textbooks have reminded us at least since Bastiat, great cities manage, without a great deal of centralized control, to attract daily provisions in a tolerably orderly way . . . That the market obviously works is perhaps the most significant lesson of modern history. Experiences in the past several decades have pressed this lesson into the consciousness of men on both sides of the Iron Curtain.
>
> (Kirzner 1992: 35)

The paramountcy of the tendency to market equilibration is a *sine qua non* for Kirzner's case for the free market, to which we turn next.

Entrepreneurship and economic order

In several papers on economic order, Kirzner (1971; 1980; 1983; 1984) recommends *laissez-faire*. The basis for Kirzner's argument is '*that human beings tend to notice that which it is in their interest to notice*' (Kirzner 1980: 28).

The argument runs as follows:

> Potential alertness may be (and so often is) untapped and inert. We know, certainly, that individuals display vastly different degrees of entrepreneurial alertness. Some are quick to spot as yet unnoticed opportunities, others notice only the opportunities revealed by the discoveries of others . . .
>
> (Ibid.: 25)

> Two individuals walk through the same city block teeming with hundreds of people in a variety of garbs, with shops of different kinds, advertising signs for many goods, buildings of different architectural styles. Each of these individuals will notice a different set of items out of these countless impressions impinging on his senses. What is noticed by one is not noticed by the other. The difference will not merely be one of chance. It is a difference that can be ascribed, in part, to the *interests* of the two individuals. Each tends to notice what is of interest to *him*.
>
> (Ibid.: 28)

It follows that '*In order to "switch on" the alertness of a potential discoverer to socially significant opportunities, they must offer gain to the potential discoverer himself*' (*ibid.*: 29).

In a free market economy, characterized by freedom of entrepreneurial entry,

> unexploited opportunities for reallocating resources from one (low market valued) use to another of higher value offer the opportunity for pure entrepreneurial gain. A misallocation of resources occurs because, so far, market participants have not noticed the price discrepancy involved. This price discrepancy presents itself as an opportunity to be exploited by the discoverer. *The most impressive aspect of the market system is the tendency for such opportunities to be discovered.*
>
> (*Ibid.*: 30)

It should be noted that the 'price discrepancy' mentioned in this quotation does not necessarily involve existing prices or products, so that the term can be applied to any profit opportunity arising from arbitrage, speculation or innovation.

In Kirzner's eyes, this is a decisive advantage of the free market in comparison to the socialized economy. Kirzner concedes that it may occur that socialist officials notice socially beneficial opportunities without the incentive of personal financial gain. However,

> It is doubtful in the extreme if ideals such as benevolence or patriotism can be relied upon, in general, to enable a potential discoverer to identify his own personal interest with that of the discovery of an opportunity for a reallocation of resources desirable for society.
>
> (Ibid.: 33)

This is a substantive proposition that goes beyond the proposition that 'human beings tend to notice that which it is in their interest to notice'. Here, something is being said about human motivation itself. Both propositions are necessary premises in Kirzner's case for the free market.

INCONSISTENCIES IN KIRZNER'S WORK

As the attentive reader will have noticed, there are a number of inconsistencies in Kirzner's ideas.

To begin with, there are contradictions within the framework of praxeology. First, does the 'first basic tenet of Austrian methodology', the axiom of action, mean nothing more than 'people have purposes', or is its true meaning 'all behavior that is not purely reflexive is consistent with preferences'? I have argued that we can understand this contradiction only if we recognize the circularity in Kirzner's concept of preferences. Second, although Kirzner claims that the action axiom is sufficient for the derivation of praxeological theorems, it is not. There is at least one necessary praxeological premise that cannot be derived from the action axiom, namely, the assumption of constant preferences.

Another contradiction is that Kirzner's later work in several respects is not praxeological, although he has never renounced praxeology. First, Kirzner has introduced a number of propositions into his analyses that cannot be arrived at aprioristically. The most important of these are that the equilibrating influence of entrepreneurial alertness in general is strong enough to be considered significant, in spite of strong disruptive forces that prevent the *attainment* of equilibrium;[35] that people tend to notice what it is in their interest to notice; and that unselfish motivations in general cannot be relied upon to ensure that socially beneficial opportunities will be noticed. Second, if psychological research on entrepreneurship will come up with conclusions, Kirzner is willing to incorporate them into economic theory, in spite of the praxeological principle that psychology cannot reveal general truths. Third, an important aspect of Kirzner's concept of entrepreneurship is that decision-making involves the identification of ends. This is inconsistent with the notion of constancy of preferences.

Finally, if we disregard Kirzner's earlier statements on praxeology, there remains one important internal inconsistency in Kirzner's later work. Kirzner contends that his entrepreneur may have a variety of motivations; yet in Kirzner's conceptualization of the entrepreneur as well as in all of his analyses, entrepreneurship is inextricably bound up with profit maximization. While it is true that profits, once earned, can serve a variety of purposes, profit maximization may contradict the attainment of certain purposes. Moreover, although the alleged essence of the entrepreneurial decision-maker is said to be the identification of the decision-maker's means–ends framework, Kirzner's entrepreneurs do not identify their own ends (they may identify the ends, or preferences of the consumers) – all they do is identify the means for the attainment of their intermediate end of profit maximization.

In Kirzner's earlier work, a conception of economics can be found, namely, the praxeological conception that is by and large Mises'. Kirzner still adheres to subjectivism, and he still believes in purposefulness. However, I have been unable to find in his more recent publications[36] anything that resembles a conception of economics or of economic methodology, or some element of these, including a definition of economics, opinions concerning the relationship with applied economics and with the other social sciences and the relevance of empirical data, ideas about how to derive premises and so on. The unequivocal abandonment of praxeology and the development of a solid epistemological and methodological alternative would contribute to the further development of Kirzner's valuable ideas on entrepreneurship and market processes.

NOTES

1 Several authors, such as W. Duncan Reekie (1984: ix and 188) and H. Barreto (1986: 529) explicitly acknowledge Kirzner's 'leadership' of the latest generation of Austrian economists.

2 The text immediately preceding this quotation (from the introductory chapter to the *Economic Point of View*) runs as follows: 'It will be seen in subsequent chapters that the classification of definitions of the economic point of view into Types A and B is far from an exhaustive one. The voluminous literature since the turn of the century dealing with the problem of definition reveals, indeed, the entire range of formulations that are discussed in this essay. Nevertheless, it remains true that the most outstanding development . . .' (Kirzner 1960: 17). Kirzner arranged the material for his book in a *topical*, rather than a *chronological*, manner. Thus, in each of the 'subsequent chapters' Kirzner refers to the history of a particular category of conceptions of 'the economic' as its subject matter. Chapters 2, 6 and 7, respectively, are about Types A and B definitions, and the praxeological conception of economics. Some, but not all, of the approaches set forth in Chapters 3, 4 and 5, can be subsumed under Types A and B.

3 In the German edition of Mises (1949), which appeared in the 1930s, Mises first used the term *praxeology*.

4 In fact, *The Economic Point of View* was in part based on the doctoral dissertation Kirzner had written under the guidance of Mises.

5 Kirzner here refers to V.C. Walsh (1970: 17).

6 The second part of this definition can be found in Yeager (1987: 22). However, Yeager refrains from attempting to define 'subjectivism' (*ibid.*: 1).

7 Although Kirzner seeks to adhere to this principle throughout his works, he has himself described *subjectivism* rather differently: 'The foundation of subjectivism in the analysis of social phenomena consists, of course, in the insight that these phenomena are generated by deliberate, purposeful human action' (Kirzner 1979: 151). Here, subjectivism is being confused with praxeology. As we will see, 'purposeful human action' is the foundation of praxeology.

8 Most recently in Kirzner (1992: 121).

9 For example Rothbard (1976: 19): 'Praxeology is the distinctive methodology of the Austrian school', and Reekie (1984: 27–32).

10 Kirzner uses the term *history* in the narrower meaning. His readership probably is more familiar with – namely, excluding anthropology, psychology and some other disciplines.

11 Thus, Kirzner rightly considers anthropology and psychology (see previous note) incapable of yielding general laws akin to the laws of the natural sciences.

12 Kirzner mostly uses 'economics' as a shorthand for economic *theory*, except in those cases where he explicitly refers to *applied* economics or the like.

13 Probably Rothbard here adds the adjective *verbal* because he does not consider the use of economic models compatible with praxeology; see next paragraph.

14 'The uncertainty of the future is already implied in the very notion of action. That man acts and that the future is uncertain are by no means two independent matters. They are only two different modes of establishing one thing . . . If man knew the future, he would not have to choose and would not act. He would be like an automaton, reacting to stimuli without any will of his own' (Mises 1949: 105).

15 The reader is referred to Mises' (1949: 131–133) laborious defense of the labour disutility axiom.

16 The only exception to this rule is Kirzner's (1963) *Market Theory and the Price System*, which, however, is intended as an intermediate microeconomics textbook. Since mainstream economics involves models and mathematics, students must get acquainted with it. Furthermore, in this book Kirzner uses (simple) mathematics in order to describe equilibrium conditions that are normally not met in reality (as he explains in the accompanying text). One reason for Kirzner to include mathematics is that a *tendency* towards equilibrium is important to his theory.

17 See Rothbard's quotation in the previous paragraph.

18 For example, psychology necessarily involves reference to empirical facts. Therefore, if the premises are based on psychological theory, indirect reference to empirical facts cannot be avoided.

19 For example, as recently as 1981 Robbins remarked: 'our explanations must to some extent be *teleological*. This is not to argue with von Mises and some of his followers that we must regard human action, if not purely vegetative, as at all times *rational* in the sense that, given belief in the range of technical knowledge available to individuals or collections of individuals action must be *consistent*. I confess that I have never been able to understand this contention.' Quoted by Reekie (1984: 28).

20 'Rationality [or purposefulness] . . . consists . . . in the consistent pursuit of one's own purposes' (Kirzner 1960: 165). Hence, *purposefulness* means 'consistency between behavior and purposes'. However, further exegesis is necessary to find out what these 'purposes' are. If Kirzner talks about a man 'who has . . . budgeted all his money for other, more highly valued purposes' (see the 'Rhine wine' case, below), 'purposes' obviously designates 'things on which the man's money (or any other resources he possesses) can be spent'. But if we substitute this formula for 'purposes' in the phrase 'consistent pursuit of one's own purposes', we obtain a meaningless statement. This riddle is solved if we realize that 'one's own purposes' is a shorthand for 'one's own *more highly valued* purposes'. Thus, the most concise definition of Kirzner's *purposefulness* is 'consistency between preferences and behavior'.

21 The 'Rhine wine' case originates from the Pareto-Croce correspondence at the turn of the century. In 1945, Tagliacozzo published on the issue. Kirzner (1960: 169–172) supports the latter's views on the nature of economics and rationality.

22 The 'best interests' are, at least 'latently', already 'present' in the subject's psyche. In other words, the subjects themselves already '*know*' what their 'true' interests are, but in order to be *fully conscious* of them, they must be in a state of sufficient mental clarity.

23 The praxeological term 'unconscious' should not be confused with the psychoanalytical terms 'unconscious' and 'subconscious' (Mises 1949: 12).

24 See Kirzner (1973: 137–140). 'The Product as an Economic Variable' in fact is the title of a 1953 essay by E.H. Chamberlin. Kirzner criticizes Chamberlin, however, for neglecting the importance of entrepreneurial alertness and the competitive-entrepreneurial process to the analysis of product change (*ibid.*: 140).

25 Although Kirzner does not use the terms 'first-order' and 'higher-order' knowledge, the following account is a faithful representation of this important aspect of Kirzner's concept of the entrepreneurial element in decision-making.

26 Witteloostuijn (1988: 302, n. 8) calls this 'the infinite regress problem'.

27 A more precise formulation is 'opportunities *and threats*'.

28 For example, ignorance concerning current prices should not be confused with uncertainty. Once obtained, such information is certain. Buchanan and Pierro (1980: 695) have coined an adequate term for this type of ignorance: *potential cognitive certainty*.

29 Information about uncertain events is incomplete by definition; therefore the expression '*elements* of information' is used. One may speak, however, of *maximal* information concerning an uncertain event. Such information, for example, data pertaining to future prices (such as movements in key cost or demand indicators), may of course be highly valuable; a haphazard gambler and a well-informed speculator are as different as night and day.

30 Kirzner does not use the term *intuition*, but he clearly refers to it when he talks of entrepreneurs having 'hunches' (Kirzner 1979: 167–168; 1985: 22).

31 'A person walks along a street and sees a store with signs offering to sell apples for one dollar; but, perhaps thinking of other things, he enters a second store where he pays two dollars for identical apples. He may have seen the signs in the first store, but his perception of them was so weak as to mean that, when he paid two dollars in the second store he did not, in fact, know that he was rejecting a preferred opportunity for one less preferred . . . *There is nothing in purposeful action that by itself guarantees that every available opportunity must be instantaneously perceived*' (Kirzner 1978: 129–130).

32 To be precise, profit accrual is interpreted to be an element of Kirzner's narrower (see above) definition of entrepreneurship. There cannot be found in Kirzner's work a *definition* of entrepreneurship in the sense of one particular concise statement of the meaning of the word. In order to find out what Kirzner means, elements from various publications must be combined.

33 The price discrepancies to which Kirzner refers include discrepancies between input prices and output prices in possible modes of production. This means that Kirzner uses the term 'price discrepancy' as a synonym for 'profit opportunity'.

34 However, entrepreneurs of course may err in assessing the 'underlying realities'. Kirzner even mentions the following problem. Entrepreneur A's future scenario is based on a correct assessment of 'underlying realities', for example the scarcity of some resource. Part of A's future scenario is their anticipation of the correct reaction of entrepreneur B to those underlying realities. A decides on some investment, based on their 'correct' assessment. Entrepreneur B, however, does not assess those same realities correctly, and makes an investment decision based on this 'wrong' assessment. The result may be that A's scenario is rendered invalid (Kirzner 1992: 29–34). This implies a *fortiori* that Kirzner has to rely on the assumption that entrepreneurs are able to assess the 'underlying realities' correctly.

35 Radical subjectivists would probably argue that Kirzner's acknowledgement of the importance of ignorance, uncertainty, error, creativity and change, is inconsistent with the postulated overall equilibrating tendency.

36 By 'recent' I mean from 1973 onwards. In Kirzner's (1976) paper 'On the Method of Austrian Economics', he proposes to amend the 'second basic tenet of Austrian methodology'. However, Kirzner does not say *how* he wants to amend it; all he says is that the 'second basic tenet' is inadequate if Hayekian learning is to be included into theory.

REFERENCES

Barreto, H. (1986) Review of Kirzner (1985), *Southern Economic Journal* 53: 529–530.

Buchanan, J. M. and A. di Pierro (1980) 'Cognition, Choice, and Entrepreneurship', *Southern Economic Journal* 46: 693–701.

Dolan, E. G. (ed.) (1976) *The Foundations of Modern Austrian Economics*, Kansas City: Sheed & Ward.

Garrison, R. W. (1982) 'Austrian Economics as the Middle Ground: Comment on Loasby', in Kirzner (1982), ch. 11.

High, J. (1982) 'Alertness and Judgment: Comment on Kirzner', in Kirzner (1982), ch. 13.

Kirzner, I.M. (1960) *The Economic Point of View; An Essay in the History of Economic Thought*, 2nd edn (1976), edited with an introduction by L.S. Moss, Kansas City: Sheed & Ward.

Kirzner, I.M. (1963) *Market Theory and the Price System*, Princeton, New Jersey: Van Nostrand.

Kirzner, I.M. (1971) 'Entrepreneurship and the Market Approach to Development; in F.A. Harper (ed.) *Toward Liberty: Essays in Honor of Mises*, Menlo Park, California: Institute for Humane Studies, ch. 7.

Kirzner, I.M. (1973) *Competition and Entrepreneurship*, Chicago & London: University of Chicago Press.

Kirzner, I.M. (1976) 'On the Method of Austrian Economics', in Dolan (1976), 40–51. Reprinted in Littlechild (1990), ch. 30.

Kirzner, I.M. (1978) 'Economics and Error', in L.M. Spadaro (ed.) *New Directions in Austrian Economics*, Kansas City: Sheed Andrews and McMeel. Reprinted in Kirzner (1979), ch. 8.

Kirzner, I.M. (1979) *Perception, Opportunity and Profit: Studies in the Theory of Entrepreneurship*, Chicago & London: University of Chicago Press.

Kirzner, I.M. (1980) 'The Primacy of Entrepreneurial Discovery', in A. Seldon (ed.) *The Prime Mover of Progress: The Entrepreneur in Capitalism and Socialism.* Reprinted in Kirzner (1985), ch. 2.

Kirzner, I.M. (ed.)(1982) *Method, Process, and Austrian Economics: Essays in Honor of Ludwig Von Mises*, Lexington (Massachusetts): D.C. Heath & Co.

Kirzner, I.M. (1983) 'Entrepreneurship and the Future of Capitalism', in Jules A. Backman (ed.) (1983) *Entrepreneurship and the Outlook for America*, New York & London: Macmillan. Reprinted in Kirzner (1985), ch. 7.

Kirzner, I.M. (1984): 'Economic Planning and the Knowledge Problem', *Cato Journal* 4: 407–425. Reprinted in Kirzner (1992).

Kirzner, I.M. (1984a) 'The Entrepreneurial Process', in Calvin A. Kent (ed.) (1984) *The Environment for Entrepreneurship*, Lexington, Massachusetts: D.C. Heath & Co. Reprinted in Kirzner (1985), ch. 4.

Kirzner, I.M. (1985) *Discovery and the Capitalist Process*, Chicago & London: University of Chicago Press.

Kirzner, I.M. (1986) 'Ludwig von Mises and Friedrich von Hayek: The Modern Extension of Austrian Subjectivism', in N. Leser (ed.) *Die Wiener Schule der Nationalökonomie*, Vienna: Hermann Böhlau. Reprinted in Kirzner (1992), ch. 7.

Kirzner, I.M. (1990a) 'Knowledge Problems and Their Solutions: Some Relevant Solutions', in Kirzner (1992) ch.10. Originally published in the journal *Cultural Dynamics.*

Kirzner, I.M. (1990b) 'Self-interest and the New Bashing of Economics: A Fresh Opportunity in the Perennial Debate?' in Kirzner (1992), ch. 12. Originally published in *Critical Review* 4(1–2) (Winter–Spring).

Kirzner, I.M. (1992) *The Meaning of Market Process: Essays in the Development of Modern Austrian Economics*, London & New York: Routledge.

Littlechild, S. (ed.) (1990) *Austrian Economics* (3 vols), Aldershot (UK) and Brookfield (Vermont): Edward Elgar.

Mises, L. von (1933) *Epistemological Problems of Economics* (first English edn 1960, first German edn 1933), foreword by L.M. Lachmann, New York and London: New York University Press.

Mises, L. von (1949) *Human Action: A Treatise on Economics*, 3rd revised edn (first English edn 1949), Chicago: Contemporary Books/Henry Regnery.

Mises, L. von (1957) *Theory and History*, New Haven, Connecticut: Yale University Press.

Mises, L. von (1962) *The Ultimate Foundation of Economic Science: An Essay on Method*, 2nd edn with a foreword by I.M. Kirzner (first edn 1962). Kansas City: Sheed Andrews & McMeel.

Reekie, W.D. (1984) *Markets, Entrepreneurs, and Liberty: An Austrian View of Capitalism*, Brighton: Harvester Wheatsheaf.

Robbins, L. (1935) *An Essay on the Nature and Significance of Economic Science*, 2nd edn (1st edn 1932), London: Macmillan.

Rothbard, M.N. (1976) 'Praxeology: The Methodology of Austrian Economics', in Dolan (1976), 19–39.

Walsh, V.C. (1970) *Introduction to Contemporary Micro-economics*, New York: McGraw Hill.

Witteloostuijn, A. van (1988) 'Maximising and Satisficing: Opposite or Equivalent Concepts?', *Journal of Economic Psychology* 9: 289–313.

Wubben, E.F.M. (1992) 'Austrian Economics and Uncertainty: On a Non-Deterministic but Non-Haphazard Future', Contribution to the European Conference on Austrian Economics of April 1992; see the Conference Collection of Papers *History and Relevance of the Austrian School of Economics*, Maastricht, The Netherlands: University of Limburg.

Yeager, L.B. (1987) 'Why Subjectivism?', *Review of Austrian Economics* 1: 5–29.

11

ON THE NON-NEUTRALITY OF MATHEMATICAL FORMALIZATION: AUSTRIAN VS. NEW CLASSICAL BUSINESS CYCLE THEORIES

*Rudy van Zijp and Hans Visser**

INTRODUCTION

Presumably the main characteristic of post-war (macro)economics has been its use of mathematics. In this sense one might agree with Lucas and Sargent's (1978: 296) claim that '[t]he Keynesian Revolution was . . . a revolution in method'. Courses in mathematics have therefore become an important part of the training of any economist who wants to master their subject in a more than perfunctory manner. Hence the question about the usefulness and appropriateness of mathematical formalization seems to be rather archaic, and it is tempting to conclude that the question is not worth raising.[1] Nevertheless, it has been raised several times in the post-war era.

Almost forty years ago Novick (1954: 357) argued that '[t]he current use of mathematical language in social science is largely a form of intellectual shorthand and in no way demonstrates that the methods heretofore so successful in the physical sciences have suddenly become adaptable to the social sciences'. He even went so far as to label 'the present efforts to apply mathematics in economics and the social sciences as simply an addition to the esoterica of the sciences' (p. 358). This view received severe criticism from a number of famous contemporaries, such as Paul Samuelson (1954), Lawrence Klein (1954), James Duesenberry (1954), Jan Tinbergen (1954), Tjalling Koopmans (1954), and Robert Solow (1991). They advanced that formalization is not merely pursued for cosmetic and esoteric reasons, but that it stimulates scientific progress in economics. The reasoning behind this view was stated most strongly by Solow (1954: 373–374), who argued that 'a large and growing fraction of what is interesting and valuable in the

* The authors wish to thank Jack Birner, Ben Elzas, Harry Garretsen, Willem Keizer and Emiel Wubben for their useful comments on an earlier version of this paper. Of course, the usual disclaimer applies.

economic theory of the last twenty years . . . has been produced by theorists who do at least some of their theorizing in mathematics'. He predicted that '[i]f mathematical techniques continue to produce good economics then . . . long before the appendix has disappeared from the human digestive tract most people will as a matter of course learn some mathematics'. This argument can be restated in the form of a syllogism, which consists of one major and two minor premises. The former holds that the development of any science results in a gradual and cumulative increase in knowledge. The two minor premises state that economics is a science, and that the development of economics has been advanced by increased formalization. The conclusion of the syllogism then is that mathematical formalization *causes* progress in economics.[2] McCloskey (1991: 6) considered this conclusion valid only if it means that formalization 'has brought transparency to many hundreds of economic arguments'. In his view, though, the use of mathematical techniques has gone too far, and nowadays economists (like mathematicians) are inclined to conduct 'a search through the hyperspace of conceivable assumptions' (p. 11). This view thus holds that the problem does not lie with formalization *per se* but rather with the *use* made of it. Consequently, the 'archaic' question posed above is better transformed into the question of what consequences mathematical formalization may (but need not) have for the domain of (economic) analysis. Stated more strongly, is mathematical formalization (non)neutral for this domain?

The present paper is organized as follows. The next section discusses the relationship between mathematical formalization and the introduction of simplifying assumptions. It will list several types of simplifying assumptions, some of which have repercussions for the domain of economic analysis. The remainder of the paper tries to illuminate these repercussions by comparing the respective business cycle theories of two rival research traditions, namely Austrian and New Classical economics. The reason for choosing these traditions is twofold. First, they are related to each other, in that they explain cyclical fluctuations in terms of optimizing behaviour on the part of the economic agents, attributing a crucial role to the incompleteness of information.[3] Second, Austrians and New Classicals differ considerably on the role of mathematical formalization in economics. The former downplay or even reject its usefulness, whereas the latter claim that formalization constitutes the main source of progress in economics. Consequently, their use of mathematical techniques may illustrate the relationship between formalization and the domain of economics. The conclusions of the study are given on pp. 188–189.

MATHEMATICAL FORMALIZATION AND SIMPLIFYING ASSUMPTIONS

Theories apply to a part of reality only. Hence all theories include simplifying assumptions. Following Musgrave (1981), these assumptions may be interpreted in three ways. First, *negligibility assumptions* hold that the variable assumed away is irrelevant for the phenomenon under consideration, in the sense that its influence on the phenomenon is negligible. Obviously, the validity of such an assumption may be tested, at least in principle. Second, *domain assumptions* specify the domain of applicability of the theory. As Musgrave (1981: 381) noted, '[w]hat begins as a negligibility assumption may, when it gets refuted, turn into a domain assumption'. Such a shift must be considered undesirable, because it means that a more testable theory is replaced by a less testable one. The theory thus becomes more protected from falsification. Third, *heuristic assumptions* hold that a particular variable may be relevant, but that *for the moment* it is assumed away. Such assumptions may be regarded as temporary domain assumptions. They are particularly useful in the so-called 'method of successive approximation', which develops a highly complicated theory in successive stages. In each stage the degree of complexity (e.g. the number of variables) is increased.

It may be argued that the process of formalizing a particular theory involves the adoption of *additional* simplifying assumptions. In this regard at least two reasons may be discerned. The one applies to formalization *per se*, whereas the other refers to the particular use made of mathematical techniques. As Katzner (1986: 141) explained, 'formalist analysis usually begins with the specification of variables and relations among them. But before even arriving at this starting gate, considerable abstraction and discipline of thought are required just to be able to accomplish the necessary specifications.' Such abstraction is particularly involved in translating concepts and relations from verbal into mathematical language. Georgescu-Roegen (1971: 43–47) argued that these languages differ, in that verbal language allows for concepts that cannot be translated into mathematics without loss of content. As Katzner (1986: 142) puts it, such *dialectic concepts* are multi-faceted, with some facets overlapping with those of other dialectic concepts. He illustrates this type of concept with the example of the notions of 'democracy' and its negation 'non-democracy'. The question of where democracy ends and non-democracy begins can only be answered arbitrarily, because some facets of 'democracy' overlap with some of 'non-democracy'. This overlap means that the dividing line between the two concepts must be established arbitrarily. In the case of economics, the concept of 'competition' may be more illuminating. It may be considered a dialectical concept because it can be characterized by many facets, such as the number of suppliers and demanders, the nature of the goods under consideration, the occurrence of transaction and information costs, etc. Contrary to dialectical concepts, *arithmomorphic concepts* are single-faceted, so that their boundaries can be sharply delineated. As Katzner's examples 'length' and 'weight' make clear, arithmomorphic concepts can be easily formalized mathematically, whereas dialectical concepts cannot. The translation of concepts from verbal into mathematical language thus involves the extraction of single-faceted concepts from multi-faceted ones. In other words, formalization is possible only if some simplifying assumptions are adopted.

The second reason for adopting simplifying assumptions is related to the particular use made of mathematical techniques. After constructing mathematical models, scientists may want to solve them analytically. However, this is possible only if they introduce some *additional* simplifying assumptions. As Weintraub (1985: 146) points out, the availability of mathematical problem-solving techniques may play an important role in this regard. They may suggest simplifying assumptions which assume away those features of the phenomenon under consideration that cannot be addressed with the available techniques. If these simplifying assumptions are (temporary) domain assumptions, this availability affects the domain of analysis.

The remainder of the paper will be concerned with the second reason for introducing simplifying assumptions. It will give an example of how the availability of the technique of optimization under constraints has led at least some economists to assume away relevant problems that cannot be solved with the aid of this technique. As already explained in the introduction, it will do so by comparing Austrian and New Classical business cycle theories.

THE ANALYSIS OF CANTILLON EFFECTS: AUSTRIAN BUSINESS CYCLE THEORY

Austrian business cycle theory starts from an intertemporal perfect-information general equilibrium, which can be defined as a series of situations in which economic agents have complete information and perfect foresight about preferences and the means of production at every point of time during the planning period (Hayek 1928: 76). Such an equilibrium is maintained if the agents do not make expectational errors (p. 85). However, Austrians recognize that in reality agents do not have complete information, and hence cannot avoid making such errors. In fact, they argue that agents make *similar* expectational errors, suggesting that this similarity follows from the fact that the agents base their actions on signals which as a rule prove reliable (p. 141). The most important signals in this regard are provided by the price system.

Disregarding the fact that Austrian business cycle theory comes in several versions, it can be reconstructed as follows. The theory concentrates on the variable that figures most prominently in investment decisions, namely the interest rate. Austrians adopt Wicksell's (1898) distinction between the natural and the market rate of interest. The former is defined as the long-run equilibrium rate of interest, which reflects the time-preferences of the economic agents. The 'market' (or money) rate of interest is the rate at which the supply of loanable funds equals the demand for loans. It need not equal the natural rate, and thus need not reflect the agents' time-preferences. The difference results from either a change in the natural rate, or a change in the market rate. In both cases, though, the resulting adjustment processes are similar.[4] In what follows, we adopt Austrian practice and concentrate on monetary expansion only. This expansion means that additional money enters the economy on the loan market, reducing the market rate of interest below the natural rate. Consequently, the present value of all investment projects rises, resulting in general overinvestments. The gap between planned savings and planned investment is filled by *forced savings*.[5] This phenomenon follows if the expenditure of entrepreneurs who borrow money to increase production makes prices rise and in that way brings about a reduction in real consumption. If preferences and patterns of expenditure differ between economic agents, forced savings and the implied distribution effects may even bring about a shift in the relevant general equilibrium and hence in the natural rate of interest.[6] Austrians argue that eventually the boom will come to a halt for two reasons. First, when the additional money stops flowing into the economy, entrepreneurs will recognize that they have made expectational errors about the profitability of their investment projects. The ensuing elimination of overinvestments will lead to a fall in the demand for producer goods, which will spread throughout the economy, reducing economic activity. As Wilson (1940) pointed out, though, this recession is by no means inevitable, because it can be postponed by continuing to increase the money supply.[7] This means that the upper turning point still has to be explained. Therefore, Austrians (and Hayek in particular) turned to a second effect of the initial fall in the market rate of interest.

As O'Driscoll and Rizzo (1985: 205) showed, the fall in the market rate of interest does not affect all projects in the same degree. That is, it does not only affect the volume of investment but also its composition. Before discussing this effect, we must first discuss the framework in which it takes place. Following Menger (1871: 8–10), capital goods can be classified according to the functions they perform in the process of production, using their 'remoteness' from consumption as a criterion for classification. Consumer goods are called 'goods of the first order', capital goods which are used in the production of these first-order goods are called second-order goods, capital goods which produce second-order goods are called third-order goods, and so forth. Hence there is a vertical relationship between *heterogeneous* capital goods. Analogously, it is possible to distinguish stages of production which can be classified in a manner similar to that of capital goods. Jointly, these stages form a *vertical* structure of production, in which production takes place in *successive* stages, so that production in a given stage depends on production in a higher-order stage.

The influence of the fall in the market rate of interest on the structure of production can now be explained as follows. This fall will affect different orders of goods differently. If entrepreneurs mistakenly interpret the fall in the market rate of interest as reflecting a fall in the natural rate, they will conclude that the agents' time-preferences have decreased. This means that they expect current consumption demand to fall and future consumption demand to rise. It will then appear to be more profitable to invest in productive activities that yield consumption output in the more distant future. In other words, the present value of investment projects that involve higher-order goods has increased, whereas that of others has decreased. This induces entrepreneurs to reallocate capital from the lower to the higher stages of production. In Austrian language, the structure of production is 'lengthened' (or has become more 'roundabout'). However, eventually this process of lengthening will be checked by a shortage of resources. Hayek (1939: 11) argued that during the later stages of the boom 'the prices of consumer goods do as a rule rise and real wages fall'.[8] The rise in consumer prices increases the profit margins on these goods, and hence induces entrepreneurs to reallocate capital from the production of capital goods to that of consumer goods. The fall in real wages makes 'shorter' methods of production more profitable, so that there will be a tendency to use more labour with the existing machinery (by working overtime, double shifts, etc.), and to invest in less expensive, less labour-saving or less durable machinery. Hayek argued that the implied decrease in the demand for capital goods will become so strong as to turn the boom into a recession. This effect is called the *Ricardo effect*.[9] During the recession entrepreneurs will correct their investment errors by reallocating their capital from higher- to lower-order goods.[10] The recession ends either because of an increase in the supply of money, or because of the reverse operation of this so-called Ricardo effect.

The above suggests that Hayek's business cycle theory contains at least two unique features. First, it adopts the Mengerian framework of the structure of production. This means that capital goods are heterogeneous, and that they stand in a vertical relationship to each other, in which a time dimension is involved. Second, the theory incorporates Cantillon effects, in the sense that an increase in the supply of money leads to redistributions between the owners of different factors of production and between the entrepreneurs in different stages of production.[11] As Foss (1990: 6, italics in original) pointed out, 'Hayek's argument is . . . dependent . . . on the time path of real factor incomes relative to the linear representation of productive activities [i.e. the vertical structure of production] and the lags *this* implies.' It takes time before the additional money is spread out evenly throughout the economy.[12] The ensuing distortion of the structure of relative prices follows from the fact that economic agents differ from each other. These differences may concern: (a) their utility functions, (b) their abilities to gather information (and hence their information sets), (c) their expectations formation functions, and/or (d) their productive activities (i.e. the order of goods that they produce). In his work on business cycles, Hayek did not explicitly discuss the heterogeneity of the first three issues, but merely stressed the fourth. The heterogeneity of production goods and productive activities accounts for the *mal*investments and the ensuing distortion of the structure of production. In his later work, Hayek increasingly recognized the importance of the dispersion of knowledge, which implies heterogeneity of information as well as expectations.

The above description of Austrian business cycle theory reflects the view that social life is extremely complex. Unfortunately, though, the Austrian attempt to do justice to this complexity has rendered the theory somewhat ambiguous: too much seems to be possible, in the sense that the theory does not yield definite conclusions and predictions. This ambiguity may even be regarded as the main reason for a debate between Hayek and his neoclassical opponents on what was called the Ricardo effect. In the 1940s the logical validity of this effect was questioned. The ensuing debate did not lead to conclusive results, although neoclassical economics was generally considered victorious. The debate could perhaps have been avoided if Hayek had been able to formalize his theory. However, it should also be noted that the mathematical techniques available at the time would have transformed his attempt to give a dynamic analysis of the effects of monetary disturbances into an exercise of comparative statics. And such an exercise was precisely what he tried to avoid. In other words, mathematical formalization would have unduly restricted the domain of his analysis.

Generally speaking, Austrians thus refuse to adopt simplifying assumptions that merely serve to facilitate mathematical formalization. Instead, they stress the complexity of social life. In contrast, New Classicals argue that economic theories should be formulated as mathematical models. These models may be called 'analogue models', because they must mimic the behaviour of the time-series of those variables that are considered most relevant for the phenomenon to be explained. New Classical economists thereby claim that mathematical formalization provides one of the main sources of scientific progress, if not the most important one. Their business cycle theory makes clear, though, that the availability of mathematical techniques, and particularly the technique of optimizing under constraints, may affect the domain of economics.

THE ELIMINATION OF CANTILLON EFFECTS: NEW CLASSICAL BUSINESS CYCLE THEORY

New Classical Economics (NCE) started as an attempt to formalize Friedman's (1968) and Phelps' (1967) explanation of the relationship between the rate of inflation and (the rate of change of) the unemployment rate, the so-called Phillips curve.[13] This explanation adopts the Natural Rate Hypothesis (NRH), according to which the economy will tend towards its 'natural rate of output' or 'natural rate of unemployment'.[14] The resulting full-information general equilibrium is called the *Natural Rate Equilibrium* (NRE). Given the absence of money illusion on the part of the economic agents, it implies that there is no relationship between real and purely monetary variables, so that money is neutral in the comparative-static sense.[15] However, this clearly conflicts with the Phillips curve, which does reflect such a relationship. Friedman and Phelps had argued that deviations of the NRE reflect expectational errors, due to incomplete information. Phelps (1970) additionally suggested that this incompleteness of information could be explained in a general-equilibrium framework in which local markets are spatially and informationally separated. The NCE elaborated this suggestion.

New Classicals adopt at least four crucial assumptions. First, economic agents are considered to be price-takers. A Walrasian *tâtonnement* process is assumed to ensure perfect price flexibility and hence continuous market-clearing. Second, aggregate real output is formulated as the 'Lucas supply function'. This function holds that deviations from the NRE can only result from unanticipated nominal price changes and hence from expectational errors. However, these errors are rational in the sense that they only differ randomly from actual realizations of economic variables. This Rational Expectations Hypothesis (REH) is the third assumption. The fourth assumption is that economic agents have incomplete information about relevant economic variables.

The NCE explains expectational errors in terms of exogenous shocks, which are either real or monetary in nature. The shocks are reflected in the prices that agents observe. Given the fourth (informational) assumption, agents must act on the basis of incomplete information. This means that they will make expectational errors. According to the REH, rational economic agents do not make systematic expectational errors, because such errors are easily detectable. The problem then arises of how unsystematic, serially uncorrelated shocks can account for the persistence that characterizes the economic data over the business cycle. The NCE solves this problem by adopting a solution which had already been given in the 1930s. Slutzky (1937) and Frisch (1933) had already shown that random shocks could lead to serially correlated movements of the variables in the system under consideration, due to some propagation mechanism. Thus, the crucial distinction, as Lucas and Sargent (1978: 313) noted, is that between *impulses* and *propagation mechanisms*. The latter ensure that serially uncorrelated disturbances will have serially correlated effects. Instances of such mechanisms have been provided by Lucas (1975), Blinder and Fischer (1981) and Kydland and Prescott (1980), among others. They give what Barro (1981b: 48) called *adjustment costs explanations* of persistence, whereby persistence is explained in terms of *friction* in the economic system.

The above description of New Classical business cycle theory already indicates that New Classicals formulate their views as mathematical models. However, mathematical formalization usually involves the introduction of additional simplifying assumptions, at least when the models are supposed to be analytically solvable. These assumptions will depend on the modelling strategy followed. New Classicals use two such strategies, namely the *representative agent approach* and the *islands approach*.

The representative agent approach defines the *representative agent* as the *mathematical* mean of the (sub)system as a whole.[16] This means that the concept is used as a hypostatization of this system.[17] As Hoover (1988: 242) observed, this means that this approach treats aggregates and index numbers as if they obey the principles of microeconomics. Its analysis is therefore restricted to the mathematical mean. Deviations from this mean are accounted for by adding a probability distribution. The resulting explanation of business cycles can be formulated as follows. Consider the following Lucas supply function:

$$y_t = z + \alpha\,(1 - \beta)\,(p_t - p_t^e) \qquad (11.1)$$

in which y is the actual aggregated level of real output, z is the 'natural rate of output', p_t is the actual general price level, p_t^e is the expected general price level, α is a parameter indicating the extent to which a deviation of p_t^e from p_t influences y_t, and β is a parameter indicating that the higher the volatility of changes in p_t the less output differs from its natural rate. The function shows that an unanticipated change in the general price level will induce representative agents to change their output. Given the New Classical assumption of comparative-static neutrality of money, this indicates that unanticipated changes in the money supply can bring actual output above its natural rate (and equivalently actual unemployment below its natural rate). In this case, the incompleteness of information ensures that the representative agent makes an expectational error about the nature of the change in the actual general price level, believing that it reflects real instead of monetary changes in the economy. However, agents will adjust their actions as soon as the correct information becomes available. This does not mean, though, that the economy immediately returns to its new NRE, because propagation mechanisms may hamper this adjustment by transmitting the effects of the random expectational errors to subsequent periods. This transmission yields a business cycle.

Incomplete information may thus explain why monetary changes have real effects. The representative agent's information set therefore plays a crucial role in the New Classical approach under consideration.[18] Given this set, the representative agent, by definition, forms rational expectations which equal the mathematical mean of the aggregate expectations, albeit in a probabilistic sense. That is, the 'representative agent approach' assumes away systematic differences between economic agents. This may be based on the argument that the expectational deviations will cancel out, presumably due to the 'Law of Large Numbers'.[19] This 'law' is a statistical regularity which applies only if the elements of the population under consideration belong to the same 'class', i.e. if they do not differ from each other in any relevant aspect. The assumption that the agents are identical will be called the *homogeneity postulate*. It is adopted in New Classical 'representative agent models', so that these models concentrate on the magnitude of aggregates, disregarding (changes in) their composition. This implies that redistributions between economic agents are considered to be irrelevant in the explanation of industrial fluctuations. This restriction of the domain of the NCE could be circumvented by introducing several 'representative agents'. This strategy is adopted in the 'islands approach'. The islands approach can be regarded as a more sophisticated version of the 'representative agent approach'. It uses Phelps' (1970) suggestion that markets can be seen as islands. In particular, it was adopted by Lucas (1972, 1975), Lucas and Prescott (1974) and Barro (1976, 1980). These models consider an economy in which a single output is produced, which must be divided between private consumption, government consumption and next period's capital. The population consists of identical households, so that their utility functions do not differ. The conjunction of these two assumptions implies that economic agents are also identical with respect to their productive activities. However, this does not mean that there are no differences at all between them. As Lucas (1975: 180) stated, the 'islands' or markets are 'imperfectly linked both physically and informationally', so that information is assumed to be homogeneous across agents in a given market, but heterogeneous across markets.[20] The 'island approach' thus assumes that economic agents only differ from each other as regards their information sets. Hence, it disregards 'intra-market' distributional effects. But what about the study of such effects *between* markets?

As was stated above, New Classical business cycle theory explains industrial fluctuations in terms of expectational errors. These errors are caused by discrepancies between changes in the relative prices and in the general price level. That is, the economic agents must determine how much of a given change in their respective local prices must be attributed to a change in the general price level, and how much of the change in local prices reflects changes in real factors. Agents must therefore form expectations about the *difference* between their local price level and the general (global) price level. Given the assumption of complete local and incomplete global information, the agents' information sets include $p_t(z)$ but not p_t. They must then form expectations about the latter, so that their output decision can be described as follows:

$$y_t(z) = z + \alpha\,(1 - \beta)\,(p_t\,(z) - p_t^e) \tag{11.2}$$

where the subscripts denote the time period under consideration, and z is an index of location. Since expectations are Muth-rational, agents are assumed to know the 'true' probability distribution of p_t^e and hence the difference between $p_t(z)$ and p_t^e. According to Pesaran (1989: 57), this means that the problem of heterogeneity of information across markets is circumvented. After all, the relevant decision variable is $d_t(z) = p_t(z) - p_t$, and all agents are assumed to know its 'true' distribution. As there can only be one 'true' distribution, this means that their respective information sets do not differ in any *relevant* (i.e. systematic) manner.[21] Information about the relevant decision variable turns out to be homogeneous across markets. The problem of the heterogeneity of information across markets in the 'islands models' is thus circumvented by assuming that all economic agents know the 'true' probability distribution of $d_t(z)$.

In conclusion, the 'islands approach' and the 'representative agent approach' assume that economic agents do *not* differ with respect to their utility functions, their abilities to gather information (and hence their relevant information sets), their expectations formation functions (and, given the information sets, their expectations) and their productive activities. This means that distribution effects, such as Cantillon effects, cannot be analysed. Their elimination from the domain of economics is the price to be paid by New Classicals for their heuristic prescription to translate economic theory into analogue models that can be solved mathematically using the technique of optimizing under constraints.

CONCLUSIONS

According to Blaug (1962: 155), 'the Cantillon effect . . . denies "the homogeneity postulate" by asserting that changes in prices produced by cash injections vary with the nature of the injection and, moreover, that changes in absolute prices are almost always associated with alterations in relative prices'. Our analysis allows for a more explicit formulation of this homogeneity postulate. In particular, New Classicals assume that agents are homogeneous with respect to (a) the utility functions, (b) the abilities to gather information (and hence the information sets), (c) the expectations formation processes (and, given (b), the expectations) and (d) their productive activities (i.e. the order of goods they produce). These assumptions reflect that New Classical business cycle theory explains cyclical fluctuations in terms of aggregate variables, thereby implying that distributional effects do not play an important role. In contrast, Hayekian business cycle theory also incorporates changes in the composition of aggregate variables. It stresses the complexity of social reality, but in doing so it completely surrenders to the impossibility of modelling the economy in full.[22] Hayek's business cycle theory allows for the inclusion of Cantillon effects and it does so at the cost of mathematical rigour. In contrast, the NCE attempts to build analogue models which are analytically solvable. In doing so it eliminates Cantillon and other distribution effects from its domain. As a result, the New Classical heuristic prescription of mathematical formalization is non-neutral, in the sense that its use of mathematical techniques, and particularly of the technique of optimization under constraints, restricts the domain of economics.

NOTES

1 Following Katzner (1991: 18), formalization is defined as 'the development and analysis of relations among variables that constitute part (or all) of an economic model'. As he noted, '[i]t is not necessary that these relations be expressed in mathematical form'. In turn, mathematization can be defined as formalization in mathematical terms. We shall restrict our analysis to the latter type of formalization.

2 Caldwell (1991: 28) himself restated the argument somewhat differently, in the sense that his second minor premise holds that the development of economics has been *accompanied* by increased formalization. However, Solow's statement that mathematical techniques *produce* good economics suggests a causal relation between these techniques and the quality of economics.

3 This is not to say, of course, that they are variations on a theme (see Van Zijp 1993).

4 Austrians usually argue that real disturbances alter the relevant intertemporal equilibrium and that the resulting adjustment process constitutes a movement towards that equilibrium. In their view, such equilibrating processes differ from business cycles, in the sense that the latter may occur, even if the relevant equilibrium would remain unchanged. That is, Austrian business cycle theory holds that, by definition, business cycles are caused by monetary expansion.

5 For a history of the notion of forced savings, see Hayek (1932), Viner (1964: 187–197) and Humphrey (1991: 9–11).

6 It is interesting to note that this ties in with modern analyses of 'hysteresis', or the phenomenon that deviations from an equilibrium growth path change the equilibrium path itself. This emphasis on the deviations-amplifying tendencies of shocks rather than the stability of any growth path can also be found in new developments in economic theory, such as 'endogenous growth theory' (see FitzGerald Scott 1989, Romer 1986 and Lucas 1988 and 'chaos theory' (see Butler 1990 and Kelsey 1990).

7 Hayek (1933d: 180) considered this possibility very unlikely.

8 He defined the real wage rate as the ratio of the money wage rate and the prices of the consumer goods produced by the labour under consideration (1939: 8).

9 This effect derives its name from Ricardo's (1817:ch. I, sec. V, 26ff.) statement that 'with every rise in the price of labour, new temptations are offered to the use of machinery'. It is designed to show that the boom will come to an end

even if the market rate of interest were to remain constant. Hayek (1931) had already shown that the boom would cease in a situation in which the market rate of interest was perfectly flexible.

10 It should be noted that the Ricardo effect assumes that entrepreneurs expect the relatively higher prices of consumer goods and the relatively lower real wages to persist for a period of time that is long enough to make it worthwhile to change their methods of production. Hayek (1939: 16–18) acknowledged this. Moreover, he also addressed the case in which entrepreneurs expect that the prices of consumer goods continue to rise. This will merely reinforce the effect, due to the continuing fall in real wages.

11 Cantillon (1755: part 2, ch. 10) explained that money that enters into circulation through money lenders brings with it a lowering of the rate of interest, while money that enters into circulation through consumptive expenditure by the rich makes the rate of interest rise, because the producers of consumer goods face an increase in the demand and have to borrow money in order to increase production. In the latter case, the phenomenon of forced savings will occur (see above).

12 In order to clarify his views Hayek (1969: 281) compared a situation of continuous credit creation to a situation in which a viscous liquid, such as honey (read: money), is poured into a vessel (the economy): 'if the stream hits the surface at one point, a little mound will form there from which the additional matter will slowly spread outward'. This analogy reflects that there is no such thing as 'helicopter money'. It leaves the question unanswered as to why the liquid is viscous (i.e. why it takes so long for the additional money to spread throughout the economy).

13 The main new classical proponents are Robert Lucas, Jr., Thomas Sargent, Neil Wallace, Robert Barro, Edward Prescott and Finn Kydland.

14 As Maddock (1979: 158, n. 4) observed, '[i]t is quite common in this [i.e. new classical] literature to switch back and forth between income and unemployment by replacing log unemployment for log income minus log trend income'.

15 For instance, see Sargent and Wallace (1975: 221–224). For a more general discussion of monetary neutrality, see Visser (1971, 1974).

16 For instance, Lucas and Rapping (1969: 25) deflate the aggregate labour supply function by an index of the number of households. Lucas (1972: 68) assumes that each period N identical individuals are born who each supply n units of labour which yield n units of output. Sargent (1972; 1973; 1976) uses aggregates only. His work builds on the microfoundations as provided by Lucas.

17 This was already stressed by Runde and Torr (1985: 217), who argued that the rational expectations approach (i.e. the NCE) does not analyse individual, but rather the market's, behaviour. In a general-equilibrium analysis this means that the representative individual is merely another way of depicting the system as a whole.

18 Lucas (1987: 94) emphasized this property of the NCE when discussing the (New-) Keynesian assumption that nominal prices are rigid because of some form of collective bargaining. He objected that '[t]he central issue for a theory of nominal price rigidity . . . is not the nature of the game agents are assumed to be engaged in, but rather the *information* agents are assumed to have about the state of the system at each date'.

19 Haltiwanger and Waldman (1989) argue that this will only hold under very special circumstances which concern the nature and intensity of the interrelations between the actions of the individuals. They distinguish two types of

interrelations, namely *congestion* and *synergism*. The former applies when the incentive for agent *i* to engage in an activity will be lower if the number of participants is higher. In the case of *synergism* the reverse holds. Agent *i*'s costs and benefits of participating in an activity can therefore be modelled as a function of the number of participants. Their analysis comes to the conclusion that '[o]nly under very special conditions do standard [i.e. microtype] rational expectations and aggregate rational expectations yield equivalent results' (p. 631). It turns out that '[t]he size of the difference [between the two equilibria] will be larger (i) the larger is the divergence in expectations under aggregate rational expectations, and (ii) the more synergistic is the environment' (p. 631). This means that new classicals implicitly assume that there is no congestion or synergism. The number of participants does not influence the individuals' cost–benefit analysis.

20 According to Pesaran (1989: 57), this feature follows from the New Classical assumption that '[a]ll firms [or individuals] observe current equilibrium prices in their local markets'. Such prices clear the market under consideration, thus conveying all information on that market. As on a given market individuals derive their information from observing the same equilibrium price, they will have identical information. That is, information will be homogeneous on that market, but heterogeneous across markets.

21 For instance, Barro (1976: 85) explicitly assumed that 'all markets have the same *ex ante* distribution of price'.

22 This emphasis is consistent with the Austrian view that economic agents differ from each other in relevant aspects. These differences may even concern the 'models' that agents use.

REFERENCES

Barro, R.J. (1976) 'Rational Expectations and the Role of Monetary Policy', *Journal of Monetary Economics* 2: 1–32. Reprinted in Barro (1981a), 79–110.

Barro, R.J. (1980) 'A Capital Market in an Equilibrium Business Cycle Model', *Econometrica* 48: 1393–1417. Reprinted in Barro (1981a), 111–136.

Barro, R.J. (1981a) *Money, Expectations, and Business Cycles*, New York: Academic Press.

Barro, R.J. (1981b) 'The equilibrium approach to business cycles', in Barro (1981a), 41–78.

Blaug, M. (1962) *Economic Theory in Retrospect*, Cambridge: Cambridge University Press, 1990.

Blinder, A.S., and S. Fischer (1981) 'Inventories, Rational Expectations, and the Business Cycle', *Journal of Monetary Economics* 8: 277–304.

Butler, A. (1990) 'A Methodological Approach to Chaos: Are Economists Missing the Point?', *Review*, Federal Reserve Bank of St Louis, 72 (2).

Caldwell, B.J. (1991) 'Has Formalization Gone too Far in Economics: A Comment', *Methodus* 3: 27–29.

Cantillon, R. (1755) *Essai sur la nature du commerce en général* (edited and translated into English by H. Higgs, New York: A.M. Kelley, 1964). Reprint of a 1931 edition. Originally written between 1730 and 1734.

Duesenberry, J.S. (1954) 'The Methodological Basis of Economic Theory', *The Review of Economics and Statistics* 36: 361–363.

FitzGerald Scott, M. (1989) *A New View of Economic Growth*, Oxford: Oxford University Press.

Foss, N.J. (1990) 'A Note on the Lag-structure in Austrian Business Cycle Theory', unpublished paper, Copenhagen: Center for Educational Research.

Friedman, M. (1968) 'The Role of Monetary Policy', *American Economic Review* 58: 1–17.

Frisch, R.A. (1933) 'Propagation Problems and Impulses Problems in Dynamic Economics', in *Economic Essays in Honour of Gustav Cassel*, London: Allen & Unwin, 171–205.

Georgescu-Roegen, N. (1971) *The Entropy Law and the Economic Process*, Cambridge, Massachusetts: Harvard University Press.

Haltiwanger, J.C., and M. Waldman (1989) 'Rational Expectations in the Aggregate', *Economic Inquiry* 27: 619–636.

Hayek, F.A. von (1928) 'Intertemporal Price Equilibrium and Movements in the Value of Money', in F.A. von Hayek (1984) *Money, Capital & Fluctuations*, ed. R. McCloughry, London: Routledge, 71–117.

Hayek, F.A. von (1931) *Prices and Production*, London: Routledge & Kegan Paul, 1935.

Hayek, F.A. von (1932) 'A Note on the Development of the Doctrine of "Forced Saving"', *Quarterly Journal of Economics* 47 (3).

Hayek, F.A. von (1933a) *Monetary Theory and the Trade Cycle*, Clifton, New Jersey, 1975. First published in German as *Geldtheorie und Konjunkturtheorie*, Wien: Hölder-Pichler-Tempski (reprint Salzburg: Wolfgang Neugebauer, 1976).

Hayek, F.A. von (1933b) 'Über "neutrales Geld"', *Zeitschrift für Nationalökonomie 4*. Reprinted as 'On "Neutral Money"', in F.A. von Hayek (1984) *Money, Capital & Fluctuations*, ed. Roy McCloughry, London: Routledge.

Hayek, F.A. von (1933c) 'Price Expectations, Monetary Disturbances and Malinvestments', in Hayek (1939), 135–156.

Hayek, F.A. von (1933d) 'The Present State and Immediate Prospects of the Study of Industrial Fluctuations', in Hayek (1939), 171–182.

Hayek, F.A. von (1939)(1950) *Profits, Interest and Investment*, London: Routledge & Kegan Paul.

Hayek, F.A. von (1942) 'The Ricardo Effect', *Economica* IX: 127–152. Reprinted in F.A. von Hayek (1949)(1976) *Individualism and Economic Order*, London: Routledge & Kegan Paul.

Hayek, F.A. von (1969) 'Three Elucidations of the Ricardo Effect', *Journal of Political Economy* 77: 274–285. Reprinted in F.A. von Hayek (1978) *New Studies in Philosophy, Politics, Economics and the History of Ideas*, London: Routledge, 165–178.

Hoover, K.D. (1988) *The New Classical Macroeconomics*, Oxford: Basil Blackwell.

Humphrey, T.M. (1991) 'Nonneutrality of Money in Classical Monetary Thought', *Economic Review*, Federal Reserve Bank of Richmond, 77 (2).

Katzner, D.W. (1986) 'The Role of Formalism in Economic Thought, with Illustration drawn from the Analysis of Social Interaction in the Firm', in P. Mirowski (ed.) *The Reconstruction of Economic Theory*, Dordrecht: Kluwer/Nijhoff.

Katzner, D.W. (1991) 'In Defense of Formalization in Economics', *Methodus 3*: 17–24.

Kelsey, D. (1990) 'An Introduction to Nonlinear Dynamics and its Application to Economics', in F. Hahn (ed.) *The Economics of Missing Markets, Information, and Games*, Oxford: Oxford University Press.

Klein, L.R. (1954) 'The Contributions of Mathematics in Economics', *The Review of Economics and Statistics* 36: 359–361.

Koopmans, T.C. (1954) 'On the Use of Mathematics in Economics', *The Review of Economics and Statistics* 36: 377–379.

Kydland, F.E., and E.C. Prescott (1980) 'A Competitive Theory of Fluctuations and the Feasibility and Desirability of Stabilization Policy', in S. Fischer (ed.) (1980) *Rational Expectations and Economic Policy*, Chicago: Chicago University Press.

Lucas, R.E., Jr. (1972) 'Expectations and the Neutrality of Money', *Journal of Political Economy* 83: 1113–1144. Reprinted in Lucas (1981), 66–89.

Lucas, R.E., Jr. (1975) 'An equilibrium model of the business cycle, *Journal of Political Economy* 83: 1113–1144. Reprinted in Lucas (1981), 179–214.

Lucas, R.E., Jr. (1981) *Studies in Business Cycle Theory*, Oxford: Basil Blackwell.

Lucas, R.E., Jr. (1987) *Models of Business Cycles*, Oxford: Basil Blackwell.

Lucas, R.E., Jr. (1988) 'On the Mechanism of Economic Development', *Journal of Monetary Economics* 22 (1).

Lucas, R.E., Jr., and E.C. Prescott (1974) 'Equilibrium Search and Unemployment', *Journal of Economic Theory* 7: 188–209. Reprinted in Lucas (1981) 156–178.

Lucas, R.E., Jr., and L.E. Rapping (1969) 'Real Wages, Employment, and Inflation', *Journal of Political Economy* 77: 721–754. Reprinted in Lucas (1981), 19–58.

Lucas, R.E., Jr., and T.J. Sargent (1978) 'After Keynesian Macroeconomics', Federal Reserve Bank of Boston, *After the Phillips Curve: Persistence of High Inflation and High Unemployment.* Reprinted in Lucas and Sargent (1981), 295–319.

Lucas, R.E., Jr., and T.J. Sargent (eds) (1981) *Rational Expectations and Econometric Practice*, London: Allen & Unwin.

Maddock, R. (1979) *Rational Expectations, Political Business Cycles and the Course of Macroeconomic Theory*, unpublished PhD dissertation, Duke University, Durham.

McCloskey, D.N. (1991) 'Economics Science: A Search through the Hyperspace of Assumptions?', *Methodus* 3: 6–16.

Menger, C. (1871) (1968) *Grundsätze der Volkswirtschaftslehre*, Gesammelte Werke, Band I, Tübingen: J.C.B. Mohr (Paul Siebeck).

Musgrave, A. (1981) '"Unreal Assumptions" in Economics: The F-twist Untwisted', *Kyklos* 34: 377–387.

Novick, D. (1954) 'Mathematics: Logic, Quantity, and Method', *The Review of Economics and Statistics* 36: 357–358.

O'Driscoll, G.P., Jr., and M. Rizzo (1985) *The Economics of Time and Ignorance*, Oxford: Basil Blackwell.

Pesaran, M.H. (1989) *The Limits of Rational Expectations*, Oxford: Basil Blackwell, 2nd revised edn.

Phelps, E.S. (1967) 'Phillips Curves, Expectations of Inflation and Optimal Unemployment over Time', *Economica* 34: 254–281.

Phelps, E.S. (1970) 'The New Microeconomics in Employment and Inflation Theory', in E.S. Phelps (ed.) (1970) *Microeconomic Foundations of Employment and Inflation Theory*, New York: Norton.

Ricardo, D. (1817)(1978) *The Principles of Political Economy and Taxation*, London: Everyman's Library.

Romer, P.M. (1986) 'Increasing Returns and Long-run Growth', *Journal of Political Economy* 94: 1002–1037.

Runde, J., and C. Torr (1985) 'Divergent Expectations and Rational Expectations', *South African Journal of Economics* 53: 217–225.

Samuelson, P.A. (1954) 'Some Psychological Aspects of Mathematics and Economics', *The Review of Economics and Statistics* 36: 380–382.

Sargent, T.J. (1972) 'Anticipated Inflation and the Nominal Rate of Interest', *Quarterly Journal of Economics* 86: 212–225.

Sargent, T.J. (1973) 'Rational Expectations, the Real Rate of Interest, and the Natural Rate of Unemployment', *Brookings Papers on Economic Activity* 2: 429–472. Reprinted in Lucas and Sargent (1981), 159–198.

Sargent, T.J. (1976) 'A Classical Macroeconometric Model for the United States', *Journal of Political Economy* 84: 207–238. Reprinted in Lucas and Sargent (1981), 521–551.

Sargent, T.J., and N. Wallace (1975) '"Rational" Expectations, the Optimal Monetary Instrument and the Optimal Money Supply Rule', *Journal of Political Economy* 83: 241–254. Reprinted in Lucas and Sargent (1981), 215–228.

Slutzky, E. (1937) 'The Summation of Random Causes as the Source of Cyclical Processes', *Econometrica* 5: 105–146.

Solow, R.M. (1954) 'The Survival of Mathematical Economics', *The Review of Economics and Statistics* 36: 372–374.

Solow, R.M. (1991) 'Discussion Notes on "Formalization"', *Methodus* 3: 30–31.

Tinbergen, J. (1954) 'The Functions of Mathematical Treatment', *The Review of Economics and Statistics* 36: 365–369.

Van Zijp, R.W. (1993) *Austrian and New Classical Business Cycle Theories*, Aldershot: Edward Elgar.

Viner, J. (1964) *Studies in the Theory of International Trade*, London: George Allen & Unwin.

Visser, H. (1971) 'Neutraal geld, een overzicht', *De Economist* 119 (4).

Visser, H. (1974) *The Quantity of Money*, London: Martin Robertson.

Weintraub, E.R. (1985) *General Equilibrium Analysis: Studies in Appraisal*, Cambridge: Cambridge University Press.

Wicksell, K. (1898) *Geldzins und Güterpreise*, Jena: Gustav Fischer. First translated in English as *Interest and Prices* (1936). Reprinted 1962 by A.M. Kelley, New York.

Wilson, T. (1940) 'Capital Theory and the Trade Cycle', *Review of Economic Studies* 7: 169–179.

Part IV

POLITICAL APPLICATIONS OF AUSTRIAN ECONOMICS

12

ECONOMIC THEORY AND COMPETITION POLICY IN THE NETHERLANDS

J.A.H. Maks

INTRODUCTION

To the surprise of politicians, journalists and many economists, competition policy in the Netherlands is increasingly coming under attack from EC competition policy. A subject that has for decades received almost no attention in the mass media and the financial and even professional media, is suddenly a news item. Not a very hot item maybe, but one can now regularly read articles on the subject.[1] The prestigious Dutch paper *NRC* even published a series of articles under the heading *Nederland: Kartelland* (The Netherlands: Nation of Cartels).

Hence, it might be worthwhile to analyse Dutch competition policy under two headings: what is its nature and how does it relate to economic theory? To be able to answer these questions we will sketch in this paper the essentials of various economic theories, evaluate them from a welfare economic point of view, describe Dutch competition policy and characterize its nature. In the next section we will discuss the theories of the Neo-Austrians, the Chicago School, the Ordo-Liberals and traditional and new industrial economics. On pp. 203–209 we will focus on the 'third-best' welfare economic theory and establish the merits, in terms of welfare economics, of each of the theories discussed. The subsequent section is devoted to Dutch competition policy in the past decades and relates this policy to economic theory and welfare economics.

ECONOMIC THEORIES

In this section we discuss the theories of the Neo-Austrians, the Chicago School, the Ordo-Liberals and traditional and new industrial economics.

The Neo-Austrians[2]

Entrepreneurship plays an essential role in the market process. Starting from utter ignorance, entrepreneurs discover opportunities. They expect that these opportunities will be profitable. The profit opportunities alert them and give them incentives to participate in the market. If entrepreneurs decide to offer an item of a certain quality for a certain price, they will learn that this offer leads to a certain volume of sales. Perhaps the volume is disappointing, due to competitors offering the item on terms that are better in the eyes of the buyers. They may respond by improving their offer: a better quality or a lower price. Or perhaps the volume surpasses their expectations: they may raise their price and increase their profits. This higher price, however, stimulates competition: other entrepreneurs try to offer the item on better terms (lower prices or better quality) so as to divert the profits in their direction. The market process not only reveals information about the scarcities but also satisfies them as well as it can be done.

Entrepreneurship and the competition caused by entrepreneurship are the driving forces of the market process. Since profitable opportunities indicate mismatches or disequilibria, the functioning of the market, in discovering and attempting to remove them, tends towards a moving, temporary equilibrium.[3] The equilibrium is hypothetical, it will never be reached. There will always remain disequilibrium states to discover, because, for example, preferences and technology change. So the market process communicates information on disequilibria and at the same time moves towards a better co-ordination of demand and supply.

The ownership of capital goods is not a prerequisite for acting as an entrepreneur. But it might be profitable to be the sole owner of a necessary resource. Entry by other entrepreneurs is then blocked, so one is able to monopolize the particular productive activity. The benefits of this sole ownership must be distinguished in cause: entrepreneurial profit versus monopoly rent. If producers established their monopoly position by buying up all the rights to the resource, the benefits are entrepreneurial profits. The monopoly may also be a consequence of a 'given' distribution of resource ownership. In this case the benefit is a rent. To capture such a rent the owners need only to sell their resource to an entrepreneur. The monopoly benefits will usually be only temporary, because they will attract competition from production techniques not using the monopolized resource.

Nevertheless it might seem to be in the interest of the consumers to 'confiscate' entrepreneurial monopoly profits using some social policy. *Prima facie* this might work. The costs of establishing the monopoly position are sunk costs: as long as the marginal revenue exceeds the marginal cost of the monopolists they will continue to supply it. The problem is that when entrepreneurs experience systematic confiscation of such profits their alertness will diminish and so the improvements in the market co-ordination generated by monopoly positions will not be forthcoming. So, in the long run the consumer may lose.

The Chicago School[4]

The central assumption of the Chicagoans is that, in the absence of sufficient evidence to the contrary, observed prices and quantities are good approximations of their long-run (perfect) competitive values. Moreover they assume rational behaviour. Whereas the Neo-Austrians supplement the *homo oeconomicus* with the creative 'entrepreneur', the Chicago school assumes that maximizing behaviour is sufficient. But like the Neo-Austrians they claim that monopoly is transitory and that freedom of entry eliminates the 'bad' influence of monopoly on price and quantity within a fairly short time.

On the basis of profit maximization they argue that the firm has hardly any opportunity to enhance monopoly power through instruments such as tie-ins, vertical integration, resale price maintenance or predatory pricing.[5] They also hold that cartels are highly unstable because of the propensity to cheat in the absence of legal enforcement. Moreover they are assumed to be futile in the long run in the absence of effective barriers to entry. Only tacit collusion at very high levels of market concentration and explicit price fixing are of serious concern for competition policy.

However, if we add to this picture Stigler's influential regulation theory, not much hope is left for any beneficial effect from intervention. In this view political decision-makers are endogenous participants in the political process. Their behaviour is a response to their voters, and the lobbying of interest groups. They are unlikely to act on advice so as to promote the general welfare.

We will discuss the traditional industrial economics below. Part of this tradition is the Harvard School. This school is very much associated with the concentration doctrine. In this doctrine, concentration reflects market power and leads to allocative inefficiency through excessively high prices and persistent excess profits. Chicagoans stress that market power depends on barriers to entry caused by product heterogeneity, cost flexibility, the state of technology, etc. Moreover they contend that concentration is more often a consequence of efficiency than a cause of allocative inefficiency. In empirical research they present evidence corroborating this position and try to demonstrate that higher profits tend to vanish in most cases in a fairly short time.

Chicagoans see in principle a task for competition or anti-trust policy in tackling overt price fixing and tacit collusion at very high levels of market concentration, and advise in the general interest that this policy should be directed at consumer welfare. They are at least sceptical that such a policy can be applied. So Neo-Austrians and Chicagoans share in the end a position that shows hardly any 'trust' in competition or anti-trust policies.

The Ordo-Liberals[6]

Whereas the Chicago School economists assume that real-world competition normally generates results close to the long-term perfect competition equilibrium, the Ordo-Liberals are less confident of the nature of the real world. They hold that government should be fairly active in installing an institutional setting, an economic order, which produces a real world with perfect competitive results.

The Ordo-Liberals do not believe in an *ordre naturel* which arises spontaneously. The state must produce a set of legal institutions. This is the framework, *i.e.* economic order, within which the economic process functions. The desired economic order must lead to (approximate) perfect competition and Pareto optimality and to a just income distribution. Moreover it should correct external effects.

Grossekettler distinguishes seven basic structuring principles guiding the construction of such an economic order. Those that are important for this discussion are as follows:

(a) comprehensive striving towards competitive prices;
(b) keeping markets open;
(c) the right to enter into contracts in conformity with competition.

For day-to-day economic policy, Eucken lists four regulating principles, of which two are relevant here:

(a) containment and correction of market power;
(b) correction of anomalous supply reactions.

Traditional industrial economics

One of the important roots of traditional industrial economics is the Harvard School.[7] Whereas Chicago economics was based on maximization and microeconomic theory, traditional industrial economics was until the early 1960s characterized by case studies and a loose, often incoherent use, if any, of theoretical tools. There are two essential concepts: the Structure–Conduct–Performance (SCP) paradigm and the workable competition concept.

In the SCP paradigm, market structure (mainly: number of sellers and distribution of market shares) determines conduct (mainly: price, research and development, investment, co-operation among sellers) and conduct generates performance (mainly efficiency, ratio of price to marginal cost, profits, innovation rate). The paradigm entails a basically one-way causation scheme, but conduct and performance may alter structure. According to the SCP paradigm, a highly concentrated market structure may lead to co-operation between the sellers and thus to monopoly-like conduct: this conduct leads to high profits and a high price to marginal cost ratio. This is basically the concentration doctrine already discussed above.

The workable competition concept poses norms for structure (e.g. an appreciable number of traders, at least as many as economies of scale permit, with none dominant), conduct (e.g. there should be no unfair, exclusionary, predatory or coercive tactics) and performance (profits should be at levels that reward investment and induce innovation). The number of norms suggested varies from about six to thirteen per paradigm aspect. It is assumed that the norms can be aggregated to a rating: thus a market may be judged to be 'almost workable' or as 'optimum'.

The workable competition concept provoked criticism. It was not operational, not consistent and it lacked a solid theoretical foundation. The results of empirical research intended to support the concentration doctrine came under attack. Research from the Chicago School and elsewhere indicated that despite high concentrations, profits fade away over time and should be seen as a consequence of efficiency and entrepreneurial skill.[8] Moreover the lack of theory or the loose use of it in empirical research was more and more seen as a weak point. So, one might say that all this criticism around the mid-1960s and early 1970s was the basis for a reformation leading to the new industrial economics, which we will discuss below.

New industrial economics[9]

This approach is characterized by the criticism of the concentration doctrine mentioned above and an important increase in the use of the formal economic theory of imperfect competition. Moreover attention focuses on the dynamics of the market structure.

Theoretical analysis concentrates on oligopolistic interaction (game theory) and entry barriers. New models of entry deterrence are developed. The contestable market emerges. Attention is also given to imperfect information, product differentiation and innovation. Econometric research is able to include many more variables and thus can be adapted to the specific characteristic of particular markets. The results, so far as they are now clear, show that higher profits require not only high concentration but also barriers to entry (see e.g. Scherer 1984). But it is still a matter of debate what kinds of barriers offer this profit protection and for how long. So far as innovation is concerned, the findings suggest that the rate of innovation is higher with market forms between pure competition and monopoly. A market in which there is hardly any room for technological innovation (the standard example is brick making) should contain less competitors, whereas a market with ample innovation potential (standard example: computer hardware and software) should have more competitors

(Scherer and Ross 1990: ch. 17). Of course, this finding is also not generally accepted and still under discussion.

The contestable market approach clarifies how entry barriers such as increasing returns to scale fail to have an impact on prices. With potential competition and in the absence of sunk costs, Ramsey welfare optimality can be obtained. Of course, the contestability approach has been criticized (see e.g. Shepherd 1984). The approach assumes total entry with Bertrand–Nash price setting (price setting with the conjecture that other firms will keep their prices fixed) without any timely response from the expelled firm. But recent research attempts to relax the strictness of contestability to quasi-contestability. One tries to develop Edwards-like scenarios (Edwards 1967: ch. 2, especially 21–23) in which, despite barriers to entry and sunk costs, prices are in the neighbourhood of Ramsey optimality (see e.g. Maks 1986, Maks and Witteloostuijn 1988, Witteloostuijn 1990, Wegberg 1994).

As indicated above, in the new industrial economics simple general conclusions that meet general acceptance are scarce. If there is a trend one might point to the insight that smaller price–cost margins are often achieved at a high cost, such as sacrificing economies of scale, a lower rate of innovation and the like. Therefore the policy implications are rather fuzzy. Attention is focusing on barriers to entry in a growing awareness that certain levels and kinds of barriers might be socially beneficial (see e.g Weizsäcker 1980). If one explicitly analyses the welfare effects of market performance, the commonly used concepts are consumers' surplus and producers' surplus. These instruments are always applied in partial analyses of the market(s) under consideration.

Summary

The Neo-Austrians hold that imperfect competition generally produces welfare results through improvements in the co-ordination of supply and demand. Chicago adherents declare perfect competition as the norm, saying that it leads to Pareto optimality and that real-world competition emulates perfect competition under normal conditions. Ordo-Liberals also take perfect competition as the norm, but say that the government should establish an economic order such that perfect competitive results are closely approximated. The Harvard School explicitly departed from perfect competition as the norm and strove towards a rating of the various forms of imperfect competition in markets by the workable competition concept, but got stuck in cruder studies of the concentration doctrine. The new industrial economics has also come to the insight that some forms of imperfect competition may be socially beneficial. It tries to identify the effects of the various types of barriers to entry. Welfare measurement is performed with consumers and producers. So all in all, the trend is towards a certain room for the concept of imperfect competition.

THIRD-BEST WELFARE ECONOMICS

Imperfect information and welfare economics

Standard welfare economics centres around perfect competition, general equilibrium and Pareto optimality. In this sub-section we will first devote some attention to the received extensions of general equilibrium theory and discuss its implications for second- and third-best welfare economics.

The received extensions of general equilibrium theory relate to time, space, state and risk. If an economy with n commodities exists for a given number of periods, say t, and is partitioned in a given number of regions, say s, the general equilibrium model remains applicable. Only the commodity space is enlarged (from n to $n \times t \times s$) and so the number of excess demand equations and equilibrium prices increases. If all agents have perfect foresight of all equilibrium prices, spot markets may exist in all periods and all regions for each commodity. Risk may be brought in by expressing the probabilities of a finite number of 'states of the world' in each period and each region. A state may be characterized by, for example, its particular technologies, preferences and climate. Each state, in each period, has a chance to prevail. If such an economy is equipped with a complete system of future (insurance) markets, trade can be allowed at the beginning of this economy against equilibrium insurance premiums. Then again we may obtain a general intertemporal equilibrium. Both these models also have in each period a temporary equilibrium. In fact we can see the intertemporal equilibrium over several periods as a sequence of temporary equilibria in each of the consecutive periods.[10]

These extensions of the general equilibrium theory make it utterly clear that one really needs to be omniscient to know the general equilibrium. They also demonstrate the need of a welfare economics based on incomplete information, the so-called third-best welfare economics. Third-best welfare economics is an offspring of second-best welfare economics. Lipsey and Lancaster (1956) clearly proved that, if in some parts of the economy we do not have first-best optimum conditions (price = marginal costs, etc.), a piecemeal realization of a first-best condition in a particular market does not necessarily improve social welfare (Lipsey and Lancaster 1956). What is socially optimal for this particular market can in principle be calculated, if we have precise information on the situations in all the other markets. But as indicated above such omniscience, especially in an economy with time, regions and various states of the world and risk, is conspicuous by its absence, and out of reach even for contemporary, almighty governments. At this point third-best welfare economics may offer a way out. The version of it that we are going to discuss has been developed by Ng (1975, 1983). He distinguishes between informational poverty and informational scarcity.

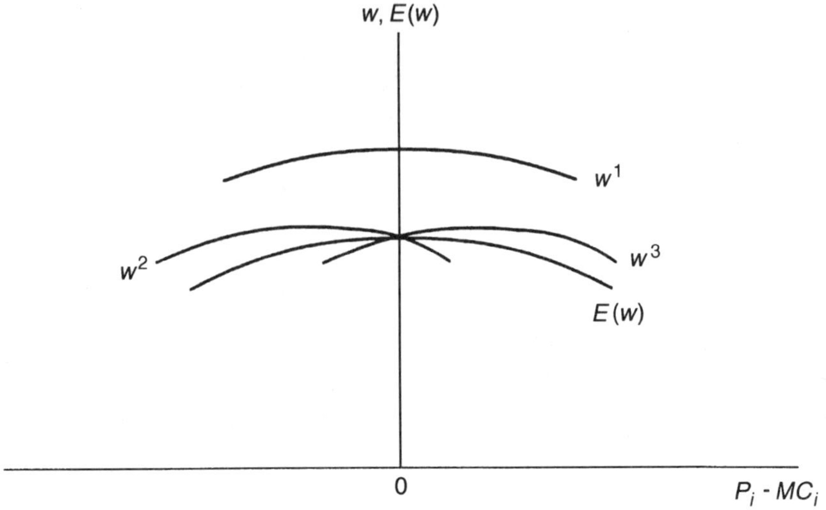

Figure 12.1 'Third-best' informational poverty: 'first-best' optimum rules.

Informational poverty is defined as a situation in which we know nothing about the differences between prices and marginal costs (and about all the other first-best optimality rules). But we can proceed if we make a very simple assumption. If one assumes that the chance of a given positive deviation of the welfare function equals the chance of an equal negative deviation and that the social welfare function is symmetric around its maximum, the expected value of the social welfare is maximized by a piecemeal realization of 'first-best' optimum conditions. This idea is illustrated in Figure 12.1.

Figure 12.1 shows the influence of the situation on the market for good i on social welfare (w). If first-best optimum conditions hold in all other markets in the economy, the social welfare is described by the curve w^1. It has its maximum value if the price of good i (P_i) equals marginal cost (MC_i). But, if we have on an unknown large number of markets unknown deviations from first-best optimum conditions, we do not know what the impact of these deviations on the social welfare in market i will be. This implies that in Figure 12.1 the social welfare maximum may lie to the right- or left-hand side of the maximum of w^1. So, if we now invoke the help of the very simple assumption formulated above, we may obtain the equally probable welfare functions w^2 and w^3. Maximization of the expected value of social welfare $E(w)$ is achieved where:

$$\text{Max}_{P_i - MC_i}: E(w) = cw^2(P_i - MC_i) + cw^3(P_i - MC_i) \tag{12.1}$$

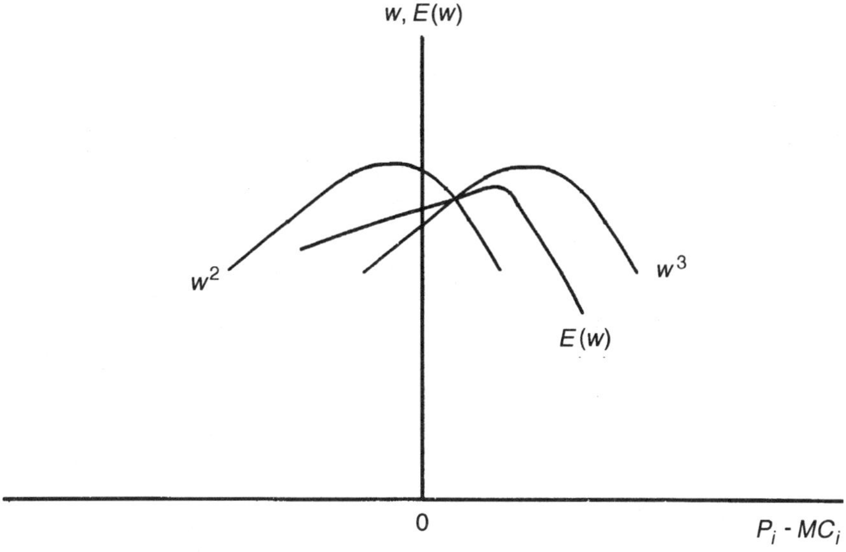

Figure 12.2 'Third-best' informational scarcity: 'third-best' optimum rules.

where c denotes the probability of w^2 and w^3 ($2c \leqslant 1$). This gives a maximum value of $E(w)$ if $P_i = MC_i$. The curve of $E(w)$ is drawn in Figure 12.1. It follows that the expected value of social welfare is maximized by a piecemeal realization of a first-best optimum condition on any particular market, even if we do not have first-best optimum conditions on other markets.

Informational scarcity denotes a situation in which one does have some information, say an estimation of the likelihood of a given positive and negative deviation of the welfare function on a market for good i and a guesstimate of its form. Figure 12.2 illustrates such a situation.

Suppose one has information allowing a guesstimate of an asymmetric form of the welfare function[11] on market i, as depicted in Figure 12.2 with w^2 and w^3. Moreover, one is able to estimate that w^2 and w^3 have equal probabilities. The sum of w^2 and w^3, weighted by this probability, generates $E(w)$. Then it follows that the expected value of social welfare can be found at the maximum of $E(w)$. This determines the expected optimal deviation of P_i and MC_i, the socially optimal third-best condition.

The question now is, which approach should be chosen? This choice depends naturally on the quality of the available information. A distinction should be drawn between market-specific and general information. A conjecture on the form of the welfare function on a market can be made if we have information on demand and costs (Ng 1975, 1983). However, the notorious problems of market frontiers and cost allocation remain.

Whether the likely optimum lies to the right or left of 'first best' may be more generally guesstimated as follows. Second-best social welfare maximization demonstrates that, under certain conditions, it is not too far from optimal to equate the price to marginal cost ratio to the average in the economy. The conditions required are that the commodity under consideration should not be highly complementary to or substitutable by goods offered under highly monopolized market conditions.

So, if we do not have any such indications the likelihood of socially optimal price to marginal cost ratios in the neighbourhood of the average in the economy is greater than for values further from the average. From this it follows that, under these conditions, if the average in the economy indicates a positive price to marginal cost ratio, the expected social optimum will also be positive and equal to this average. Ng considers this and similar reasoning to be the beginning of an operational third-best piecemeal approach, based on informational scarcity. Note that maximum social welfare in this approach is not related to perfect competition but to the average imperfect market in the economy.

At the end of the previous section we observed a trend towards a certain room for imperfect competition. Now we see again that imperfect competition might be compatible with optimal social welfare.

Economic theories and welfare economics

The easiest way to link Neo-Austrian economics with welfare theory is the Pareto criterion. If, for example, entrepreneurs discover a disequilibrium between consumers who have unequal marginal rates of substitution, they may arrange an exchange. Consumers and the entrepreneur benefit from the transactions, so a full-blown Pareto improvement is obtained. However, a snake in the grass may spoil this simple image. In our discussion of the intertemporal general equilibrium in the preceding sub-section it turned out that it is highly unlikely that a series of consecutive temporary equilibria will constitute an intertemporal general equilibrium: a good co-ordination of supply and demand over time. Unforeseen changes in preferences, technologies and 'states of the world' make the temporary equilibrium move. Moreover on pp. 197–198 it was observed that improvements in the co-ordination brought about by entrepreneurs tend towards a moving, temporary equilibrium. Therefore, what at the time appeared to be a Pareto improvement may, seen in hindsight and in the light of new information and disappointed expectations, prove to one or other party to be no improvement at all.

Since imperfect information and even utter ignorance are core concepts in the Neo-Austrian method, one may wonder whether a relation can be established between this economics and third-best welfare theory. In answering this question it must be explicitly stated that the moving, temporary equilibrium probably is a temporary, long-term Ramsey competition equilibrium. It is temporary because it does not assume 'omniscience' as Kirzner makes perfectly clear.[12] It is long-term because 'decisions currently made reflect the most up to date intelligence'. 'Ramsey competition' includes all those competition models that, in long-term equilibrium, end up in a situation of no more than normal profit. So it includes perfect competition, Chamberlin's monopolistic competition, (quasi)-contestability, etc. It is called 'Ramsey' because all costs are covered. The resulting allocation is a second-best Ramsey optimal allocation. We note that entrepreneurial competition erodes profits and that Neo-Austrian equilibrium is characterized by the absence of profit opportunities. If this reasoning is viable one may conclude that the market process is moving towards such a Ramsey optimal equilibrium.

We may now have a ground to establish a link between the reference point of Ramsey optimal equilibrium and third-best welfare economics. First, it must be emphasized that, of course, in Neo-Austrian eyes, this reference point can never be calculated.[13] The question remains: are we able to link this approach to informational scarcity or poverty?

Can we make the link with the informational scarcity model? One is tempted to decide this on an empirical basis. One would like to look, for example, at the average profit in an economy. But in the Neo-Austrian theory this information is scattered throughout the economy and cannot be gathered. Calculations of average profits in the economy cannot with confidence be regarded as revealing the true profit situation. Reported profits are, on the one hand, reflections of disequilibria and, on the other hand, biased by accounting conventions. Hence there is no way of discovering a likely third-best optimal price–cost margin in a particular market on the basis of informational scarcity, nor can we recommend market forms that would generate such an optimal margin.

A similar line of argument applies to the informational poverty model, leading to a rejection of the possibility of calculating optimal prices (equal to marginal costs). If Neo-Austrians are willing to accept the very simple assumption of the preceding sub-section they may also be prepared to recommend market conditions that lead in the end to prices equal to marginal costs. Of course it must immediately be added and emphasized that this insight is still not operational in the sense that recommendations can be derived on market form and entrepreneurial conduct. For such a result we have to find out what stimulates market processes in disequilibrium to converge on such a 'first-best result' and at what speed. But then again we do not need this 'third-best first-best' approach at all, because we may directly focus on the question of how to stimulate the market process in disequilibrium towards Ramsey price–cost situations.

So we end with the paradoxical conclusion that we cannot link third-best welfare imperfect information economics with Neo-Austrian economics, in which imperfect information plays such an essential role. The results seem to be meagre. Nonetheless one should realize what has been achieved. Entrepreneurial action leads to a welfare improvement according to the Pareto criterion. This improvement is a movement towards an equilibrium. We have identified this equilibrium as a second-best Ramsey allocation. Hence entrepreneurial action brings us closer to a Ramsey optimal allocation. An important question for further research emerges: what forces stimulate the market process to converge towards its equilibrium, or, to rephrase this question in Neo-Austrian terms, how can entrepreneurial action be stimulated (see Kirzner 1985: ch. 4)? Clearly the Neo-Austrians do not put their trust in traditional 'anti-trust' policies. Finally it must be repeated and emphasized that in Neo-Austrian eyes imperfect competition is a necessary condition for co-ordination improvements and increases in welfare.

The intended link with Chicago is not so difficult to untangle. Strictly speaking, Chicagoans see long-term perfect competition and Pareto optimality as the norm. Real-world competition normally generates in a short time results that look very similar to those of long-term perfect competition. It is probably very much in the spirit of Chicago to extend their ideal to Ramsey competition and Ramsey optimal allocation, as these are defined above. Like the Austrians they will probably not attach much value to the imperfect information third-best approach, since they will maintain that imperfect real-world markets normally produce Ramsey equilibria with rare exceptions. Consequently they will probably not worry much about the second-best or third-best problem. This attitude is only justifiable if indeed no market in the long term normally manifests persistent excess profits.

Ordo-Liberals seem formally attached to perfect competition and Pareto optimality. However, considering the structuring and regulating principles mentioned on p. 200, one could easily defend the replacement of Pareto optimality by second-best Ramsey optimality. This implies that all markets with Ramsey competition, as defined above, are socially optimal. But even after such a replacement Ordo-Liberals might be expected to believe that an active and alert piecemeal competition policy in accordance with the regulating principles is necessary, even if the economic order satisfies all structuring principles. Since assuming an omniscient government is not in the spirit of the Ordo-Liberals, third-best welfare economics might provide a suitable guiding policy. The informational scarcity model seems to be the natural candidate. Ordo-Liberal methodology does not oppose attempts to guesstimate the situation in an economy and on a particular market.

As stated, the relation between theory and traditional industrial economics is rather cumbersome. It is probably hardly an overstatement to assert that there is no relation between the workable competition concept and welfare economics. But to be able to grasp and operationalize the concept of workable competition, to rate the workability of markets, one needs some sort of a social welfare function. As we have observed above, the lack of theoretical content in traditional industrial economics is one of the main reasons for the emergence of the new industrial economics.

If welfare economics instruments are applied in the new industrial economics, it is usually to consumers' and producers' surplus and dead-weight loss. These concepts have the advantage that they can be used to compare the welfare effects of changes in the performance of one or more markets. They are normally used in partial analyses of one market. This means that side effects in other markets or for the whole of the economy are neglected, so that the second-best problem is very relevant. One may, for example, analyse or measure a positive welfare effect on a given market. But such an exercise does not in general tell us whether social welfare increases. It may even decrease. It might be very worthwhile or even necessary to supplement such a partial welfare analysis with a piecemeal third-best informational scarcity guesstimate of the socially optimal situation on the market. Only in this way can one know whether the welfare change on the market has a positive social welfare effect. This means *in concreto* that if, for example, one is analysing the welfare drawbacks of a change to a monopoly situation on a market, the reference point for a socially optimal outcome is not the first-best Pareto optimal price to marginal cost ratio but the expected third-best optimal average price to marginal cost ratio in the economy. This simple example clarifies our point: a partial analysis may show a welfare loss if a market price moves above marginal cost, but in fact such a change may well increase social welfare.

All in all we observe that welfare economics proves to be a useful if not necessary instrument. Entrepreneurial action in the Neo-Austrian approach leads to a Pareto improvement towards a second-best Ramsey allocation. The Chicago School position can be improved by the replacement of perfect competition Pareto optimal allocation by socially optimal Ramsey competition. Ordo-Liberals may prefer to ground competition policy on informational scarcity third-best insights. New industrial economists can improve their welfare analysis using the same insights. It is to be noted that this conclusion can be stated, despite the fact that third-best welfare economics, based on imperfect information and compatible with imperfect competition, is just beginning to explore its potential.

COMPETITION POLICY IN THE NETHERLANDS

Empirical nature[14]

Competition policy in the Netherlands has its legal base in the *Wet Economische Mededinging* of 1956. It is an abuse system: agreements to diminish competition are allowed unless forbidden. In the United States and the EC a prohibition system is applied: agreements to diminish competition are banned with some exceptions allowed. The main characteristics of the Dutch system are as follows:

(a) Agreements to diminish competition should be notified to the Minister of Economic Affairs, who may forbid the arrangement or declare it a generally binding agreement (section 2 of the law).
(b) Market positions with economic power can be made public and/or forced to curtail their negative consequences (section 24).
(c) Collective resale price maintenance is banned with the notable exception of books. Individual resale price maintenance is forbidden for certain consumer durables (section 9).

The guiding principle for the Minister is the general interest. This gives him or her considerable discretionary power. From the explanation and defence of this law in the early 1950s by Minister J. Zijlstra,[15] we can deduce that general interest can be construed as 'healthy' and 'effective' competition, i.e. markets should manifest a reasonable balance of economic power. This balance should produce a level of competition that serves expansion, diminishes stagnation and generates acceptable price to cost ratios. Monopoly profits stimulate progress only if they are not long-lasting, but erode through the dynamic process of monopoly formation and destruction. This construction cannot conceal the considerable discretionary power of the Minister. However, before making a decision, he or she is obliged to consult an advisory Committee on Economic Competition.

The practice of competition or anti-trust policy in the Netherlands grows out of these legal principles. There are some 500 notified cartel agreements with nationwide effects on prices, supply and market division. Moreover the number of agreements with regional or local significance is approximately 750, and there are about 100 notified cartel agreements on collective sales offices, technical co-operation, joint ventures and collective exclusive trade arrangements. Finally, of course, there are an unknown number of non-notified secret settlements. As far as cartel agreements on prices, etc., are concerned there has only been one prohibition, leaving aside the two bans on resale price maintenance already mentioned above. If there is an anti-trust policy in the Netherlands it is almost hidden away. There have been quite a number of cases in which the Minister has asked advice from the Committee on Economic Competition. It is said that objections raised during this procedure are normally met by the cartels. Moreover the Ministry discusses notified arrangements informally with the cartel representatives. As it turns out, this 'informal policy' often makes further 'formal policy' superfluous. Hence, one cannot know for certain what the nature of the Dutch anti-trust policy is, since the relevant direct information is missing. Nonetheless most experts would agree that the competition policy in the Netherlands has been quite permissive. The Ministry of

Economic Affairs has a well-known reputation as the 'Ministry of the Entrepreneurs', and there is a remarkable lack of concern with competition on the part of politicians and interest groups, who could have corrected this attitude. In Brussels' EC bureaucracy the Netherlands is well known if not infamous for its relatively high number of cartels and their persistence and importance. The EC anti-trust policy has increasingly attempted to correct the Dutch anti-trust policy. This EC effort has made such an impact that recently a politician held it possible that all Dutch notified cartels would be banned within a few years.

Theoretical nature

The explanation and defence of the *Wet Economische Mededinging* by Minister Zijlstra in the early 1950s could *prima facie* be considered as compatible with either a Neo-Austrian and Chicagoan position or an Ordo-Liberal position. He does not reject or disapprove of monopolies. He even mentions their positive influence on progress on the condition that their extra profits erode over time. But being a Neo-Austrian one would not need such a competition law, and a Chicagoan would need it only under certain limited conditions. So, on second thoughts, his position might have been closer to the Ordo-Liberals, in favour of an active competition policy directed towards the rapid erosion of monopoly positions (Zijlstra 1956: 45–46 and 75–76). But most probably he was inspired by the traditional industrial economics concept of workable competition aiming at sufficient profits to reward investments and encourage innovation.

Looking back on the practice of Dutch anti-trust policy over the past decades, we can evaluate its performance according to the various points of view. It is pretty clear that Neo-Austrians and Chicagoans would give high marks to the permissive practice noted above and that Ordo-Liberals would be severely disappointed. Traditional industrial economists, however badly equipped with market rating instruments, would emphasize the increase in the concentration in Dutch industries in the period 1950–1970 and expect higher profits. If they found these profits higher than necessary in some industries they would have argued for a more active policy.[16] New industrial economists would probably like to start an extensive research programme to investigate the question. They would, however, not hesitate to identify a likely shortcoming of the Dutch policy, in the law's lack of identified goals for the competition policy. If one looks at the EC Anti-trust law one observes that agreements to diminish competition are forbidden but that exceptions may be allowed if such agreements lead to production improvements or to improvements in technical or economic progress. This is similar in spirit to Zijlstra's explanation and defence of his competition law. But then an explicit condition is added in article 3 of section 85 of the treaty of Rome: a fair share of any benefit should go to the users of the products. The cartel should benefit not only the cartel members but also the consumer. Given the increasing attention and effort devoted by the EC to correct Dutch competition policy, a possible, systematic negligence of the consumer interest in defining the general interest may be a factor that the new industrial economist who is concerned with producer *and* consumer surplus and optimal social welfare would want to give explicit interest.

SUMMARY AND CONCLUSION

The Neo-Austrians hold that imperfect competition generally produces welfare results through improvements in the co-ordination of supply and demand. Chicago adherents declare perfect competition as the norm, saying that it leads to Pareto optimality and that real-world competition emulates perfect competition under normal conditions. Ordo-Liberals also take perfect competition as the norm, but say the government should establish an economic order such that perfect competitive results are closely approximated. The Harvard School explicitly departed from perfect competition as the norm and strove towards a rating of the various forms of imperfect competition in markets by the workable competition concept, but got stuck in cruder studies of the concentration doctrine. The new industrial economics has also come to the insight that some forms of imperfect competition may be socially beneficial. It tries to identify the effects of the various types of barriers to entry. Welfare measurement is performed with consumers and producers. So all in all, the trend is towards a certain room for the concept of imperfect competition.

We observe that welfare economics proves to be a useful if not necessary instrument. Entrepreneurial action in the Neo-Austrian approach leads to a Pareto improvement towards a second-best Ramsey allocation. The Chicago School position can be improved by the replacement of perfect competition Pareto optimal allocation by socially optimal Ramsey competition. Ordo-Liberals may prefer to ground competition policy on informational scarcity third-best insights. New industrial economists can improve their welfare analysis using the same insights. It is to be noted that this conclusion can be stated, despite the fact that third-best welfare economics, based on imperfect information and compatible with imperfect competition, is just beginning to explore its potential.

It is pretty clear that Neo-Austrians and Chicagoans would give high marks to the permissive practice of Dutch competition policy and that Ordo-Liberals would be severely disappointed. Traditional industrial economists would emphasize the increase in the concentration in Dutch industries in the period 1950–1970 and expect higher profits. If they found these profits higher than necessary in some industries they would have argued for a more active policy. New industrial economists would probably like to start an extensive research programme to investigate the question. They would, however, not hesitate to identify a likely shortcoming of the Dutch policy, in the law's lack of identified goals for the competition policy. A possible, systematic negligence of the consumer interest in defining the general interest may be a factor that the new industrial economist who is concerned with producer and consumer surplus and optimal social welfare would want to give explicit interest.

Whatever economic point of view one may favour, we have demonstrated the value of the various economic theories in grounding and evaluating competition (anti-trust) policy. Moreover they demonstrate the necessity and usefulness of welfare economics in economic theory: without welfare economics the *raison d'être* for the economic science ceases to exist.

NOTES

1 See e.g. Maks and Witteloostuijn (1987). Even a serious monograph on Dutch competition policy has been published: see Uitermark (1990).
2 The leading contemporary Neo-Austrian is I.M. Kirzner. This section is based on Kirzner (1973), (1985) and (1990).
3 Kirzner (1973: 235–236), states: 'the spotlight is focused not on the degree of conformity to the ideal allocation as seen from the perspective of omniscience, but on the degree to which currently known information is deployed' and 'one will recognize that decisions currently being made reflect the most up to date intelligence gathered by alert, profit-motivated entrepreneurs and that decisions will in turn effectively communicate the information to others'. It is remarkable that Léon Walras also holds that a market economy tends to develop towards a moving, temporary equilibrium; see Walras (1874). See also Maks and Witteloostuijn (1989) and (1990).
4 Leading Chicago economists are M. Friedman and G. Stigler.
5 Of course, these claims did not remain without criticism.
6 Also known as the Freiburg School. Its main founders were W. Eucken and F. Boehm. For an extensive discussion see Meijer (1988) or Borchert and Grossekettler (1985).
7 Leading names: J.M. Clark, E.S. Mason and J.S. Bain.
8 See Stigler (1963), Brozen (1970, 1971), Phlips (1971), Demsetz (1973) and Pagoulatos and Sorensen (1976).
9 See Scherer and Ross (1990), Tirole (1988) and Schmalensee and Willig (1989).
10 Note that such a series of temporary equilibria need not behave as a stationary equilibrium in the sense that each temporary equilibrium is an exact duplicate of its predecessor. Nor is it necessary that such a sequence manifests itself in steady state growth in, say, the value of the goods consumed.
11 For an explanation of such an asymmetric form see Mamuth (1992: 194–195).
12 See note 3, above.
13 One should bear in mind the neo-Austrian point of view in the so-called calculation debate.
14 For more extensive reports on Dutch competition policy, see Uitermark (1990) and Mamuth (1992: ch. 11).
15 See *Wet Economische Mededinging*, 4th edn: XXIII–XXIV. Note the Chicagoan or even Neo-Austrian flavour of this explanation.

16 But see Zeelenberg (1985). He does not observe a positive profit–concentration correlation in the Netherlands.

REFERENCES

Borchert, M. and H. Grossekettler (1985) *Preis- und Wettbewerbstheorie*, Stuttgart: W. Kohlhammer.

Brozen, Y. (1970) 'The Antitrust Task Force Deconcentration Recommendation', *Journal of Law and Economics* 13: 279–292.

Brozen, Y. (1971) 'Concentration and Structural and Market Disequilibria', *Antitrust Bulletin* 16: 241–248.

Demsetz, H. (1973), 'Industry Structure, Market Rivalry and Public Policy', *Journal of Law and Economics* 16: 1–10.

Edwards, C.D. (1967) *Control of Cartels and Monopolies: An International Comparison*, New York: Oceana.

Groenveld, K., Maks, J.A.H. and J. Muysken (1990) *Economic Policy and the Market Process: Austrian and Mainstream Economics*, Amsterdam: North-Holland.

Kirzner, I.M. (1973) *Competition and Entrepreneurship*, Chicago: Chicago University Press.

Kirzner, I.M. (1985) *Discovery and the Capitalist Process*, Chicago: Chicago University Press.

Kirzner, I.M. (1990) 'The Market Process: An Austrian View', in Groenveld, Maks and Muysken (1990), 23–39.

Lipsey, R.G. and K. Lancaster (1956) 'The General Theory of Second Best', *Review of Economic Studies*, 24: 11–32.

Maks, J.A.H. (1986) 'On the Compatibility of the Welfare State and the Market Economy', in W. Albeda (ed.) *The Future of the Welfare State and the Market Economy*, Maastricht: Presses Interuniversitaires Européennes.

Maks, J.A.H. and A. van Witteloostuijn (1987), 'Concurrentie en mededingingsbeleid: de barrièremarkt als een microfundering van werkbare concurrentie', *Maandschrift Economie* 51: 448–461.

Maks, J.A.H. and A. van Witteloostuijn (1988) 'Workable Competition and the Barrier Market', *European Journal of Political Economy* 4: 117–135.

Maks, J.A.H. and A. van Witteloostuijn (1989) 'Walras, a Hicksian *avant la lettre*', *Economie appliquée* 41: 595–608.

Maks, J.A.H. and A. van Witteloostuijn (1990) 'Walras on Temporary Equilibrium and Dynamics', *History of Political Economy* 22: 223–237.

Mamuth, H.A. (1992) *Markteconomie, Analyse en evaluatie*, Utrecht.

Meijer, G. (1988) *Het neoliberalisme: Neoliberalen over economische orde en economische theorie*, Assen/Maastricht: Van Gorcum.

Ng, Yew-Kwang (1975) 'Non-economic Activities, Indirect Externalities, and Third-best Policies', *Kyklos* 29: 507–525.

Ng, Yew Kwang (1983) *Welfare Economics*, London: Macmillan.

Pagoulatos, E. and R. Sorensen (1976) 'Foreign Trade, Concentration and Profitability in Open Economics', *European Economic Review* 8: 255–267.

Phlips, L. (1971) *Effects of Industrial Concentration: A Cross-section Analysis for the Common Market*, Amsterdam: North-Holland.

Scherer, F.M. (1984) 'On the Current State of Knowledge in Industrial Economics', *Discussion Paper IIM/IP*: 84–24, Wissenschafszentrum Berlin.

Scherer, F.M. and D. Ross (1990) *Industrial Market Structure and Economic Performance*, 3rd edn, Boston: Houghton Mifflin Company.

Schmalensee, R. and R.D. Willig (eds) (1989) *Handbook of Industrial Organization*, Amsterdam: North-Holland.

Shepherd, W.G. (1984) 'Contestability vs. Competition', *American Economic Review* 74: 572–587

Stigler, G. (1963) *Capital and Rates of Return in Manufacturing Industries*, Princeton: National Bureau of Economic Research.

Tirole, J. (1988) *The Theory of Industrial Organization*, Cambridge: MIT Press.

Uitermark, P.J. (1990) *Economische mededinging en algemeen belang: Een onderzoek naar de economisch-theoretische fundering van de mededingingspolitiek*, Groningen: Wolters-Noordhoff.

Walras, L. (1874) *Eléments d'économie politique pure: ou théorie de la richesse sociale*, Lausanne: Corbaz. English translation of the definitive (1926) edition by W. Jaffé, 1954, *Elements of Pure Economics*, Homewood, Illinois: Irwin.

Wegberg, M. van (1994) *Multimarket Competition: A Conceptual Framework*, Maastricht: Universitaire Pers Maastricht.

Weizsäcker, C.C. von (1980) *Barriers to Entry: A Theoretical Treatment*, Berlin: Springer.

Wet Economische Mededinging (law on economic competition) (1988) *Nederlandse Staatswetten nr. 12*, 4th edn, edited by A.D. Ham.

Witteloostuijn, A. van (1990) *Rationality, Competition and Evolution*, Maastricht: Datawyse/Kreps Repro Meppel.

Zeelenberg, C. (1985) *Industrial Price Formation*, Amsterdam: North-Holland.

Zijlstra, J. (1956) *Economische orde en economische politiek*, Leiden: Stenfert Kroese.

13

EARLY VIEWS ON THE SOCIALIST ECONOMY

Wladyslaw Sztyber

FUNDAMENTAL PRINCIPLES OF THE SOCIALIST SYSTEM OF ECONOMY AS SEEN BY K. MARX AND F. ENGELS

Starting from criticism of the capitalist economic system, K. Marx and F. Engels have formulated fundamental principles of the socialist system of economy. One of those principles has been nationalization of capital (Marx and Engels 1848; included in 1949, Vol. I: 44). However, their attitude towards small private property was quite different: they saw its future in terms of voluntary associations (Engels 1894; included in 1949, Vol. II: 414).

Transformation of the capitalist ownership of the means of production into the socialist one implies substitution of profit as the basic criterion of allocation of the factors of production by a planned regulation of production 'according to the needs of the community and of each individual' (Engels 1877; included in 1949, Vol. II: 138). As stated by Marx and Engels, the market with all its mechanisms and the related categories lose any sense in the socialist economy.

> The society will be obliged to know how much labour is needed to produce any object of use. It will be obliged to set up a plan of production including, in particular, the labour force. The plan will be determined ultimately by effective benefits that will be obtained from the various objects of use weighted against each other and in relation to the quantities of labour required for their production. People will do all that quite simply, without the famed 'value'.
>
> (Engels 1878; included in 1949: 304)

Another fundamental principle of the socialist system of economy is the principle of distribution of the part of the social product designed to be distributed among workers, according to their labour. 'The claim of producers to their product is proportional to the labour supplied by them; equality consists in that a unique measure – labour, is applied' (Marx 1875;

included in 1949, Vol. II: 14). Workers acquire the right to take from social stores various use values, the amount of which must be less than the quantity of labour they supplied to the society. Following the law of distribution according to labour, however, all are subject to the same principle of participation in the social product in proportion to their own labour.

The two fundamental principles of the socialist system of economy mentioned above were subject to a vigorous discussion. Two periods may be distinguished therein: the 'prior to Mises' period and the 'Mises' period. Within both, various currents appeared. In the first one, however, there was only a controversy on the concept of the socialist economy. Depending on the way of looking at the fundamental principles of the socialist economy as formulated by Marx and Engels, two currents of views may be distinguished. The one, approving those principles, tended to concretize and to develop them as well as to modify them to a certain degree. The other one modified essentially at least some of them, tending to construct a different concept of the socialist economic system.

In the second period, which began with L. von Mises who argued that the socialist system of economy was void of rationality, the controversies expanded and intensified considerably. In response to the objections put forward by the critical current, various concepts of the socialist system of economy emerged. In both periods, the contribution of the Austrian socio-economic thought to all those discussions was of a distinctive importance.

In the 'prior to Mises' period, a more or less orthodox current was predominating in the socialist economic thought. Its main representatives were A. Bebel and R. Hilferding. Although there were some small differences in their views, they accepted the principles as formulated by Marx and Engels.

THE ORTHODOX, 'PRIOR TO MISES' CURRENT IN SOCIALIST ECONOMIC THOUGHT

In the view of A. Bebel – just like Marx and Engels – in the socialist economy, production is directly subordinated to satisfaction of needs: the use values produced have lost their character of commodities, money has left the stage and the social outlays are expressed directly in quantities of the socially necessary labour time.

The society sets up itself the volume of effective needs on the basis of requests for particular use values, and the latter are transmitted to individuals according to the principle of equivalence. The needs are not static: they change over time and the new ones, not known so far, appear. The sole possible limit to their satisfaction is, in Bebel's opinion, scarcity of labour power.

The degree of satisfaction of needs depends, to a certain extent, upon the decision of the society. Having learned from experience and expectations the volume of the needs and the productivity of labour, it settles the necessary length of the working day.

It is a particular merit of A. Bebel to have distinctly recognized the importance of problems of technical substitution and to have emphasized the related role of economic calculus whose aim is to economize the outlays of resources in the process of production.

> The question of a 'cheaper' transportation on waterways, the one so important for the present society, will not be so for the future society which will not know of what is 'cheap' or 'expensive', but nevertheless it will have to pay attention to waterways which offer comfortable opportunities of transportation and may be used with the minimum outlays of power and materials.
>
> (Bebel 1883, see 1907: 263)

A criterion for the selection of production from among the various use values which satisfy a given need, will be the volume of the social outlay. The principle governing the process of decision-making will be that of minimization of outlays.

In the sphere of satisfaction of needs, freedom prevails. However, the society does not passively subordinate itself to the wishes of consumers, and it is far from devoting its resources of production means and labour force to the production of goods such as alcohol, which damage the health. In the society to come, says Bebel, all those stupidities and extravagances in the field of fashion which are associated with competition among women and take root in pride and the need to display publicly one's fortune, will also disappear.

The aim of the new system, says Bebel, is not only growth in production and a just distribution of the use values produced, but also an active contribution to the rationalization of needs. As a result of a purposeful organization of economic processes the society will become rich, just and rational.

R. Hilferding (1910) puts all the forms of social production which, in principle, produce exclusively for their own needs, on an equal footing while treating in the same way the primitive commune and patriarchal family as well as the modern socialist society. He does not discern the various relationships between production and consumption in each of those forms of society, which correspond to certain, highly differentiated levels of production forces.

In Hilferding's concept of the socialist economy, the production is subordinated to the needs of community which are known thanks to the organized statistical research. How much, where and how the goods are to be produced is decided upon by the representatives elected by the socialist society. The agencies of regulation and management of the national economy, created to represent the social consciousness, specify the amounts and directions of production and provide for distribution of the social product among members of the society. The distribution, subject to corresponding rules, is carried out in the form of allocation of products.

The distribution through allocation is corrected by exchange between members of the socialist society. In view of the supposedly small size of that exchange, its acts would occur in a completely incidental way, and it would be difficult to find any objective regularities in that sphere. It is mainly subjective tastes and likings of consumers not suitable for any economic analysis, that manifest themselves in that exchange. It has therefore, in Hilferding's opinion, no influence on production, like an exchange of toys between Mary and Johnny in the children's room (1904/5, Vol. I: 106).

In Hilferding's system money does not exist. Orders adressed by the society to the social product do not even remind one of money, since they resemble rather the theatre tickets with specified numbers of places. In this way also the concept of 'labour money' is rejected, the use of which had to facilitate the choice of products by consumers in the non-commodity socialist society.

The position of Hilferding, who denies the existence of exchange of commodities as a means connecting production with consumption, is all the more incomprehensible as, at the same time, he assumes the existence of private small peasant holdings and industrial firms. The pretended indirect socialization of small enterprises thanks to the direct socialization of big industry does not yet eliminate the private ownership of the means of production from that area, so it does not remove the basis underlying the exchange of commodities.

THE INNOVATIVE, 'PRIOR TO MISES' CURRENT IN SOCIALIST ECONOMIC THOUGHT

Unlike in the case of A. Bebel and R. Hilferding, the commodity character of the socialist economy with the related functioning of the market mechanism is recognized by K. Kautsky, though to a limited extent and under social control.

K. Kautsky rejects both the natural calculus and the concept of 'labour money', considering the latter as too difficult to be realized in practice. Diversity of types of labour, different degrees of their intensities, systematic changes in labour outlays, difficulties with calculation of amounts of labour outlays of different types – all those factors make the realization of that concept impossible (Kautsky 1920).

In the modern society an economy without money would be possible, in Kautsky's view, in two particular cases. One is represented by the existence of one big factory embracing all existing workshops, subject to a central management which assigns to each enterprise definite production targets and provides it with the corresponding amount of the means of production and labour force and also takes care of allocation of the various consumption goods to consumers. The other case means a high level of labour productivity and output which assures the abundance of goods. In such a society, people work as much as they can and receive as much as they need.

After having introduced the two theoretically possible cases of economy without money, K. Kautsky concludes that commodity production and money will be maintained in the socialist system. This results, first of all, from the fact that households are separated from the modern industry.

There will be two kinds of exchange in the socialist society. Between the socialist enterprises there will be exchange of the necessary means of production, and between workshops and households there will be circulation of consumer goods for the purposes of personal consumption. The latter will be based on the previous transfer of labour force to the disposal of the firm.

However, money will be of a different character in the socialist system than under capitalism. The predominance of the social ownership of the means of production will prevent the possible transformation of money into capital and so it will cease to be a means for individuals to become wealthy. Instead, the positive aspects of money, namely its quality as a means to facilitate and accelerate circulation, and to make possible the use of the right of choice, will be maintained.

The value forms will be largely used, both at the level of the whole economy and in a single firm. A careful accounting necessitates the use of money forms. Accounting in natural units would be very troublesome and the results would lack any comparability. Computing the outlays on production and the results of its realization in money terms makes it possible to calculate profit or loss of the firm. The real rentability can, of course, be calculated only when pricing is correct and not arbitrary. This is why Kautsky proposes to adopt for the initial period 'prices as transmitted by history'. Although such prices are not a perfect and exact form of measuring labour outlays, they are sufficient for an efficient functioning of circulation.

The value forms and the resulting regularities play, in Kautsky's system, an important role also in the sphere of economic equilibrium. However, the law of value does not control the production in an anarchic way. Neither the volume of production nor the level of prices is determined by a spontaneous process of supplying a more or less known, but still uncertain, market.

Shifts in the allocation of labour to particular branches are made in a purposeful way. If the intended increase in production targets of a branch cannot be obtained through technical improvements, it will be obtained through cutting the targets of other branches.

Changes in prices will also be made, if needed, but they cannot be reduced below the level that would lead to a reduction in wages of the workers producing the given commodities. They will be made mainly as a result of changes in labour productivity.

Under socialism the producers, in Kautsky's belief, know the market and this simply results from the fact that a contract was made with all the consumers by which the producers were obliged to deliver a given quantum of various commodities at fixed prices.

> The consumers as a whole following their knowledge of economic conditions, reach in advance an agreement with producers in each branch of production, thereby determining the volume of output and its prices. Since then both production and prices develop within more uniform limits. Workers do not suffer, either as consumers because of high prices, or as producers because of unemployment.

While admitting the possibility of a loss of rentability by a firm or even a whole branch of production, Kautsky emphasizes that this cannot happen to the whole economy. It is not the non-existence of profit, he states, that is a characteristic of the socialist system, but its destination.

In the sphere of wages there will appear, in Kautsky's view, equalization tendencies not observed so far. The immense disparities in income levels inherited from the previous system will be eliminated. This does not mean, however, that the wage differentials which are justified by the requirements of production will completely disappear. The tendencies toward equalization of wages will manifest themselves mainly in raising the lower wages.

The distribution among the members of the society will be limited, in principle, to the consumption goods only. This will not be an arbitrary process: it will have to allow for incentives for the workers to perform their tasks carefully and accurately, as well as for the interests of firms in obtaining satisfactory results. It is both workers and the management staff who benefit from increased effects of the process of production. The feeling of power and freedom stemming from their status of co-managers of the firm makes, in Kautsky's belief, for growth in their diligence, ambitions and readiness to work hard and enjoy their work.

The role of the law of value in the field of prices, wages and production is extensively presented in Kautsky's writings. After having discussed its influence in each of those fields separately, he concludes: 'We may thus expect that though private production and private competition will disappear, there will be the law of labour value which generally governs the socialist society' (1920: 219).

CRITICISM OF THE SOCIALIST SYSTEM OF ECONOMY

The author who may be considered as the one who initiated a new stage in the discussion of the socialist system of economy, is L. von Mises. His works have gained the largest resound (1920, 1924, 1928). He is the most advanced author in criticism of the socialist economic system. He does not limit his argument to the rejection of the labour theory of value. In addition, he tries to prove that there are no conditions under socialism for a correct operation of the value mechanism.

As a consequence of the substitution of the social ownership of production means (which is identified by Mises with state ownership) for the private one, the exchange loses any sense. And without exchange of the production means, Mises argues, no prices can exist. Although the means of consumption may still continue to be commodities and to be exchanged, their prices in view of no prices for production means would be arbitrary; they could not be correctly determined. Although money still remains in circulation, it does not fulfil its most essential function – that of the standard of value. Accordingly, it no longer plays any role in the economic calculus.

To withdraw from the private ownership of production means is identical, in Mises' belief, with restricting the applicability of the category of money and, at the same time, with withdrawal from the rational economy. His conclusion is unambiguous. The system in which there are no conditions for economic calculus, is deprived of the compass that shows the direction of a rational behaviour. And with no criterion of rational behaviour one cannot conduct a rational economy at all.

Mises then considers other possible economic calculations and concludes that they are either inapplicable or misleading. He stresses limitations of the calculus *in natura* and rejects any attempt to substitute it for monetary calculus in money. In the socialist economy, he argues, consumption means only could be subject to calculus *in natura*, but this cannot be the case of goods of a higher order.

Mises' position was a little different in relation to calculus in labour. He put forward two theoretical objections against it. First, it does not allow for the role of material factors of production. The surpluses supplied by nature with no additional labour outlays should be ascribed, in his opinion, to the factors that produced them and, in view of their scarcity, they should be taken into account in that calculus. Second, the calculus in labour ignores different qualities of labour. As opposed to an exchange economy where the rate of substitution between the simple and composed labour is expressed in the wage rate, the calculation in terms of labour time under socialism would be based, in his view, on proportions of substitution arbitrarily fixed by a central body.

Another proposal that was contested by Mises is the adoption of the price system which the socialist economy inherited from capitalism. This method, according to Mises, could be applied only for the short term, but it could not be recommended for the long term because, in this case, the inherited price system would have to be modified, whereas the socialist system does not offer any criteria on which those corrections could be based.

At almost the same time a similar view on the limited possibility for a rentability calculus in the socialist economy was expressed by M. Weber (1956). Such a calculus can be made only in terms of money whereas the latter is unimaginable without existence of prices, not only for consumer goods but also for the factors of production. In order to have correct prices it is required that there exist autonomous economic units and that they compete with one another. For market prices are a result of fight and compromise, so they reflect the prevailing system of relative forces.

The rentability calculus is a condition of rationality which is called formal by Weber. The formal rationality says nothing about the manner of distribution of goods. Besides the concept of formal rationality, the concept of material rationality is introduced by M. Weber in which the economic problems are viewed from social, political and ethical standpoints. The social ownership of the means of production hampers, in the opinion of M. Weber, the orientation as far as the formal rationality is concerned, but it does not hamper the use of material rationality.

The line of criticism of the socialist system of economy as taken up by Mises has been continued by F.A. Hayek (1935: chs. 1 and 5). The central problem that, in his view, has to be solved by the socialist economy, as by any other economy, is a rational allocation of scarce means among competing claims. Realization of that task does not meet any difficulties under conditions of private ownership of the means of production. Through its price system the market mechanism offers to economic units a set of alternatives for their choices. No such mechanism exists in the socialist economy.

Unlike Mises, Hayek does recognize the possible existence of a decentralized model of the socialist economy, but he believes that the centralized model is more convenient to the character of the planned economy, and this is incompatible with the freedom of choice of consumption and employment. In the latter case, allocation of resources does not depend upon the mechanism of the market.

In response to the development of models of the socialist economy in which the market was given an important place, Hayek tried to extend the platform of criticism so far practised by considering two variants of the functioning of that economy. In one model purchases and sales are performed by a body heading an industrial branch, in the other one the transactions are made by single firms.

The first system is compared with a monopoly where the tendency to profit maximization is identical with the most rational use of resources. In the second case the firm does not possess a full autonomy. Distribution of durable means of production and investments, on the one hand, and the choice of directors and control of their activities, on the other, are parts of the legal capacity of a central body. Any distribution of functions in the field of investments between the central body and the firm would obscure, in the author's opinion, the problem of responsibility for the errors committed. And it is exactly the lack of responsibility of the heads of the firm that, in the view of Hayek, stands in the way of a rational utilization of resources available to the firm.

Acting in the name of a social interest gives rise, according to Hayek, to another deficiency of competitive socialism, namely risk aversion. Social ownership of the means of production does not create conditions for full competition, it only makes possible the introduction of a system of quasi-competition where the responsibility rests with the supervising body rather than with the firm itself. The negative phenomena accompanying such a system are found to be due to lacking conditions for development of free initiative and responsibilities.

It is true that the second model considered by Hayek includes elements of competition but the author himself does not see any possibility to reconcile it with planning. The socialist system in which such elements of competition are present, is full of contradictions and inconsistencies, and therefore it is seen by the author as less effective than a fully competitive system. In the best case it could achieve results resembling those obtained under conditions of the private ownership of production means.

Positive characteristics of the socialist system are seen by Hayek in the area of income distribution. But the benefits from a more just distribution of incomes are paid for, in his belief, at a price excessively high for society, in the form of a lower effectiveness of the economy.

Finally, it is worthwhile to add that Hayek did admit the theoretical possibility of a rational allocation of resources in the socialist economy based on the mathematical method of general equilibrium. But, at the same time, he pointed to the lack of practical possibilities to gather the immense quantities of information needed to construct, and then to solve, such a mathematical model.

THE MARKET MODELS OF THE SOCIALIST ECONOMY

In response to the criticism of the orthodox system of the socialist economy, attempts were undertaken to construct a socialist system based on the market and the functioning of its mechanism. The early attempts of that kind are, first of all, those by J. Marschak and K. Polanyi.

In the guild system of J. Marschak (1924) the role of the market is limited. Production units create economic associations. The firm is, in principle, autonomous but certain decisions may be reserved in favour of bodies at higher levels of the economic hierarchy, and the possible solutions of that problem may vary and depend upon actual conditions and needs.

There are no principal obstacles, in Marschak's opinion, that would make the use of economic calculus in money terms impossible. For both prices and calculus of rentability there exist, in fact, analogous sets of conditions.

The guild system would not hamper any adjustment of the means of production to the given needs. The latter would be based on the known demand for final products, on the one hand, and would allow, on the other hand, for all the interrelationships between the various production processes and for the related technical production coefficients. Equilibrium becomes thus endogenous to the system.

But the areas in which, according to the author, the actual price system and the related economic calculus not only do not matter but may even have negative effects on the economy, is the sphere of dynamics. Here, a strict keeping with actual or even foreseen prices may be, in his opinion, highly dangerous for socio-economic progress. A release from that dependence would facilitate the realization of present as well as future economic targets.

The development of new economic regions would be greatly promoted by a correct policy of transportation tariffs. Prices can be used to influence the introduction and diffusion of new methods of production. Decisions that, from the point of view of a narrowly conceived profitability, are found irrational may appear highly rational from the standpoint of the whole economy. The example of land improvements is quoted by the author as a means of related revenues of the state budget, as well as the general welfare of the whole society.

A concept of the socialist market economy is put forward also by K. Polanyi (1924). In the opinion of this author, the socialist economy is faced with two fundamental tasks, one being the maximization of production in the area of technology of production, and the other related to the socio-economic sphere – submission of the directions of production and the distribution of the goods produced to the social criteria.

Although the author admits that both tasks may be realized alternatively using directive methods or the mechanism of competition, he is decidedly in favour of the market solution. It seems that, besides the social considerations, it is the factors enabling the economic calculus to be made that induced the author to take that position. The economic calculus is, in his conviction, the central problem of the socialist economy.

The system of guild organization of the economy creates sufficient conditions for correct economic calculations. The existence of at least two parallel centres of decision-making seems sufficient to give rise to the emergence of certain dissimilarities underlying the development of contradictory interest which are the necessary premises for the formation of effective prices.

The system of a competitive economy based on the social ownership of production means has taken, with K. Polanyi as with J. Marschak, the form of guild socialism, in which an attempt is made to combine the actual mechanism of the functioning of the capitalist economy with challenges resulting from the fact of socialization of the ownership of the means of production. According to this concept the most penetrating changes seem to take place in the sphere of distribution. It is only from there that they expand on the sphere of production, the structure of which undergoes accordingly only such modifications that result from the disappearance of incomes stemming from private property.

In the later period more developed models of the socialist market economy were elaborated, i.e. those by H.D. Dickinson (1933) and O. Lange (1938). Besides the criticism of the orthodox socialist economy, it is also the above early concepts of market forms of the socialist economy that contributed to their elaboration.

The development of economic thought relative to the socialist economy as presented above has been, first of all, of a cognitive nature. Only little of it was applied in the practice of the functioning of the socialist economy. This is particularly the case of the theoretical achievements in the concepts of the socialist market economy. The system of real socialism based on orthodox principles was showing a very limited ability to learn from experience in spite of its clear ineffectiveness in many areas. Imposed by force by a dogmatic authority which confessed priority of ideology and politics also in the matters related to the economy, the system continued to exist for many years, and the multiple attempts at its reform were doomed to failure.

REFERENCES

Part of the references are given in the Polish language. The titles of the corresponding German original versions are added.

Bebel, A. (1883) *Die Frau und der Sozialismus*, in (1907) *Kobieta i socjalizm*, Kraków: Towarzystwo Wydawnictw Ludowych.

Dickinson, H.D. (1933) 'Price Formation in a Socialist Community', *Economic Journal*, June.

Engels, F. (1877) *Die Entwicklung des Sozialismus von der Utopie zur Wissenschaft*, in (1949) *Rozwój socjalizmu od utopii do nauki.* Ksiazka i Wiedza. Dziela Wybrane, II.

Engels, F. (1878) *Herrn Eugen Dührings Umwälzung der Wissenschaft ("Anti-Dühring")*, in (1949) *Anty-Dühring.* Ksiazka i Wiedza.

Engels F. (1894) *Die Bauernfrage in Frankreich und Deutschland*, in (1949) *Kwestia chlopska we Francji i Niemczech.* Ksiazka i Wiedza, Dziela Wybrane, II.

Hayek F.A. (1935) *Collectivist Economic Planning*, London: Routledge and Kegan Paul.

Hilferding, R. (1904/5) 'Zur Problemstellung der theoretischen Okonomie bei Karl Marx', *Neue Zeit*, Vol. I.

Hilferding, R. (1958) *Kapital finansowy*. Pastwowe Wydawnictwo Naukawe.

Hilferding, R. (1910) *Das Finanzkapital.*

Kautsky, K. (1920) *Sozialisierung und die Arbeiterräte. Rede Proletariatsrevolution und ihres Programm*; *Socjalizacja i rady robotnicze*. Ludowe Towarzystwo Wydawnicze 1920, Lwów. Oraz Rewolucja proletariacka i jej programu.

Lange, O. (1938) 'On the Economic Theory of Socialism', in O. Lange and F. M. Taylor, *On the Economic Theory of Socialism*, ed. B. E. Lippincott, Minneapolis: University of Minnesota Press. (Originally 1936).

Marschak, J. (1924) 'Wirtschaftsrechnung und Gemeinwirtschaft-zur Mises'schen These von der Unmöglichkeit sozialistischer Wirtschaftsrechnung', *Archiv für Sozialwissenschaft und Sozialpolitik*, Vol. 51.

Marx, K. and F. Engels (1848) *Manifest der Kommunistischen Partei*, in (1949) *Manifest Komunistyczny*. Ksiazka i Wiedza. Dziela Wybrane, I.

Marx, K. (1875) *Kritik des Gothaer Programms*, in (1949) *Krytyka Programu Gotajskiego.* Ksiazka i Wiedza. Dziela Wybrane, II.

Mises, L. von (1920) 'Die Wirtschaftsrechnung im sozialistischen Gemeinwesen', *Archiv für Sozialwissenschaft und Sozialpolitik*, Vol. 47.

Mises, L. von (1924) 'Neue Beiträge zum Problem der sozialistischen Wirtschaftsrechnung', *Archiv für Sozialwissenschaft und Sozialpolitik*, Vol. 51.

Mises, L. von (1928) 'Neue Schriften zum Problem der sozialistischen Wirtschaftsrechnung', *Archiv für Sozialwissenschaft und Sozialpolitik*, Vol. 60.

Polanyi, K. (1924) 'Die funktionelle Theorie der Gesellschaft und das Problem der sozialistischen Rechnungslegung', *Archiv für Sozialwissenschaft und Sozialpolitik*, Vol. 52.

Weber, M. (1956) *Wirtschaft und Gesellschaft*, Tübingen: Mohr (originally 1922).

14

ENTREPRENEURSHIP AND THE ECONOMIC ANALYSIS OF SOCIALISM

Jesús Huerta de Soto

This article attempts to show that the theory of entrepreneurship, as developed by Israel M. Kirzner, must be an essential element of any analysis on the impossibility of socialism. As a consequence of this analysis, a new definition of socialism is proposed, based on the concept of entrepreneurship, which seems to be more generally and analytically fruitful than the standard definition. In the first section, the essence of entrepreneurship is explained. On pp. 238–242, a new definition of socialism is introduced. After that, in the subsequent three sections, the analysis of its impossibility from the point of view of entrepreneurial theory is developed. On pp. 247–250 a critique of the alternative and traditional concepts of socialism is included in the section. Special attention is paid to the relationship between socialism and interventionism in the final section.

THE ESSENCE OF ENTREPRENEURSHIP

In a general or broad sense, entrepreneurship coincides with *human action* itself (Mises 1966: 11–29 and 251–256).[1] In this respect, it can be said that any person who *acts* to modify the present and to obtain their objectives in the future is practising entrepreneurship. Although, at first sight, this definition may appear too broad and to be out of line with current linguistic usage, it must be remembered that it corresponds to a concept of entrepreneurship which is being constantly worked upon and studied by economic science[2] and which, moreover, is fully in line with the original etymological meaning of the term *entrepreneur*.

In fact, both the English word *enterprise* (in French *entreprise*, in Spanish *empresa*) and the French and English *entrepreneur* (in Spanish *empresario*) have their etymological origin in the Latin verb *in prehendo-endi-ensum*, which means to discover, see, perceive, realize, trap. The Latin expression *in prehensa* clearly implies the idea of *action*, meaning to take, grasp or seize.

In short, the Spanish word *empresa* is synonymous with action and in France the term *entrepreneur* has been used since medieval times to refer to people entrusted with the performance of important actions, generally connected with warfare or with great projects for the construction of cathedrals. In English, *The Oxford English Dictionary* (1989: 293, meanings 3 and 1) defines *enterprise* as the '*action* of taking in hand' and also as 'the bold, arduous, or momentous undertaking'. And in Spanish, one of the meanings of *empresa* given in the *Dictionary of the Spanish Royal Academy* is 'arduous and difficult *action* which is valiantly commenced'.

This word was also used in medieval times to refer to the insignias of certain orders of knighthood, which indicated the pledge, under oath, to carry out a certain important *action.*

In any case, the meaning of *enterprise* as action is necessarily and inexorably linked to an enterprising, go-ahead attitude, which consists of continuously seeking, discovering, creating or becoming aware of new ends and means (all of which is in line with the etymological meaning stemming from the Latin verb *in prehendo*).

Entrepreneurship and alertness

Entrepreneurship, in the strict sense of the term, consists basically of discovering and appreciating (*prehendo*) the opportunities of attaining an end or, if one prefers, of obtaining a gain or profit, which arises in one's environment, acting in consequence in order to take advantage of them. Kirzner (1973: 65–69) says that the performance of entrepreneurship implies a special *alertness* (in Spanish *perspicacia*), i.e. continually being *alert*, which makes it possible for human beings to discover and become aware of what is happening around them. Perhaps Kirzner uses the English term 'alertness' because the term *entrepreneurship* is of French origin and does not automatically imply in the Anglo-Saxon language the idea of *prehendo* which is present in the continental European Roman languages.

In any case, in Spanish, the adjective *perspicaz* is most appropriate to describe entrepreneurship, as it applies, according to the *Dictionary of the Spanish Royal Academy*, 'to the very acute glance or look which is far-reaching'. Furthermore, *speculator* etymologically comes from the Latin noun *specula*, which means watchtower or high vantage point from which to discover or see in the distance. This idea fits in perfectly with the activity carried out by the entrepreneur when deciding what actions to take and estimating the effect thereof in the future. Being alert is also acceptable as a feature of entrepreneurship as it implies the idea of attention or watchfulness.

Information, knowledge and entrepreneurship

The nature of entrepreneurship in the form in which we have been discussing it cannot be understood in depth without understanding how it modifies or produces changes in the information or knowledge that the actor possesses. First, perceiving or becoming aware of new ends and means leads to a modification of the actor's knowledge, in the sense that the actor creates or discovers new information. Second, this discovery modifies the whole map or context of information or knowledge that the subject possesses.

We may, therefore, pose the following essential question: what are the relevant characteristics of the information or knowledge discovered by the performance of entrepreneurship? We will study in detail six basic characteristics of this type of knowledge:

(a) it is subjective knowledge of a practical, non-scientific nature;
(b) it is private or exclusive knowledge;
(c) it is dispersed over the minds of all people;
(d) most of it is tacit knowledge and, therefore, is not articulable;
(e) it is knowledge that is created *ex nihilo*, from nothing, precisely by entrepreneurship; and
(f) most of it is transmissible in a form that is not conscious, through very complex social processes, the study of which constitutes the research subject of economic science.

Subjective and practical non-scientific knowledge

First, the knowledge we are analysing, the most important or relevant to the practice of human action, is, above all, *subjective* knowledge of a *practical*, non-scientific nature. Practical knowledge is all knowledge that cannot be formally represented, but that the subject acquires or learns through practice, i.e. from human action itself carried out in its corresponding contexts. It is, as Hayek says, the knowledge relevant to all kinds of particular circumstances as regards its subjective co-ordinates in time and space.[3] In short, we are talking about knowledge of specific human valuations, i.e. both of the ends desired by the actors and of their knowledge about the ends which they believe other actors desire or pursue.

In the same way, it is practical knowledge of the means that the actors believe to be within their reach to attain their ends and, in particular, of all the circumstances, personal or otherwise, that the actor considers may be relevant within the context of each specific action (see Hayek 1972: 33–56 and 77–91).

Private and dispersed knowledge

Practical knowledge has an exclusive and dispersed nature. This means that each actor possesses only some of what we could call 'atoms' or 'bits' of the information that is globally generated and transmitted at the social level,

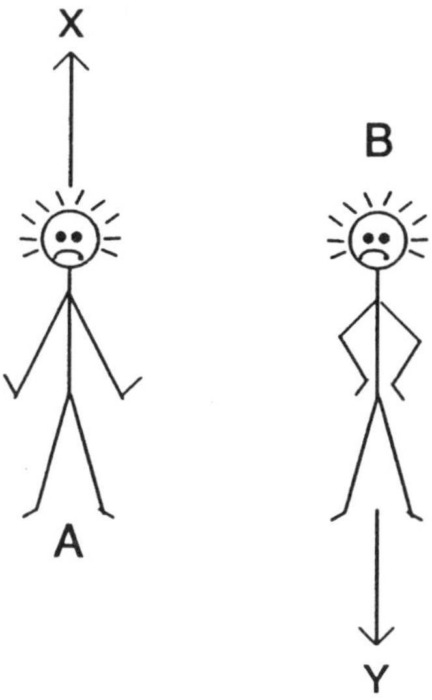

Figure 14.1

but that, paradoxically, only he or she possesses, i.e. which only he or she consciously knows and consciously interprets. Therefore, each person who acts and practises entrepreneurship does so in a strictly personal and unrepeatable way, as his or her starting point is an attempt to attain ends or objectives in accordance with a vision and knowledge of the world which only he or she possesses with all its richness and variety of nuances and which cannot be exactly repeated in any other human being.

Therefore, the knowledge to which we refer is not something which is *given*, available to everybody by some material means of information storage (newspapers, specialized journals, books, computers, etc.). On the contrary, the relevant knowledge for human action is basically practical and strictly exclusive, which can only be 'found' spread over the minds of each and every one of the men and women who act and constitute humanity.

In Figure 14.1, we will introduce some stickmen, with the sole objective of helping us to make the analysis contained herein more graphic.

In this figure we wish to represent two real human beings of flesh and blood, whom we call A and B. Each of the people represented by A and B possesses their own exclusive knowledge, i.e. knowledge that the other does not have. What is more, from the point of view of an external observer, we may say that there 'exists' knowledge that we, as observers, do not possess and which is dispersed between A and B, inasmuch as A has part of it and B another part.

Thus, for example, let us assume that the information that A has is that he aims to attain an end X (which we represent by the arrow above his head pointing towards X) and that, with a view to attaining this end, he possesses certain practical information which is relevant in the context of the action (this knowledge or practical information is represented by the 'halo' which A has around his head). B's case is similar, except that the end he pursues is very different, in this case, Y (represented by the arrow at his feet pointing towards Y). The practical information that the actor B considers relevant in the context of his action is also represented by the 'halo' around his head.

In some simple actions the actor, individually, possesses the information necessary to attain the proposed end without the need to relate to other actors at all. In these cases, whether or not the action is undertaken is the result of an *economic calculation* or estimative judgement made by the actor, weighing up and *directly* comparing the subjective value placed on the end he or she aims to attain with the cost or value placed upon what would be renounced if he or she pursues the chosen end.

However, the actions on which the actor can take this type of decision directly are few and very simple. The majority of actions in which we are involved are much more complex, as we will now explain. Let us imagine, as represented in Figure 14.1, that A has a great desire to reach end X but, in order to do so, requires the existence of a means M which he does not have at his disposal and which he *does not know* either where or how to obtain. Simultaneously, let us suppose that B is somewhere else, that he aims to attain a very different end (end Y), to which he devotes all his efforts, and that he knows, or 'knows of' or has at his disposal a large quantity of a means M which he does not consider useful or suitable for attaining his end but which, by coincidence, is the means that A would need to enable him to reach the objective he desires (X). What is more, it must be emphasized that, as is true in most real cases, X and Y are *contradictory*, *i.e.* each actor pursues different ends, with a different degree of intensity and with a relative degree of knowledge regarding the ends and regarding the means within his realm which do not coincide with or are not adjusted to his needs (this explains the disconsolate expression with which we have drawn our stickmen). Later on, we will see how the practice of entrepreneurship makes it possible to overcome this kind of contradictory or *unco-ordinated* behaviour.

Tacit, inarticulate knowledge

Practical knowledge is mostly *tacit* and *inarticulate*. This means that the actor knows how to do or carry out certain actions (*know how*) but does not know what the elements or parts of what he or she is doing are, or if they are true or false (*know that*) (see Ryle 1949).[4]

Thus, for example, when a person learns to play golf, one is not learning a set of objective, scientific rules which permit one to make the necessary movements as a result of the application of a series of formulae of mathematical physics. The learning process rather consists of the acquisition of a series of practical habits of conduct. In the same way, we may quote, as Polanyi does, the example of the person who learns to ride a bicycle, trying to keep their balance by moving the handlebar to the side towards which he is beginning to fall, thus causing a centrifugal force which tends to keep the bicycle upright. However, practically no cyclist is aware of or knows the physical principles on which their ability is based. On the contrary, the cyclist is rather using their 'sense of balance' which, in some way, indicates to them the way in which they should behave at any given moment in order not to fall. Polanyi (1959: 24–25) even states that tacit knowledge is, in fact, the dominant principle of all knowledge.

Even the most highly formalized and scientific knowledge is always the result of an intuition or act of creation, which are simply manifestations of tacit knowledge. The new formalized knowledge, which we can acquire thanks to formulae, books, graphs, maps, etc., helps to reorganize all our information. The information from different points of view becomes richer and more productive. This opens up new possibilities for using creative intuition.

A type of inarticulable knowledge which plays an essential role in the development of society is that which is made up of a set of habits, traditions, institutions and legal rules which constitute law and make society possible and which humans learn to obey without being able to theorize or articulate in detail the precise role played by such rules and institutions in the different situations and social processes where they intervene. The same may be said of language and also, for example, of the financial and cost accounting used by entrepreneurs to guide their actions and which is simply a practical knowledge or technique which, used within a determined context of market economy, is a generalized guideline for entrepreneurs to help them attain their objectives, without their being able, in the majority of cases, to formulate a scientific theory of accounting and, even less, to explain how such a theory helps in the complicated processes of co-ordination which make life in society possible (Lavoie: 1985).[5]

We can, therefore, conclude that the practice of entrepreneurship as we have defined it (the capacity to discover and appreciate opportunities for profit, undertaking a conscious line of behaviour in order to take advantage thereof) consists of a type of knowledge which is basically tacit and inarticulable.

The essentially creative nature of entrepreneurship

Entrepreneurship does not require any means for its execution. This means that entrepreneurship does not imply any cost and, therefore, is essentially creative. The creative nature of entrepreneurship is shown by the fact that it gives rise to profits which, in a certain sense, arise from nowhere and which we will call *pure entrepreneurial profits*.

To obtain entrepreneurial profits it is not necessary, therefore, to have any prior means available, but merely to practise entrepreneurship well. We can illustrate this fact starting from the situation described in Figure 14.1. It is sufficient to *become aware of* the situation of *lack of adjustment or of co-ordination* which exists between A and B for the opportunity of pure entrepreneurial profit to arise.

Thus, in Figure 14.2, it is assumed that it is a third person, in this case C, who practises entrepreneurship on discovering the lack of adjustment or of co-ordination shown in Figure 14.1 (we represent the fact that C becomes aware of such opportunity by a 'bulb' which lights up). Logically, in practice, entrepreneurship could be practised by A or B or by both of them simultaneously, with the same or differing intensities, although, for our purposes, it is more illustrative to consider that it is carried out by a third person C.

In fact, it is sufficient for C to contact B and offer to buy the resource, which he (the latter) possesses in abundance and upon which he places practically no importance, for a certain amount, let us say 3 monetary units, which B will find enormously satisfactory, as he never imagined he could obtain so much for his resource. Later, once the exchange has been made, C will be able to contact A and sell him the resource which A so intensely needs to attain the end he is pursuing, selling it to him for, let us say, 9 monetary units (if C does not have any money, he can obtain it, for example, by persuading someone to make him a temporary loan). As a consequence, therefore, of the practice of entrepreneurship by C, he has obtained, *ex nihilo*, pure entrepreneurial profit of 6 monetary units.

It is now of special interest to emphasize that, as a consequence of this act of entrepreneurship, there have been three effects of extraordinary importance. First, entrepreneurship has *created* new information which did not exist previously. Second, this information has been *transmitted* throughout the market. Third, as a consequence of the entrepreneurial act, the economic agents involved *have learnt* to act in accordance with each other. These consequences of entrepreneurship are so important that it is worth studying each of them separately in detail.

Creation of information

All entrepreneurial acts imply the creation *ex nihilo* of new information. This creation takes place in the mind of the person, in our example the person represented by stickman C, who is the first to practise entrepreneurship. Effectively, when C becomes aware that there exists a situation such as the one described, in which A and B are involved, new information, which he did not previously have, is created in his mind. But moreover, once C

Figure 14.2

undertakes the action and enters into contact with A and B, new information is also created in the minds of A and B.

Thus, A becomes aware of the fact that the resource that he lacked and of which he had such a need in order to attain his end is available in other parts of the market in greater abundance than he thought and that, therefore, he may undertake, now without problems, the action that he did not begin due to the lack of the resource. B, for his part, becomes aware that the resource that he possessed in such abundance and upon which he placed no value is very much wanted or desired by other people and that, therefore, he can sell it at a good price. Moreover, part of the new practical information which originated in the mind of C on practising entrepreneurship and which later arises in the minds of A and B, is included, in a very summarized form, in a series of *prices* or historical exchange *ratios* (i.e. B sold at 3 and A bought at 9).

Transmission of information

The entrepreneurial creation of information implies a simultaneous *transmission* thereof in the market. In fact, transmitting something to someone is to make that person generate or create in their own mind part of the information that we created or discovered previously. In our example, strictly speaking, not only the idea has been transmitted to B that his resource is important and should not be wasted, and to A the idea that he may go ahead with the pursuit of the end he desired but could not pursue in view of the lack of such resource. Also, through the respective prices, which are a potent transmission system, since they transmit a large amount of information at very low cost, it is communicated to the whole market or society that the resource in question should be kept and saved, as there is a demand for it. Simultaneously it is communicated that all those who do not undertake actions, because they think the said resource does not exist, can obtain it and go ahead with their respective plans of action.

Logically, the relevant information is always subjective and only exists within the persons who are capable of interpreting or discovering it, meaning that it is always human beings who create, perceive and transmit information. The erroneous idea that information is objective originates from the fact that part of the entrepreneurial-created subjective information is set out 'objectively' in signals (prices, institutions, rules, 'firms', etc.) which may be discovered and subjectively interpreted by many people in the context of their specific actions, thus facilitating the creation of new subjective information, richer and more complex. However, in spite of appearances, the transmission of social information is basically tacit and subjective, *i.e.* it is not express and articulated, and takes a very summarized form (in fact, the minimum information indispensable to co-ordinate the social process is transmitted and subjectively captured), which, in addition, permits full advantage to be taken of the limited capacity of the human mind to constantly discover and create new knowledge.

Learning effect: co-ordination and adjustment

Finally, it is necessary to stress how agents A and B have learnt to act in accordance with each other. In other words, B, as a consequence of the entrepreneurial act originally undertaken by C, does not now squander or waste the resource he has at his disposal but, in his own interest, keeps and conserves it. A, as he has the resource at his disposal, can attain his end and undertake the action that he did not undertake previously. Both, therefore, learn to act in co-ordination, i.e. to modify and discipline their behaviour in accordance with the other human beings. Moreover, they learn in the best possible way: without realizing that they are learning and *motu proprio*, i.e. voluntarily and within the context of a plan in which each of them pursues his own ends and interests. This, and nothing else, is the *nucleus* of the process, both marvellous and simple and effective, which makes life in society possible. Finally we observe that the practice of entrepreneurship by C makes possible not only a co-ordinated action between A and B which did not exist previously, but also that the latter two carry out an *economic calculation* in the context of their respective actions, with data or information which they did not have before and which permits them to attain, with a much greater chance of success, their respective ends. In short, the economic calculation by each actor is made possible thanks precisely to the information generated in the entrepreneurial process. Or, in other words, without the practice of entrepreneurship, the information necessary for each actor to calculate or estimate appropriately the value of each alternative course of action is not generated. That is, without entrepreneurship, economic calculation is not possible.

The above observations constitute the social science teachings that are, at the same time, the most important and the most elementary and which allow us to conclude that entrepreneurship is, without any doubt, the social function *par excellence*, given that it makes life in society possible, as it adjusts and co-ordinates the individual behaviour of its members. Without entrepreneurship, it is impossible to conceive of the existence of any society.

The essential principle

Now the really important point from a theoretical point of view is not who, specifically, practises entrepreneurship (although, in practice, this is precisely the most important point), but that, as there are no institutional or legal restrictions on the free practice of entrepreneurship, each person may put into practice their entrepreneurial activities as best they can, creating new information and taking advantage of the practical, exclusive information that they have discovered in the circumstances of any given moment.

It does not correspond to the economist, but rather to the psychologist, to study in detail our innate force which moves us entrepreneurially in all our fields of action. Here and now, we are only interested in stressing the essential principle that people tend to discover the information which is of interest to them. Therefore, if there is freedom with regard to the attainment of ends and interests, these will act as an incentive. This will make it possible for the person practising entrepreneurship, motivated by such incentive, to continuously perceive and discover the relevant practical information for the attainment of the proposed ends. And, vice versa, if for any reason the field in which entrepreneurship may be practised is limited or closed in a determined area of life in society (by legal, institutional or traditional restrictions), then human beings will not even consider the possibility of attaining or reaching ends in these forbidden or limited areas and, therefore, as the end is not possible, it will not act as an incentive. In consequence, no practical relevant information for the attainment of such end will be perceived or discovered. What is more, not even the affected persons *will be conscious* under these circumstances of the enormous value and great number of ends that cannot be attained as a result of the situation of institutional restriction.

That is, within the stickman scheme of Figures 14.1 and 14.2, we realize how, if there is freedom for human action to be carried out, the 'entrepreneurial bulb' can freely light up in any circumstance where there is lack of social adjustment or co-ordination, thus producing the process of creation and transmission of information which will lead to the co-ordination of the disorder, allowing and making possible life in society. On the other hand, if in a certain area the practice of entrepreneurship is prevented, it is never possible for the 'entrepreneurial bulb' to light up, i.e. it is not possible for the entrepreneur to discover the existing situation of disco-ordination which, therefore, will be able to continue unaltered indefinitely or may even get worse.

ENTREPRENEURSHIP AND THE CONCEPT OF SOCIALISM

Our discussion of entrepreneurship in the previous section was necessary because we propose a new definition of socialism which is based on the concept of entrepreneurship. In fact, we will define socialism as any *system of institutionalized aggression against the free practice of entrepreneurship*. *Aggression* or *coercion* must be understood to mean any physical violence or threat of physical violence which is originated towards and performed on an individual by another human being or group of human beings. As a consequence of this coercion, the individual, who would otherwise have freely carried on their entrepreneurship, is, in order to avoid a greater evil, forced to act differently to the way they would have acted under other circumstances, thus modifying their behaviour and adapting it to meet the ends of the person or persons who are coercing them.[6]

We may consider aggression, thus defined, to be the anti-human action *par excellence*. This is so because coercion prevents a person from freely carrying on their entrepreneurship, i.e. from seeking the objectives they have set using the means that, according to their information and to the best of their knowledge, they believe or consider to be accessible to them for reaching these objectives. Aggression is, therefore, an evil because it prevents the human being from carrying on the activity that is most characteristic of him or her and which essentially and most intimately corresponds to him or her.

There are two types of aggression: systematic or institutionalized and non-systematic or non-institutionalized. The latter type of coercion, which is, in nature, dispersed, arbitrary and more unpredictable, affects the carrying on of entrepreneurship to the extent that the individual considers there to be a greater or lesser probability that, in the context of a specific action, force will be used upon them by a third party, who may even appropriate the results of his entrepreneurial creativity.

Although non-systematic outbreaks of aggression are more or less serious, depending on the circumstances, institutionalized or systematic aggression is far more serious as regards co-ordinated human interaction. As we have seen, this type of aggression constitutes the essence of our definition of socialism. We do not, of course, consider the concept of

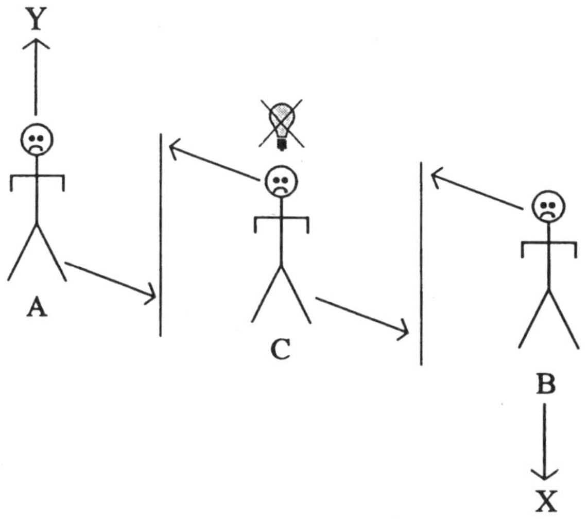

Figure 14.3

systematic aggression to include the minimum level of institutionalized coercion necessary to guard against and correct the negative effects produced by non-institutionalized or non-systematic aggression. This minimum level of institutionalized coercion is that which even non-institutionalized aggressors would wish to be provided for them, outside the scope of his non-systematic aggression, in order to pacifically take advantage thereof.

In fact, institutionalized coercion is characterized by being highly predictable, repetitive, methodical and organized. The main consequence of this systematic aggression against entrepreneurship is to make largely impossible and perversely divert the carrying on of entrepreneurship in all the areas of society where said aggression is effective.

In Figure 14.3, we show the typical situation resulting from the systematic practice of coercion. We assume that, in an organized and systematic way, the free human action of C in relation to A and B in a specific area of life in society is prevented by coercion. This is represented by the lines that separate C from A and B. As a consequence, it is not possible, as systematic coercion prevents it by the threat of serious evils, for C to discover and take advantage of the profit opportunity that he would have if he could interact freely with B and with A. It is very important to clearly understand that the aggression does not only prevent him from taking advantage of the profit opportunity, but even prevents the discovery of this opportunity.

The possibility of obtaining gains or profits acts as an incentive to the discovery of these opportunities. Therefore, if a determined area of life in society is restricted by systematic coercion, the actors tend to adapt to said situation, they take it for granted and, therefore, do not even create, discover or become aware of the opportunities that are latent. We represent this situation in Figure 14.3 by crossing out the light bulb which, in accordance with our convention, indicates the creative act of pure entrepreneurial discovery.

If the aggression falls systematically upon one social area and, as a consequence, entrepreneurship cannot be carried out in that area, none of the other effects typical of the pure entrepreneurial act explained on pp. 228–238 will take place. In fact, in the first place, new information will neither be created nor transmitted from actor to actor. Second, and this is a cause for even more concern, the adjustment necessary in cases of a lack of social co-ordination will not occur. As the discovery of opportunities for profit are not permitted, there will be no incentive for the actors to become aware of situations of lack of adjustment or co-ordination that arise. In short, information will not be created, it will not be transmitted from one agent to another and the different human beings will not learn to discipline their behaviour in accordance with that of their peers.

Thus, in Figure 14.3, we see how, as C cannot carry on entrepreneurship, the system is maintained continuously unco-ordinated: A cannot pursue end Y due to lack of a resource which B has in abundance and does not know what to do with. He therefore squanders and misuses it, unaware that an A exists and needs it urgently. In accordance with our analysis, we can, therefore, conclude that the main effect of socialism, as we have defined it, is to prevent the action of the co-ordinating forces which make life in society possible.

Does this mean that the proposers of socialism are advocating a chaotic or unco-ordinated society? On the contrary, apart from a few exceptions, the proposers of the socialist ideal defend it because, tacitly or explicitly, they believe or suppose that the system of social co-ordination not only will be undisturbed by the existence of the institutionalized and systematic violence which they favour, but will be made much more effective by the fact that the systematic coercion is performed by a controlling organism which is supposed to possess knowledge (regarding both the ends and the means) and valuations which are better, both quantitatively and qualitatively, than those that the coerced actors may possess at a lower level.

From this perspective, we may now complete the definition of socialism given at the beginning of this heading, stating that *socialism is all systematic and institutionalized aggression that restricts the free performance of entrepreneurship in a determined social area and that is carried out by a controlling organism which is in charge of the tasks of social co-ordination necessary in said area.* Under the following heading we will analyse the point to which socialism, in the terms with which we have defined it, is or is not an intellectual error.

SOCIALISM AS AN INTELLECTUAL ERROR

Life in society is possible thanks to the fact that individuals, spontaneously and without realizing it, learn to modify their behaviour, adapting it to the needs of other people. This unconscious learning process is the natural result of the practice of entrepreneurship by human beings. This means that, upon interaction with one's peers, each person spontaneously initiates a process of adjustment or co-ordination in which new information – tacit, practical and dispersed – is continually being created, discovered and transmitted from one mind to others.

The problem posed by socialism is whether it is possible, by the coercive mechanism, to verify the processes of adjustment and co-ordination of the conduct of different human beings, which depend upon each other and which are indispensable if life in society is to function. All the foregoing take place within a framework of constant discovery and new creation of practical information which makes it possible for civilization to advance and develop.

The ideal put forward by socialism is, therefore, highly daring and ambitious,[7] as it implies the belief that not only the mechanism of co-ordination and social adjustment may be made effective by the controlling organism which performs the institutionalized coercion in the social area in question but that, in addition, this adjustment may even be improved by the coercive procedure.

Figure 14.4 is a schematic representation of the concept of socialism as we have defined it. On the 'lower level' are human beings, endowed with

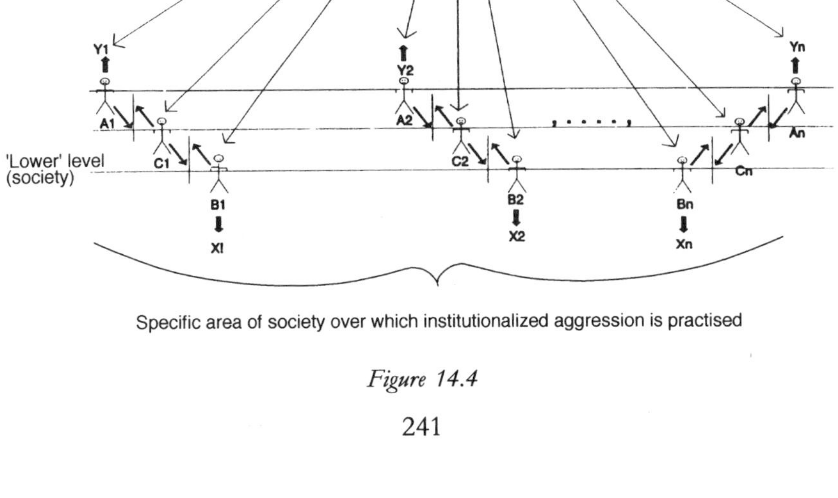

Figure 14.4

knowledge or practical information, who, for this reason, try to interact freely among themselves, although such interaction is not possible in some areas due to institutionalized coercion. This coercion is represented by the vertical lines which separate the figures forming each group. On the 'upper level', we show the controlling organism which, as an institution, practices coercion in determined areas of life in society. The vertical arrows in opposite directions, which come from the figures on the left and right of each group, represent the existence of unadjusted personal plans which are typical of a situation where there is a lack of social co-ordination. Cases of lack of co-ordination cannot be discovered and eliminated by entrepreneurship because of the barriers imposed by the effect of institutionalized coercion on entrepreneurship. The arrows which go from the head of the controlling figure towards each human being on the lower level represent the coercive commands which comprise the aggression typical of socialism, aimed to compel the citizens to act in a co-ordinated way and to pursue end 'F' which is considered 'right' by the controlling organism.

The command may be defined as any specific instruction or stipulation, the contents of which are clearly defined, which, regardless of the legal form it takes, prohibits or compels determined actions to be taken under specific circumstances. The command is characterized by the fact that it does not allow human beings to freely carry on their entrepreneurship in the social area to which it refers.

Commands are, moreover, deliberate decisions of the controlling organism practising institutionalized aggression and are aimed to force all the actors to fulfil or pursue not their personal ends, but the ends of those who govern or control.

In view of the foregoing, socialism is an intellectual error because it is not theoretically possible that the organism in charge of practising institutionalized aggression possesses sufficient information to endow its commands with contents of a co-ordinating nature. We will examine this simple argument with a certain amount of detail. It can be developed from two different, but complementary, points of view: first, from the overall perspective of the human beings who constitute society and who are coerced; and second, from the standpoint of the coercive organization which practises aggression systematically. Below we analyse separately the problem posed by socialism from each of these viewpoints.

THE IMPOSSIBILITY OF SOCIALISM FROM THE PERSPECTIVE OF SOCIETY

The static argument

First, from the point of view of human beings who interact among themselves and constitute society (the so-called 'lower' level of Figure

14.4), it must be remembered that each of them possesses exclusive practical and dispersed information, the majority of which is tacit and, therefore, cannot be articulated. This means that it is logically impossible to conceive of its possible transmission to the controlling organism (the so-called 'upper' level in Figure 14.4).

In fact, it is not only that the total volume of practical information sensed and handled by all human beings at an individual level is so enormous that its conscious acquisition by the controlling organism is inconceivable, but, above all, this volume of information is disseminated among the minds of all people in the form of tacit information which cannot be articulated and, therefore, cannot be formally expressed nor explicitly transmitted to any controlling centre.

We already saw on pp. 238–242 how information relevant to life in society is created and transmitted implicitly in a disseminated way, i.e. neither consciously nor deliberately. In this way the different social agents learn to discipline their behaviour in relation to that of other people but are not aware that they are the protagonists of this learning process nor that, therefore, they are adapting their behaviour to that of other human beings: they are simply conscious that they are acting, i.e. trying to obtain their personal ends using the means they believe to be within their reach. Therefore, the knowledge we are discussing is a knowledge that is only possessed by human beings acting in society which, in view of its intrinsic nature, cannot be explicitly transmitted to any central controlling organism. As this knowledge is indispensable if different individual behaviours are to be co-ordinated socially, thus making society possible, and cannot be transmitted to the controlling organism given the fact that it cannot be articulated, it is logically absurd to think that a socialist system can work.

The dynamic argument

Socialism is impossible not only because the information possessed by the actors is intrinsically unable to be transmitted explicitly, but because, moreover, from a dynamic point of view, human beings, on carrying out entrepreneurship, i.e. on acting, constantly create and discover new information.

It would be very difficult to transmit to the controlling organism information or knowledge that has not yet been created, but which is continually arising as a result of the social process itself to the extent that the latter is not attacked.

Figure 14.5 represents the actors who are continually creating and discovering new information throughout the social process. As time, in its subjective sense, elapses, those who perform their entrepreneurship in interaction with their peers are constantly becoming aware of new profit opportunities, of which they try to take advantage. Consequently, the

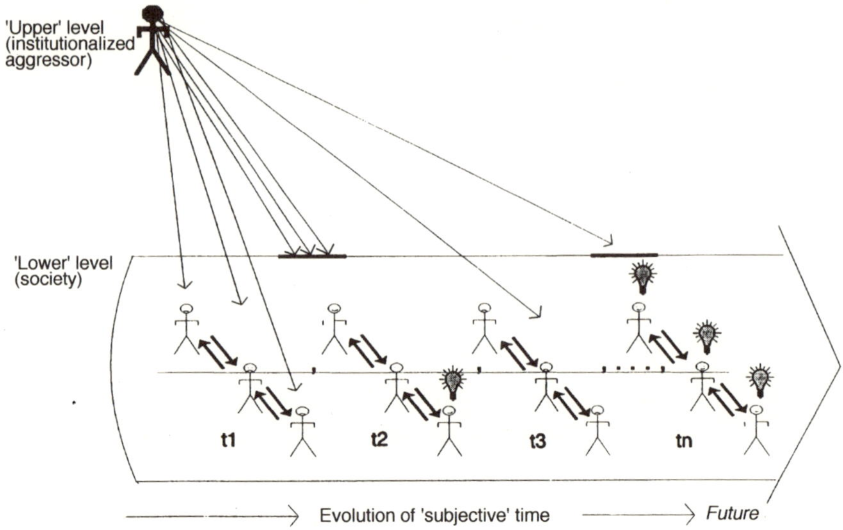

Figure 14.5

information possessed by each of them is constantly undergoing modification. This is represented in Figure 14.5 by the different bulbs which light up as time passes.

It is clear that not only will it be impossible for the controlling organism to have all the information necessary to co-ordinate society by commands at its disposal, given that this information is, as we have seen, dispersed, exclusive and impossible to articulate, but that, moreover, it will be continually modified and will arise *ex nihilo* as time passes. It is highly unlikely that it is possible to transmit to the controlling organism information that is at each moment indispensable for the co-ordination of society but which has not even yet been created by the entrepreneurial process itself.

Thus, for example, when it looks rainy at dawn or there is any other series of meteorological circumstances, farmers realize that, as a result of the change in the situation, they will have to modify their decision on the different tasks that should be done on the farm on that day, without being able to formally articulate the reasons for which they are taking such a decision. It is not possible, therefore, to transfer this information, which is the result of many years of experience and work on the farm, to a hypothetical controlling organism (for example, a ministry of agriculture in the capital) and await instructions. The same may be said of any other person who carries on their entrepreneurship in a determined environment, be it a decision as to whether they should invest in a certain company or sector, or whether they should buy or sell certain stocks or shares, or whether they should contract certain persons to collaborate in their work, etc. We may, therefore, consider that the practical information is not only, as it were, in a capsule, in the sense that it is not accessible to the controlling organism which practises institutionalized aggression, but in addition to being in a capsule, is continually being modified and regenerated in a new form, as the future is created and made step by step by the actors.

Lastly, let us remember that, to the same extent as the socialist coercion is practised on a more continual and effective basis, the free pursuit of individual ends will be made increasingly impossible and, therefore, the latter will not act as an incentive and it will not be possible to discover or generate the practical information necessary to co-ordinate society through entrepreneurship. The controlling organism is, therefore, faced with a dilemma impossible to eradicate, as it has an absolute need of the information generated in the social process, which it cannot obtain under any circumstance, as, if it intervenes coercively in such process, it will destroy the capacity to create information and, if it does not intervene, it will not obtain the information either.

In short, we may conclude that, from the perspective of the social process, socialism is an intellectual error, as, for the following reasons, it is not possible to conceive that the controlling organism in charge of intervening with commands can obtain the information necessary to co-ordinate society:

- *First*, because of the volume (it is impossible for the intervening organism to consciously assimilate the enormous volume of practical information that is spread over the minds of human beings).
- *Second*, because the necessary information is essentially impossible to transfer to the central organism (as it is tacit and impossible to articulate).
- *Third*, because, in addition, it is not possible to transfer information which has not yet been discovered or created by the actors and which only arises as a result of the free process of the practice of entrepreneurship.
- *Fourth*, because the practice of coercion prevents the entrepreneurial process from discovering and creating the information necessary to co-ordinate society.

THE IMPOSSIBILITY OF SOCIALISM FROM THE PERSPECTIVE OF THE CONTROLLING ORGANISM

Now from the perspective of what we have called the 'upper' level in the figures, i.e. from the standpoint of the person or group of persons, organized to a greater or lesser extent, who systematically and institutionally carry out aggression against the free practice of entrepreneurship, we should make a series of considerations which confirm, even more, if that is possible, the conclusion that socialism is simply an intellectual error.

We will begin by accepting for dialectic purposes, as did Mises (1966: 696), that the controlling organism (regardless of whether it is a dictator or leader, an elite, a group of scientists or intellectuals, a ministerial department, a group of representatives elected democratically by 'the people' or, in short, any combination, of a greater or lesser complexity, of all or some of these elements) is endowed with the maximum technical and intellectual capacity, experience and wisdom, together with the best intentions, that is humanly conceivable (we will soon see that these hypotheses are not true in reality and the reason for this). However, what cannot be accepted is that the controlling organism is endowed with superhuman capacities nor, specifically, that it has the gift of omniscience,[8] i.e. that it is capable of assimilating, knowing and interpreting simultaneously all the scattered and exclusive information that is dispersed over the minds of all the beings who act in society and which is continually being generated and created *ex novo* by these beings.

The reality is that the greater part of the controlling organism, sometimes also called the planning organism or organism of central or partial intervention, does not know, or only has a very vague idea as to the knowledge that is available dispersed among the minds of all the actors who may be submitted to its orders. There is, therefore, a small or nonexistent possibility that the planner may come to know, or know where to look for and find, the elements of dispersed information that are being generated in the social process and of which it has such a great need in order to control and co-ordinate such process.

Moreover, the controlling organism will unavoidably have to be composed of human beings with all their virtues and defects, who, like any other actor, will have their own personal ends which will act as incentives and lead them to discover the information relevant to their personal interests. Most probably, therefore, the people who constitute the controlling organism, if they use their entrepreneurial intuition correctly from the point of view of their own ends or interests, will generate the information and experience necessary to, for example, keep themselves in power indefinitely and justify and rationalize their acts to themselves and to third parties, practise coercion in an increasingly sophisticated and effective way, present their aggression to the citizens as something inevitable and attractive, etc.

To the contrary of the 'well-intentioned' hypothesis set out at the beginning of the preceding paragraph, these will generally be the most common incentives and will prevail over others, particularly over interest in discovering the practical, specific and relevant information that exists at each moment dispersed over society and which is necessary to make the co-ordinated functioning of the latter possible through commands. This lack of motivation will determine, moreover, that the controlling organism does not even realize, i.e. become conscious, of the degree of its own ineradicable ignorance, sinking into a process that distances it more and more from the social realities that it is trying to control.

In addition, the controlling organism will become incapable of making any kind of economic calculation, inasmuch as, regardless of its ends (and we may again imagine that they are the most 'human' and 'morally elevated' ones), it cannot know whether the costs incurred in pursuing such ends have, for itself, a value even greater than the value that it attributes subjectively to the ends pursued. The cost is merely the subjective value which the actor attributes to what must be renounced in pursuit of a determined end. It is obvious that the controlling organism cannot obtain the knowledge or information necessary to become aware of the true cost incurred in accordance with its own scale of values, as the information necessary to estimate costs is spread over the minds of all the human beings or actors who make up the social process and who are coerced by the controlling organism (democratically elected or otherwise) in charge of systematically practising aggression against the body of society.

In this respect, if we define the concept of responsibility as the quality of the action that is executed once the actor has come to know the cost thereof and takes such cost into account by the corresponding estimated economic calculation, we may conclude that the controlling organism, regardless of its composition, system of choice and value judgements, as it is unable to see and appreciate the costs incurred, will always tend to act irresponsibly. There exists, therefore, the unresolvable paradox that the more the controlling organism tries to plan or control a determined area of life in society, the less possibilities it will have of reaching its objectives, as it cannot obtain the information necessary to organize society, creating, moreover, new, serious imbalances and distortions to the precise degree that its coercion is carried out more effectively and limits the entrepreneurship of human beings.

We must, therefore, draw the conclusion that it is a serious error to think that the controlling organism can make economic calculations in the same way as the individual entrepreneur. On the contrary, the more developed the socialist organization, the more practical first-hand information which is indispensable for economic calculation will be lost, making economic calculation completely impossible to the precise degree to which obstacles to free human action are placed by the organism practising institutionalized coercion.

CRITICISM OF THE ALTERNATIVE CONCEPT OF SOCIALISM

Traditionally, socialism has been defined as the system of social organization based on state ownership of the means of production. This definition has for a long time been the most generalized definition for historical and political reasons. It was the original definition used by Mises in his critical treatise on socialism in 1922[9] and was later considered by Mises and the rest of his school as a reference point throughout the subsequent controversy as to the impossibility of socialist economic calculation.

However, since its origin, this traditional definition of socialism could be seen to be unsatisfactory. First, it was of an evidently static nature, as it depended on the existence or otherwise of a determined legal institution (property rights) in relation to a specific economic category (the means of production). Therefore, the use of this definition of socialism required a prior explanation of what was understood by property rights and the implications of such a concept in the economic area. Moreover, the controversy on the impossibility of socialism showed how the different scientists involved had serious communication difficulties among themselves, precisely due to the different meaning and contents they considered implicit in their concept of property rights. Finally, the traditional definition appeared to exclude interventionism and economic control from its scope. However, notwithstanding the fact that it did not demand full state ownership of the means of production, interventionism produced effects of lack of co-ordination which were qualitatively very similar. For all these reasons, it seemed advisable to continue searching to find a definition of socialism that went to the very root of its essence, was as free as possible of concepts liable to ambiguous interpretation and which, as was the case of the social processes to which it would be applied, had a markedly dynamic nature.

Second, one of the most important consequences of the controversy on the impossibility of socialist economic calculation was the development and refinement by the economists of the Austrian school (Mises, Hayek and, above all, Kirzner) of a theory in which entrepreneurship appeared as the protagonizing and creative force of all social processes. The discovery that it was precisely our innate entrepreneurial capacity, visible through our own creative action, which made life in society possible, as it discovered social imbalances and created and transmitted the information necessary for each actor to learn to discipline their own behaviour in accordance with their peers, indicated definitively the path along which the preparation of a truly scientific concept of socialism should travel.

The following most important step in the process of the formation of a definition of socialism was given by Hans-Hermann Hoppe. Hoppe (1989) has shown that the essential characteristic of socialism is that it is based on an aggression or institutionalized interference against property rights. He (Hoppe 1989: 2) states that 'Socialism, by no means an invention of XIX century Marxism but much older, must be conceptualized as an institutionalized interference with or agression against private property and private property claims.' His definition is more dynamic and, therefore, much more operative than the traditional definition. He does not talk about the existence or otherwise of something called property rights, but about whether institutionally, i.e. in a repetitive and organized way, coercion or physical violence is practised against property rights.

Although we consider Hoppe's definition to be an important advance, it does not seem completely satisfactory as, first, it requires that what is understood by property rights be explained or defined *ab initio* and, second, it does not make any mention of the practise of entrepreneurship as the essential protagonist of all social processes.

Combining Hoppe's definition, in the sense that all socialism implies the systematic use of coercion, with the contributions in the field of the theory of entrepreneurship of Kirzner, we reach the conclusion that the most appropriate definition of socialism is that which has been proposed and used in this article, according to which socialism is any organized system of institutionalized aggression against entrepreneurship and human action. This definition has, in the first place, the advantage of being easily understood by anybody, without the need for an *a priori* detailed explanation of what is understood by property rights and what their contents should be. Anybody can understand that human action may or may not be aggressive and that, when it is not so, except in the specific case of a person defending oneself from arbitrary non-systematic external aggression, such action is the most intimate and typical manifestation of the human being and, therefore, is something completely legitimate which must be respected.

In other words, we consider our definition of socialism to be the most appropriate because it is established in terms of the concept of human action and, therefore, in terms of the most intimate essence of humankind. Moreover, socialism is conceived as an institutionalized aggression against the precise forces that make life in society possible and, in this respect, it is only apparently paradoxical to state that there is nothing more anti-social than the socialist system itself. Bringing this reality to light is one of the greatest virtues of the definition of socialism we propose. Without any doubt, the process of social interaction free from aggression requires compliance with a whole series of rules, guidelines or behaviour habits. All of these together constitute law in the traditional sense, i.e. the framework within which human actions may pacifically be carried out. Law, however, is not something that arises prior to the practise of human action, but a result of the evolution and customs of the social process of interaction itself. Therefore, according to our definition, socialism is not a system of institutionalized aggression against an evolutionary consequence of entrepreneurship (property rights), but a system of aggression against human action or entrepreneurship itself.

Our definition of socialism allows the theory of society to relate directly to a theory on law, its origins, development and evolution. Moreover, it is perfectly compatible with our posing the questions, on a theoretical level, of what property rights arise from a non-coercive social process, what the just property rights are, and to what point socialism is ethically admissible or otherwise.

SOCIALISM AND INTERVENTIONISM

Another advantage of the definition of socialism we have proposed is that it includes or incorporates within its scope the social system based on interventionism. In fact, whether interventionism is considered one of the typical features of socialism or, as is more usual, an intermediate system between 'real socialism' and the free social process, it is evident that, as any interventionist measure consists of an institutional aggression coercively practised in a certain social area, interventionism, regardless of its degree, type or cause, is socialism from the standpoint of our definition.

The use of the terms 'socialism' and 'interventionism' as synonyms, far from being an unjustified broadening of the sense that they normally have, is an analytic requirement for the theory of social processes. In fact, although originally the first Austrian school theorists who dealt with interventionism considered it to be a different conceptual category from socialism,[10] as the controversy on the impossibility of socialist economic calculation advanced, the borderlines between the two concepts were erased and this definition process has continued up to the present day, when it has become evident to those who cultivate the theory of entrepreneurship that there is no qualitative difference between socialism and interventionism,[11] although it may be admitted that, in colloquial usage, one term or the other is sometimes used to refer to the different degrees to which the same reality becomes manifest.

In addition, the proposed definition of socialism permits science to play the important role of revealing the attempts, very habitual nowadays in many political, social and cultural spheres, to immunize interventionism against the natural and inevitable effects of the economic, social and political decay of 'real socialism', which is, in fact, its predecessor and intellectual inspiration. Real socialism and interventionism are, at most, only two manifestations of different degrees of intensity of the same coercive and institutionalized reality and they fully share the same essential intellectual error and the same pernicious social consequences.

NOTES

1 With regard to the concept of human action and its main elements, L. von Mises (1966: 11–29 and 251–256) should be especially consulted. Mises textually states that 'every actor is always an entrepreneur and a speculator' (p. 252) and that 'entrepreneur means *acting man* in regard to the changes occurring in the market' (p. 254).

2 The main writer on the concept of entrepreneurship discussed in this article is I.M. Kirzner, Professor of Economics at the University of New York. He is the author of a trilogy (*Perception, Opportunity and Profit, Competition and Entrepreneurship* and *Discovery and the Capitalist Process*, 1973, 1979 and 1985, respectively), in which he expands upon and makes an impeccable in-depth study of the different aspects of the concept of entrepreneurship which was initially developed by L. von Mises and F.A. Hayek. Moreover, Kirzner has written a fourth book, *Discovery, Capitalism and Distributive Justice* (1989), which studies the implications of his concept of entrepreneurship in the field of *social ethics.*

3 Saint Thomas of Aquinas (1954: 293–294 and 301) defines particular circumstances as *accidentia individualia humanorum actuum* (i.e. the individual accidents of human acts) and states that, apart from time and place, the most important of such particular circumstances is that which refers to the end pursued by the actor (*principalissima est omnium circunstantiarum illa quae attingit actum ex parte finis*). In addition, it must be pointed out that we owe the distinction between practical knowledge and scientific knowledge to M. Oakeshott (1962, 1975, 1991: 12, 15, 23–25, 36, 78–79 and 119–121).

4 This distinction has become generalized since it was given in 1949 by Gilbert Ryle in his well-known article 'Knowing How and Knowing That', included in Ryle (1949).

5 Lavoie (1985: 103–104) adds that, if costs were something that could be established objectively, scientifically and universally, the taking of decisions in economic life could be reduced to obeying a series of completely articulated and specified rules but, given that costs are something subjective and can only be known within the context of each specific action by the actor, the practice of entrepreneurship cannot be articulated in detail or replaced by any objective criterion of a scientific nature.

6 The *Dictionary of the Spanish Royal Academy* defines coercion (in Spanish: 'coacción') as 'force or violence performed upon a person to make him execute something'. It comes from the Latin *cogere*, to impel, and *coactionis*, which refers to the collection of taxes. Regarding the concept of coercion and its effects on the human actor, the reader should consult Hayek (1959: 20–21).

7 L. von Mises (1981: 40) has already stated that 'the idea of socialism is at once grandiose and simple. We may say, in fact, that it is one of the most ambitious creations of the human spirit, so magnificent, so daring, that it has rightly aroused the greatest admiration. If we wish to save the world from barbarism we have to refute socialism, but we cannot thrust it carelessly aside.'

8 Mises (1966: 696) even states that the director (or controlling organism) 'has at his disposal all the technical knowledge of his age. Moreover, he has a complete inventory of all the material factors of production available and a roster enumerating all manpower employable. In these respects the crowd of experts and specialists which he assembles in his offices provide him with *perfect information* and answer correctly all questions he may ask them. Their voluminous reports accumulate in huge piles on his desk.' Furthermore, Mises assumes that 'the director has made up his mind with regard to the valuation of ultimate ends' and that 'everyone agrees with one another and with the director in the valuation of ultimate ends' (*ibid.*). However, when Mises refers to 'perfect information' and to the availability of 'a complete inventory of all the factors of production', this must be understood in its technological sense ('all the technological knowledge of his age') and as a concession referring only to the first reason against socialism that we have given in the text (it is impossible to assimilate the enormous volume of information spread over

society, even if it is correctly articulated, i.e. without errors, as Mises concedes). But Mises is not making any concessions regarding the other three reasons for the impossibility of socialism, which could only be solved assuming *perfect knowledge* (in the neoclassical sense), i.e. an *omniscient* capability to have (a) inarticulate knowledge; (b) knowledge not yet created by the entrepreneurs; and (c) knowledge that can only be created by the entrepreneurs if not coerced. So, Mises explicitly states that 'it would be nothing short of idiocy to assume that (the directors) are omniscient and infallible', adding that the question is 'whether any *mortal* man, equipped with the logical structure of the *human* mind, can be equal to the tasks incumbent upon a director of a socialist society, (*ibid.*). He concludes that 'It is vain to comfort oneself with the hope that the organs of the collective economy will be "omnipresent" and "omniscient". We do not deal in praxeology with the acts of the omnipresent and omniscient Deity, but with the actions of man endowed with a human mind only. Such a mind cannot plan without economic calculation' (p. 710). This long note was necessary because very recently some Austrian economists, in their obsession with dehomogenizing Mises and Hayek, have concluded that Mises was assuming that socialism was impossible even under 'perfect knowledge' (i.e. 'omniscient' conditions), as if Mises' argument were a mere computational problem inside the static framework of the pure logic of choice. (See Salerno 1990a: 36–41; 1990b: 51–71; 1993: 113–146; Rothbard 1991: 51–76; 1992: 4–5).

9 For Mises (1981: 211; originally German 1922), 'The essence of socialism is this: all the means of production are in the exclusive control of the organized community. This and this alone is socialism. All other definitions are misleading.' Three years earlier (1919), he wrote almost exactly the same definition in *Nation, State and Economy*, (1983: 172; originally German 1919). For the reasons put forward in the text, we believe that Mises was mistaken to make such an emphatic statement.

10 The first one to use the term 'interventionism' in its economic sense was L. von Mises (1929, 1976). See also Lavoie (1982).

11 Thus, for example, Lavoie (1981: 5) concludes that interventionism '*can be shown to be self-defeating and irrational on much the same grounds on which Mises pronounced complete central planning impossible* . . . piecemeal government interference into the price system must be seen as similarly obstructive of this same necessary discovery procedure, and therefore as distortive of the knowledge which it generates. Thus the calculation argument may be used to explain many of the less-than-total failures resulting from government *tinkering* with the price system, in fundamentally the same way that it explains the utter economic ruin inevitably resulting from the attempted *abolition* of the price system'. Kirzner (1985: 121), for his part, has referred on several occasions to the *parallelism* between socialism and interventionism. We must criticize the idea, even defended by Mises on occasions, that economic calculation is possible in interventionist systems, as such calculation is impossible precisely in the areas where intervention takes place and if, in general, some calculations may be made, it is because the system does not extend its intervention to the whole society (at least to the degree that characterizes real socialism).

REFERENCES

Aquinas, T. (1954) *Suma Teólogica*, Part I–II, Q7, Art. 1 & 2, Vol. IV, Madrid: BAC.

Hayek, F.A. (1959) *Constitution of Liberty*, London: Routledge.

Hayek, F.A. (1972) *Individualism and Economic Order*, Chicago: Henry Regnery Company.
Hoppe, H-H. (1989) *A Theory of Socialism and Capitalism*, Boston: Kluwer Academic Publishers.
Kirzner, I.M. (1973) *Competition and Entrepreneurship*, Chicago: University of Chicago Press.
Kirzner, I.M. (1979) *Perception, Opportunity and Profit*, Chicago: University of Chicago Press.
Kirzner, I.M. (ed.) (1982), *Method, Process and Austrian Economics: Essays in Honor of Ludwig von Mises*, Massachusetts: Lexington Books.
Kirzner, I.M. (1985) *Discovery and the Capitalist Process*, Chicago: University of Chicago Press.
Kirzner, I.M. (1989) *Discovery, Capitalism and Distributive Justice*, Oxford: Basil Blackwell.
Lavoie, D. (1981) 'Introduction', *The Journal of Libertarian Studies* V (1).
Lavoie, D. (1982) 'The Development of the Misesian Theory of Interventionism', in Kirzner (1982).
Lavoie, D. (1985) *Rivalry and Central Planning*, Cambridge: Cambridge University Press.
Mises, L. (1919) *Nation, Staat und Wirtschaft*, Wien/Leipzig: Manzsche. English translation by L.B. Yeager (1983) *Nation, State and Economy*, New York and London: New York University Press.
Mises, L. (1929) *Kritik des Interventionismus*, Jena: Gustav Fischer Verlag.
Mises, L. (1966) *Human Action: A Treatise on Economics*, 3rd edn, Chicago: Henry Regnery Company.
Mises, L. (1976) *A Critique of Interventionism*, New York: Arlington House.
Mises, L. (1981) *Socialism: An Economic and Sociological Analysis*, Indianapolis: Liberty Classics; originally published in German in 1922.
Oakeshott, M. (1962) *Rationalism in Politics*, London: Methuen.
Oakeshott, M. (1975) *On Human Conduct*, Oxford: Oxford University Press. Re-edited 1991, Oxford: Clarendon Paperbacks.
Oakeshott, M. (1991) *Rationalism in Politics and Other Essays*, Indianapolis: Liberty Press.
Oxford English Dictionary (1989), 2nd edn, Vol. V, Oxford: Clarendon Press.
Polanyi, M. (1959), *The Study of Man*, Chicago: University of Chicago Press.
Rothbard, M.N. (1991) 'The End of Socialism and the Calculation Debate Revisited', *Review of Austrian Economics* 5 (2): 51–56.
Rothbard, M.N. (1992) *The Present State of Austrian Economics*, Auburn, Alabama: Ludwig Mises Institute.
Ryle, G. (1949) *The Concept of Mind*, London: Hutchinson's University Library.
Salerno, J.T. (1990a) 'Ludwig von Mises as Social Rationalist', *Review of Austrian Economics* 4: 36–41.
Salerno, J.T. (1990b) 'Postscript: Why a Socialist Economy is "Impossible"', in L. Mises, *Economic Calculation in the Socialist Commonwealth*, Auburn, Alabama: Praxeology Press.
Salerno, J.T. (1993) 'Mises and Hayek Dehomogenized', *Review of Austrian Economics* 6 (2): 113–146.

15

THE AUSTRIAN PERSPECTIVE FOR THE EUROPEAN ECONOMY TODAY*

Roel P. Zuidema

> The Good Society is one in which the chances of anyone selected at random are likely to be as great as possible.
>
> (F.A. Hayek 1976: 132)

INTRODUCTION

Reflection on the history and relevance of the Austrian school in economics can take different forms. There is some reason nowadays to frame that reflection in the following, more specific way. The part of the world from which Austrian economics originated is of late more or less unstable. The various political–economic institutions that had become so familiar in the course of forty years, with a sharp dividing line between a Western and an Eastern part of Europe, are no longer taken for granted. In the former a certain renewal of the political–economic order seems to be getting under way. In the latter the old order has been rapidly falling apart, but the hopefully expected introduction of adequate new socio-economic arrangements has proven to be difficult both in design and application. As yet an underlying concept for a new political–economic order for the whole of Europe seems lacking. In this context it may be asked: what message does (neo-)Austrian economic thinking have for (re-)shaping the economic institutions of this part of the world to the benefit of all the peoples concerned?

Of course it is not the purpose to discuss that generally formulated problem fully. The intention is to investigate in a rather preliminary way if and in what sense a kind of optimal economic regime, based on an Austrian point of view, could be aimed at (and ultimately installed) in Europe. More particularly it will be discussed what kind of questions should be considered and which possible answers could be given, in the context of the history of

* This article is an elaboration of a paper presented at a European Conference on Austrian Economics in Maastricht, April 9–10, 1992. Comments on an earlier draft by two anonymous referees are gratefully acknowledged.

Europe. Is there something of great importance with regard to the political–economic future of Europe that at this very moment should not be overlooked, according to the (Neo-)Austrians?

The first section of this paper summarizes the development of Austrian ideas on political economy in general. It is followed by a simple model of the message of the (Neo-)Austrian economists for taking a historically proper viewpoint on the possibility of a market economy which would seize every known opportunity for an effective use of economic resources in full accordance with personal preferences.

The next section discusses the institutional features of present-day Europe-in-transition and the suitable content of an Austrian program. Finally, some tentative conclusions are presented regarding the presumed Austrian message and its chance of realization.

THE DEVELOPMENT OF AUSTRIAN THINKING ON POLITICAL ECONOMY

For the purpose of this article it is appropriate to give a simple outline of the development of the Austrian view on political–economic matters. There were in fact certain differences of opinion not only among members of different generations, but also among representatives of the same generation. With that reservation, we look at the history of the Austrian School to give a rough picture of the original content and later formulation of its political–economic way of thinking.

The first generation

The founders of the Austrian School were more or less close to each other in their way of economic thinking. Menger and his early disciples, Wieser and Böhm-Bawerk, strongly advocated the idea of subjective value. They really proved to be masters in their explanation and use of the, at that time, conceived 'marginal method' for understanding economic phenomena in a market setting.

Streissler (1990) has concluded from the lectures given by Menger to the Austrian crown prince (such as reflected in the notebooks of the latter) that he certainly was a minimalist as regards state action. But in the opinion of Kirzner (1990), one should distinguish between his central vision of the economic system, and complicating considerations regarding error and property rights, when he was moving from the realm of economic theory to that of social policy. He acknowledges that Menger's basic vision has a strong classical–liberal ring, which he prefered to stress in those lectures to Crown Prince Rudolph, that being the central message for an introductory course; but that, furthermore, there is also a Mengerian 'fine print', in which on occasion he assigns important interventionist responsibilities to the state. Menger, in the view of Hutchison, 'was critical of would-be reformers who failed to perceive or appreciate the possibly, or even frequently, beneficent workings of some originally spontaneous, unplanned social institutions', but 'he was also critical of the unqualified conservative defence or exaltation . . . of such "natural" institutions and processes'.[1] With regard to the two other early Austrians, Böhm-Bawerk on the one hand could be perceived as a defender of the so-called capitalist economic system, while Wieser, according to Hutchison (1981: 207), 'was highly critical of free-market capitalism, attached great importance to the growth of monopoly, and was highly sympathetic to social-democratic and reformist ideas'.

The power of the market as an institution to exploit the available economic means, in their view, could both principally be understood and historically demonstrated. Next to their academic work this first generation has played an important role in government service in the imperial Vienna of their time. It is not entirely correct to suggest one uniform whole of economic analysis in so far as they quarrelled with each other while developing their main ideas and spelling out their theories. Nevertheless, together they have given a coherent picture of their school's general view concerning the proper organization of society. This may be considered as a vision of a liberal political content in conjunction with an authentic subjective value approach in economics.

From the beginning the Austrian School also had followers outside its country of origin. Gradually it became less attached to its Vienna base and this geographical centre was lost at the end of the 1930s. Certain economists have carried forward the Austrian flag to recent times, although each of them did so in their own way. In this connection one also sees Schumpeter mentioned, but we may consider Mises and Hayek as the two main representatives. Their opinions will be discussed in more detail in order to arrive at a comprehensive picture of the 'Austrian' message for political economy.

But first a few remarks here are in order about Schumpeter, in so far as he may be considered as an Austrian economist. He presented a competitive and a monopolistic interpretation of the capitalist economic process successively. The former centres around a dynamic vision of the role of entrepreneurs, to realize the innovations necessary for economic development, while the latter stresses the role of established large-sized firms for carrying on the economic development of society.[2] In the end, according to Schumpeter, socialism and (guided) capitalism would perhaps not make such a great difference to the way in which production will be organized. In his final expectations for the future political–economic order he seems to let them almost converge to some kind of melted system.[3]

Mises' free and prosperous commonwealth

The essence of Mises' view on political economy has been comprehensively formulated in his book on *Liberalismus* (1927).[4] He presented it as a doctrine which could be seen as the central tenet of his whole work. With the term 'liberalism' he refers to the social order endorsed by the philosophy of the Enlightenment. It implies that a condition of society described as capitalism entails the best economic prospects for all its members. His explanation is as follows.

At least in the tradition of the Classical School in economics, political economy should be understood as the scientific examination of different ways of organizing society on the basis of the division of labour. From such an inquiry it follows that there seems to be a choice between two basic arrangements: communal and private ownership of the means of production. In opposition to liberalism, socialism implies a preference for the former, but in the end cannot deliver what its adherents promise. Liberalism favours capitalism because it is the only workable system to produce the fruits of social co-operation. There is indeed no other way to arrive at rational economic calculations. The institution of the market is indispensable to get a common (monetary) denominator to compare and decide on alternatives in the use of means.[5]

The material interests of the members of a society can only be secured, Mises concludes, by allowing them to make economic decisions on the basis of private property. It is impossible to conceive of a central body, exercising overall authority over the use of the means of production, to make all the necessary decisions in the pursuit of public welfare. In other words, capitalism is the proper system of social organization for a modern economy, if no return to medieval or ancient levels of material provision for the population is desired. It is enhanced by peaceful conditions in which everyone receives equal treatment under the law. Liberalism involves a restrictive view on government and, at the same time, does not restrict the application of its principles to national boundaries. The role of the state is to secure a peaceful order within its territory. The state should, however, refrain from acts of interventionism in the economic sphere. The grasping for immediate benefits by interference with the market for some political attractive goal neglects the provisional costs of such a measure (in terms of the provisional benefits of non-interference).

In particular, protectionism should not reign in international economic relations. In Mises' view it is this kind of policy, whatever its motives, that could finally lead to war. It also may be considered the explanation for the relative economic backwardness of the continental states of Europe in the first quarter of this century as compared to the United States. People striving for a United States of Europe then already seemed to have that in mind. But what they forgot, according to Mises (at the end of the 1920s), is the higher goal of a world-wide free economic system to produce the fruits of division of labour on the widest possible level. The behaviour of states in the past impeded such a development.

Hayek on politics and economics

Besides Mises, Hayek also expressed ideas on politics and economics from an 'Austrian' point of view over a long period. In the collection of essays published in 1949 under the title *Individualism and Economic Order*, he admits these to be 'fragments, products which have emerged in the pursuit of a distant goal, which for the time being must serve in place of the finished product'. They were in fact preliminary to his fuller treatment of various issues in later publications. But these essays clearly contain many insights which, although from a somewhat different angle, may be called consistent with those found in the work of Mises. It is therefore justified to consider the essence of Hayek's thought as at least complementary to that of Mises'.

First of all he rejects the pragmatic attitude that became dominant in the first half of this century and then led to precisely the state of affairs that nobody wanted (in the period 1914–1945).[6] The principles of true and false individualism should be clearly distinguished instead. He describes 'false individualism' as the rationalistic pseudo-individualism, of Cartesian origin, which leads us to believe that no order in society can be reached if not properly designed according to some well-conceived plan. He considers this manner of thinking (for which he later introduced the term 'constructivism') to be fundamental to 'socialism'. True individualism, on the contrary, is based on an anti-rationalistic approach and regards a human as 'a very irrational and fallible being, whose individual errors are corrected only in the course of a social process, and aims at making the best of a very imperfect material'. But, at the same time, it is believed that 'if left free, men will often achieve more than individual human reason could design or foresee'. In Hayek's opinion the contrast between these two types of individualism permeates all social thought.

How then could a rational economic order according to Hayek be constructed?[7] On certain familiar assumptions, so Hayek remarks, the answer is simple enough. If we have all the necessary information concerning preferences and available means at hand, it is purely a problem of logic. But for a whole society the data from which we start with our economic calculus are never given to a single mind and can never be so given. Therefore the economic problem of a society is how to utilize knowledge, which in its totality is not given to anyone. The real function of the price mechanism is precisely that it is a mechanism for communicating information throughout the economic system to the individual economic actors. The price system is indispensable for any rational calculation in a complex society. In the meantime, this has also become clear to adherents of '(market) socialism'. Therefore the problem at hand is how to make the best use of that price system, and how to stimulate the spread of relevant knowledge in the economic system.

How can one extend this kind of economic order on an international level? In the aforementioned collection of essays Hayek considers the possibility of a federation between states as leading to less government interference, and therefore favourable or desirable. Furthermore, in (a reprint of) an article from the early 1940s he discussed the attractiveness of 'A Commodity Reserve Currency' for an international monetary system which is not controlled in an arbitrary manner, but based on some kind of mechanical and predictable rule. After 1975 Hayek has even pleaded for the denationalization of money and instead a competition between currencies supplied by private issues (e.g. Hayek 1984). He expects that under complete freedom of the money supply, every money supplier is inclined to deploy a price index of a bundle of commodities for keeping the purchasing power of the deposits they offer constant (see also Visser 1993). Concerning the prospects of international order he remarked in the same period:

> An international authority which effectively limits the powers of the state over the individual will be one of the best safe-guards of peace. The international Rule of Law must become a safeguard as much against the tyranny of the state over the individual as against the tyranny of the new super-state over the national communities.[8]

THE (NEO-)AUSTRIAN POLITICAL–ECONOMIC MESSAGE

Both Mises and Hayek elaborated their views in various other publications. After some more or less lonely decades they got company from their intellectual offspring: the Neo-Austrians. The kernel of their political–economic message may be expressed in the form of a (consistent) 'model' of strongly held beliefs or contentions with regard to the socio-economic organization.

The principle for choosing the socio-economic order

The basic Austrian viewpoint from which to discern between various types of socio-economic organization is that of 'liberalism'.[9] This leaves it to all to decide how to use their knowledge for their own purposes, to act freely and to pursue whatever aims they have according to the values they adhere to. Under unpredictable circumstances, this facilitates the growth of reason for society as a whole. In this way full use is made of the creative powers of a free civilization. This could also explain the tremendous advancements in technology and the material provision for needs in the past.[10] From this viewpoint of liberalism it follows that, contrary to socialism, private property must not only be allowed for consumer goods but should also be extended to the means of production. The 'socialist' alternative of collective ownership of the means of production will lead to a waste of resources because of the impossibility of economic calculation, in the absence of information on which to base decisions, and because it will imply coercion by the state with regard to people's actions.[11]

The use and diffusion of relevant economic information

Under circumstances of capitalism the markets provide price signals to allow individual entrepreneurs to make their calculations for activities that, depending on their profitability, will also serve the needs of their customers and thus society at large. With changing conditions of scarcity, the necessary adjustments will almost automatically take place because information about these changes will be adequately communicated in the economic system through price alterations; that is to say, provided that the government does not directly interfere with the market process and price formation, and also abstains from a progressive income taxation.[12]

The proper role of government in society

For true law to be anchored in society, Hayek indicated three cornerstones in his *Constitution of Liberty* (1960). These are: the rule of law (government must never coerce an individual except in the enforcement of a known rule), that law must be known and certain, and that law should apply equally to all. Next to coercive activities government can also pursue several service functions, and it may provide general regulations specifying conditions which certain activities must satisfy.[13]

The use of the government apparatus to promote a so-called distributive justice is not consistent with the functioning of markets, nor with the aforementioned cornerstones of true law, as guarantees for individual freedom of the members of society. There is a great difference between equality 'before the law' and 'by the law'. Government should also take additional action to promote the diffusion of economic knowledge in society. In the supply of money, it has the duty to respect the need for a stable currency. Therefore, liberalism should not be identified with *laissez-faire*, as far as certain functions in a society should be fulfilled by government.

The shaping of the international economic order

Concerning the right international economic order, and at the same time to advance the realization of the above guidelines on a national scale, the striving for political and economic union between states has positive and negative aspects: positive in so far as that, within such a union, there will be a tendency for the task of the local and central government authorities to be restricted to their proper functions; but there is a negative counterpart, in so far as this could be accompanied by a further obstacle, from the side of government, in the sense of protectionism by which such a union would be shielded from (the fruits of) international trade.

The above 'model' of the political–economic message of the Austrian heritage clearly shows that it is not possible to exclude one element from it.

INSTITUTIONAL DISARRAY, TRANSITION AND RESHAPING

Taking the above message as a starting point, its relevance to the prospects for the economy in the whole of Europe today should be considered.

The present political–economic situation in Europe

The political–economic outlook for Europe at the moment may roughly be summarized as follows. In the former Soviet Union a situation of disarray exists. In the heart of continental Europe this is accompanied by a certain institutional transition already under way. In the so-called western side of Europe, moreover, a continuous reshaping in the direction of a further political–economic integration takes place.

The Commonwealth of Independent States, as the major part of the Soviet Union since 1992 came to be known, officially remains on the track of a market economy. But no one seems to be sure that this can be realized in the near future after upheavals in the political sphere and recent setbacks in its economic implementation. Of course much will depend on what will happen in Russia proper, as the supposed political–economic locomotive of the whole area. The freeing of all prices occurred rather chaotically. That was not preceded, as preferably should have been the case, and also not immediately accompanied, by the decollectivization of state enterprises.

In the various other countries of central and eastern Europe, which used to belong to the Comecon group, developments make an actual transition to a kind of market economy in a not-too-distant future possibly more likely. Although their shorter period of communist rule may facilitate this process, it is as yet not clear at what exact kind of economic order they ultimately will arrive. Poland, Czechoslovakia and Hungary, because of their earlier renewing of the social–economic order, are closely watched by the other countries in this region for lessons to be learned from their experience. The three newly independent Baltic republics, Romania and Bulgaria, not to mention the war-plagued remnants of former Yugoslavia and Albania, are all experiencing rather bad economic conditions.

The members of the ('old') European Community, though keenly observing the turmoil on its eastern flank, are fully concentrating their efforts on the completion of a common market, and the reshaping of their own region into a political–economic union before the end of the century. This 'European Union' in itself could be appreciated as enhancing the chances of arriving at a type of socio-economic organization as outlined by the Austrians. However, considering what is going on in the rest of Europe, it is questionable whether that partial (or should we say 'piecemeal') realization of Austrian ideas should govern the policies of the twelve countries of the Community. It may be noticed that Sweden, Finland and Austria, traditionally neutral countries, became uneasy in their second-class position. Together with Norway they have applied for full membership which is expected soon to be honoured. This stays in sharp contrast to the case of other interested countries which are not allowed to join. By now striving for a separate political–economic union at the western side of the old cold war frontier, perhaps some larger and more worthy goal may be lost. There is a certain parallel with the formation in the 1950s of trading blocks in non-communist Europe. Austrians such as Haberler and Röpke did not like at all the creation of the EEC and of the EFTA as its counterpart. This would surely have a negative impact on the idea of an Atlantic Community; furthermore it could divide 'free' Europe into two separate blocks; and it would certainly not be in the interest of the Third World if protectionism were to be thus enhanced (Meijer, 1988: 168).

If it is correct to distinguish three regions in this way, more or less differing in political–economic circumstances, how are these to be put in line to provide the kind of prospects contained in the Austrian message for Europe as a whole? Let us try to describe what programme from that angle should now be recommended.

The content of an Austrian programme for Europe today

First of all, the instalment of a constitution of liberty (in the terminology of Hayek) should be contemplated. If that is not yet conceivable to apply to all of Europe, then at least it should be recommended to govern the relations between the European states, so as to let the Rule of Law reign everywhere. An extended European Court of Justice may be one of the conditions to the fulfilment of this.

Second, as a prerequisite for the socio-economic organization ultimately intended, there should be a free flow of goods in the whole continent as soon as possible. No specific economic barriers should be put in the way of trade, to protect whatever purpose by individual states. Incidentally, that should also apply to the agricultural objectives and policies adopted by the European Community in the past. Furthermore, it implies the breaking up of all tariffs in inter-European trade, also in the disguised forms that states are capable of thinking up.

Third, private property must become fully recognized throughout the whole of Europe, as the central cornerstone for implementing the market economy and to get all the possible fruits of that institution. This will eventually lead to re-allocation of investment funds, from the richer western side to the poorer eastern side, promoting a more equal socio-economic development.

Fourth, the provision of stable currencies is of course not only in the interest of the present members of the European Community, but will be of equal importance to other European countries. Therefore the introduction of the ECU as the main European currency, if it comes to that, should not be restricted to a part of Europe.[14]

Finally, it should not be the ultimate purpose to construct a kind of political–economic fortress Europe. But one may in the end settle for some loose European League of Nations, guaranteeing political freedom to citizens, equality for all under a basic law of rights, a free trade throughout the domain, an independent monetary authority and mutual economic assistance in supporting the overall infrastructure. As for the so-called distributive justice, it will become clear that, far from being just a national cause, it should only be pursued by indirect measures in terms of equal opportunities for all European citizens under the law. Everything else considered useful should then be based on voluntary co-operation between the member-states.

WHAT POLITICAL-ECONOMIC ORDER WILL EMERGE IN EUROPE?

Can we now reach some tentative conclusions, not only concerning the presumed Austrian political–economic message, but also regarding its chance of realization in the present circumstances in Europe? In this context yet another and possibly more important question arises, namely: what kind of political–economic order do we expect to emerge in Europe?

In the coming years political developments and socio-economic events may take their own course, but for at least a small part they can be influenced by a change in the vision of the politicians and the public at large. In the broader sense of the word such as has been propagated by members of the Austrian School, liberalism may be seen as a kind of social philosophy, which is attractive to more groups in a society than those united under a political umbrella with that name (see for instance Machlup 1969).

According to Buchanan (1990), himself not being an 'Austrian' economist, Europe in the 1990s finds itself historically in an analogous setting to that of the United States two centuries ago. More particularly, referring to the pre-Lincoln period, he considers that an historical example for creating an effective federal union for Europe. Buchanan emphasizes that the opportunity is in place and the time is ripe. 'Europe waits for its own James Madison, who understands the constitutional economics of competition and . . . appreciates the nuances of persuasive argument, bargaining and compromise required to generate agreement among apparently divergent interests.' Buchanan stresses that checks must be included in the constitutional contract that defines the federal structure. Formal rules will not be sufficient as the American experience has demonstrated, in his opinion, and therefore he recommends some explicit acknowledgement of the rights of citizens in the separate units to secede from union. That in itself, together with a guarantee that the economy both internally and externally remains open, will result in a factual limitation of the power of the central union; it is then forced to prevent secession becoming a viable option. His approach, incidentally, in many ways resembles the exposed (Neo-)Austrian line of thought.

Is there, in a conscious effort to improve the whole structure of European politics and economics in the next century, anything in particular that, according to the Austrian heritage, can be considered as being of crucial importance? Although it may appear an exaggeration, to the present author it seems to be their idea that somehow the shortsightedness of economic policies of government authorities must in fact be overcome as the main obstacle.[15]

Political–economic shortsightedness could indeed be the fundamental barrier to the creation and working of a benign political–economic order: not only in so far as politicians, both before and after elections, are inclined to give short-run promises and by all means try to show short-term results; but also because the combined action of these politicians tends to complicate the socio-economic order, in such a way that it fulfils its functions even less well than it could have if left to itself. Over longer periods of time this may also lead to an erosion not only of the market system proper, but also of the trust of people in a democratically chosen government to fulfil its rightful duties. The latter then should be considered only a part of, instead of somehow standing above, the socio-economic political order.

Over centuries, history has shown that governments have quite often acted to the detriment of their subjects. In modern states, even when the government is controlled by a democratically elected parliament, wisdom has not always led to the design and the implementation of benevolent economic policies. Although the best scenario for solving the actual political–economic problems in Europe may not be clear, it may be concluded that the Austrians still have much historical evidence in support of their main points of view. It has been their speciality to advise for the effective use of unpredictable opportunities.

NOTES

1 Hutchison (1981: 186) adds that Menger rejected both a kind of extreme liberalism and conservative 'mysticism', and in this context concluded (in the *Untersuchungen* of 1883): 'But never, and this is the essential point in the question under review, may science dispense with testing for their suitability those institutions which have come about 'organically'. It must, when careful investigation so requires, change and better them according to the measure of scientific insight and the practical experience at hand. No era may renounce this duty.'

2 Schumpeter's approach of the role of the entrepreneur with regard to the developing market economy has been criticized by Kirzner (1971). It was, namely, contended that development is initiated by innovators who are *generating* new opportunities, and in that way act to *disturb* a former existing state of equilibrium. Kirzner, on the contrary, stresses that entrepreneurship fulfils already *existing* but not yet recognized opportunities in a society. By this fulfilment of the potential for economic development, they must be considered an *equilibrating* force, as there was no satisfaction of all conditions for equilibrium consistent with available information before.

3 According to Halm (1969), Schumpeter and others are wrong in considering the increase of superficial similarities to be an indication of the convergence of economic systems. In his opinion, it is not in progress, if convergence means a symbiosis of market and central plan, with an emerging system that combines what is good and eliminates what is bad in the pure systems. 'The way to improve our system is not to combine principles and policies that are incompatible.'

4 In 1962 the book was reprinted in an English translation: *The Free and Prosperous Commonwealth*. Of this version a second edition has been published in 1976, under a title which came closer to that of the original: *Liberalism: A Socio-Economic Exposition*.

5 This critique of Mises, concerning the possibility and prospects of a collectivistic type of economy, gave rise to the socialist calculation debate. For a recent overview of the debate, and the several issues related to it, see W. Keizer (1989).

6 F.A. Hayek, 'Individualism: True and False' (1945), in Hayek (1949).

7 F.A. Hayek, 'The Use of Knowledge in Society' (1945), in Hayek (1949).

8 See the last chapter of Hayek (1944).

9 Mises (1962) rejects the philosophy of what he calls the *American* self-styled 'liberal'. 'Every measure aiming at confiscating some of the assets of those who own more than the average or at restricting the rights of the owners of property is considered as liberal and progressive.'

10 Hayek (1960: ch. 2). Concerning the performance of what he calls the liberal (international) economic order in the nineteenth century, Haberler has remarked that even Karl Marx, in the *Communist Manifesto* of 1848, has shown to be impressed by the productive achievements of the bourgeoisie: 'It has been the first to show what man's activity can bring about' (Haberler 1979). According to Kirzner, Austrian economists adhere to two basic tenets, two distinct insights about the economic world: that human action is purposeful, and that there is an indeterminacy and unpredictability inherent in human preferences, human expectations, and human knowledge (Kirzner 1976a).

11 At the end of his life, Oscar Lange, the direct opponent of Mises in the debate on the possibility of economic calculation under socialism, has come more

closely in the direction of Mises according to Rothbard. He refers to Lange's appreciation for the concept and elaboration of economic theory as (one form of) praxeology, which Lange defined as the science of rational activity. 'Lange's remarkable adoption of Misesian praxeology as the major base for economics, onto which Marxian and other approaches were then hastily grafted, met predictably mixed reaction in Marxian circles' (Rothbard 1971: 317).

12 Hayek (1960: ch. 15). With regard to Mises' 'hints' concerning the market process as a fundamental concept instead of equilibrium, see Lachmann (1971). And on the role of entrepreneurship in that market process, see Kirzner (1976b).

13 '. . . the basic principles of a liberal society may be summed up by saying that in such a society all coercive functions of government must be guided by the overruling importance of what I like to call THE THREE GREAT NEGATIVES: PEACE, JUSTICE AND LIBERTY. Their achievement requires that in its coercive functions government shall be confined to the enforcement of such prohibitions (stated as abstract rules) as can be equally applied to all, and to exacting under the same uniform rules from all a share of the costs of the other, non-coercive services it may decide to render to the citizens with the material and personal means thereby placed at its disposal' (Hayek 1967: ch. 11, 177).

14 In the last fifteen years Hayek pleaded for denationalization of money and competition between currencies supplied by private issuers (see e.g. Hayek 1984).

15 Both Mises and Hayek made this point very clear. In Hayek's (1978: 222) words: 'in the course of a long life my opinion of governments has steadily worsened: the more intelligently they try to act (as distinguished from simply following an established rule), the more harm they seem to do – because once they are known to aim at particular goals (rather than merely maintaining a self-correcting spontaneous order) the less they can avoid serving sectional interests' and furthermore 'The politician, acting on a modified Keynesian maxim that in the long run we are all out of office, does not care if his successful cure of unemployment is bound to produce more unemployment in the future' (*ibid.*: 223).

REFERENCES

Buchanan, J.M. (1990) 'An American Perspective on Europe's Constitutional Opportunity', paper presented at the Mont Pèlerin Society General Meeting (on the subject 'Europe in an Open World Order'), Munich, September 2–8.

Haberler, G. (1979) 'The Liberal International Economic Order in Historical Perspective', in R.C. Amacher, G Haberler and T.D. Willett (eds), *Challenges to a Liberal International Economic Order*, Washington DC: American Enterprise Institute for Public Policy Research, 43–65.

Halm, G.N. (1969) 'Will Market Economies and Planned Economies Converge?', in Streissler, E. (ed.) *Roads to Freedom: Essays in Honour of F.A. von Hayek*, London: Routledge & Kegan Paul, 75–88.

Hayek, F.A. (1944) *The Road to Serfdom*, London: George Routledge & Sons.

Hayek, F.A. (1949) *Individualism and Economic Order*, London: Routledge & Kegan Paul.

Hayek, F.A. (1960) *The Constitution of Liberty*, London: Routledge & Kegan Paul.

Hayek, F.A. (1967) *Studies in Philosophy, Politics and Economics*, Chicago: Chicago University Press.

Hayek, F.A. (1976) *Law, Legislation and Liberty: A New Statement of the Liberal Principles of Justice and Political Economy*, Volume 2: *The Mirage of Social Justice*, London: Routledge & Kegan Paul.

Hayek, F.A. (1978) *New Studies in Philosophy, Politics, Economics and the History of Ideas*, London: Routledge & Kegan Paul.

Hayek, F.A. (1984) 'The Future Unit of Value', in P. Salin, *Currency Competition and Monetary Union*, The Hague: Martinus Nijhoff, 29–41.

Hutchison, T.W. (1981) *The Politics and Philosophy of Economics, Marxians, Keynesians and Austrians*, Oxford: Basil Blackwell.

Keizer, W. (1989) 'Recent Reinterpretations of the Socialist Calculation Debate', in J.J. Krabbe, A. Nentjes and H. Visser (eds), *Austrian Economics: Roots and Ramifications Reconsidered*, Part 2, Bradford: MCB University Press, 63–83.

Kirzner, I.M. (1971) 'Entrepreneurship and the Market Approach to Development', in F.A. Harper, F.A. Hayek, H. Hazlitt, L.E. Read and G.R. Velasco (eds), *Toward Liberty: Essays in Honor of Ludwig von Mises on the Occasion of his 90th Birthday*, Volume II, Menlo Park, California: Institute for Humane Studies, 194–208.

Kirzner, I.M. (1976a) 'On the Method of Austrian Economics', in E.G. Dolan (ed.) *The Foundations of Modern Austrian Economics*, Kansas: Sheed & Ward.

Kirzner, I.M. (1976b) 'Equilibrium versus Market Process', in E.G. Dolan (ed.) *The Foundations of Modern Austrian Economics*, Kansas: Sheed &Ward.

Kirzner, I.M. (1990) 'Menger, classical liberalism, and the Austrian School of Economics', in J.B. Caldwell (ed.) *Carl Menger and his Legacy in Economics*, annual supplement to Volume 22, *History of Political Economy*, Durham and London: 93–106.

Lachmann, L.M. (1971) 'Ludwig von Mises and the Market Process', in Harper, F.A. *et al.* (ed.) *Toward Liberty: Essays in Honor of Ludwig von Mises on the Occasion of his 90th Birthday*, Volume II, Menlo Park, California: Institute for Humane Studies, 38–52.

Machlup, F. (1969) 'Liberalism and the Choice of Freedoms', in Streissler, E. (ed.) *Roads to Freedom: Essays in Honour of F.A. von Hayek*, London: Routledge & Kegan Paul, 117–146.

Meijer, G. (1988) *Neoliberalisme: Neoliberalen over economische orde en economische theorie (Neoliberalism: Neoliberals on Economic order and Economic Theory)*, Assen/Maastricht: Van Gorcum.

Mises, L. von (1962) *The Free and Prosperous Commonwealth*, English translation of *Liberalismus* (1927), Jena: Gustav Fischer.

Mises, L. von (1976) *Liberalism: A Socio-Economic Exposition*, 2nd edn, Kansas City: Sheed Andrews & McMeel.

Rothbard, M.N. (1971) 'Lange, Mises and Praxeology: The Retreat from Marxism' in Harper, F.A., *et al.* (eds.), *Toward Liberty: Essays in Honor of Ludwig von Mises on the Occasion of his 90th Birthday*, Volume II, Menlo Park, California: Institute for Humane Studies, 307–321.

Streissler, E. (1990) 'Carl Menger on Economic Policy: The Lectures to Crown Prince Rudolf', in B.J. Caldwell (ed.), *Carl Menger and his Legacy in Economics*, Annual Supplement to *History of Political Economy* 22, Durham and London: Duke University Press.

Visser, H. (1993) 'Currency Competition, the EMU and Constructivism' in *International Journal of New Ideas* II (1).: 27–35.

16

COMMENT ON ROEL P. ZUIDEMA'S 'THE AUSTRIAN PERSPECTIVE'

Aad van Mourik

Professor Zuidema has provided us with a valuable and instructive survey of the relevance of Austrian ideas for the present and future ordering of the European economies. Although I find myself in agreement with most of his analysis, Zuidema's paper leaves some urgent problems of international ordering untouched, and therefore may not be able to fulfil its promise to discuss the Austrian economic message for '(re-)shaping the economic institutions' of Europe. In the following, I shall try to make explicit what I mean by this comment.

Being myself a student of the European integration process, I read Zuidema's paper with 'European' eyes. I could not avoid asking myself the question of how an Austrian would evaluate this integration process in general and its most important details in particular. Since Zuidema gives us but few clues on these issues, I shall try to complement his paper on this score.

If one reads Chapter 15 in *The Road to Serfdom*, it becomes clear that Hayek considered the nineteenth-century liberal idea of an international federation of states as the best form of international ordering. A federation is a form of government wherein certain powers have been transferred to the international authority, and wherein individual states remain fully responsible for their internal affairs. In fact, Hayek considers a federation the only viable form of international ordering which is able to secure a democratic rule. However, pointing at the experiences made with the League of Nations, he admits that a world federation of countries inhabited by free individuals would probably be hard to achieve, and that one might consider as a first step the establishment of regional federations which could be restricted to certain parts of the world. To avoid the possibility of war, these regional arrangements would have to be embedded in a larger arrangement covering the entire world.

Hayek did not favour any kind of international ordering that would not be subjected to some fundamental principles. In its most ideal form, the international organization would be able to seriously restrict the discretionary coercive powers of the nation-state over its individuals. The international rule of law would have to offer substantial guarantees that would shelter the individual from discretionary actions of the nation-state government, but also from discretionary actions of the international authority. Individuals should be the basis of the international order. If this were not the case, international competition between individuals and markets would be replaced by a power struggle between states. In addition, the international order would have to guarantee a nation's right to independence, no matter what the size of that nation might be.

Now what should be the implication of all these principles for our opinion of the European integration process? Recently, the EC ended the 1992 process to complete the internal market and signed the Maastricht Treaty. Both events might be viewed quite pessimistically through Hayekian eyes. The 1992 process would produce a planned order for Europe, in which many disretionary powers have been transferred from nations to the EC Commission. One would only have to think of the tremendous efforts that have been contemplated to define and impose European standards. In addition, there are many who would contend that the European integration process has created and stimulated a kind of artificial economic solidarity between the member states and has resulted in the emergence of new blocks with opposed interests. Furthermore, the EC has turned into a powerful trade bloc, which, according to some, narrow-mindedly defends its trade interest *vis-à-vis* the rest of the world. Finally, and perhaps most importantly, the democratic content of the European administration is desperately lacking.

Hayek was extremely critical of those who favour an economic ordering that would take place through deliberate plans to create a supra-national authority which would possess far-reaching powers. Having no strong confidence in deliberate attempts to create national social orders, he could only be sceptical about attempts to do the same on an international scale. In this respect, he argues that the economic ordering of western Europe lacks any moral foundation that would justify it. He does not believe in the solidarity of the Dutch worker who would want to pay a higher price for his or her bike in order to secure the job of a Coventry worker. Yet this European distributive justice has been an essential characteristic of the EC throughout its entire existence. And the Maastricht Treaty envisages an even larger role for the regional policies of the EC.

One cannot escape the impression that Hayek must have been extremely sceptical about the post-war European efforts to create a kind of regional 'federation'. Although the Maastricht Treaty envisages the creation of a true European federation of states and adopted the subsidiarity principle as a basis for further integration, things have got pretty much out of hand in a direction away from Hayek's ideal international economic order.

This conclusion becomes all the more obvious if one considers the constituant elements of the integration process. The trade liberalization process in Europe itself was, of course, a good idea. But inherent in that process was a discrimination towards Third World countries, which seems incompatible with Austrian ideas. One need also only look at the Common Agricultural Policy (CAP) to find evidence in support of the claim that the integration process has gone in the wrong direction. The CAP is probably the area where all Austrian policy prescriptions are flagrantly violated. Being a policy of market intervention, it has succeeded in the elimination of competition between individuals on the one hand and between markets on the other. Also, it created gross distributive injustice, in that richer farmers and countries have been able to secure the main benefits for themselves, and that small farmers from the poorer countries are only minor beneficiaries. It has resulted in tensions in the international arena, particularly with the United States and developing countries, through its disruptive effect on the agricultural world markets. And finally, the CAP has created a formidable tax burden for the citizens of the EC.

Another area where the realities of the EC are at odds with the Austrian policy prescriptions concerns the industrial policy of the EC. Although it is frequently maintained that this policy intended to stimulate competition between industrial firms in the EC, it has in the past frequently been directed towards the survival of 'old champions'. The steel, textiles, shipbuilding, etc., industries have all been sheltered from international competition by both national and EC subsidies and trade policies. This prohibited the market from correcting the inefficiencies that have existed in these sectors.

Finally, the competition policy is worth mentioning. The competition policy grants the EC Commission the power to intervene when EC trade is affected in two major areas. First, it prohibits agreements and other 'concerted practices' which may affect trade between states and which have as their purpose or effect 'the prevention, restriction or distortion of competition within the common market'. Second, undertakings that are an abuse of a dominant position are considered to violate the EC rules of competition. The purpose of the EC competition law is therefore to stimulate competition as much as possible. Although Austrians might in principle be sympathetic to this idea, they would probably not bother very much about the implications of dominant positions and they would reject the EC competition policy. In their view, the success of dominant firms would eventually and automatically attract competitors. The Austrians would probably argue against the need to regulate monopolies at all, and therefore consider the competition policy, which lies at the heart of the 1992 process, as superfluous.

If one overlooks the above arguments, then the conclusion cannot be other than that, although some principles of the post-war international order in Europe (federation, subsidiarity, competition) might pass an

Austrian test, the application of this principle has gone in totally the wrong direction. Needless to say, the post-war international order stands far apart from the Austrian ideal. Unfortunately, the present changes in Europe do not seem to bring significant changes in the right direction.

INDEX